Quran and Wisdom
of
Hazrat Inayat Khan

Farzana Moon

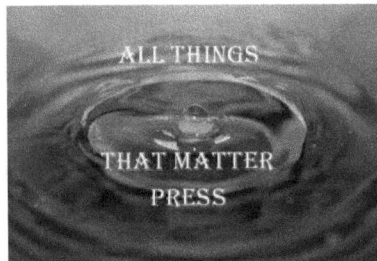

ISBN 13: 9780999524374
Library of Congress Control Number: 2018955028
Cover Photos: Photo by Marcus Löfvenberg on Unsplash

Cover design © by All Things That Matter Press
Published in 2018 by All Things That Matter Press

For Hazrat Inayat Khan in Abode of Bliss. His lamp of wisdom my guiding light.

Foreword

And Quran is not such as could ever be invented in despite of Allah, but it is a confirmation of that which was before it and an exposition of that which is decreed for mankind. Therein is no doubt—from the Lord of the Worlds. (10:38 Quran)

This book gets its breath of life from the wisdom of Hazrat Inayat Khan. A little over century ago he came from India to US, then travelled to Europe to unite east and west in love, peace, and harmony. Divinely inspired in music and in knowledge of esoteric and exoteric religions, he strove toward teaching God-realization, not promoting any particular faith, not even his own in which he was born, Islam. This book contains a selection of verses from the Quran which extremists ignore, picking only the ones which they can distort to suit the fever of their hate, malice, injustice, intolerance. The names of one hundred and fourteen Surahs in the Quran serve as chapters, a few verses from each chapter highlighting the purity of Islam for the benefit of Muslims and non-Muslims to gain knowledge and understanding.

These verses need no clerics, scholars or theologians to interpret or misinterpret by the very virtue of their all-encompassing rhythm of mercy, justice, compassion. Each Surah begins with a quote from Hazrat Inayat with clear explanation. At the end of each chapter are chunks of his lectures or contemplations, most of those un-published. This book reveals the pearl of unity in diversity. Blissfully and astonishingly, the seeds of love which Hazrat Inayat Khan planted a century ago have grown into tall saplings, lending afresh the cool shade of kindness and compassion.

Also, I have taken the liberty to share only the verses from the Quran which filled my heart with so much love and gratitude that I am hoping they would be a source of as much guidance to others as they are to me in recitation and contemplation. These verses speak to me of peace and compassion. Sheer poetry of their message sings to all of beauty and inspiration. They became my divine guides in my dark hours of pain and despair. It is comforting to embrace these verses as friends who speak through the tongues of angels, softly and tenderly.

(Note: A Surah is the term for a chapter of the Quran)

This is a brief biography of Hazrat Inayat Khan.

Hazrat Inayat Khan was born July 5, 1882 in Baroda, India. He died February 5, 1927 in Tilak Lodge north of Delhi's Red fort in India. His ancestry can be traced back to King Tipu Sultan. His family was both spiritual and musical, and growing up as a young man he was interested in studying and exploring all religions. Mentored by great musicians and saints and sages of India, finally he met his Sufi teacher, to whose teaching his whole life was indebted. The name of that Sufi teacher was Madani, who instructed him to leave his hometown and venture abroad. 'Fare forth into the world, my child, and harmonize the East and the West with the harmony of thy music. Spread the wisdom of Sufism abroad, for to this end thou art gifted by Allah, the most Merciful and Compassionate.' In obedience to his teacher, Hazrat Inayat Khan came to America Year 1910 to promote the message of God realization. While giving lectures and concerts, he fell in love with an American girl by the name of Ora Ray Baker. They were married in London March 20, 1913. Their first daughter Nurunnisa was born in Russia, 1914, and they returned to London at the inception of WW1. They had three more children, two boys and another girl. They settled in Suresness, Paris, but after his death and much later at the inception of WW11, the family moved to London. Nurunnisa became a British spy against Nazi Germany invasion of Paris. She was captured by Gestapo, then killed in Nazi concentration camps. Hazrat Inayat Khan's legacy still lives in Fazal Manzil in Suresness, Paris, where he lived with his family and where his wife Ora Ray Baker, titled as Pirani, died, but their daughter Nurunnisa embalmed as Spy Princess in a movie is alive on world stage.

Quran and Wisdom

Surah One

Al Fatihah

Misbelief alone misleads; single-mindedness always leads to the goal.

He who sincerely seeks his real purpose in life is himself sought by that purpose. As he concentrates on that search a light begins to clear his confusion, call it revelation, call it inspiration, call it what you will. It is mistrust that misleads. Sincerity leads straight to the goal. Hazrat Inyat Khan

In the name of Allah, the Beneficent, the Merciful

Praise be to Allah, Lord of the Worlds

The Beneficent, the Merciful

Owner of the Day of Judgment

Thee alone we worship, Thee alone we ask for help

Show us the straight path

The path of those whom Thou hast favored

Not the path of those who earn Thine anger, nor of those who go astray. (1:7 Quran)

The wise man should keep the balance between love and power; he should keep the love in his nature ever increasing and expanding, and at the same time strengthen the will so that the heart may not easily be broken.

Many seek protection from all hurting influences by building some wall around themselves. But the canopy over the earth is so high that a wall cannot be built high enough, and the only thing one can do is to live in the midst of all inharmonious influences, to strengthen his will power and to bear all things, yet keeping the fineness of character and a nobleness of manner together with an ever-living heart. To become cold with the coldness of the world is weakness, and to become broken by the hardness of the world is feebleness, but to live in the world and yet to keep above the world is like walking on the water. There are two essential duties for the man of wisdom and love; that is to keep the love in our nature ever increasing and expanding and to strengthen the will so that the heart may not be easily broken. Balance is ideal in life; man must be fine and yet strong, man must be loving and yet powerful. Hazrat Inayat Khan

Surah Two

Al Baqarah

Failure comes when will surrenders to reason. For instance, when a person tries to unravel a knot, and then he thinks, 'No use giving time to it,' he loses an opportunity of strengthening the will and attaining the object desired. However small a thing may appear to be, when once handled, one must accomplish it, not for the thing itself, but for what benefit it gives. Hazrat Inayat Khan

In the name of Allah, the Beneficent, the Merciful

This is the Scripture whereof there is no doubt a guidance unto those who ward off evil. (2:2 Quran)

And who believe in that which is revealed unto thee Muhammad and that which was revealed before thee, and are certain of the Hereafter. (2:4 Quran)

These depend upon guidance from their Lord. These are the successful. (2:5 Quran)

And of mankind are some who say: We believe in Allah and the Last Day, when they believe not. (2:8 Quran)

And when it is said unto them. Make not mischief in the earth, they say: We are peacemakers only. (2:11 Quran)

O mankind! Worship your Lord Who hath created you and those before you, so that you may ward off evil. (2:21 Quran)

And give glad tidings O Muhammad unto those who believe and do good works that theirs are gardens underneath which rivers flow, as often as they are regaled with food of the fruit thereof, they say: This is what was given us aforetime and it is given to them in resemblance. There for them are pure companions, there forever they abide. (2:25 Quran)

How disbelieve ye in Allah when you were dead and He gave life to you. Then He will give you death, then life again and then unto Him ye will return. (2:28 Quran)

And believe in that which I reveal, confirming that which ye possess already of the Scripture and be not first to disbelieve therein, and part not with My revelations for a trifling price and keep your duty unto me. (2:41 Quran)

Confound not truth with falsehood, nor knowingly conceal the truth. (2:42 Quran)

Establish worship, pay the poor due and bow your heads with those who bow in worship. (2:43 Quran)

Enjoin ye righteousness upon mankind when ye yourself forget to practice it. And ye are the reader of the Scripture! Have ye then no sense? (2:44 Quran)

Seek help in patience and prayer, and truly it is hard save for the humble-minded. (2:45 Quran)

Who know that they will have to meet their Lord and that unto Him they are returning. (2:46 Quran)

Lo, those who believe in that which is revealed unto thee, Muhammad, and those who are Jews and Christians and Sabaeans—whosoever believeth in Allah and the Last Day and doeth right—surely their reward is with their Lord, and there shall be no fear come upon them, neither shall they grieve. (2:62 Quran)

And those who believe and do good works, such are rightful owners of the Garden. They will abide therein. (2:82 Quran)

And when we made with you a covenant saying: Shed not the blood of your people, nor turn a party of your people out of your dwellings. Then you ratified our covenant and ye were witness thereof. (2:84 Quran)

Say, O Muhammad, to mankind: who is an enemy to Gabriel? For he it is who hath revealed this Scripture to thy heart by Allah's leave, confirming that which was revealed before it, and a guidance and glad tidings to believers. (2:97 Quran)

Unto Allah belong the East and the West, and withersoever you turn, there is Allah's countenance. Lo, Allah is All-Embracing, All-Knowing. (2:115 Quran)

And when We made the House at Mecca a resort for mankind and a sanctuary, saying: Take as your place of worship the place where Abraham stood to pray. And we imposed a duty upon Abraham and Ishmael, saying: Purify My House for those who go around and those who meditate therein and those who bow down and prostrate themselves in worship. (2:125 Quran)

And when Abraham and Ishmael were raising the foundations of the House, Abraham prayed: Our Lord accept from us this duty. Lo, Thou, only Thou art the Hearer, the Knower. (2:127 Quran)

Our Lord! And make us submissive unto Thee and our seed a nation submissive unto Thee, and show us our ways of worship, and relent toward us. Lo, Thou, only Thou art the Relenting, the Merciful. (2:128 Quran)

Our Lord! And raise up in their midst a messenger from among them, who shall recite unto them Thy revelations and shall instruct them in Scripture and in wisdom and shall make them grow. Lo, Thou, only Thou art the Wise, the Mighty. (2:129 Quran)

And who forsaketh the religion of Abraham save him who befooleth himself? Verily We chose him in the world, and lo, in the Hereafter he is among the righteous. (2:130 Quran)

When his Lord said to him: Surrender. He said: I have surrendered to the Lord of the Worlds. (2:131 Quran)

The same did Abraham enjoin upon his sons, and also Jacob, saying: O my sons! Lo, Allah hath chosen for you the true religion, therefore die not save as men who have surrendered unto Him. (2:132 Quran)

Or were ye present when death came to Jacob, when he said unto his sons: What will ye worship after me? They said: We shall worship thy God, the God of thy fathers, Abraham and Ishmael and Isaac, One God and unto Him we have surrendered. (2:133 Quran)

Those are people who have passed away. Theirs is that which they earned, and yours is that which ye earn. And ye will not be asked of what they used to do. (2:134 Quran)

Say O Muslims: We believe in Allah and that which is revealed unto us and that which was revealed unto Abraham and Ishmael, and Isaac, and Jacob, and the tribes, and that which Moses and Jesus received, and that which the Prophets received from their Lord. We make no distinction between any of them, and unto Him we have surrendered. (2:1136 Quran)

Say unto the People of the Scripture: Dispute ye with us concerning Allah, when He is our Lord and your Lord? Ours are our works and yours your works. We look to Him alone. (2:139 Quran)

And each one hath a goal toward which he turneth, so vie with one another in good works. Wheresoever you may be, Allah will bring you all together. Lo, Allah is able to do all things. (2:148 Quran)

Lo, the mountains As-Safa and Al-Marwah are among the indications of Allah. It is therefore no sin for him who is on pilgrimage to the House of God or visiteth it, to go around them as the pagan custom is. And he who doeth good of his own accord, for him, lo, Allah is Aware, Responsive. (2:158 Quran)

O ye who believe! Eat of the good things wherewith We have provided you, and render thanks to Allah if it is indeed He whom you worship. (2:172 Quran)

It is not righteousness that ye turn your face to the East and the West, but righteous is he who believeth in Allah and the Last Day and the angels and the Scripture and the Prophets. And giveth his wealth for love of Him to kinsfolk and to orphans and the needy and the wayfarer, and to those who ask, and to set slaves free, and observeth proper worship and payeth the poor due. And those who keep their treaty when they make one, and the patient in tribulation and adversity and time of stress. Such are they who are sincere. Such are the God-fearing. (2:177 Quran)

Fight in the way of Allah against those who fight against you, but begin not hostilities. Lo, Allah loveth not aggressors. (2:190 Quran)

The pilgrimage is in the well-known months and whoever is minded to perform the pilgrimage therein, let him remember that there is to be no lewdness nor abuse nor angry conversation on the pilgrimage. And whatsoever good ye do Allah knoweth it. So make provisions for yourselves hereafter, for the best provision is to ward off evil. Therefore keep your duty unto Me, O men of understanding. (2:197 Quran)

Mankind were one community and Allah sent unto them Prophets as bearers of good tidings and as warners and revealed therewith the Scripture with the truth that it might judge between mankind concerning that wherein they differed. And only those to whom the Scripture was given differed concerning it, after clear proofs had come unto them, through hatred one of another. And Allah by His will guided those who believe unto the truth of that concerning which they differed. Allah guideth whom He will unto a straight path. (2:213 Quran)

They question thee O Muhammad with regard to warfare in sacred month. Say: Warfare is a great transgression. (2:217 Quran)

Lo, those who believe and those who emigrate to escape the persecution and strive in the way of Allah, those have hope of Allah's mercy. Allah is Merciful, Forgiving. (2:218 Quran)

They question thee about strong drink and game of chance. Say: In both is great sin and some utility for men, but the sin of them is greater than their usefulness. And they ask thee what they ought to spend. Say: That which is superfluous. Thus Allah maketh plain to you His revelations that haply ye may reflect. (2:219)

And make not Allah by your oaths a hindrance to your being righteous and observing your duty unto Him and making peace among mankind. Allah is Hearer, Knower. (2:224 Quran)

Allah will not take you to task which is unintentional in your oaths. But He will take you to task for that which your hearts have garnered. Allah is Clement, Forgiving. (2:225 Quran)

There is no compulsion in religion. The right direction is henceforth distinct from error. (2:256)

Those who spend their wealth for the cause of Allah and afterward make not reproach or injury to follow for which they have spent, their reward is with their Lord. And there shall no fear come upon them, neither shall they grieve. (2:262 Quran)

A kind word with forgiveness is better than almsgiving followed by injury. Allah is Clement, Absolute. (2:263 Quran)

The guiding of them is not your duty, O Muhammad, but Allah guideth whom He will. And whatsoever good thing ye spend, it is for yourselves, when you spend not save in search of Allah's countenance, and whatsoever good thing ye spend, it will be repaid to you in full, and ye will not be wronged. (2:272 Quran)

The messenger believeth in that which hath been revealed unto him from his Lord and so do the believers. Each one believeth in Allah and His angels and His Scriptures and His messengers—We make no distinction between any of His messengers—and they say: We hear and we obey. Grant us Thy forgiveness, our Lord. Unto Thee is the journeying. (2:285 Quran)

Success comes when reason, the store of experience, surrenders to will.

A learned person without will power is like a head without a body. Common sense is necessary in the path of attainment, but not to such an extent that the reason should dominate and lead the will. The will, in action, must lead the reason, whereas if the reason is allowed to lead the will, the will many times becomes paralyzed. But when in cooperation the will leads the reason, then the path of attainment becomes illuminated.

Reason is learned from the ever changing world, but wisdom comes from the essence of life. Reason is the master of the unbeliever and the servant of the believer. In order to see this question more clearly one must picture oneself as two beings, one the king and the other the servant. When one of them expresses a wish, it is the king who wishes. And the part that says, 'I cannot,' is the servant. If the servant has his way, then the king is in the place of the servant. And the more the servant has his way, the more the servant rules and the king obeys. In this way naturally conflict arises and that reflects upon the outer life. One's whole life becomes unlucky. One may be pious or good or religious, it makes no difference. If man does not realize the kingdom of God within himself nor realize his spirit to be a king, he does not accomplish the purpose of life. Hazrat Inyat Khan

Surah Three

Ali Imran

There is an answer to every call; those who call on God, to them God comes.

There is nothing that you ask that this universe will not answer. For it is the nature of this universe to answer your soul's call. When a person seeks for something in the universe and he cannot find it, it is not true that it is not there. The fact is that he does not see it. Hazrat Inyat Khan

In the name of Allah, the Beneficent, the Merciful

He hath revealed unto thee, Muhammad, the Scripture with truth, confirming that which was revealed before it, even as He revealed the Torah and the Gospel. (3:3 Quran)

He it is Who hath revealed unto thee, Muhammad, the Scripture wherein are clear revelations—They are the substance of the Book—and others which are allegorical. But those in whose hearts is doubt pursue, forsooth, that is allegorical, seeking to cause dissention by seeking to explain it. None knoweth its explanation save Allah, and those who are of sound instruction say: We believe therein, the whole is from our Lord, but only men of understanding really heed. (3:6 Quran)

Beautified for mankind is love of the joys that come from women and offspring and stored up heaps of gold and silver and horses and cattle and land. That is the comfort of the life of the world. Allah, with Him is a more excellent abode. (3:14 Quran)

Say: Shall I inform you of something better than that? For those who keep from evil, with their Lord, are Gardens underneath which rivers flow, and pure companions, and contentment from Allah. Allah is Seer of His bondmen. (3:15 Quran)

Say, O Muhammad, to mankind, if you love Allah, follow me. Allah will love you and forgive you your sins. Allah is Merciful, Forgiving. (3:31 Quran)

And remember when the angels said: O Mary! Lo, Allah giveth thee glad tidings of a word from Him, whose name is the Messiah, Jesus, Son of Mary, illustrious in the world and the Hereafter, and one of those brought near unto Allah. (3:45 Quran)

He will speak unto mankind in his cradle and in his manhood, and he is of the righteous. (3:46 Quran)

She said: My Lord! How can I have a child when no mortal hath touched me? He said: So, it will be. Allah createth what He will. If He decreeth a thing He saith unto it only: Be, and it is. (3:47 Quran)

And He will teach him the Scripture, the Torah and the Gospel. (3:48 Quran)

And will make him a messenger unto the children of Israel, saying: Lo, I come unto you with a sign from your Lord. Lo, I fashion for you one of the clay the likeness of a bird, by Allah's leave. I heal him who was born blind, and the leper, and I raise the dead, by Allah's leave. And I announce unto you what ye eat and what ye store up in your houses. Lo, herein verily is a potent for you, if ye are to be believers. (3:49 Quran)

And I come confirming that which was before me of the Torah and to make lawful some of that which was forbidden unto you. I come unto you with a sign from your Lord, so keep your duty to Allah and obey me. (3:50 Quran)

So Allah is my Lord and your Lord, so worship Him. This is a straight path. (3:51 Quran)

And remember when Allah said: O Jesus! Lo, I am gathering thee and causing thee to ascend unto Me, and I am cleansing thee of those who disbelieve and am setting those who follow thee above those who disbelieve until the Day of Resurrection. Then unto Me you will all return, and I shall judge between you as to that wherein ye used to differ. (3:54 Quran)

Lo, the likeness of Jesus with Allah is as the likeness of Adam. He created him of dust, then He said unto Him, Be, and he is. (3:59 Quran)

This is the truth from thy Lord, O Muhammad, so be not thou of those who waver. (3:60 Quran)

Say: O People of the Scripture! Come to an agreement between us and you: that we shall worship none but Allah, and that we shall ascribe no partner unto Him, and that none of us shall take others for lords beside Allah. And if they turn away, then say: Bear witness we are they who have surrendered unto Him. (3:64 Quran)

Lo, those of mankind who have the best claim to Abraham are those who followed him, and this Prophet and those who believe with him, and Allah is the Protecting Friend of the believers. (3:68 Quran)

Nay, but the chosen of Allah is he who fulfilleth his pledge and wardeth off evil, for lo, Allah loveth those who ward off evil. (3:76 Quran)

And lo, there is a party of them who distort the Scripture with their tongues that ye may think that what they say is from the Scripture, when it is not from the Scripture. And they say: It is from Allah, when it is not from Allah. And they speak a lie concerning Allah knowingly. (3:78 Quran)

It is not possible for any human being unto whom Allah had given the Scripture and wisdom of the Prophethood that he should afterwards have said unto mankind: Be slaves of me instead of Allah, but he said was: Be ye faithful servants of the Lord by virtue of your constant teaching of the Scripture and of your constant study thereof. (3:79 Quran)

When Allah made His covenant with the Prophets, He said: Behold that which I have given you of the Scripture and knowledge. And afterward there will come unto you a messenger, confirming that which ye possess. Ye shall believe in him and ye shall help him. He said: Do you agree, and will you take up my burden which I lay upon you in this matter? They answered: We agree. He said: Then bear you witness. I will be a witness with you. (3:81 Quran)

Say O Muhammad: We believe in Allah and that which is revealed unto us and that which was revealed unto Abraham and Ishmael and Isaac, and Jacob and the tribes, and that which we vouchsafed unto Moses and Jesus and the Prophets from their Lord. We make no distinction between any of them, and unto Him we have surrendered. (3:84 Quran)

Ye will not attain unto piety until ye spend of that which ye love. And whatsoever ye spend, Allah is aware thereof. (3:92 Quran)

Lo, the first Sanctuary appointed for mankind was that at Becca, a blessed place, a guidance to the peoples. (3:96 Quran)

Wherein are plain memorials of Allah's guidance the place where Abraham stood up to pray, and whosoever entereth it is safe. And pilgrimage to the House is a duty unto Allah for mankind for him who can find a way thither. And for him who disbelieveth, let him know that, lo, Allah is Independent of all creatures. (3:97 Quran)

Unto Allah belongeth whatsoever is in the heavens and whatsoever is in the earth. He forgiveth whom He will and punisheth whom He will. Allah is Merciful, Forgiving. (3:129 Quran)

Those who spend of that which Allah hath given them in ease and adversity, those who control their wrath and are forgiving toward mankind, Allah loveth the good. (3:134 Quran)

It was the mercy of Allah that thou wast lenient with them, O Muhammad, for if thou hadst been stern and fierce of heart they would have dispersed from round about thee. So pardon them and ask forgiveness of them and consult with them upon the conduct of affairs. And when thou art resolved, then put thy trust in Allah. Lo, Allah loveth those who put their trust in Him. (3:159 Quran)

And their Lord hath heard them and He saith: I suffer not the work of any worker, male or female, to be lost. Ye proceed one from another. So those who fled and were driven forth from their homes and suffered damage for My cause and fought and were slain. Verily, I shall remit their evil deeds from them and verily I shall bring them into Gardens underneath which rivers flow — A reward from Allah. And with Allah is the fairest of rewards. (3:195 Quran)

He who thinks against his own desire is his own enemy.

When one considers the psychology of failure and success, failure follows failure. And why is it? Because the consciousness reflecting success is full of success, and the activity which goes out from that consciousness is creating productive activity; so if the consciousness has success before its view, then the same reflection will work and bring success. Whereas if the consciousness is impressed with failure, then failure will work constantly, bringing failure after failure.

Very often pessimistic people speak against their own desire. They want to undertake some work, and they say, 'I will do this, but I don't think I shall succeed in it.' Thus they hinder themselves in their path. Man does not know that every thought makes an impression on the consciousness and on the rhythm with which the consciousness is working. According to that rhythm that reflection will come true and happen; and a man proves to be his own enemy by his ignorance of these things.

Man's attitude is the secret of life, for it is upon man's attitude that success and failure depend. Both man's rise and fall depend upon his attitude. By attitude I mean that impulse which is like a battery behind the mechanism of thought. There is hidden in our heart a wonderful power. It is a divine power, a sacred power, and it can be developed and cherished by keeping our attitude right. *Hazrat Inyat Khan*

Surah Four

An-Nisa

The brain speaks through words; the heart in the glance of the eyes; and the soul through a radiance that charges the atmosphere, magnetizing all.

The heart of man is like a globe over the light of the soul. When the globe is dusty, naturally the light is dim. When it is cleaned, the light increases. In fact, the light is always the same. It is the fault of the globe when it is not clear. When this radiance shines out, it shows itself not only through the countenance and expression of a man, but even in the man's atmosphere. The soul-power, so to speak, freely projects outward, and the surroundings feel it. Hazrat Inyat Khan

In the name of Allah, the Beneficent, the Merciful

O mankind! Be careful of your duty to your Lord Who created you from a single soul and from it created its mate and from them twain hath spread abroad a multitude of men and women. Be careful of your duty toward Allah in whom ye claim your rights of one another, and toward the wombs that bore you. Lo, Allah hath been a watcher over you. (4:1 Quran)

Give unto orphans their wealth. Exchange not the good for the bad in your management thereof, nor absorb their wealth into your own wealth. Lo, that would be a great sin. (4:2 Quran)

And if ye fear that ye will not deal fairly by the orphans, marry of the women who seem good to you, two or three or four, and if ye fear you cannot do justice to so many, then one only. Thus is it more likely that ye will not do injustice. (4:3 Quran)

And give unto women whom you marry free gift of your marriage portion, but if they of their own accord remit unto you a part thereof, then ye are welcome to absorb it in your wealth. (4:4 Quran)

Allah would make the burden light for you, for man was created weak. (4:28 Quran)

O ye who believe! Squander not your wealth among yourselves in vanity, except it be a trade by mutual consent, and kill not one another. Lo, Allah is ever Merciful unto you. (4:29 Quran)

Whoso doeth that through aggression and injustice, We shall cast him into Fire and that is very easy for Allah. (4:30 Quran)

And covet not the thing in which Allah hath made some of you excel others. Unto men a fortune from that which they have earned, and unto women a fortune from that which they have earned. Envy not one another, but ask Allah of His bounty. Lo, Allah is ever Knower of all things. (4:32 Quran)

And if ye fear a breach between them twain, the wife and husband. Appoint an arbiter from her folk and an arbiter from his folk. If they desire amendment, Allah will make them of one mind. Lo, Allah is ever Knower, Aware. (4:35 Quran)

Lo, Allah wrongeth not even the weight of an ant, and if there is a good deed, He will double it and will give the doer from His presence an immense reward. (4:40 Quran)

Allah knoweth best who are your enemies. Allah is sufficient as a Friend and Allah is sufficient as a Helper. (4:45 Quran)

We sent no messenger save that he should be obeyed by Allah's leave. And if when they have wronged themselves, they had but come unto thee and asked forgiveness of Allah, and asked forgiveness of the messenger, they would have found Allah Merciful, Forgiving. (4:64 Quran)

Whatever of good befalleth thee O man, it is from Allah, and whatever of ill befalleth thee, it is from thyself. We have sent thee Muhammad as a messenger unto mankind and Allah is sufficient as witness. (4:79 Quran)

When ye are greeted with a greeting, greet ye with a better than it or return it. Lo, Allah taketh count of all things. (4:86 Quran)

It is not for a believer to kill a believer unless it be by mistake. (4:92 Quran)

Whoever slayeth a believer of set purpose, his reward is Hell for ever. Allah is wroth against him and He hath cursed him and prepared for him an awful doom. (4:93 Quran)

Degrees of rank from Him, and mercy and forgiveness. Allah is ever Merciful, Forgiving. (4:96 Quran)

And seek forgiveness of Allah. Lo, Allah is ever Merciful, Forgiving. (4:106)

Yet whoso doeth evil or wrongeth his own soul, then seeketh pardon of Allah, will find Allah Merciful, Forgiving. (4:110 Quran)

And whoso doeth good works, whether male of female and he or she is a believer, such will enter paradise and they will not be wronged the dint in a date-stone. (4:124 Quran)

Who is better in religion than he who surrendereth his purpose to Allah while doing good to men and followeth the tradition of Abraham, the upright. Allah Himself chose Abraham as friend. (94:125 Quran)

Unto Allah belongeth whatsoever is in the heavens and whatsoever is in the earth. Allah ever surroundeth all things. (4:126 Quran)

If a woman feareth ill-treatment from her husband or desertion, it is no sin for them twain if they make terms of peace between themselves. Peace is better. But greed hath been present in the minds of men. If ye do good and keep from evil, lo, Allah is ever Informed of what ye do. (4:128 Quran)

Unto Allah belongeth whatsoever is in the heavens and whatsoever is in the earth. And We charged those who received the Scripture before you, and We charge you that ye keep your duty toward Allah. And if ye disbelieve, lo, unto Allah belongeth whatsoever is in the heavens and whatsoever is in the earth, and Allah is ever Absolute, Owner of Praise. (4:131 Quran)

Unto Allah belongeth whatsoever is in the heavens and whatsoever is in the earth, and Allah is sufficient as Defender. (4:132 Quran)

O ye who believe! Be ye staunch in justice, witnesses for Allah even though it be against yourselves or your parents or your kindred, whether the case be of a rich man or a poor man, for Allah is nearer unto both than ye are. So follow not passion lest ye lapse from truth and if ye lapse or fall away, then lo, Allah is ever informed of what ye do. (4:135 Quran)

O ye who believe! Believe in Allah and His messenger and the Scripture which He hath revealed unto His messenger and the Scripture which He hath revealed aforetime. Whoso disbelieveth in Allah and His angels and His Scriptures and His messengers and the Last Day, he verily hath wandered far away. (4:136 Quran)

What concern hath Allah for your punishment, if ye are thankful for His mercies and believe in Him? Allah is ever Aware, Responsive. (4:147 Quran)

And Allah loveth not utterance of harsh speech save by one who hath been wronged. Allah is ever Hearer, Knower. (4:148 Quran)

If ye do good openly or keep it secret, or forgive evil. Lo, Allah is Powerful, Forgiving. (4:149 Quran)

Those who believe in Allah and His messengers and make no distinction between any of them, unto them Allah will give their wages. And Allah was forever Merciful, Forgiving. (4:152 Quran)

And because of their saying: We slew the Messiah Jesus son of Mary, Allah's messenger—they slew him not, nor crucified, but it appeared so unto them, and lo, those who disagree concerning it are in doubt thereof. They have no knowledge thereof save pursuit of a conjecture, they slew him not for certain. (4:157 Quran)

But Allah took him up unto Himself. Allah was ever Wise, Mighty. (4:158 Quran)

Those who are firm in knowledge and the believers believe in that which is revealed unto thee, and that which was revealed before thee. Especially the diligent in prayer and those who pay the poor-due, the believers in Allah and the Last Day. Upon these We shall bestow immense rewards. (4:162 Quran)

Lo, We inspire thee as We inspired Noah and the Prophets after him, as We inspired Abraham and Ishmael and Isaac and Jacob and the tribes, and Jesus and Job and Johah and Aaron and Solomon, and We imparted unto David the Psalms. (4:163)

And messengers we have mentioned unto thee before and messengers We have mentioned unto thee, and Allah spoke directly unto Moses. (4:164 Quran)

Messengers of good cheer and of warning in order that mankind might have no argument against Allah after the messengers. Allah was ever Wise, Mighty. (4:165 Quran)

But Allah Himself testifieth concerning that which He hath revealeth unto thee, in His knowledge hath He revealed it, and the angels also testify. And Allah is sufficient witness. (4: 166 Quran)

O mankind! The messenger hath come unto you with the truth from your Lord. Therefore believe, it is better for you. But if ye disbelieve, still, lo, unto Allah belongeth whatsoever is in the heavens and the earth. Allah is ever Wise, Knower. (4:170 Quran)

The Messiah will never scorn to be a slave unto Allah, nor will the favored angels. Whoso scorneth His service and is proud, all such will He assemble unto Him. (4:172 Quran)

O mankind! Now hath a proof from your Lord come unto you, and We have sent down unto you a clear light. (4:175 Quran)

As for those who believe in Allah, and hold fast unto Him, them, He will cause to enter into his grace and mercy. He will guide them unto Him by a straight road. (4:176 Quran)

Love is the merchandise which all the world demands; if you store it in your heart, every soul will become your customer.

In reality the greatest miracle of Christ that any wise man can see is the miracle of Christ's living heart; not wonderworking, but the living God presented to the world; it was the lighted faith which helped the darkness to vanish, not dogmas, or doctrines, or theories; all that came afterwards. He went to fishermen and said to them, 'Come hither, I will make you fishers of men'. What does it mean? Does 'fishers of men' mean fishers of money? No, he meant by this: Let love be alive in your hearts, that the whole world may become your customers. Hazrat Inayat Khan

Surah Five

Al Maidab

Sincerity is the jewel that forms in the shell of the heart.

The more sincerity is developed, the greater share of truth you will have. And however much sincerity a person may have, there is always a gap to fill, for we live in the midst of falsehood, and we are always apt to be carried away by this world of falsehood. Therefore we must never think we are sincere enough, and we must always be on our guard against influences which may carry us away from that sincerity which is the bridge between ourselves and our ideal. No study, no meditation is more helpful than sincerity itself. Hazrat Inayat Khan

In the name of Allah, the Beneficent, the Merciful

O ye who believe! Profane not Allah's monuments, nor the Sacred Month, nor the offerings, nor the garlands, nor those repairing to the Sacred House, seeking the grace and pleasure of Allah. But when you have left the sacred territory, then go hunting if ye will. And let not your hatred of a folk who once stopped your going to the Inviolable Place of Worship seduce you to transgress, but help ye one another unto pious duty and righteousness. Help not one another unto sin and transgression, but keep your duty to Allah. Lo, Allah is severe in punishment. (5:2 Quran)

This day I have perfected your religion for you and complet4ed my favor unto you and have chosen you as religion Al-Islam. Whosoever is forced by hunger, not by will to sin, for him, lo, Allah is Merciful, Forgiving. (5:3 Quran)

This day all good things made lawful for you. The food of those who have received the Scripture is lawful for you, and your food is lawful for them. And so are the virtuous women of the believers and the virtuous women of those who received the Scripture before you, lawful for you, when ye give them their marriage portions and live with them in honor, not in fornication, nor taking them as secret concubines. Whoso denieth the faith, his work is vain and he will be among the losers in the Hereafter. (5:5 Quran)

O ye who believe! Be steadfast witness for Allah in equity, and let not hatred of any people seduce you that ye deal not justly. Deal justly, that is nearer to your duty. Observe your duty to Allah. Lo, Allah is informed of what ye do. (5:8 Quran)

Allah hath promised those who believe and do good works: Theirs will be forgiveness and immense reward. (5:9 Quran)

O People of the Scripture! Now hath our messenger come unto you, expounding unto you much of that which ye used to hide in the Scripture, and forgiving much. Now hath come unto you light from Allah and a plain Scripture. (5:15 Quran)

Whereby Allah guideth him who seeketh. His good pleasure into paths of peace. He bringeth them out of darkness unto light by His decree, and guideth them unto a straight path. (5:16 Quran)

For that cause We decreed for the Children of Israel that whosoever killeth a human being for other than manslaughter or corruption in the earth, it shall be as if he had killed all mankind, and whoso saveth the life of one, it shall be as if he had saved the life of all mankind. Our messengers came unto them of old with clear proofs of Allah's sovereignty, but afterwards, lo, many of them became prodigals in earth. (5:32 Quran)

O ye who believe! Be mindful of your duty to Allah, and seek the way of approach unto Him, and strive in His way in order that ye may succeed. (5:35 Quran)

Lo! We did reveal the Torah, wherein is guidance and a light, by which the Prophets who surrendered unto Allah judged the Jews, and the rabbis and the priests judged for such as Allah's Scripture as they were bidden to observe, and thereunto they were witnesses. So fear not mankind, but fear Me. And barter not my revelations for a little gain. Whoso judgeth not by that which Allah hath revealed, such are disbelievers. (5:45 Quran)

And We caused Jesus, son of Mary, to follow in their footsteps, confirming that which was revealed before him, and We bestowed on him the Gospel wherein is guidance and a light, confirming that which was revealed before it in the Torah—a guidance and an admonition unto those who ward off evil. (5:46 Quran)

And unto thee have We revealed the Scripture with the truth, confirming whatever Scripture was before it, and a watcher over it. So judge between them by which Allah hath revealed, and follow not their desires away from the truth which hath come unto thee. For each, We have appointed a divine law and a traced-out way. Had Allah willed He would have made you one community. But that He may try you by that which He hath given you, He hath made you as ye are. So vie one with another in good works. Unto Allah ye will all return, and He will then inform you of that wherein ye differ. (5:48 Quran)

Is it a judgment of the time of pagan ignorance that they are seeking? Who is better than Allah for judgment to a people who have certainty in their belief. (5:50 Quran)

Say O People of the Scripture! Ye have naught of guidance till ye observe the Torah and the Gospel and that which was revealed unto you from your Lord. That which is revealed unto thee Muhammad from thy Lord is certain to increase contumacy and disbelief of many of them. But grieve not for the disbelieving folk. (5:68 Quran)

Lo! Those who believe and those who are Jews, and Sabaeans and Christians—Whatsoever believeth in Allah and the Last Day and doth right—there shall no fear come upon them, neither shall they grieve. (5:69 Quran)

Will they rather not turn unto Allah and seek forgiveness of Him? Allah is Merciful, Forgiving. (5:74 Quran)

O People of the Scripture! Stress not in your religion other than the truth, and follow not the vain desires of folk who erred of old and led many astray, and erred from a plain road. (5:77 Quran)

O ye who believe! Forbid not good things which Allah hath made lawful for you, and transgress not. Lo, Allah loveth not transgressors. (5:87 Quran)

Eat of that which Allah hath bestowed on you as food lawful and good, and keep your duty to Allah in whom ye are believers. (5:88 Quran)

Allah will not take you to task for that which is unintentional in your oaths, but He will take you to task for the oaths which ye swear in earnest. The expiation thereof is the feeding of the ten of the needy with the average of that wherewith ye feed your own folk, or the clothing of them, or the liberation of a slave, and for him who findeth not the wherewithal to do so, then a three days fast. This is the expiation of your oaths when ye have sworn, and keep your oaths. Thus Allah expoundeth unto you His revelations in order that ye may give thanks. (5:89 Quran)

Obey Allah and obey the messenger, and beware! But if ye turn away, then know that the duty of Our messenger is only plain conveyance of the message. (5:92 Quran)

There shall be no sin imputed unto those who believe and do good works for what they may have eaten in the past. So be mindful of your duty to Allah, and do good works, and again be mindful of your duty and believe, and once again, be mindful of your duty, and do right. Allah loveth the good. (5:93 Quran)

Allah hath appointed Kaaba, the Sacred House, a standard for mankind, and the Sacred Month and offerings and the garlands. That is so that ye may know that Allah knoweth whatsoever is in the heavens and whatsoever is in the earth, and that Allah is Knower of all things. (5:97 Quran)

Know that Allah is severe in punishment, but that Allah also is Merciful, Forgiving. (5:98 Quran)

The duty of the messenger is only to convey the message. Allah knoweth what ye hide and what ye proclaim. (5:99 Quran)

Say: The evil and good are not alike even though the plenty of evil attract thee. So be mindful of your duty to Allah, O men of understanding that ye may succeed. (5:100 Quran)

O ye who believe! Ask not of things which, if they were made known unto you, would trouble you, but if ye ask of them when the Quran is being revealed, they will be made known unto you. Allah pardoneth this, for Allah is Clement, Forgiving. (5:101 Quran)

A folk before you asked for such disclosures, and then disbelieved therein. (5:102 Quran)

O ye who believe! Ye have charge of your own souls. He who erreth cannot injure you if ye are rightly guided. Unto Allah ye will all return, and then He will inform you of what ye used to do. (5:105 Quran)

When Allah saith: O Jesus, son of Mary! Remember my favor unto thee and unto thy mother. How I strengthened thee with the Holy Spirit, so that thou speakest unto mankind in the cradle as in maturity. And how I taught thee the Scripture and Wisdom, and theTorah and the Gospel. And how thou didst shape of clay as if it were the likeness of a bird by My permission, and how I restrained the Children of Israel from harming thee when thou comest unto them with clear proofs, and those of them who disbelieved exclaimed: This is naught else but mere magic. (5:110 Quran)

And when I inspired the disciples, saying: Believe in Me and My messenger. They said: We believe. Bear witness that we have surrendered unto thee. (5:111 Quran)

When the disciples said: O Jesus, son of Mary! Is thy Lord able to send down for us a table spread with food from heaven? He said: Observe your duty to Allah, if ye are true believers. (5:112 Quran)

They said: We wish to eat thereof, that we may satisfy our hearts and know that thou hast spoken truth to us, and that thereof we may be witnesses. (5:113 Quran)

Jesus, son of Mary, said: O Allah, Lord of us! Send down for us a table spread with food from heaven that it may be a feast for us, for the first of us and for the last of us, and a sign from thee. Give us sustenance, for Thou art the Best of Sustainers. (5:114 Quran)

And Allah said: Lo, I send it down for you. And whoso disbelieveth of you afterward, him surely will I punish with a punishment therewith I have not punished any of My creatures. (5:115 Quran)

And when Allah saith: O Jesus, son of Mary! Didst thou say unto mankind: take me and my mother for two gods beside Allah? He saith: Be glorified! It was not mine to utter that which I had no right. If I used to say it, then Thou knewest it. Thou knowest what is in my mind, and I know not what is in Thy Mind. Lo, Thou, only Thou are the Knower of Things Hidden. (5:116 Quran)

I spake unto them only that which Thou commandest me, saying: Worship Allah, my Lord and your Lord. I was a witness of them while I dwelt among them and when Thou tookest me Thou was the Watcher over them. Thou art Witness over all things. (5:117 Quran)

If Thou punish them, lo, they are Thy slaves, and if thou forgive them, lo, they are Thy slaves. Lo, Thou, only Thou are the Wise, the Mighty. (5:118 Quran)

Allah saith: This is a day in which their truthfulness profiteth the truthful, for theirs are Gardens underneath which rivers flow, wherein they are secure forever. Allah taking pleasure in them and they in Him. This is the great triumph. (5:119 Quran)

Unto Allah belongeth the Sovereignty of the heavens and the earth and whatsoever is therein, and He is Able to do all things. (5:120 Quran)

It is more important to know the truth about one's self than to try to find out the truth of heaven and hell.

It is more important to find out the truth about oneself than to find out the truth about heaven and hell, or about many other things which are of less importance and are apart from oneself. However, every man's pursuit is according to his state of evolution, and so each soul is in pursuit of something but he does not know where it leads him. The first sign of realization is tolerance towards others. There are the words of Christ: 'In the house of my father are many mansions' and those of the Prophet: 'Each soul has its own religion' This means that according to his evolution so man knows the truth and the more a man knows, the more he finds there is to learn. In order to attain truth one must make one's own life truthful. This is life in its moral aspect. The more truthful one is in one's everyday life the more one practices this moral despite its great difficulty, the more one approaches the only religion which there is. Truth is the very self of man. Truth is the divine element in man. Truth is every soul's seeking. Therefore as soon as the clouds of illusion are scattered, that which man now begins to see is nothing but the truth which has been there all the time. He finds that the truth was never absent; it was only covered by clouds of illusion. By changing his own nature, by making himself more truthful, he disperses the clouds of falsehood within and without, and begins to see life as it really is both inwardly and outwardly. From this time onwards, the meaning of religion becomes clear. When a person really wants to find the way, it is not very far from him. It depends on the sincerity of the desire to find it whether it is far or not. What is necessary for finding it is not much reading, or discussion or argument, but a practical study of self. One questions one's own self: what am I? Am I a material body, or a mind, or something behind a mind? Am I myself or my coat? Is this object "me," or something different? Is this body my cover, or myself?

There is One Truth, the true knowledge of our being, within and without, which is the essence of all wisdom. Hazrat Ali says, 'Know thyself, and thou shalt know God.' The Sufi recognizes the knowledge of self as the essence of all religions; he traces it in every religion, he sees the same truth in each, and therefore he regards all as one. Hence he can realize the saying of Jesus; 'I and my Father are one.' The difference between creature and Creator remains on his lips, not in his soul. This is what is meant by union with God. It is in reality the dissolving of the false self in the knowledge of the true self, which is divine, eternal, and all pervading. 'He who attaineth union with God, his very self must lose,' said Amir. Hazrat Inyat Khan

Surah Six

Al Anam
The real abode of God is in the heart of man; when it is frozen with bitterness or hatred, the doors of the shrine are closed, the light is hidden.

The soul is the Spirit of God, and the Spirit of God lives within the shrine of the heart; this shrine can be closed or it can be open. There are some things in life that open it and some that close it. The things that close the heart are those which are contrary to love, tolerance and forgiveness, such as coldness, bitterness and ill-will, and a strong element of duality. The world is more upset today than ever before; in many ways man seems to go from bad to worse, and yet he thinks that he is progressing. It is not lack of organization or of civilization; both these things he has. What he lacks is the expression of the soul. He closes his door to his fellow man, he closes the shrine of the heart and by doing so he is keeping God away from himself and others. Nation is set against nation, race against race, religion against religion. Therefore today more than ever before there is a need for the realization of this philosophy. What we need is not that all religions should become one nor all races; that can never be. But what is needed is undivided progress, and making ourselves examples of love and tolerance. By talking about it, by discussing and arguing it will not come, but by self-realization, by making ourselves the examples of what should be, by giving love, taking love, and showing in our action gentleness, consideration and the desire for service for the sake of God in whom we can all unite beyond the narrow barriers of race and creed. Hazrat Inayat Khan

In the name of Allah, the Beneficent, the Merciful

Repel not those who call upon their Lord at morn and evening, seeking His countenance. Thou art not accountable for them in aught, nor are they accountable for thee in aught, that thou shouldst repel them and be of the wrong-doers. (6:52 Quran)

Farzana Moon

And when those who believe in Our revelation come unto thee, say: Peace be unto you! Your Lord hath prescribed for himself mercy, that whoso of you doeth evil and repenteth afterward thereof and doeth right, for him, lo, Allah is Merciful, Forgiving. (6:54 Quran)

He it is who gathereth you at night and knoweth which ye commit by day. Then He raiseth you again to life therein, that the term appointed for you may be accomplished. And afterward unto Him is your return. Then He will proclaim unto you what ye used to do. (6:60 Quran)

He it is Who created the heavens and the earth in truth. In the day when He saith: Be! It is. (6:73 Quran)

His word is the truth, and His will be the Sovereignty on the day when the trumpet is blown. Knower of the visible and the invisible, He is the Wise, the Aware. 6:74 Quran)

Those who believe and obscure not their belief by wrongdoing, theirs is safety, and they are rightly guided. (6:83 Quran)

That is Our argument. We gave it unto Abraham against his folk. We raise unto degrees of wisdom whom We will. Lo, thy Lord is Wise, Aware. (6:84 Quran)

And we bestowed upon him Isaac and Jacob; each of them We guided. And Noah did We guide aforetime, and of his seed We guided David and Solomon and Job and Joseph and Moses and Aaron. Thus do We reward the good. (6:85 Quran)

And Zachariah and John and Jesus and Elias. Each one of them was the righteous. (6:86 Quran)

And Ishmael and Elisha and Jonah and Lot. Each one of them did We prefer above Our creatures. (6:87 Quran)

Some of their forefathers and their offspring and their brethren. And We chose them and guided them unto a straight path. (6:88 Quran)

Those are they whom Allah guideth, so follow their guidance. Say O Muhammad unto mankind: I ask of you no fee for it. Lo, it is naught but a Reminder to His creatures. (6:91 Quran)

And this is a blessed Scripture which We have revealed, confirming that which was revealed before it, that thou mayest warn Mother of Villages and those around her. Those who believe in the Hereafter believe herein, and they are careful of their worship. (6:93 Quran)

And He it is Who hath produced you from a single being and hath given you a habitation and a repository. We have detailed Our revelations for a people who have understanding. (6:99 Quran)

Such is Allah, your Lord. There is no God save Him, the Creator of all things, so worship Him. And He taketh care of all things. (6:103 Quran)

Vision comprehendeth Him not, but He comprehends all vision. He is the Subtile, the Aware. (6:104 Quran)

Proofs have come unto you from your Lord, so whose seeth, it is for his own good, and whoso is blind is blind to his own hurt. I am not a keeper over you. (6:105 Quran)

Thus do We display Our revelations that they may say unto thee, Muhammad: Thou hast studied, and that We may make it clear for people who have knowledge. (6:106 Quran)

Revile not those unto whom they pray beside Allah, lest they wrongfully revile Allah through ignorance. Thus unto every nation have We made their deed seem fair. Then unto their Lord is their return, and He will tell them what they used to do. (6:109 Quran)

Shall I seek other than Allah for judge, when He it is Who hath revealed unto you this Scripture fully explained? Those unto whom We gave Scripture aforetime know that it is revealed from thy Lord in truth. So be not thou, O Muhammad, of the waverers. (6:115 Quran)

Perfected is the word of thy Lord in truth and justice. There is naught that can change His words. He is the Hearer, the Knower. (6:116 Quran)

Forsake the outwardness of sin and the inwardness thereof. Lo, those who garner sin will be awarded that which they have earned. (6:121 Quran)

This is the path of thy Lord, a straight path. We have detailed Our revelations for a people who take heed. (6:127 Quran)

For them is the abode of peace with their Lord. He will be their Protecting Friend because of what they used to do. (6:128 Quran)

Say O Muhammad: O my people! Work according to your power. Lo, I too am working. Thus ye will come to know for which of us will be the happy sequel. Lo, the wrong-doers will not be successful. (6:136 Quran)

They are losers who besottedly have slain their children without knowledge, and have forbidden that which Allah bestowed upon them, inventing a lie against Allah. They indeed have gone astray and are not guided. (6:141 Quran)

Again, We gave the Scripture unto Moses, complete for him who would do good, an explanation of all things, a guidance and a mercy, that they might believe in the meeting of their Lord. (6:155 Quran)

And this is a blessed Scripture which We have revealed. So follow it and ward off evil, that ye may find mercy. (6:156 Quran)

Lest ye should say: The Scripture was revealed only to two sects before us, and we in sooth were unaware of what they read. (6:157 Quran)

Lo, as for those who sunder their religion and become schismatics, no concern at all hast thou with them. Their case will go to Allah, Who then will tell them what they used to do. (6:160 Quran)

Whoso bringeth a good deed will receive tenfold the like thereof, while whoso bringeth an ill deed will be awarded but the like thereof, and they will not be wronged. (6:161 Quran)

He it is Who placed you as viceroys of the earth and hath exalted some of you in rank above others, that He may try you by the test of that which He hath given you. Lo, thy Lord is swift in prosecution, and lo, He is Merciful, Forgiving. (6:166 Quran)

Our virtues are made by love, and our sins caused by the lack of it.

There is one moral; the love that springs forth from self-denial and blooms in deeds of beneficence. The orthodox say, 'This is good, that is bad. This is right, that is wrong,' but to a Sufi the source of all good deeds is love. Someone may say that this is the source of bad deeds also, but that is not so; it is lack of love. Our virtues are made of love, and our sins are caused by lack of it. Love turns sins into virtues, and its lack makes virtues meaningless. Christ said when a woman was brought before Him accused of sin, 'Her sins are forgiven, for she loved much.' Heaven is made so beautiful with love, and life becomes a hell through the lack of it. Love in reality creates harmony in one's life on earth and peace in heaven. *Hazrat Inayat Khan*

Surah Seven

Al Araf

The fire of devotion purifies the heart of the devotee, and leads unto spiritual freedom.

The heart developed by religion and morality becomes first capable of choosing and then of retaining the object of devotion without wavering for a moment. Devotion sweetens the personality, and is the light on the path of the disciple. Those who study mysticism and philosophy while omitting self-sacrifice and resignation grow egoistic and self-centered. Such persons are apt to call themselves either God or a part of God, and thus make an excuse for committing any sins they like. Regardless of sin or virtue they misuse and malign others, being utterly fearless of the hereafter. Yet they forget that 'strait is the gate, and narrow is the way, which leadeth unto life', as the Bible says. The fire of devotion purifies the heart of the devotee and leads to spiritual freedom.

Devotees by their power of concentration, by their purity of life, and by their divine love become wonderful healers. Their every tear and sigh become a source of healing for themselves and those around them. Devotion is the fire in which all infirmities are consumed.

Hazrat Inayat Khan

In the name of Allah, the Beneficent, the Merciful

And unto man: O Adam! Dwell thou and thy wife in the Garden and eat from whence ye will, but come not nigh this tree lest ye become wrong-doers. (7:19 Quran)

Then Satan whispered to them that he might manifest unto them which was hidden from them of their shame, and he said: Your Lord forbade you from this tree only lest ye should become angels or become of the immortals. (7:20 Quran)

And he swore unto them, saying: I am a sincere adviser unto you. (7:21 Quran)

Thus did he lead them on with guile. And when they tasted of the tree, their shame was manifest on them and they began to hide by heaping on themselves some of the leaves of the Garden. And their Lord called them, saying: Did I not forbid you from that tree and tell you: Lo, Satan is an open enemy to you? (7:22 Quran)

They said: Our Lord! We have wronged ourselves. If Thou forgive us not and have not mercy on us, surely we are of the lost! (7:23 Quran)

He said: Go down from hence, one of you a foe to another. There will be for you on earth a habitation and a provision for a while (7:24 Quran)

He said: There shall ye live and there shall ye die, and thence shall ye be brought forth. (7:25 Quran)

O Children of Adam! We have revealed unto you the raiment to conceal your shame, and splendid vesture, but the raiment of restraint from evil that is best. This is of the revelations of Allah, that they may remember. (7:26 Quran)

O Children of Adam! Look to your adornment at every place of worship, and eat and drink, but be not prodigal. Lo! He loveth not the prodigal. (7:31 Quran)

Say: Who hath forbidden the adornment of Allah which he hath brought forth for His bondmen, and the good things of His providing? Say: Such, on the Day of Resurrection, will be only for those who believed during the life of the world. Thus do We detail Our revelations for people who have knowledge. (7:32 Quran)

Say: My Lord forbiddeth only indecencies, such of them as are apparent and such as are within, and sin and wrongful oppression, and that ye associate with Allah that for which no warrant hath been revealed, and that ye tell concerning Allah that which ye know not. (7:33 Quran)

And every nation hath its term, and when its term cometh, they cannot put it off an hour nor yet advance it. (7:34 Quran)

O Children of Adam! If messengers of your own come unto you who narrate unto you my revelations, then whosoever refraineth from evil and amendeth—there shall be no fear come upon them, neither shall they grieve. (7:35 Quran)

Lo! Your Lord is Allah Who created the heavens and the earth in six days, then mounted He the Throne. He covereth the night with the day, which is in haste to follow it, and hath made the sun and the moon and the stars subservient by His command. His verily is all creation and commandment. Blessed by Allah, the Lord of the Worlds! (7:54 Quran)

O mankind! Call upon your Lord humbly and in secret. Lo! He loveth not aggressors. (7:55 Quran)

Work not confusion in the earth after the fair ordering thereof, and call on Him in fear and Hope. Lo, the mercy of Allah is nigh unto the good. (7:56 Quran)

And if there is a party of you which believed in that wherewith I have been sent, and there is a party which believeth not, then have patience until Allah judge between us. He is the best of all who deal in judgment. (7:87 Quran)

Those who follow the messenger, the Prophet who can neither read nor write, whom they will find described in the Torah and the Gospel which are with them. He will enjoin on them that which is right and forbid them that which is wrong. He will make lawful for them all good things and prohibit for them only the foul, and he will relieve them of their burden and the fetters they used to wear. Then those who believe in him, and help him, and follow the light which is sent down with him, they are the successful. (7:157 Quran)

Say O Muhammad: O mankind! Lo, I am the messenger of Allah to you all—the messenger of Him unto Whom belongeth the Sovereignty of the heavens and the earth. There is no God save Him. He quickeneth and He giveth death. So believe in Allah and His messenger, the Prophet who can neither read, nor write, who believeth in Allah and in His Words, and follow him that haply you may be led aright. (7:158 Quran)

And as for those who make men keep the Scripture and establish worship, lo, We squander not the wages of reformers. (7:170 Quran)

Allah's are the fairest names. Invoke Him by them. And leave the company of those who blaspheme His names. They will be requited what they do. (7:180 Quran)

They ask thee of the destined Hour, when will it come to port. Say: Knowledge thereof is with my Lord only. He alone will manifest it at its proper time. It is heavy in the heavens and the earth. It cometh not to you save unawares. They question thee if thou couldst be well informed thereof. Say: Knowledge thereof is with Allah only, but most of mankind know not. (7:187 Quran)

Say: For myself I have no power to benefit, nor power to hurt, save that which Allah willeth. Had I knowledge of the Unseen, I should have abundance of wealth, and adversity would not touch me. I am but a warner, and a bearer of good tidings unto folk who believe. (7:188 Quran)

He it is Who did create you from a single soul and therefrom did make his mate that he might take rest in her. And when he covered her she bore a light burden and she passed unnoticed with it, but when it became heavy they cried unto Allah, their Lord, saying: If thou givest unto us aright we shall be of the faithful. (7:189 Quran)

Lo! My Protecting Friend is Allah who revealeth the Scripture. He befriendeth the righteous. (7:196 Quran)

Keep to forgiveness, O Muhammad, and enjoin kindness, and turn away from the ignorant. (7:199 Quran)

And thou O Muhammad remember thy Lord within thyself humbly and with awe, below thy breath, at morn and evening. And be not thou of neglectful. (7:205 Quran)

Lo! Those who are with thy Lord are not too proud to do Him service, but they praise Him and adore Him. (7:206 Quran)

Man does not see beyond what he sees.

Ah! How desirous I was to see the divine Beloved! It is not the fault of the Beloved that you do not see; He is before you! It is the fault of you who recognize Him not. Everything, whatever you see is nothing else but The Presence of God!

Men have differed in all ages because they have called their Deity by different names. There have existed wars, fights and family feuds for ages, men dividing themselves merely for the difference of the names given to their Deity. Man always sees just what he sees; he cannot see beyond it. When an ordinary or an illiterate person meets a poet, he sees the man-part and not the poet-part. But if he is told that this person is a poet he may see the poet-part when he meets him. He now sees that he is a poet in his actions and in his words; in everything about him he sees the poet, whereas otherwise he would not have been able to see this. Thus a great poet may go among a crowd and the people will only see the man in him; they do not see the poet, and they do not know how profound his thoughts are. So once a person begins to recognize God in man he does not see the man any more but God. The man is the surface, while God is deep within him. Such recognition brings a person into touch with everyone's innermost being, and then he knows more about people than they know themselves. It is said, 'By the vision of God, their self will become God.' This happens when we come to see God in everybody. We develop goodness in our actions; our words become God's words because we are impressed with all that reflects only goodness and is mirrored around us. Then we become a museum or a picture of goodness. We reflect it from morning till evening, we reflect forgiveness, we reflect tolerance, and we reflect all these lovely qualities. As it is said, 'If my Beloved is in every kind of man, how considerate I ought to be towards all!' The lover is always very careful when he is with his beloved; he becomes thoughtful and tender. Divine perfection is perfection in all powers and mysteries. All these are manifested without specially striving for them. Perfection and annihilation is that stage where there is no longer 'I' and no longer 'you', where there is what there is. *Hazrat Inayat Khan*

Every man's pursuit is according to his evolution.

Everyone says or does or thinks only according to his own particular evolution, and he cannot do better. Why not, therefore tolerate? Why not, therefore, forgive?

Moses once passed by a farm and saw a peasant boy talking to himself, saying, 'O Lord, Thou art so good and kind that I feel if Thou wert here by me I would take good care of Thee, more than of all my sheep, more than of all my fowls. In the rain I would keep Thee under the roof of my grass-shed, when it is cold I would cover Thee with my blanket, and in the heat of the sun I would take Thee to bathe in the brook. I would put Thee to sleep with Thy head on my lap, and would fan Thee with my hat, and would always watch Thee and guard Thee from wolves. I would give Thee bread of manna and would give Thee buttermilk to drink, and to entertain Thee I would sing and dance and play my flute. O Lord my God, if Thou wouldst only listen to this and come and see how I would tend Thee.' Moses was amused to listen to all this, and, as the deliverer of the divine message, he said, 'How impertinent on thy part, O boy, to limit the unlimited One, God, the Lord of hosts, who is beyond form and color and the perception and comprehension of man.' The boy became disheartened and full of fear at what he had done. But immediately a revelation came to Moses: 'We are not pleased with this, O Moses, for We have sent thee to unite Our separated ones with Us, not to disunite. Speak to everyone according to his evolution.' Every man's pursuit is according to his state of evolution, and so each soul is in pursuit of something but he does not know where it leads him. The first sign of realization is tolerance towards others. There are the words of Christ: 'In the house of my father are many mansions' and those of the Prophet: 'Each soul has its own religion' This means that according to his evolution so man knows the truth and the more a man knows, the more he finds there is to learn. *Hazrat Inayat Khan*

Surah Eight

Al Anfal

Those who throw dust at the sun, the dust falls in their own eyes.

Raise not dust from the ground; it will enter into your eyes. Sprinkle some water on it that it may settle down and lie under your feet.

To delve into a matter which matters little, is like raising dust from the ground.

Man forms his future by his actions. His every good or bad action spreads its vibrations and becomes known throughout the universe. The more spiritual a man is, the stronger and clearer are the vibrations of his actions, which spread over the world and weave his future. The universe is like a dome: it vibrates to that which you say in it, and echoes the same back to you. So also is the law of action: we reap what we sow.

Hazrat Inyat Khan

In the name of Allah, the Beneficent, the Merciful

They only are the true believers whose hearts feel fear when Allah is mentioned, and when the revelations of Allah are recited unto them they increase their faith, and who trust in their Lord. (8:2 Quran)

Who establish worship and spend of that We have bestowed on them. (8:3 Quran)

Those are they who are in truth believers. For them are grades of honor with their Lord, and pardon, and a bountiful provision. (8:4 Quran

O ye who believe! If you keep your duty to Allah, He will give you discrimination between right and wrong and will rid you of your evil thoughts and deeds, and will forgive you. Allah is of infinite bounty. (8:29 Quran)

And obey Allah and His messenger, and dispute not one with another lest ye falter and your strength depart from you, but be steadfast. Lo, Allah is with the steadfast. (8:46 Quran)

Be not as those who came forth from their dwellings boastfully and to be seen of men, and debar men from the way of Allah, while Allah is surrounding all they do. (8:47 Quran)

That is because Allah never changeth the grace He hath bestowed on any people until they first change that which is in their hearts, and that is because Allah is Hearer, Knower. (8:53 Quran)

And if they incline to peace, incline thou also to it, and trust in Allah. Lo! He is the Hearer, the Knower. (8:61 Quran)

Now enjoy what ye have won as lawful and good, and keep your duty to Allah. Lo, Allah is Merciful, Forgiving. (8:69 Quran)

O Prophet, say unto those captives who are in your hands: If Allah knoweth any good in your hearts He will give you better than that which hath been taken from you, and will forgive you. Lo, Allah is Merciful, Forgiving. (8:70 Quran)

Lo, those who believed and left their homes and strove with their wealth and their lives for the cause of Allah, and those who took them in and helped them: those are protecting friends of one another. And those who believed, but did not leave their homes, ye have no duty to protect them till they leave their homes, but if they seek help from you in the manner of religion, then it is your duty to help them except against a folk between whom and you is a treaty. Allah is Seer of what ye do. (8:72 Quran)

And those who disbelieve are protectors one of another—If ye do not so, there will be confusion in the land, and great corruption. (8:73 Quran)

Those who believed and left their homes and strove for the cause of Allah, and those who took them in and helped them—these are the believers in truth. For them is pardon, and a bountiful provision. (8:74 Quran)

And those who afterwards believed and left their homes and strove along with you, and those who are slain are nearer one to another in the ordinance of Allah. Lo! Allah is Knower of all things. (8:75 Quran)

The source of truth is within man; he himself is the object of his realization.

In point of fact truth is simple; it is man who makes it difficult for himself. For all other aspects of knowledge he has to get from outside, but truth is something which is within man himself. It is something which is nearest to us though we imagine it to be farthest; it is something which is within, though we imagine it to be outside; it is knowledge itself we want to acquire. Thus the seeker is engaged in a continual struggle: struggle with himself, struggle with others, and struggle with life. And at the end of the journey he always finds that he has traveled because it was his destiny to travel, and he discovers that his starting-point is the same as his final goal. Then the question arises: what is the way to attain the truth? Can it be attained through study? The answer is that the source of realizing the truth is within man. But man is the object of his realization. Man, absorbed from morning till evening in his occupations which engage his every attention to the things of the earth and of self-interest, remains intoxicated. Seldom there are moments in his life, brought about by pain or suffering, when he experiences a state of mind which can be called soberness. Hindus call this state of mind sat, which is a state of tranquility. Man then begins to become conscious of some part of his being which he finds to have almost covered his eyes. When we look at life from this point of view we find that an individual who claims to be a living being is not necessarily living a full life. It is only a realization of inner life which at every moment unveils the soul, and brings before man another aspect of life in which he finds fullness, a greater satisfaction, and a rest which gives true peace. Heaven is not a country or a continent; it is a state, a condition within oneself, only experienced when the rhythm is in perfect working order. If one knows this, one realizes that happiness is man's own property. Man is his own enemy: he seeks for happiness in the wrong direction and never finds it. It is a continual illusion. Man thinks, 'If I had this or that I should be happy for ever', and he never arrives at happiness because he pursues an illusion instead of the truth. Happiness is only to be found within, and when man tunes himself he finds all for which his soul yearns within himself. *Hazrat Inayat Khan*

You cannot be both horse and rider at the same time.

The ego has two sides: the first one is the one we know, and the next one we must discover. The side we know is the false ego which makes us say, 'I'. What is it in us that we call 'I'? We say, 'This is my body, my mind, these are my thoughts, my feelings, my impressions, this is my position in life.' We identify our self with all that concerns us and the sum total of all these we call 'I'. In the light of truth this conception is false, it is a false identity. By reasoning with oneself and by trying to study oneself analytically it is possible to get nearer to the true knowledge of one's being. If we consider that every part that constitutes our being has its own name -- the hand, the foot, every part of our being has a different name, quality and purpose, and even a separate form -- what is it then in man which says 'I' and identifies itself with what it sees? It is not our head, hand or foot which says 'I' nor is it the brain. It is something that we cannot point out which identifies itself with all these different parts and says 'I' and mine and knows itself to be the person who sees. This in itself is ignorance, and it is this which the Hindus have called avidya.

How can you be that which you possess? You cannot be the horse and rider at the same time, nor can you be carpenter and tool at the same time. Herein lies the secret of mortality and immortality. What has taken possession of this accommodation? A deluded ego that says, 'I.' It is deluded by this body and mind and it has called itself an individual. When a man has a ragged coat he says, 'I am poor'. In reality his coat is poor, not he. What this capacity or accommodation contains is that which becomes his knowledge, his realization, and it is that which limits him. It forms that limitation which is the tragedy of every soul. Now, this capacity may be filled with self, or it may be filled with God. There is only room for one. Either we live with our limitation, or we let God reign there in His unlimited Being. *Hazrat Inyat Khan*

Surah Nine

At Taubah

He who can live up to his ideal is the king of life; he who cannot live up to it is life's slave.

The ideal life is at least to try to live up to one's ideal. But in order to have an ideal one must first awaken to an ideal. Not everyone possesses an ideal; many people do not know of it. It is no exaggeration to say that the wars and disasters we have gone through, the unrest that all feel, and the disagreement among the people which is sometimes seen and sometimes not seen, are all caused by one thing and that is the lack of an ideal.

Is it power which is the object of the spiritual person, or is it inspiration after which he seeks? It is in fact neither of these things which he pursues, but all such things as power and inspiration follow him as he proceeds on his path towards the spiritual goal. The goal of the spiritual person is self-realization, and his journey is towards the depth of his own being, his God, his ideal. God is the ideal that raises mankind to the utmost reach of perfection. There is no ideal that can raise the moral standard higher than the God-ideal, although love is the root of all and God is the fruit of this. Love's expansion and love's culmination and love's progress all depend upon the God-ideal. That which makes us esteem those whom we esteem is their ideal. That which raises man from earth to heaven is his ideal. And that which pulls man down from the heavens to the earth is also his ideal. When he does not live up to his ideal, he falls to earth. And when he raises his ideal he goes from earth to heaven. He can rise to any height, according to the stature of his ideal. *Hazrat Inayat Khan*

At Taubah is the only verse in the Quran without an invocation.

Freedom from obligation is proclaimed from Allah and His messenger toward those of the idolaters with whom you made a treaty. (9:1 Quran)

And if anyone of the idolaters seeketh thy protection, O Muhammad, then protect him so that he may hear the word of Allah, and afterward convey him to his place of safety. That is because they are a folk who know not. (9:6 Quran)

Say: Naught befalleth us save that which Allah hath decreed for us. He is our Protecting Friend. In Allah let believers put their trust. (9:51 Quran)

The alms are only for the poor and the needy and those who collect them, and those whose hearts are to be reconciled. And those who free the captives and the debtors, and for the cause of Allah, and for the wayfarer, a duty imposed by Allah. Allah is Wise, Knower. (9:60 Quran)

The hypocrites, both men and women, proceed one from another. They enjoin the wrong, and they forbid the right, and they withhold their hands from spending for the cause of Allah. They forget Allah as He hath forgotten them. Lo, the hypocrites, they are the transgressors. (9:67 Quran)

And the believers, men and women, are protecting friends one of another, they enjoin the right and forbid the wrong, and they establish worship and they pay the poor due, and they obey Allah and His messenger. As for these, Allah will have mercy on them. Lo, Allah is Wise, Mighty. (9:71 Quran)

Allah promiseth to the believers, men and women Gardens underneath which rivers flow, wherein they will abide—blessed dwellings in Garden of Eden. And—greater far—acceptance from Allah. That is the supreme Triumph. (9:72 Quran)

Not unto the weak nor unto the sick nor unto those who can find naught to spend is any fault to be imputed though they stay at home, if they are true to Allah and His messenger. Not unto the good is there any road of blame. Allah is Merciful, Forgiving. (9:91 Quran)

And of the wandering Arabs there is he who believeth in Allah and the Last Day, and taketh that which he expendeth and also the prayers of the messenger as acceptable offerings in the sight of Allah. Lo, verily, it is an acceptable offering for them. Allah will bring them into His mercy. Lo, Allah is Merciful, Forgiving. (9:99 Quran)

And the first to lead the way, of the Muhajirin and the Ansar, and those who followed them in goodness—Allah is well pleased with them and they are well pleased with Him. And He hath made ready for them Gardens underneath which rivers flow, wherein they will abide forever. That is the supreme triumph. (9:100 Quran)

And there are others who have acknowledged their faults. They mixed a righteous action with another that was bad. It may be that Allah will relent toward them. Lo, Allah is Merciful, Relenting. (9:102 Quran)

Take alms of their wealth, wherewith thou mayest purify them and mayest make them grow, and pray for them. Lo, thy prayer is an assuagement for them. Allah is Hearer, Knower. (9:103 Quran)

Know they not that Allah is He Who accepteth repentance from His bondmen and taketh the alms, and that Allah is He Who is the Merciful, the Relenting. (9:104 Quran)

And say unto them: Act! Allah will behold your actions and so will His messenger and the believers, and ye will be brought back to the Knower of the invisible and the visible, and He will tell you what ye used to do. (9:105 Quran)

Triumphant are those who turn repentant to Allah, those who serve him, those who praise him, those who bow down, those who fall prostrate in worship, those who enjoin the right and who forbid the wrong and those who keep the limits ordained of Allah—And give glad tidings to the believers. (9:112 Quran)

It was never Allah's path that he should send a folk astray after He had guided them until He had made clear unto them what they should avoid! Lo, Allah is aware of all things. (9:115 Quran)

Lo, Allah! Unto Him belongeth the sovereignty of the heavens and the earth. He quickeneth and He giveth death. And ye have, instead of Allah, no protecting friend, nor helper. (9:116 Quran)

Allah hath turned in mercy to the Prophet, and to the Muhajirin and the Ansar, who followed him in the hour of hardship. After the hearts of a party of them had almost swerved aside, then turned He unto them in mercy. Lo, He is full of Pity, Merciful for them. (9:117 Quran)

And to the three also, did He turn in mercy, who were left behind, when the earth, vast as it is, was straitened for them, and their own souls were straitened for them till they bethought them that there is no refuge from Allah save toward Him. Then turned He unto them in mercy that they too might turn repentant unto Him. Lo, Allah! He is the Merciful, the Relenting. (9:118 Quran)

O ye who believe! Be careful of your duty to Allah, and be with the truthful. (9:119 Quran)

There hath come unto you a messenger, one of your own selves, unto whom aught that ye are overburdened is grievous, full of concern for you, for the believers full of pity, merciful. (9:128 Quran)

Now if they turn away, O Muhammad, say: Allah sufficeth me. There is no God save Him. In Him I have put my trust, and He is Lord of the Tremendous Throne. (9:129 Quran)

God is truth, and truth is God.

Many intellectual people, with their various ideas, differ from one another in their opinions and in their way of looking at things, in their speculations, but do the prophets differ from one another? No, they cannot differ. The reason is that it is the various minds which differ, not the souls. The one who lives in his mind, is conscious of his mind; the one who lives in his soul is conscious of the soul. When a person is living in his mind, he is living through the darkness of the night. The moment he rises above his mind and awakens in the light of the soul he becomes spiritual. And if a thousand spiritual people speak, they will say the same thing, perhaps in different words but with only one meaning, for they have one and the same vision. This is why spiritual realization is called the truth. There are many facts but only one truth. The facts can be put into words but not the truth, for God is truth, the soul is truth, the real self of man is truth. We generally confuse truth with fact, and we often use the word fact for truth. When we look at it from the mystic's point of view we find that words are too intricate ever to explain what is truth. Truth is that which cannot be pointed out, because all things that can be compared have their opposite, but neither God nor truth has an opposite. Names are to point out forms, and words are to distinguish one thing from another, while definitions come from the pairs of opposites or at least from differences. That which is all-pervading and is in all things and beings, that which every word explains and yet no word can explain, is God and is truth. The seeker after truth goes out into the world and he finds innumerable different sects and religions. He does not know where to start. Then he desires to find out what is hidden under these sects, these different religions, and he begins to seek the object which he wishes to gain through wisdom. Wisdom is a veil over truth, even wisdom cannot be called truth. God alone is truth, and it is truth that is God. And truth can neither be studied nor taught nor learned; it is to be touched, it is to be realized; and it can be realized by the unfoldment of the heart. Truth is one, God is one, life is one. To me there is no such thing as two. Two is only one plus one.

Man creates his own disharmony.

Feelings such as pride, conceit, selfishness, jealousy, envy and contempt are all feelings which hurt others and which destroy one's own life making it full of the misery which springs from that selfish personal feeling, that ego of man. The more egoistic, the more conceited he is, the more miserable a life he has in the world, the more he makes the lives of others miserable. It is in the world that, growing up, he creates all this and this creation is called nafs or ego. Yet at the same time in the depth of the heart there is that goodness which is the divine goodness, that righteousness which man has inherited from the Father in heaven. Man creates his own disharmony in his soul and then treats others in the same way; therefore he is not satisfied with his own life, nor is he satisfied with others because he feels that he has a complaint against others, although mostly it is caused by himself. What he gives he receives back, but he never sees that. He always thinks: what the depth of his being yearns for -- love, goodness, righteousness, harmony and peace — everybody must give to him. But for him when it comes to giving he does not give because he lives in the other life he has created.

But when a revolution comes in the life of a man, as soon as he begins to see deeply into life, to acquire goodness — not only to get but to give — as soon as he begins to enjoy not only the sympathy of others but giving sympathy to others, then comes a period when he begins to see this Satan-spirit as apart from his real original being, standing before him constantly in conflict with his natural force, freedom and inclination. The mystery of perfection lies in annihilation — not in annihilation of the real self, but of the false self, of the false conception which man has cherished in his heart and always has allowed to torture his life. God speaks to everyone, not only to the messengers and teachers. He speaks to the ears of every heart, but it is not every heart which hears it. His voice is louder than the thunder, and His light is clearer than the sun — if one could only see it, if one could only hear it. In order to see it and in order to hear it man should remove this wall, this barrier which he has made of the self. Then he becomes the flute upon which the divine Player may play the music of Orpheus which can charm even the hearts of stone; then he rises from the Cross into the life everlasting. *Hazrat Inayat Khan*

Surah Ten

Jonah

As man rises above passion, so he begins to know what is love.

To an angelic soul love means glorification. To a jinn soul love means admiration. To a human soul love means affection. To an animal soul love means passion. One need not fall in love, one must rise through love. Pour out floods of love, yet keeping your garment of detachment from being wet. To what does the love of God lead? It leads to that peace and stillness which can be seen in the life of the tree which flowers and bears fruit for others and expects no return. A person who is able to help others should not hide himself but do his best to come out into the world. 'Raise up your light high', it is said. All that is in you should be brought out, and if the conditions hinder you, break through the conditions!

Hazrat Inyat Khan

In the name of Allah, the Beneficent, the Merciful

Lo, those who believe and do good works, their Lord guideth them by their faith. Rivers will flow beneath them in the Gardens of Delight. (10:10 Quran)

Their prayer therein will be: Glory be to Thee, O Allah! And their greeting therein will be: Peace. And the conclusion of their prayer will be: Praise be to Allah, Lord of the Worlds! (10:11 Quran)

The similitude of the life of the world is only as water which We send down from the sky, then the earth's growth of that which men and cattle eat mingleth with it still, when the earth hath taken on her ornaments and is embellished and her people deem that they are masters of her, Our commandment cometh by night or by day and we make it as reaped corn as if it had not flourished yesterday. Thus do we expound the revelations for people who reflect. (10:25 Quran)

And Allah summoneth to the abode of peace, and lendeth whom He will to a straight path. (10:26 Quran)

For those who do good is the best reward and more thereto. Neither dust, nor ignominy cometh near their faces. Such are rightful owners of Garden, they will abide therein. (10:27 Quran)

And if they deny thee, say: Unto me my work, and unto you your work. Ye are innocent of what I do, and I am innocent of what ye do. (10:42 Quran)

Lo, Allah wrongeth not mankind in aught, but mankind wrong themselves. (10:45 Quran)

And for every nation there is a messenger. And when their messenger cometh on the Day of Judgment, it will be judged between them fairly, and they will not be wronged. (10:48 Quran)

And they say: When will the promise be fulfilled, if ye are truthful? (10:49 Quran)

Say: I have no power to hurt or benefit myself, save that which Allah willeth. For every nation there is an appointed time. When their time cometh, then they cannot put if off an hour, nor hasten it. (10:50)

O mankind! There hath come unto you an exhortation from your Lord, a balm for that which is in the breasts, a guidance and mercy for believers. (10:58 Quran)

Say: In the bounty of Allah and in His mercy, therein let them rejoice. It is better than what they hoard. (10:59 Quran)

Say: Have ye considered what provisions Allah hath sent down for you, how ye have made of it lawful and unlawful? Say: Hath Allah permitted you, or do you invent a lie concerning Allah? (10:60 Quran)

And what think those who invent a lie concerning Allah will be their plight upon the Day of Resurrection? Lo, Allah truly is Bountiful toward mankind, but most of them give not thanks. (10:61 Quran)

And thou Muhammad are not occupied with any business and thou recitest not a lecture from this Scripture, and ye mankind perform no act, but We are witness of you when ye are engaged therein. And not an atom's weight in the earth or in the sky escapeth your Lord, nor what is less than that or greater than that, but it is written in a clear book. (10:62 Quran)

Lo, verily, friends of Allah are those on whom fear cometh not, nor do they grieve. (10:63 Quran)

Those who believe and keep their duty to Allah. (10:64 Quran)

Theirs are good tidings in the life of the world and in the Hereafter — there is no changing the Words of Allah — that is the Supreme Triumph. (10:65 Quran)

And let not their speech grieve thee, O Muhammad. Lo, power belongeth wholly to Allah. He is the Hearer, the Knower. (10:66 Quran)

And if thy Lord willed, all who are in the earth would have believed together. Wouldst thou Muhammad compel men until they are believers? (10:100 Quran)

Say: O mankind! Now hath the Truth from your Lord come unto you. So, whosoever is guided, is guided only for the good of his soul, and whosoever erreth, erreth only against it. And I am not a warder over you. (10:109 Quran)

And O Muhammad, follow that which is inspired in thee, and forbear until Allah give judgment. And He is the Best of Judges. (10:110 Quran)

He who stores evil in his heart cannot see beauty.

When someone tells another about some evil, he thinks that he himself is so good, so free from all evil. This side of human nature we see even in children. One child will come and tell how naughty the other is, thinking, 'I must be called good.' Such a tendency grows and develops. Life gathers the wickedness in people. The heart becomes impressed. In time the evil is stored up. That which is the store becomes the treasure, the world within. He who stores evil cannot see good, because there is no good in this world that has not a little spark of evil in it. There is no evil in this world that has not a little spark of good. If a person only tried to find the spark of good, he could find it. But if a person seeks to find a little spark of evil in every good, he can do that also. Someone may say of another, 'He is very good.' But the neighbor says, 'Yes, he is good, but you do not know this about him: I will just tell you what he does!' Is there anyone who never contradicts when somebody is praising another? There has never been anyone in history about whom somebody has not spoken evil. What is really good? The answer is, there is no such thing as good or evil. There is beauty. That which is beautiful, we call good. That which is ugly compared with the beautiful, we call evil: whether it is custom, idea, thought or action. This shows that this whole phenomenon of the universe is the phenomenon of beauty. Every soul has an inclination to admire beauty, to seek for beauty, to love beauty, and to develop beauty.

Once an ascetic thinker was taken to a variety show in New York, where there were all sorts of dances and acts and different amusements, the one who took him there was eager to find out what his opinion about it was and said to him, 'This must disgust you, a contemplative person, to come and see this nonsense going on the stage.' He replied, 'No, never. How can it be disgusting? Is it not my Krishna who is playing there?' It is those who have touched the inner beauty who are capable of appreciating beauty in all forms. It is not only that they appreciate it, they admire and worship it. If worship is given to anything or anyone it is given to God who is hidden in the form of beauty. *Hazrat Inyat Khan*

Surah Eleven

Hud

Love manifests towards those whom we like as love; towards those whom we do not like as forgiveness.

In the East, when we speak of saints or sages, it is not because of their miracles, it is because of their presence and their countenance which radiate vibrations of love. How does this love express itself? In tolerance, in forgiveness, in respect, in overlooking the faults of others. Their sympathy covers the defects of others as if they were their own; they forget their own interest in the interest of others. They do not mind what conditions they are in; be they high or humble, their foreheads are smiling. To their eyes everyone is the expression of the Beloved, whose name they repeat. They see the divine in all forms and in all beings. Think of the life of the great Master Jesus. One sees that from beginning to end there was nothing but love and forgiveness. The best expression of love is that love which is expressed in forgiveness. Those who came with their wrongs, errors, imperfections, before the love, that was all forgiven; there was always a stream of love which always purified. We may make an ideal in our imagination, and, whenever we see that goodness is lacking, we may add to it from our own heart and so complete the nobility of human nature. This is done by patience, tolerance, kindness, forgiveness. The lover of goodness loves every little sign of goodness. He overlooks the faults and fills up the gaps by pouring out love and supplying that which is lacking. This is real nobility of soul. Religion, prayer, and worship, are all intended to ennoble the soul, not to make it narrow, sectarian or bigoted. One cannot arrive at true nobility of spirit if one is not prepared to forgive the imperfections of human nature. For all men, whether worthy or unworthy, require forgiveness, and only in this way can one rise above the lack of harmony and beauty.

Hazrat Inyat Khan

In the name of Allah, the Beneficent, the Merciful

Lo, those who believe and do good works and humble themselves before their Lord, such are rightful owners of the Garden, they will abide therein. (11:23 Quran)

The similitude of two parties is as the blind and the deaf, and the seer and the hearer. Are they equal in similitude? Will ye not then be admonished? (11:24 Quran)

Ask pardon of your Lord and then turn unto Him in repentance. Lo, my Lord is Merciful, Loving. (11:90 Quran)

And lo, unto each thy Lord will verily repay his works in full. Lo! He is informed of what they do. (11:111 Quran)

So tread thou the straight path as thou art commanded and those who turn unto Allah with thee, and transgress not. Lo! He is seer of what ye do. (11:112 Quran)

And incline not toward those who do wrong lest the Fire touch you, and ye have no protecting friends against Allah, and afterward ye should not be helped. (11:113 Quran)

Establish worship at the two ends of the day and in some watches of the night. Lo, good deeds annul ill deeds. This is a reminder for the mindful. (11:114 Quran)

And have patience, O Muhammad, for lo, Allah loseth not the wages of the good. (11:115 Quran)

And Allah's is the Invisible of the heavens and the earth, and unto Him the whole matter would be returned. So worship Him and put thy trust in Him. Lo, thy Lord is not unaware of what ye mortals do. (11:123 Quran)

Until man loses himself in the vision of God, he cannot be said to live really.

Man wrongly identifies himself with the physical body, calling it 'myself.' And when the physical body is in pain he says, 'I am ill,' because he identifies himself with something which belongs to him but which is not himself. The first thing to learn in the spiritual path is to recognize the physical body not as one's self, but as an instrument, a vehicle, through which to experience life. Every soul seeks after beauty; and every virtue, righteousness, good action, is nothing but a glimpse of beauty. Once having this moral, the Sufi does not need to follow a particular belief or faith, to restrict himself to a particular path. He can follow the Hindu way, the Muslim way, the way of any Church or faith, provided he treads this royal road: that the whole universe is but an immanence of beauty. Therein lies the whole of religion. The mystic's prayer is to that beauty, and his work is to forget the self, to lose himself like a bubble in the water [like a drop in the ocean].As life unfolds itself to man the first lesson it teaches is humility; the first thing that comes to man's vision is his own limitedness. The vaster God appears to him, the smaller he finds himself. This goes on and on until the moment comes when he loses himself in the vision of God. In terms of the Sufis this is called fana, and it is this process that was taught by Christ under the name of self-denial. Often man interprets this teaching wrongly and considers renunciation as self-denial. He thinks that the teaching is to renounce all that is in the world. But although that is a way and an important step which leads to true self-denial, the self-denial meant is the losing oneself in God. There is a [Hadith] which says: 'Mutu kubla anta mutu', which means, Die before death. A poet says, 'Only he attains to the peace of the Lord who loses himself.' God said to Moses, 'No man shall see me and live.' To see God we must be non-existent. It is false love that does not uproot man's claim of "I"; the first and last lesson of love is "I am not".

It is not love, but the pretense of love, that imposes the claim of the self. The first and last lesson in love is, 'I am not —Thou art' and unless man is moved to that selflessness he does not know justice, right or truth. His self stands above or between him and God.

There is no greater teacher of morals than love itself, for the first lesson that one learns from love is, 'I am not, you are.' This is self-denial, self-abnegation, without which we cannot take the first step on love's path. One may claim to be a great lover, to be a great admirer, to be very affectionate, but it all means nothing as long as the thought of self is there, for there is no love. But when the thought of self is removed, then every action, every deed that one performs in life, becomes a virtue.

He who says, 'I love you but only so much, I love you and give you sixpence but I keep sixpence for myself, I love you but I stand at a distance and never come closer, we are separate beings'—his love is with his self. As long as that exists, love has not done its full work. Love accomplishes its work when it spreads its wings and veils man's self from his own eyes. That is the time when love is fulfilled, and so it is in the life of the holy ones who have not only loved God by professing or showing it, but who have loved God to the extent that they forgot themselves. Man is here on earth for this one purpose, that he may bring forth that spirit of God in him and thus discover his own perfection. The three stages towards this perfection are the following. The first stage is to make God as great and as perfect as your imagination can.

The second stage is the work of the heart. The first lesson that love teaches us is: 'I am not. Thou art.' The first thing to think of is to erase ourselves from our minds and to think of the one we love. As long as we do not arrive at this idea, so long the word love remains only in the dictionary. Many speak about love but very few know it. Is love a pastime, an amusement, a drama; is it a performance? The first lesson of love is sacrifice, service, self-effacement. To close the eyes for prayer is one thing, and to produce the love of God is another thing. That is the second stage in spiritual realization, where, in the thought of God, one begins to lose oneself in the same way that the lover loses the thought of self in the thought of the beloved. And the third stage is different again. In the third stage the Beloved becomes the Self, and the self is there no more. For then the self, as we think it to be, no longer remains. The self becomes what it really is. It is that realization which is called Self-realization. *Hazrat Inyat Khan*

Surah Twelve

Yusuf

As life unfolds itself to man, the first lesson he learns is humility.

Every moment of our life, if we can see wisely, contains some fault or error, and asking pardon is just like purifying the heart and washing it white. Only think of the joy of humbling yourself before God!, humbling yourself before that Spirit, that Ideal, who is the true Father and Mother, on Whose love you can always depend -- it is a spark of His love which expresses itself in the earthly father and mother—and in whatever manner you humble yourself before Him, it can never be enough. To humble your limited self before His Perfection, that is to deny yourself. Self-denial is not renouncing things, it is denying the self, and its first lesson is humility. This is self-denial: that a man says, 'I am not, Thou art;' or that an artist looking at his picture, says, 'It is Thy work, not mine;' or that a musician, hearing his composition, says, 'It is Thy creation, I do not exist.' That soul then is in a way crucified, and through that crucifixion resurrection comes. There is not the slightest doubt that when man has had enough pain in his life he rises to this great consciousness. But it is not necessary that only pain should be the means. It is the readiness on the part of man to efface his part of consciousness and to efface his own personality, which lifts the veil that hides the spirit of God from the view of man. As life unfolds itself to man the first lesson it teaches is humility; the first thing that comes to man's vision is his own limitedness. The vaster God appears to him, the smaller he finds himself. This goes on and on until the moment comes when he loses himself in the vision of God. *Hazrat Inyat Khan*

In the name of Allah, the Beneficent, the Merciful

We narrate unto thee Muhammad the best of narratives in that We have inspired in thee this Quran, though aforetimes thou wast of the heedless. (12:3 Quran)

And the king said: Bring him unto me. And when the messenger came unto him, Joseph said: Return unto thy lord and ask him: what was the case of the women who cut their hands? Lo, my lord knoweth their guile. (12:50 Quran)

He the king then sent for those women and said: What happened when ye asked an evil act of Joseph? They answered: Allah Blameless! We know no evil of him. Said the wife of the ruler. Now the truth is out. I asked of him an evil act, and he is surely of the truthful. (12:51 Quran)

Then Joseph said: I asked for this, that he my lord may know that I betrayed him not in secret, and that surely Allah guideth not the snare of the betrayers. (12:52 Quran)

I do not exculpate myself. Lo, the human soul enjoineth unto evil, save that whereon my Lord hath mercy. Lo, my Lord is Merciful, Forgiving. (12:53 Quran)

And the king said: Bring Joseph unto me that I may attract him to my person. And when he had talked with him he said: Lo, thou art today in our presence established and trusted. (12:54 Quran)

Joseph said: Set me over the storehouse of the land. Lo, I am a skilled custodian. (12:55 Quran)

Thus gave We power to Joseph in the land. He was the owner of it where he pleased. We reach with Our mercy whom We will. We lose not the reward of the good. (12:56 Quran)

And the reward of the Hereafter is better, for those who believe and ward off evil. (12:57 Quran)

Joseph said to his brothers: Have no fear this day! May Allah forgive you, and He is the Most Merciful of those who show mercy. (12:92 Quran)

Go with this shirt of mine and lay it on my father's face, he will become again a seer, and come to me with all your folk. (12:93 Quran)

When the caravan departed their father had said: Truly I am conscious of the breath of Joseph, though ye call me dotard. (12:94 Quran)

Those around him said: By Allah, lo, thou art in thine old aberration. (12:95 Quran)

Then, when the bearer of glad tidings came, he laid it (shirt) on his face and he became a seer once more. He said: Said I not unto you that I knew from Allah that which ye know not? (12:96 Quran)

They said: O our father! Ask forgiveness of our sins for us, for lo, we are sinful. (12:97 Quran)

He said: I shall ask forgiveness for you of my Lord. Lo, He is the Merciful, the Forgiving. (12:98 Quran)

And when they came in before Joseph, he took his parents unto him and said: Come into Egypt safe, if Allah will! (12:99 Quran)

We sent not before thee any messengers save men whom We inspired from among the folk of the townships. Have they not traveled in the land and seen the nature of the consequence for those who were before them? And verily the abode of the Hereafter, for those who ward off evil, is best. Have ye then no more sense? (12:109 Quran

In their history verily there is a lesson for men of understanding. It is no invented story but a confirmation of the existing Scripture and a detailed explanation of everything, and a guidance and a mercy for folk who believe. (12:111 Quran)

The soul brings its light from Heaven; the mind acquires its knowledge from earth. Therefore, when the soul believes readily, the mind may still doubt.

Belief is natural, and disbelief is unnatural, for belief is born in man, and unbelief is acquired. Every child born on earth is born with a tendency to believe what is told him, but the experience of the individual in this world full of falsehood teaches man to disbelieve. That shows that every soul comes from the world of truth, and opens his eyes in the world of falsehood. Every child comes into the world with that purity of heart whose natural tendency is to believe and later he acquires the tendency to doubt. The Prophet has therefore said: 'Every child is born a believer, it is afterwards that he becomes an unbeliever.' For doubt is earth-born and belief is heaven-born. The tendency to doubt, to be depressed, the tendency towards fear, suspicion and confusion, the tendency to puzzle — where does it all come from? It all comes from the thought of getting something in return: 'will another give me back what I

Farzana Moon

have given him? Shall I get the just portion back, or less?' If that is the
thought behind one's acts there will be fear, doubt, suspicion, puzzle and
confusion. For what is doubt? Doubt is a cloud that stands before the sun,
keeping it from shining its light. So is doubt: gathering around the soul it
keeps its light from shining out, and man becomes confused and
perplexed. Once selflessness is developed, it breaks through the cloud
saying, 'What do I care whether anyone appreciates it; I only know to
give my service, and that is all my satisfaction. I do not look forward to
get it back. I have given and it is finished; this is where my duty ends.'
That person is blessed, because he has conquered, he has won.
Understanding does not depend upon the head; it depends upon the
heart. By the help of the head one can make it more clear, it becomes
intelligible and one can express it better. But to begin with it must come
from the heart, not from the head. Besides, a person who only uses his
head says, 'It must be so because I think it is so', whereas the person who
has the heart quality says, 'It is so because I believe it to be so'. That is the
difference. In one person there is a doubt, in the other there is conviction.
Spiritual attainment is nothing but conviction. When a person arrives at
the stage when the knowledge of reality becomes a conviction, then there
is nothing in the world that will change it. And if there is anything to
attain to, it is that conviction which one can never find in the outside
world; it must rise from the depths of one's own heart. *Hazrat Inayat Khan*

The priest gives a benediction from the church; the branches of the
tree in bending give blessing from God.

Anyone who has some knowledge of mysticism and of the lives of the
mystics knows that what always attracts the mystic most is nature.
Nature is his bread and wine. Nature is his soul's nourishment. Nature
inspires him, uplifts him and gives him the solitude for which his soul
continually longs. Every soul born with a mystical tendency is constantly
drawn towards nature. In nature that soul finds its life's demand, as it is
said in the Vadan, 'Art is dear to my heart, but nature is near to my soul.'
Nature itself is the glory of God. The deeper we look into life the more it
unfolds itself, allowing us to see more keenly. Life is revealing. It is not
only human beings who speak; if only the ears can hear even plants and
trees and all nature speak, in the sense that nature reveals itself, reveals
its secret. In this way we communicate with the whole of life. Then we
are never alone, then life becomes worth living. What appeals to us in
being near to nature is nature's music, and nature's music is more perfect
than that of art. It gives us a sense of exaltation to be moving about in the
woods, and to be looking at the green; to be standing near the running
water, which has its rhythm, its tone and its harmony. The swinging of
the branches in the forest, the rising and falling of the waves, all has its
music. And once we contemplate and become one with nature our hearts

open to its music. When a person begins to see all goodness as being the goodness of God, all the beauty that surrounds him as the divine beauty, he begins by worshipping a visible God, and as his heart constantly loves and admires the divine beauty in all that he sees, he begins to see in all that is visible one single vision; all becomes for him the vision of the beauty of God. His love of beauty increases his capacity to such a degree that great virtues such as tolerance and forgiveness spring naturally from his heart. Even things that people mostly look upon with contempt, he views with tolerance. The brotherhood of humanity he does not need to learn, for he does not see humanity, he sees only God. And as this vision develops, it becomes a divine vision, which occupies every moment of his life. In nature he sees God, in man he sees His image, and in art and poetry he sees the dance of God. The waves of the sea bring him the message from above, and the swaying of the branches in the breeze seems to him a prayer. For him there is a constant contact with his God. *Hazrat Inyat Khan*

Surah Thirteen

Ar Rad
Believe in God with childlike faith; for simplicity with intelligence is the sign of the Holy Ones.

The question arises: what is the manner of opening the heart? The way to it is a natural life, the life of the child, smiling with the smiling one, praying with the praying one, ready to learn from everyone, ready to love. The child has enmity against no one, he has no hatred, no malice, his heart is open. It is in the child that you can see the smiles of angels; he can see through life. When the grown-up person is made ready, when he has acquired the attributes of the child, then he creates heaven within himself, he understands. The child with his innocence does not understand, but when a person with understanding develops the childlike loving tendency, the purity of heart of the child with the desire to be friendly to all—that is the opening of the heart, and it is by that blessing that he can receive all the privileges of human life, truth is simple. The more simple you are and the more you seek for simplicity, the nearer you come to truth. I remember the blessing my spiritual teacher, my murshid, used to give me every time I parted from him. And that blessing was, 'May your Iman be strengthened.' At that time I had not thought about the word Iman. On the contrary I thought as a young man, is my faith so weak that my teacher requires it to be stronger? I would have preferred it if he had said, may you become illuminated, or may your powers be great, or may your influence spread, or may you rise higher and higher, or become perfect. But this simple thing, may your faith be strengthened, what did it mean? I did not criticize but I pondered and pondered upon the subject. And in the end I came to realize that no blessing is more valuable and important than this. For every blessing is attached to a conviction. Where there is no conviction there is nothing. The secret of healing, the mystery of evolving, the power of all attainments, and the way to spiritual realization, all come from the strengthening of that belief which is a conviction, so that nothing can ever change it.

We read in the Vadan, 'Simplicity is the living beauty.' Mankind today has made life so complex that whatever one seeks after, one wants to find in complexity. All things in life which have importance, beauty and value are simple; and simplest of all things is the divine truth. *Hazrat Inayat Khan*

In the name of Allah, the Beneficent, the Merciful

Allah is he who raised up the heavens without visible supports, then mounted the Throne, and compelled the sun and the moon to be of service, each cometh into an appointed term. He ordereth the course, He detaileth the revelations that haply ye may be certain of the meeting with your Lord. (13:2 Quran)

And He it is who spread out the earth and placed therein firm hills and flowing streams and all fruits he placed therein: two spouses, male and female. He covereth the night with the day. Lo, herein, verily are portents for people who have sense. (13:3 Quran)

And in the earth are neighboring tracts, vineyards and ploughed lands, and date-palms, like and unlike, which are watered with one water. And we have made some of them to excel others in fruit. Lo, herein, verily are portents for people who have sense. (13:4 Quran)

Allah knoweth that which female beareth and that which the wombs absorb and that which they grow. And everything with Him is measured. (13:8 Quran)

He is the Knower of the invisible and the visible, the Great, the High Exalted. (13:9 Quran)

He it is who showeth you the lightning, a fear and a hope, and raiseth the heavy clouds. (13:12 Quran)

He sendeth down water from the sky, so that valleys flow according to their measure, and the flood beareth on its surface, swelling foam — from that which they smelt in the fire in order to make ornaments and tools: risheth a foam like unto it — thus Allah coineth the similitude of the true and the false. Then, as for the foam, it passeth away as scum upon the banks, while as for that which is of use to mankind, it remaineth in the earth. Thus Allah coineth the similitudes. (13:17 Quran)

Garden of Eden which they enter, along with all who do right of their fathers and their helpmates and their seed. The angels enter unto them from every gate. (13:23 Quran)

Saying: Peace be unto you because ye persevered. Ah, passing sweet will be the sequel of the heavenly Home. (13:24 Quran)

Allah enlargeth livelihood for whom He will, and straiteneth it for whom He will. And they rejoice in the life of the world, whereas the life of the world is but brief comfort as compared with the Hereafter. (13:26 Quran)

Who have believed and whose hearts have rest in the remembrance of Allah. Verily in the remembrance of Allah do hearts find rest! (13:28 Quran)

Those who believe and do right: Joy is for them, and bliss their journey's end. (13:29 Quran)

Thus We send thee, O Muhammad, unto a nation before whom other nations have passed away, that thou mayest recite unto them that which We have inspired in thee, while they are disbelievers in the Beneficent. Say: He is my Lord, there is no God save Him. In Him do I put my trust and unto Him is my recourse. (13:30 Quran)

And verily We sent messengers to mankind before thee, and We appointed for them wives and offspring, and it was not given to any messenger that he should bring a portent save by Allah's leave. For everything there is a time prescribed. (13:38 Quran)

Allah effaceth what He will, and establisheth what He will, and with Him is the source of ordinance. (13:39 Quran)

Whether We let thee see something of that which We have promised them, or make thee die before its happening, thine is but conveyance of the message, ours the reckoning. (13:40 Quran)

Nature speaks louder than the call from the minaret.

One may ask, what should one study? There are two kinds of studies. One kind is by reading the teachings of the great thinkers and keeping them in mind, the study of metaphysics, psychology, and mysticism. And the other kind of study is the study of life. Every day one has an opportunity for studying; but it should be a correct study. When a person travels in a tramcar, in the train, with a newspaper in his hand, he wants to read the sensational news which is worth nothing. He should read human nature which is before him, people coming and going. If he would continue to do this, he would begin to read human beings as though they were letters written by the divine pen, which speak of their past and future. He should look deeply at the heavens and at nature and at all the things to be seen in everyday life, and reflect upon them with the desire to understand. This kind of study is much superior, incomparably superior, to the study of books. The deeper we look into life the more it unfolds itself, allowing us to see more keenly. Life is revealing. It is not only human beings who speak; if only the ears can hear even plants and trees and all nature speak, in the sense that nature reveals itself, reveals its secret. In this way we communicate with the whole of life. Then we are never alone, then life becomes worth living. Just as there is a communication between persons who love each other very much, so the sympathy of a person whose soul has unfolded itself is so awakened that not only every person but even every object begins to reveal its nature, its character and secret. To him every man is a written letter.

We hear stories of saints and sages who talked with rocks and plants and trees. They are not only stories; it is reality. It is also told of the apostles that at the moment when the Spirit descended upon them they began to speak many languages. When they understood so many languages, they understood the language of every soul. It means that the illuminated soul understands the language of every soul. And every soul has its own language. It is that which is called revelation. All the teachings that the great prophets and teachers have given are only interpretations of what they have seen. They have interpreted in their own language what they have read from the manuscript of nature: that trees and plants and rocks spoke to them. Did nature only speak to those in the past? No, the soul of man is always capable of that bliss if he only realized it. Once the eyes of the heart are open, man begins to read every leaf of the tree as a page of the sacred Book. In the swinging of the branches, in the flying of the birds, and in the running of the water, Beloved, I see Thy waving hand, bidding me good-bye. In the cooing of the wind, in the roaring of the sea, and in the crashing of the thunder, Beloved, I see Thee weep and I hear Thy cry. In the promise of the dawn, in the breaking of the morn, in the smiles of the rose, Beloved, I see Thy joy at my homecoming. *Hazrat Inayat Khan*

Surah Fourteen

Ibrahim
He who has failed himself has failed all; he who has conquered himself has won all.

There is no reason for anyone to feel discouraged by his weaknesses or deficiencies, or by his actions that have dissatisfied him, or by anything in life that has failed. He should forget the past that has failed him, and begin to construct and mold his future as he would wish it to be. Considering that as a branch is not separate from the bough, and the bough is not separate from the stem, so with all our limitations we are not separate from the will of the Unlimited One. I remember a Persian verse made by my murshid which relates to the self: 'When I feel that now I can make peace with myself, it finds time to prepare another attack.' That is our condition. We think that our little faults, since they are small, are of no consequence; or we do not even think of them at all. But every little fault is a flag for the little self, for its own dominion. In this way battling makes man the sovereign of the kingdom of God. Very few can realize the great power in battling with and conquering the self. But what does man generally do? He says, 'My poor self, it has to withstand the conflicts of this world; should I also battle with this self?' So he surrenders his kingdom to his little self, depriving himself of the divine power that is in the heart of man. There is in man a false self and a real self. The real self contains the eternal; the false self contains the mortal. The real self has wisdom; the false self-ignorance. The real self can rise to perfection; the false self ends in limitation. The real self has all good, the false self is productive of all evil. One can see both in oneself: God and the other one. By conquering the other one, one realizes God. This other power has been called Satan; but is it a power? In reality it is not. It is and it is not. It is a shadow. We see shadow and yet it is nothing. We should realize that this false self has no existence of its own. As soon as the soul has risen above the false self, it begins to realize its nobility.

Hazrat Inyat Khan

In the name Allah, the Beneficent, the Merciful

Alif, Lam, Ra. This is a Scripture which We have revealed unto thee Muhammad and thereby thou mayest bring forth mankind from darkness unto light, by the permission of their Lord, unto the path of the Mighty, the Owner of Praise. (14:1 Quran)

And We never sent a messenger save with the language of his folk, that he might make the message clear for them. Then Allah sendeth whom He will astray, and guideth whom He will. He is the Wise, the Mighty. (14:4 Quran)

We verily sent Moses with our revelations, saying: Bring thy people forth from darkness unto light. And remind them of the days of Allah. Lo, therein are revelations for each steadfast, thankful heart. (14:5 Quran)

And those who believed and did good works are made to enter Gardens underneath which rivers flow, therein abiding by permission of their Lord, their greeting therein: Peace. (14:23 Quran)

Seest thou not how Allah coineth a similitude. A goodly saying as a goodly tree, its root: set firm, its branches reaching into heaven. (14:24 Quran)

Giving its fruit at every season by permission of its Lord. Allah coineth the similitudes for mankind in order that they may reflect. (14:25 Quran)

And the similitude of a bad saying is as a bad tree, uprooted from upon the earth, possessing no stability. (14:26 Quran)

Allah confirmeth those who believe by a firm saying in the life of the world and in the Hereafter, and Allah sendeth wrong-doers astray. And Allah doeth what He will. (14:27 Quran)

Allah is He Who created the heavens and the earth, and caused water to descend from the sky, thereby producing fruits as food for you, and maketh the ships to be of service unto you, and hath made of service unto you the rivers. (14:32 Quran)

And maketh the sun and the moon, constant in their courses, to be of service unto you, and hath made of service unto you the night and the day. (14:33 Quran)

My Lord! Lo, they have led many of mankind astray. But whoso followeth me, he verily is of me. And whoso disobeyeth me—still Thou art Merciful, Forgiving. (14:36 Quran)

Oh Lord! Lo, I (Abraham) have settled some of my posterity in an uncultivable valley near unto Thy holy House, our Lord, that they may establish proper worship, so incline some hearts of men that they may yearn toward them, and provide Thou them with fruits in order that they may be thankful. (14:37 Quran)

Our Lord! Lo, Thou knowest that which we hide and that which we proclaim. Nothing in the earth or in the heavens is hidden from Allah. (14:38 Quran)

Praise be to Allah Who hath given me, in my old age, Ishmael and Isaac! Lo, my Lord is indeed the Hearer of prayer. (14:39 Quran)

My Lord! Make me to establish proper worship, and some of my posterity also: our Lord, and accept the prayer. (14:40 Quran)

Our Lord! Forgive me and my parents and believers on the day when the account is cast. (14:41 Quran)

So think not that Allah will fail to keep His promise to His messengers. Lo, Allah is Mighty, Able to requite the wrong. (14:47 Quran)

He who arrives at the state of indifference without experiencing interest in life is incomplete and apt to be tempted by interest at any moment; but he who arrives at the state of indifference by going through interest really attains the blessed state.

It is the interest of God which has been the cause of all creation and which keeps the whole universe in harmony; nevertheless one should not be completely immersed in phenomena, but should realize oneself as being independent of interests. He who arrives at the state of indifference without experiencing interest in life is incomplete, and apt to be tempted by interest at any moment; but he who arrives at the state of indifference by going through interest, really attains the blessed state. Perfection is reached not through interest alone, nor through indifference alone, but through the right experience and understanding of both. We also see many examples in this world of how interest often limits man's power, and how indifference makes it greater. But at the same time indifference should not be practiced unless it springs naturally from the heart. There is a saying in the Hindi language, 'Interest makes kings, but indifference makes emperors.' There comes a day in the life of a person, sooner or later, the day when he no longer thinks about himself, how he eats, how he is clothed, how he lives, how anybody treats him, if anybody loves him or hates him. Every thought that concerns himself leaves him. That day comes, and it is a blessed day when it comes to a man. That day his soul begins to live. Indifference is attained by developing interest, and by developing discrimination in one's interest. Instead of going backward one should go forward in one's interest. Then one will find that a spring will rise naturally in one's heart, when the heart has touched the zenith in the path of interest. Then the fountain of interest will break up gradually, and when this happens, one should follow this trend, so that in the end one may know what interest means, and what indifference means.

Our likes and infatuations have a certain limit; when their time has expired the period of indifference commences. When the water of indifference is drunk, then there is no more wish for anything in the world. The nature of the water one drinks in this world is that one's thirst is quenched for a certain time and then comes again. When the water of divine knowledge is drunk, then thirst never comes again. Indifference, however, must be reached after interest has taken its course; before that moment it is a fault. A person without an interest in life becomes exclusive, he becomes disagreeable. Indifference must come after all experience—interest must end in indifference. Man must not take the endless path of interest: the taste of everything in the world becomes flat. Man must realize that all he seeks in the objects he runs after, that all beauty and strength, are in himself, and he must be content to feel them all in himself.

Vairagya means satisfaction, the feeling that no desire is to be satisfied any more, that nothing on earth is desired. This is a great moment, and then comes that which is the kingdom of God. Vairagya means a person who has become indifferent; and yet indifference is not the word for it. It describes a person who has lost the value in his eyes of all that attracts the human being. It is no more attractive to him; it no more enslaves him. He may still be interested in all things of this life, but is not bound to them. No affair of this world, no relation, no friendship, no wealth, no rank, position or comfort, nothing holds him. And yet that does not mean that he in any way lacks what is called love or kindness, for if ever he lives in this world it is only out of love. He is not interested in the world and it is only love that keeps him here, the love which does not express itself any more in the way of attachment, but only in the way of kindness, forgiveness, generosity, service, consideration, sympathy, helpfulness, in any way that it can; never expecting a return from the world, but ever doing all that it can, pitying the conditions, knowing the limitations of life and its continual changeability. *Hazrat Inyat Khan.*

Surah Fifteen

Al Hijr

Love brought man from the world of unity to that of variety, and the same force can take him back again to the world of unity from the world of variety.

Sufis take the course of love and devotion to accomplish their highest aim, because it is love which has brought man from the world of unity to the world of variety, and the same force can take him back again to the world of unity from that of variety. *Love is the reduction of the universe to the single being, and the expansion of a single being, even to God.* (Balzac) Love is that state of mind in which the consciousness of the lover is merged in that of the object of his love; it produces in the lover all the attributes of humanity, such as resignation, renunciation, humility, kindness, contentment, patience, virtue, calmness, gentleness, charity, faithfulness, bravery, by which the devotee becomes harmonized with the Absolute. As one of God's beloved, a path is opened for his heavenly journey: at the end he arrives at oneness with God, and his whole individuality is dissolved in the ocean of eternal bliss where even the conception of God and man disappears. Seeing the nature and character of life the Sufi says that it is not very important to distinguish between two opposites. What is most important is to recognize that One which is hiding behind it all. Naturally after realizing life the Sufi climbs the ladder which leads him to unity, to the idea of unity which comes through the synthesis of life, by seeing One in all things, in all beings. In whatever age the wise were born, they have always believed the same: that behind all is oneness, and in the understanding of that oneness is wisdom. A person who awakens to the spirit of unity, a person who sees the oneness behind all things—his point of view becomes different and his attitude therefore changes. He no longer says to his friend, 'I love you because you are my friend'; he says, 'I love you because you are my self'. *Hazrat Inyat Khan*

In the name of Allah, the Beneficent, the Merciful

No nation can outstrip its term nor can they lag behind. (15:5 Quran)

We verily sent messengers before thee among the factions of the men of old. (15:10 Quran)

And never came unto them a messenger but they did mock him. (15:11 Quran)

Thus do We make it a traverse the hearts of the guilty. (15:12 Quran)

They believe not therein, though the example of the men of old hath gone before. (15:13 Quran)

And even if We opened unto them a Gate of Heaven, and they kept mounting through it. (15:14 Quran)

They would say: Our sight is wrong—nay, but we are folk bewitched. (15:15 Quran)

And verily in the heaven, We have set mansions of the stars, and We have beautified it for beholders. (15:16 Quran)

And the earth have We spread out, and placed therein firm hills, and caused each seemingly thing to grow therein. (15:19 Quran)

And We have given unto you livelihoods therein, and unto those for whom ye provide not. (15:20 Quran)

And there is not a thing but with Us are the stores thereof. And We send it not down save in appointed measure. (15:21 Quran)

And We send the winds fertilizing, and cause water to descent from the sky, and give it to you to drink. It is not ye who are the holders of the store thereof. (15:22 Quran)

Lo, it is We, even We, Who quicken and give death, and We are the inheritor. (15:23 Quran)

And verily We know the eager among you and verily We know the laggards. (15:24 Quran)

Lo, thy Lord will gather them together. Lo, he is Wise, Aware. (15:25 Quran)

Verily We created man of potter's clay of black mud altered. (15:26 Quran)

And the Jinn did We create aforetime of essential fire. (15:27 Quran)

Announce, O Muhammad, unto My slaves that verily I am the Merciful, the Forgiving. (15:49 Quran)

We created not the heavens and the earth and all that is between them save with truth, and lo, the Hour is surely coming. So, forgive, O Muhammad, with a gracious forgiveness. (15:85 Quran)

Lo! Thy Lord! He is the All-Wise Creator. (15:86 Quran)

We have given thee seven of the oft-repeated verses and the great Quran. (15:87 Quran)

Strain not thine eyes toward that which We cause some wedded pairs among them to enjoy, and be not grieved on their account, and lower thy wind in tenderness for the believers. (15:88 Quran)

And say: Lo! I, even I am a plain warner. (15:89 Quran)

Such as We send down for those who make division. (15:90 Quran)
Those who break the Quran into parts. (15:91 Quran)
Them, by thy Lord, We will question everyone. (15:92 Quran)
Of what they used to do. (15:93 Quran)

The religion of each one is the attainment of his soul's desire; when he is on the path of that attainment he is religious; when he is off that path then he is irreligious, impious.

Religion is a need of the human soul. In all periods and at every stage of the evolution of humanity there has been a religion which people followed, for at every period the need for religion has been felt. The reason is that the soul of man has several deep desires, and these desires are answered by religion. The first desire is the search for the ideal. There comes a time when man seeks for a more complete justice than he finds among men, and when he seeks for someone on whom he can rely more surely than he can on his friends in the world. There comes a time when man feels a desire to open his heart to a Being who is above human beings and who can understand his heart. He feels the need of asking forgiveness of someone who is above human pettiness, and of seeking refuge under someone stronger than he. And to all these natural human tendencies there is an answer which is given by religion, and that answer is God.

When speaking on the subject of ideal life, the words of the Prophet of Islam may be quoted, where he says, 'Every soul has its own religion.' This means that every soul has a certain direction which it has chosen, a goal to attain during life. This goal is a certain ideal, which depends on the soul's evolution. In the Hindu language, the same word, Dharma, means both duty and religion. Both are expressed by one word. 'This is your Dharma' means: 'This is your faith.' How beautiful the thought is! Whatever kind of duty it is, so long as you have an ideal before you and are performing that duty, you are walking in the path of religion. We, with our narrowness of faith or belief, accuse others of belonging to another religion, another chapel or church. We say, 'This temple is better, that faith is better.' The whole world has kept on fighting and devastating itself just because it cannot understand that each form of religion is peculiar to itself. Therefore, the ideal life is in following one's own ideal. It is not in checking other people's ideals. The whole aim of the Sufi is, by thought of God, to cover his imperfect self even from his own eyes, and that moment when God is before him and not his own self, is the moment of perfect bliss to him. My Murshid, Abu Hashim Madani, once said that there is only one virtue and one sin for a soul on the path: virtue when he is conscious of God and sin when he is not. *Hazrat Inayat Khan*

Surah Sixteen

An Nahl

The reformer comes to plow the ground; the prophet comes to sow the seed; and the priest comes to reap the harvest.

There is the time of plowing, there is the time of sowing and there is the time of reaping the harvest. It is not all done at the same time.

Hazrat Inayat Khan

In the name of Allah, the Beneficent, the Merciful.

And the cattle hath He created, whence ye have warm clothing and uses, and whereof ye eat. (16:5 Quran)

And wherein is beauty for you, when ye bring them home, and ye take them out to pasture. (16:6 Quran)

And they bear your loads for you unto a land ye could not reach save with great trouble to yourselves. Lo! Your Lord is Full of Pity, Merciful. (16:7 Quran)

And horses and mules and asses He hath created that ye may ride them, and for ornament. And He createth that which ye know not. (16:8 Quran)

And He it is Who hath constrained the sea to be of service that ye eat fresh meat from thence, and bring forth from thence the ornaments which ye wear. And thou seest the ships ploughing it that ye mankind may seek of His bounty, and that haply ye may give thanks. (16:14 Quran)

And He hath cast into earth firm hills that it quake not with you, and streams and roads that ye may find a way. (16:15 Quran)

And landmarks too, and by the star they find a way. (16:16 Quran)

And He then Who createth as him who createth not? Will ye not then remember? (16:17 Quran)

And if ye would count the favor of Allah ye cannot reckon it. Lo! Allah is indeed Merciful, Forgiving. (16:18 Quran)

Assuredly Allah knoweth that which they keep hidden and that which they proclaim. Lo! He loveth not the proud. (16:23 Quran)

And it is said unto those who ward off evil: What hath your Lord revealed? They say: Good. For those who do good in this world there is a good reward and the home of the Hereafter will be better. Pleasant indeed will be the home of those who ward off evil. (16:30 Quran)

Gardens of Eden which they enter, underneath which rivers flow, wherein they have what they will. Thus Allah repayeth those who ward off evil. (16:31 Quran)

Those whom angels cause to die when they are good. They say: Peace be unto you! Enter the Garden because of what ye used to do. (16:32 Quran)

And Our word unto a thing, when We intend it, is only that We say unto it: Be! And it is. (16:40 Quran)

And those who became fugitives for the cause of Allah after they had been oppressed. We verily shall give them goodly lodging in the world, and surely the reward of the Hereafter is greater, if they but know. (16:41 Quran)

Such are the steadfast and put their trust in Allah. (16:42 Quran)

And We sent not our messengers before thee other than men whom We inspired—Ask the followers of the Remembrance if ye know not? (16:43 Quran)

With clear proofs and writings, and We have revealed unto thee the Remembrance that thou mayest explain to mankind that which hath been revealed for them, and that haply they may reflect. (16:44 Quran)

And if Allah were to take mankind to task for their wrongdoing, He would not leave here-on a living creature, but He reprieveth them to an appointed term, and when their term cometh they cannot put it off an hour nor yet advance it. (16:61 Quran)

And We have revealed the Scripture unto thee only that thou mayest explain unto them that wherein they differ and as a guidance and a mercy for people who believe. (16:64 Quran)

And of the fruits of the date palm and grapes, whence ye derive strong drink and also good nourishment. Lo! Therein is indeed a portent for people who have sense. (16:67 Quran)

And thy Lord inspired the bee, saying: Choose thou habitations in the hills and in the trees and in that which they thatch. (16:68 Quran)

Then eat of all fruits, and follow the ways of thy Lord, made smooth for thee. There cometh forth from their bellies a drink diverse of hues, wherein is healing for mankind. Lo, herein is indeed a portent for people who reflect. (16:69 Quran)

Lo! Allah enjoineth justice and kindness, and giving to kinsfolk, and forbiddeth lewdness and abomination and wickedness. He exhorteth you in order that ye may take heed. (16:90 Quran)

And be not like unto her who unravelleth the thread, after she had made it strong, to thin filaments, making your oaths a deceit between you because a nation being more numerous than another nation. Allah only trieth you thereby, and He verily will explain to you on the Day of Resurrection that wherein ye differed. (16:92 Quran)

Whosoever doth right, whether male or female, and is a believer, him or her verily We shall quicken with good life, and We shall pay them a recompense in proportion to the best of what they used to do. (16:97 Quran)

And when We put a revelation in place of another revelation—and Allah knoweth best what He revealeth. They say: Lo, thou art but inventing. Most of them know not. (16:101 Quran)

Say: The Holy Spirit hath revealed it from thy Lord with truth, that it may confirm the faith of those who believe, and as guidance and good tidings for those who have surrendered to Allah. (16:102 Quran)

On the Day when every soul will come pleading for itself, and every soul will be repaid what it did, and they will not be wronged. (16:111 Quran)

And speak not concerning that which your own tongues qualify as clean or unclean, the falsehood: 'This is lawful and this is forbidden.' So that ye invent a lie against Allah. Lo, those who invent a lie against Allah will not succeed. (16:116 Quran)

Then lo, thy Lord—for those who do evil in ignorance and afterward repent and amend. Lo, for them thy Lord is afterward indeed Merciful, Forgiving. (16:119 Quran)

The Sabbath was appointed only for those who differed concerning it, and lo, thy Lord will judge between them on the Day of Resurrection concerning that wherein they used to differ. (16:124 Quran)

Call unto the way of thy Lord with wisdom and fair exhortation, and reason with them in the better way. Lo, thy Lord is best aware of him who strayeth from His way, and He is Best Aware of those who go right. (16:125 Quran)

If ye punish, then punish with the like of that wherewith ye were afflicted. But if ye endure patiently, verily it is better for the patient. (16:126 Quran)

Endure thou patiently O Muhammad. Thine endurance is only by the help of Allah. Grieve not for them, and be not in distress because of that which they devise. (16:127 Quran)

Lo, Allah is with those who keep their duty unto Him and those who are doers of good. (16:128 Quran)

At every step of evolution, man's realization of God changes.

There is a time when toys are treasures. But the child who cries for a toy comes to an age when he gives it away. And at every step in a man's evolution the values of power and position and wealth change in his eyes. And so as he evolves there arises in him a spirit of renunciation which may be called the Spirit of God. Gradually he recognizes the real value of those fair and lovely qualities of the spirit that change not.

Every step in evolution makes life more valuable. The more evolved you are, the more priceless is every moment; it becomes an opportunity for you to do good to others, to serve others, to give love to others, to be gentle to others, to give your sympathy to souls who are longing and hungering for it. Life is miserable when a person is absorbed in himself.

In selfishness there is an illusion of profit, but in the end the profit attained by selfishness proves to be worthless. Life is the principal thing to consider, and true life is the inner life, the realization of God, the consciousness of one's spirit. When the human heart becomes conscious of God it turns into the sea and it spreads; it extends the waves of its love to friend and foe. Spreading further and further it attains perfection.

The one who in the shrine of his heart has seen the vision of God, the one who has the realization of truth, can only smile, for words can never really explain what truth means. The nearest explanation one can give is that truth is realization. At every step of man's evolution his realization changes, but there is a stage where man arrives at the true realization, a realization which is a firm conviction that no reason or logic can change or alter. Nothing in the world can change it anymore, and that conviction is called by the Sufis Iman.

The realization which is attained is that there is nothing to realize any more. The process of this attainment is a sincere research into truth and life, and the understanding of 'what I am the other is', together with the contemplation of God, a selfless consciousness, and a continual pursuit after the receiving of the knowledge of God. Hazrat Inayat Khan

Prayer is the greatest virtue, the only way of being free from all sin.

The first aspect of prayer is giving thanks to God for all the numberless blessings that are bestowed upon us at every moment of the day and night, and of which we are mostly unconscious. The second aspect of prayer is laying our shortcomings before the unlimited perfection of the divine Being, and asking His forgiveness. This makes man conscious of his smallness, of his limitation, and therefore makes him humble before his God.

There are many virtues, but there is one principal virtue. Every moment passed outside the presence of God is sin, and every moment in His presence is virtue. The whole object of the Sufi, after learning this way of communicating is to arrive at a stage where every moment of our life passes in communion with God, and where our every action is done as if God were before us. Is that within everyone's reach? We are meant to be so.

Prayer is a great virtue and is the only way of being free from all sin. In prayer a man reaches the Spirit of God which is all-powerful and ever-forgiving; and the power of prayer opens the doors of the heart in which God, the All-Merciful resides.

There are many different feelings which have their influence upon men, and give joy and exaltation; but there is none greater and more exalting than that of offering our faults and weaknesses before God and asking His pardon with true repentance and humility. No ethics, no philosophy, can give greater joy than this, which is sincere devotion to God; and the deepest joy is his who knows best how to humble himself before God. The proud man, ignorant of greatness of God, and of His all-sufficient power, does not know this exaltation, which raises the soul from earth to Heaven. *Hazrat Inayat Khan*

Surah Seventeen

Bani Israil

We are always searching for God afar off, when all the while He is nearer to us than our own soul.

Spirituality has become far removed from material life, and so God is far removed from humanity. Therefore, one cannot any more conceive of God speaking through a man, through someone like oneself. Even a religious man who reads the Bible every day will have great difficulty in understanding the verse, 'Be ye perfect, even as your Father in heaven is perfect.' The Sufi message and its mission are to bring this truth to the consciousness of the world: that man can dive so deep within himself that he can touch the depths, where he is united with the whole of life, with all souls, and that he can derive from that source harmony, beauty, peace and power.

When a person turns for guidance to God, to the inner Being, then all light and all knowledge are his for his guidance. "But," people say. "How can we attach ourselves with the inner Being, so as to have that guidance?" When the mind is fixed upon anything, then the person becomes linked to that, a current is established between him and it. It may be called the guidance of God or the guidance of the Self. If we look within, God is nearer to us than our mind and our body, because He is that life in which as is said in the Bible, we live and move and have our being.

'The one whom I have called God, whose personality I have recognized, and whose pleasure or displeasure I have sought, has been seeing His life through my eyes, has been hearing through my ears. It was His breath that came through my breathing, His impulse which I felt, and therefore I know that this body which I had thought to be my own is really the true temple of God. I did not realize that this body was the shrine of God.' Not knowing that God experiences this life through man, one is seeking for Him somewhere else, in some person aloof and apart from the world, whereas all the time He is in oneself. *Hazrat Inayat Khan.*

In the name of Allah, the Beneficent, the Merciful

Glorified be He Who carried His servant by night from the Inviolable Place of Worship to the Far Distant Place of Worship, the neighborhood whereof We have blessed, that We might show him of Our tokens! Lo! He, only He, is the Seer, the Hearer. (17:1 Quran)

We gave unto Moses the Scripture, and We appointed a guidance for the Children of Israel. Saying: Choose no guardian beside Me. (17:2 Quran)

They were the sea of those whom We carried in the ship along with Noah. Lo, he was a grateful slave. (17:3 Quran)

Whosoever goeth right, it is only for the good of his own soul that he goeth right, and whosoever erreth, erreth only to its hurt. No laden soul can bear another's load. We never punish until We have sent a messenger. (17:15 Quran)

Your Lord is best aware of what is in your minds. If ye are righteous, then lo! He was ever Forgiving unto those who turn unto Him. (17:25 Quran)

Give the kinsman his due, and the needy, and the wayfarer, and squander not thy wealth in wantonness. (17:26 Quran)

Slay not your children, fearing a fall to poverty. We shall provide for them and for you. Lo, the slaying of them is great sin. (17:31 Quran)

And come not near unto adultery. Lo, it is an abomination and an evil way. (17:32 Quran)

And slay not the life which Allah hath forbidden save with right. Whoso is slain wrongfully, We have given power unto his heir, but let him not commit excess in slaying. Lo, he will be helped. (17:33 Quran)

Come not near the wealth of the orphans save with that which is better till he come to strength, and keep the covenant. Lo, of the covenant it will be asked. (17:34 Quran)

Fill the measure when you measure, and weigh with a right balance, that is meet, and better in the end. (17:35 Quran)

O man, follow not that whereof thou hast no knowledge. Lo, the hearing, the sight and the heart—of each of these it will be asked. (17:36 Quran)

And walk not in the earth exultant. Lo, thou canst not rend the earth, nor canst thou stretch to the height of the hills. (17:37 Quran)

Glorified is He and High Exalted above what they say! (17:43 Quran)

The seven heavens and the earth and all that is therein praise Him, and there is not a thing but hymneth His praise, but ye understand not their praise. He is ever Clement, Forgiving. (17:44 Quran)

And thy Lord is best aware of all who are in the heavens and the earth. And We preferred some of the Prophets above others, and unto David We gave the Psalms. (17:55 Quran)

O mankind, your Lord is He Who driveth for you the ship upon the sea that ye may seek of His bounty. Lo, He was ever Merciful toward you. (17:66 Quran)

Verily We have honored the children of Adam. We carry them on the land and the sea, and have made provision of good things for them and have preferred them above many of those whom We created with a marked preferment. (17:70 Quran)

And say: My Lord! Cause me to come in with a firm incoming and to go out with a firm outgoing. And give me from Thy presence a sustaining Power. (17:80 Quran)

And say: Truth hath come and falsehood hath vanished away. Lo, falsehood is ever bound to vanish. (17:81 Quran)

And We reveal of the Quran that which is healing and a mercy for believers though it increase the evil doers in naught save ruin. (17:82 Quran)

And when We make life pleasant unto man, he turneth away and is averse, and when ill toucheth him he is in despair. (17:83 Quran)

Say: Each one doth according to his rule of conduct, and thy Lord is best aware of him whose way is right. (17:84 Quran)

They will ask thee concerning the Spirit. Say: The Spirit is by command of my Lord, and of knowledge ye have been vouchsafed but little. (17:85 Quran)

And if We willed We could withdraw that which We have revealed unto thee, then wouldst thou find no guardian for thee against Us in respect thereof. (17:86 Quran)

It is naught save mercy from thy Lord. Lo, His kindness unto thee was ever great. (17:87 Quran)

Say unto them: If ye possessed the treasures of the mercy of my Lord, ye would surely hold them back for fear of spending, for man was ever grudging. (17:100 Quran)

Say unto mankind: Cry unto Allah, or cry unto the Beneficent, unto whichsoever ye cry, it is the same. His are the most beautiful names. And thou, Muhammad, be not loud voiced in thy worship, nor yet silent therein, but follow a way between. (17:110 Quran)

To renounce what we cannot gain is not true renunciation, it is weakness.

To renounce what we cannot gain is not true renunciation, it is weakness. When the apples are so high up on the branch of the tree that we cannot reach them, we try to and cannot, if we then say, "The apples are sour. I don't want them", that is not renunciation. If we climb the tree and get the apples and cut them in half, then we may say, "They are sour", and throw them away.

If we say, "I cannot have my wish. It is not intended by the will of God. I am resigned to the will of God", that is not resignation. Why should it not be meant for us to have our wish? Behind our will there is the will of God. God desires it through us. Christ said, "If ye desire bread,

He will not give a stone". By this we see that it is natural for us to have our desire, it is natural for us to have health and riches and success and all things. It is unnatural to have illnesses and failures and miseries. But if, after gaining all the wealth in the world, position and titles, then we give it up, then that will be true renunciation.

There are two different renunciations: one is renunciation, the other is loss. True renunciation is that which a person makes who has risen above something that he once valued; or whose hunger and thirst for the thing are satisfied and it is no more so valuable as it once was; or who perhaps has evolved and sees life differently, no longer as he saw it before.

Renunciation in all these cases is a step forward towards perfection. But the other renunciation is one which a person is compelled to make when circumstances prevent his achieving what he wishes to achieve or from getting back what he has lost helplessly; or when, by weakness of mind or body, by lack of position, power, or wealth, he cannot reach the object he desires. That renunciation is a loss; and instead of leading towards perfection it drags man down toward imperfection. The final victory in the battle of life for every soul is when he has abandoned, which means when he has risen above, what once he valued most. For the value of everything exists for man only so long as he does not understand it. When he has fully understood, the value is lost, be it the lowest thing or the highest thing. It is like looking at the scenery on the stage and taking it for a palace. Such is the case with all things of the world; they seem important or precious when we need them or when we do not understand them; as soon as the veil which keeps man from understanding is lifted, then they are nothing. *Hazrat Inayat Khan*

Do not fear God, but consciously regard His pleasure and displeasure.

The religion of the Sufi is the religion of the heart. The principal moral of the Sufi is to consider the heart of others, so that in the pleasure and displeasure of his fellow-man he sees the pleasure and displeasure of God.

There are four paths or stages that lead a person to spiritual knowledge, from the limited to the unlimited. The first stage is Shariat. This is where the God-ideal is impressed upon mankind as authority, as fear of God. This really means conscientiousness, not fear as is usually thought. If we love, we do not wish to displease; love does not force us to act, but it asks us to be conscientious and take care not to cause the least disharmony with the one whose happiness we want.

This stage of Shariat is that in which a person asks himself what will please Him, or displease Him. He learns his religion from his parents, from his friends. A good action pleases, a bad action displeases, and pride displeases most; he learns everything very easily by seeing what displeases another. How easy it is; and yet they still go to a clergyman or to a priest, to ask what pleases God. And all the time it is just what pleases man that pleases God, and therefore if we please all around us, we please God; if we displease them, we displease God. A man who has attained to this stage realizes what reward comes to him when he pleases the world, and what happens when he does not. *Hazrat Inayat Khan*

Surah Eighteen

Al Kahf

It is the sincere devotee who knows best how to humble himself before God.

There are many different feelings which have an influence upon us, and which give a feeling of joy, of exaltation, but there is no sentiment greater or more effective than the feeling of bringing one's faults and weaknesses before God to ask for His pardon. To become conscious of one's shortcomings, to be sorry for them, to repent of them, and to ask His forgiveness in all humility, no ethics, no philosophy can give a greater joy than this. It is the sincere devotee of God who knows best what feeling it is to humble oneself before God. The proud one, ignorant of the greatness of God, of His all-sufficient power, does not know what is this exaltation that raises the soul from earth to heaven? To be really sorry for one's errors is like opening the gates of heaven.

The customs existing in all parts of the world of bowing and bending and prostrating are all devoted to the one Being, who alone deserves it, and no one else. There is beauty in these customs. Man is the most egoistic being in creation. He keeps himself veiled from God, the perfect Self within, by the veil of his imperfect self, which has formed his false ego. But by the extreme humility with which he stands before God and bows and bends and prostrates himself before the almighty Being, he makes the highest point of his presumed being, the head, touch the earth where his feet are, and thus in time he washes off the black stains of his false ego, and the light of perfection gradually manifests. Only then does he stand face to face with his God, the idealized Deity, and when the ego is absolutely crushed, then God remains within and without, in both planes, and none exists save He. *Hazrat Inayat Khan*

In the name of Allah, the Beneficent, the Merciful

Lo, as for those who believe and do good works—Lo, We suffer not the reward of one whose work is goodly to be lost. (18:31 Quran)

As for such, theirs will be the Gardens of Eden, wherein rivers flow beneath them, therein they will be given armlets of gold and will wear green robes of finest silk and gold embroidery, reclining upon thrones therein. Blest the reward, and fair the resting place! (18:32 Quran)

Wealth and children are an ornament of the life of the world. But the good deeds which endure are better in thy Lord's sight for reward, and better in respect of hope. (18:47 Quran)

And remember when we said to the angels: Fall prostrate before Adam, and they fell prostrate, save Iblis. He was of the Jinn, so he rebelled against his Lord's command. Will ye choose him and his seed for your protecting friends instead of Me, when they are an enemy to you? Calamitous is the exchange for evil-doers! (18:51 Quran)

Thy Lord is the Forgiver, full of Mercy. If He took them to task now for what they earn, He would hasten on the doom for them, but theirs is an appointed term from which they will find no escape. (18:59 Quran)

And when Moses said unto his servant: I will not give up until I reach the point where the two rivers meet, though I march on for ages. (18:61 Quran)

And when they reached the point where the two rivers met, they forgot their fish, and it took its way into the waters, being free. (18:62 Quran)

And when they had gone further, he said unto his servant: Bring us our breakfast. Verily we have found fatigue in this our journey. (18:63 Quran)

He said: Didst thou see, when we took refuge on the rock, and I forgot the fish—and none but Satan caused me to forget to mention it—it took its way into the waters by a marvel. (18:64 Quran)

He said: This is that which we have been seeking. So they retraced their steps again. (18:65 Quran)

Then found there one of Our slaves, unto him We have given mercy from Us, and had taught him knowledge from Our presence. (18:66 Quran)

Moses said unto him: May I follow thee, to the end of that thou mayest teach me right conduct of that which thou hast been taught? (18:67 Quran)

He said: Lo, thou canst not bear with me. (18:68 Quran)

How canst thou bear with that whereof thou canst not compass my knowledge? (18:69 Quran)

He said: Allah willing, thou shalt find me patient and I shall not in naught gainsay thee. (18:70 Quran)

He said: Well, if thou go with me, ask me not concerning aught till I myself make mention of it unto thee. (18:71 Quran)

So they twain set out till, when they were in the ship, he made a hole therein. Moses said: Hast thou made a hole therein to drown the folk thereof? Thou verily hast done a dreadful thing. (18:72 Quran)

He said: Did I not tell thee that thou couldst not bear with me? (18:73 Quran)

Moses said: Be not wroth with me that I forgot, and be not hard upon me for my fault. (18:74 Quran)

So they twain journeyed on till, when they met a lad, he slew him. Hast thou slain an innocent soul who hath slain no man? Verily thou hast done a horrid thing. (18:75 Quran)

He said: Did I not tell thee that thou couldst not bear with me? (18:76 Quran)

Moses said: If I ask thee after this concerning aught, keep not company with me. Thou hast received an excuse from me. (18:77 Quran)

So they twain journeyed on till, when they came unto a folk of certain township, they asked its folk for food, but they refused to make them guests. And they found therein a wall upon the point of falling into ruin, and he repaired it. Moses said: If thou hast wished, thou couldst have taken payment for it. (18:78 Quran)

He said: This is the parting between thee and me. I will announce unto thee the interpretation of that thou couldst not bear with patience. (18:79 Quran)

As for the ship, it belonged to poor people working on the river, and I wished to mar it, for there was a king behind them who is taking every ship by force. (18:80 Quran)

And as for the lad, his parents were believers and We feared lest he should oppress them by rebellion and disbelief. (18:81 Quran)

And We intended that their Lord should change him for one better in purity and nearer to mercy. (18:82 Quran)

And as for the wall, it belonged to two orphan boys in the city, and there was beneath it a treasure belonging to them, and their father had been righteous, and thy Lord intended that they should come to their full strength and should bring forth their treasure as a mercy from their Lord, and I did it not upon my own command. Such is the interpretation of that wherewith thou wouldst not bear. (18:83 Quran)

Say: Though the sea became ink for the Words of my Lord, verily the sea would be used up before the Words of my Lord were exhausted, even though We brought the like thereof to help. (18:110 Quran)

Say: I am only a mortal like you. My Lord inspireth in me that your God is only one God. And whoever hopeth for the meeting with his Lord, let him do righteous work, and make none sharer of the worship due unto his Lord. (18:111 Quran)

He who expects to change the world will be disappointed, he must change his view. When this is done, then tolerance will come, forgiveness will come, and there will be nothing he cannot bear.

The other day I lectured in Paris and after my lecture a very able man came to me and said, 'Have you got a scheme?' I said, 'What scheme?' 'Of bettering conditions.' I replied that I had not made such a scheme, and he said, 'I have a scheme, I will show it to you'. He opened his box and brought out a very large paper with mathematics on it and showed it to me saying. 'This is the economic scheme that will make the condition of the world better: everyone will have the same share'. I said, 'We should practice that economic scheme first on tuning our piano: instead of saying D, E, F, we should tune them all to one note and play that music and see how interesting that would be—all sounding the same, no individuality, no distinction, nothing.' And I added, 'Economy is not a plan for construction, but it is a plan for destruction. It is economics which have brought us to destruction. It is the heart quality, it is the spiritual outlook which will change the world'.

Very often people coming to hear me say afterwards, 'Yes, all you say is very interesting, very beautiful, and I wish too that the world was changed. But how many think like you? How can you do it? How can it be done?' They come with that pessimistic remark, and I tell them, 'One person comes into a country with a little cold or influenza and it spreads. If such a bad thing can spread, cannot an elevated thought of love, kindness and goodwill towards all men spread? See then that there are finer germs, germs of goodwill, of love, kindness, and feeling, germs of brotherhood, of the desire for spiritual evolution, which can have greater results than the other ones. If we all have that optimistic view, if we all work in our little way, we can accomplish a great deal'.

Many have been cross with God for having sent any misery in their lives—but we always get such experiences! Becoming cross one says, 'Why, this is not just', or 'This is not right', and 'How could God who is just and good allow unjust things to happen?' But our sight is so limited that our conception of right and wrong and good and evil is only for us— not according to God's plan. It is true that, as long as we see it as such, it is so for us and for those who look at it from our point of view, but when it comes to God the whole dimension is changed, the whole point of view is changed.

The Sufi therefore, finds the only way out of the distress of life. He rises above it, taking all things as they come, patiently. He does not mind how he is treated. His principle is to do his best, and in that is his satisfaction. Instead of depending on another person to be kind to him, the Sufi thinks if he were kind to another person that is sufficient. Every wise man in the long run through life will find in this principle the solution of happiness. For we cannot change the world, but we can change ourselves. *Hazrat Inayat Khan*

Surah Nineteen

Maryam

Our soul is blessed with the impression of the glory of God whenever our lips praise Him.

There is a necessity for praise in prayer, praise of the beauty of God, for man must learn to recognize and praise the beauty of God as manifested in all His creation. In this way he impresses beauty on his soul, and he is able to manifest it in himself, and he becomes the friend of all and is without prejudice. For this reason the Sufi cultivates his heart. The emblem of the Sufi is a heart between two wings, meaning that when the heart is cultivated man can soar up into the heights of heaven.

"Why does God need praise from me? Who am I that I should offer Him praise?" True, we can never praise Him enough; never can our praise be sufficient, but our souls are blessed with the impression of the Glory of God whenever we praise Him. The soul could praise God every moment and yet wanting to praise Him yet more, it is constantly hungering and thirsting to find the Beauty and Perfection of God. By the praise of God the soul is filled with bliss; even to utter the name of God is a blessing that can fill the soul with light, joy and happiness as nothing else can do.

One might ask what effect prayers can have upon the soul, which is pure and aloof from everything. The soul, when it sees the external self-bowing before God, rejoices and is glad. Prayer gives nobility to whoever prays, be he rich or poor. The attitude of a prayerful person towards God is that of a lover towards his beloved, of a child towards its parents, of a servant towards his master, of a pupil towards his teacher, of a soldier towards his commander.

The whole object of the Sufi, after learning this way of communicating is to arrive at a stage where every moment of our life passes in communion with God, and where our every action is done as if God were before us. Is that within everyone's reach? We are meant to be so. Hazrat Inayat Khan

In the name of Allah, the Beneficent, the Merciful

A mention of the mercy of thy Lord unto His servant Zachariah. (19:2 Quran)

When he cried unto Lord a cry in secret. (19:3 Quran)

Saying: My Lord! Lo, the bones of me wax feeble and my head is shining with grey hair, and I have never been unblest in prayers to Thee, my Lord. (19:4 Quran)

Lo, I fear my kinsfolk after me, since my wife is barren. Oh, give me from Thy presence a successor. (19:5 Quran)

Who shall inherit of me and inherit also of the house of Jacob. And make him, my Lord, acceptable unto Thee. (19:6 Quran)

It was said unto him: O Zachariah! Lo, We bring thee tidings of a son whose name is John. We have given the same name to none before him. (19:7 Quran)

He said: My Lord! How can I have a son when my wife is barren and I have reached infirm old age? (19:8 Quran)

He said: So, it will be. Thy Lord saith: It is easy for me, even as I created thee before when thou wast naught. (19:9 Quran)

He said: My Lord, appoint for me some token. He said: Thy token is that thou, with no bodily defect, shall not speak unto mankind three nights. (19:10 Quran)

Then he came forth unto his people from the sanctuary and signified to them: Glorify your Lord at break of day and fall of night. (19:11 Quran)

And it was said unto his son: O John: Hold fast the Scripture. And We gave him wisdom when a child. (19:12 Quran)

And compassion from Our presence, and purity, and he was devout. (19:13 Quran)

And dutiful toward his parents. And he was not arrogant, rebellious. (19:14 Quran)

Peace on him the day he was born, and the day he dieth, and the day he shall be raised alive! (19:15 Quran)

And make mention of Mary in the Scripture, when she had withdrawn from her people to a chamber looking East. (19:16 Quran)

And had chosen seclusion from them. Then We sent unto her Our spirit and it assumed for her the likeness of a perfect man. (19:17 Quran)

She said: Lo, I seek refuge in the Beneficent One from thee. If thou art God-fearing. (19:18 Quran)

He said: I am only a messenger of thy Lord that I bestow on thee a faultless son. (19:19 Quran)

She said: How can I have a son when no mortal flesh touched me, neither I have been unchaste? (19:20 Quran)

He said: So, it will be that We may make of him a revelation for mankind and a mercy from Us, and it is a thing ordained. (19:21 Quran)

And she conceived him, and she withdrew with him to a far place. (19:22 Quran)

And the pangs of childbirth drove her unto the trunk of the palm-tree. She said: Oh, would that I had died ere this and had become a thing of naught, forgotten! (19:23 Quran)

Then one cried unto her from below her, saying: Grieve not. Thy Lord hath placed a rivulet beneath thee. (19:24 Quran)

And shake the trunk of the palm-tree toward thee. Thou wilt cause ripe dates to fall upon thee. (19:25 Quran)

So eat and drink and be comforted and if thou meetest any mortal, say: Lo, I have vowed a fast unto the Beneficent, and may not speak this day to any mortal. (19:26 Quran)

Then she brought him to her own folk, carrying him. They said: O Mary! Thou hast come with an amazing thing. (19:27 Quran)

O sister of Aaron! Thy father was not a wicked man, nor was thy mother a harlot. (19:28 Quran)

Then she pointed to him. They said: How can we talk to one who is in the cradle a young boy? (19:29 Quran)

He spake: Lo! I am the slave of Allah. He hath given me the Scripture and hath appointed me a Prophet. (19:30 Quran)

And hath made me blessed wheresoever I may be, and hath enjoined upon me prayer and alms-giving so long as I remain alive. (19:31 Quran)

And hath made me dutiful toward her who bore me, and hath not made me arrogant, unblest. (19:32 Quran)

Peace on me the day I was born, and the day I die, and the day I shall be raised alive. (19:33 Quran)

Such was Jesus, son of Mary: This is a statement of the truth, concerning which they doubt. (19:34 Quran)

And lo, Allah is my Lord and your Lord! So serve Him. This is the right path. (19:36 Quran)

And make mention, O Muhammad, in the Scripture of Abraham. Lo, he was a saint, a Prophet. (19:41 Quran)

And make mention in the Scripture of Moses. Lo, he was chosen, and he was a messenger of Allah, a Prophet. (19:51 Quran)

We called him from the right slope of the Mount, and brought him nigh in communion. (19:52 Quran)

And We bestowed upon him Our mercy his brother Aaron, a Prophet likewise. (19:53 Quran)

And make mention in the Scripture of Ishmael. Lo, he was a keeper of his promise, and he was a messenger of Allah, a Prophet. (19:54 Quran)

He enjoined upon his people worship and almsgiving and was acceptable in the sight of his Lord. (19:55 Quran)

And make mention of the Scripture of Idris (Enoch). Lo, he was a saint, a Prophet. (19:56 Quran)

And We raised him to high station. (19:57 Quran)

These are they unto whom Allah showed favor among the Prophets of the seed of Adam and of those whom We carried in the ship with Noah, and of the seed of Abraham and Israel, and from among those whom We guided and chose. When the revelations of the Beneficent were recited unto them, they fell down weeping and adoring. (19:58 Quran)

Allah increaseth in right guidance those who walk aright, and the good deeds which endure are better in thy Lord's sight for reward and better for resort. (19:76 Quran)

Lo, those who believe and do good works, the Beneficent will appoint for them love. (19:96 Quran)

And We make this Scripture easy in thy tongue, O Muhammad, only that thou mayest bear good tidings therewith unto those who ward off evil and warn therewith the forward folk. (19:97 Quran)

Self-pity is the worst poverty; it overwhelms man until he sees nothing but illness, trouble and pain.

If one studies one's surroundings one finds that those who are happy are so because they have less thought of self. If they are unhappy it is because they think of themselves too much. A person is more bearable when he thinks less of himself. And a person is unbearable when he is always thinking of himself. There are many miseries in life, but the greatest misery is self-pity.

Man is mostly selfish, and what interests him is that which concerns his own life. Not knowing the troubles of the lives of others he feels the burden of his own life even more than the burden of the whole world. If only man in his poverty could think that there are others who are poorer than he, in his illness that there are others whose sufferings are perhaps greater than his. In his troubles that there are others whose difficulties are perhaps greater than his! Self-pity is the worst poverty. It overwhelms man and he sees nothing but his own troubles and pains, and it seems to him that he is the most unhappy person in the world, more so than anyone else.

A great thinker of Persia, Sadi, writes in an account of his life, 'Once I had no shoes, I had to walk barefoot in the hot sand, and how miserable I was. Then I met a man who was lame, for whom walking was very difficult. I bowed down to heaven at once and offered thanks that I was much better off than he who had not even feet to walk upon.' This shows that it is not a man's situation in life, but his attitude towards life that makes him happy or unhappy.

When Jesus Christ said, 'Seek ye first the kingdom of God,' this teaching was an answer to the cry of humanity: some crying, 'I have no wealth,' others crying, 'I have no rest,' others crying. 'My situation in life is difficult, My friends are troubling me,' or, 'I want a position, wealth.' The answer to them all is, 'Seek ye first the kingdom of God, and all these things shall be added unto you.' *Hazrat Inayat Khan*

Surah Twenty

Ta Ha

The heart is not living until it has experienced pain.

Those who have avoided love in life from fear of its pain have lost more than the lover, who by losing himself gains all. The loveless first lose all, until at last their self is also snatched away from their hands. The warmth of the lover's atmosphere, the piercing effect of his voice, the appeal of his words, all come from the pain of his heart. The heart is not living until it has experienced pain. Man has not lived if he has lived and worked with his body and mind without heart. The soul is all light, but all darkness is caused by the death of the heart. Pain makes it alive. The same heart that was once full of bitterness, when purified by love becomes the source of all goodness. All deeds of kindness spring from it.

A person who has never experienced pain cannot sympathize with those suffering pain. Sympathy is something more than love and affection, for it is the knowledge of a certain suffering which moves the living heart to sympathy.

Suffering is always a blessing. If it is for higher ideas, for God, for an ideal, it takes a person at once to the highest heaven. If it is for lower ideas, for the ego, for pride, for possessions, it takes a person to the lowest depth of hell. But there, after much suffering, after a long, long time, he loses these ideas and is purified. That is why the Christian religion shows the symbol of the Cross, of suffering. How high our ideal may be, how low our ideal may be, in the end each pain has its prize.

If there were no pain, one would not have the experience of joy. It is pain which helps one to experience joy. Everything is distinguished by its opposite and the one who feels pain deeply is more capable of expressing joy. If there were no pain, life would be most uninteresting; for it is by pain that penetration takes place, and the sensation after pain is a deeper joy. Without pain the great musicians, athletes, discoverers, and thinkers would not have reached the stage they have arrived at in the world. If they had always experienced joy, they would not have touched the depths of life. Hazrat Inyat Khan

In the name of Allah, the Beneficent, the Merciful

We have not revealed unto thee Muhammad this Quran in that thou shouldst be distressed. (20:2 Quran)

But as a reminder unto him who feareth. (20:3 Quran)

A revelation from Him Who created the earth and the high heavens. (20:4 Quran)

The Beneficent One, Who is established on the Throne. (20:5 Quran)

Unto Him belongeth whatsoever is in the heavens and whatsoever is in the earth, and whatsoever is between them, and whatsoever is beneath the sod. (20:6 Quran)

And if thou speakest aloud, then lo, He knoweth the secret thought and that which is yet more hidden. (20:7 Quran)

Allah! There is no God save Him. His are most beautiful names. (20:8 Quran)

Hath there come unto thee story of Moses? (20:9 Quran)

When he saw a fire and said unto his folk: Wait! Lo, I see a fire afar off. Peradventure I may bring you a brand therefrom or may find guidance at the fire. (20:10 Quran)

And when he reached it, he was called by name, O Moses! (20:11 Quran)

Lo, I, even I, am thy Lord. So take off thy shoes, for lo, thou art in the holy valley of Tuwa. (20:12 Quran)

And I have chosen thee, so hearken unto that which is inspired. (20:13 Quran)

Lo, I, even I, am Allah. There is no God save Me. So serve me and establish worship for My remembrance. (20:14 Quran)

Lo, the Hour is surely coming. But I will to keep it hidden, that every soul may be rewarded for that which it striveth to achieve. (20:15 Quran)

And he who hath done some good works, being a believer, he feareth not injustice, nor begrudging of his wage. (20:112 Quran)

Thus We have revealed it as a lecture in Arabic, and have displayed therein certain threats, that peradventure they may keep from evil or that it may cause them to take heed. (20:113 Quran)

Then exalted be Allah, the True King! And hasten not, O Muhammad, with the Quran ere its revelation hath been perfected unto thee and say: My Lord, increase me in knowledge. (20:114 Quran)

And when We said unto the Angels: Fall prostrate before Adam, they fell prostrate all save Iblis, he refused. (20:116 Quran)

Therefore We said: O Adam! This is an enemy to thee and unto thy wife, so let him not drive you both out of the Garden, so that thou come to toil. (20:117 Quran)

It is vouchsafed unto thee that thou hungerest not therein, nor art naked. (20:118 Quran)

And that thou thirsteth not therein, nor art exposed to the Sun's heat. (20:119 Quran)

But the devil whispered to him, saying: O Adam! Shall I show thee the tree of immortality and power that wasteth not away? (20:120 Quran)

Then they twain ate thereof, so that their shame became apparent unto them, and they began to hide by heaping on themselves some of the leaves of the Garden. And Adam disobeyed his Lord, so went astray. (20:121 Quran)

Then his Lord chose him, and relented toward him and guided him. (20:122 Quran)

He said: Go down hence, both of you, one of you a foe unto the other. But if there come unto you from Me a guidance, then whoso followeth my guidance, he will not go astray, nor come to grief. (20:123 Quran)

Mysticism without devotion is like uncooked food; it can never be assimilated.

Knowledge and heart are just like the positive and negative forces; it is these two things which make life balanced. If the heart quality is very strong and intellect is lacking, then life lacks balance. Knowledge and heart quality must be developed together. There are fine lights and shades in one's life that cannot be perceived and fully understood without having touched the deeper side of life, which is the devotional side.

Mystics of all ages have not been known for their miraculous powers or for the doctrines they have taught, but for the devotion they have shown throughout their lives. The Sufi in the East says to himself Ishq Allah Mabud Allah which means 'God is Love, God is Beloved', in other words it is God who is Love, Lover, and Beloved. When we hear the stories of the miraculous powers of mystics, of their great insight into the hidden laws of nature, of the qualities which they manifested through their beautiful personalities, we realize that these have all come from one and the same source, whether one calls it devotion or whether one calls it love.

Mysticism without devotion is like uncooked food and can never be assimilated. 'I am the heart of my devotees,' says Krishna in the Baghavat Gita. And Hafiz says, 'O joyous day when I depart from this abode of desolation, seeking the repose of my soul and setting out in search of my Beloved.' The life of the mystics, both the inner and the outer, is shown as a wondrous phenomenon within itself. He becomes independent of all earthly sources of life and lives in the Being of God, realizing His presence by the denial of his individual self; and he thus merges into that highest bliss wherein he finds his salvation. *Hazrat Inayat Khan*

Surah Twenty-One

Al Anbiya

The pleasures of life are blinding; it is love alone that clears the rust from the heart, the mirror of the soul.

The heart of man, as the Sufis say, is a mirror. All that is reflected in this mirror is projected upon other mirrors. When man has doubt in his heart that doubt is reflected upon every heart with which he comes in contact. When he has faith that faith is reflected in every heart. Can there be a more interesting study and a greater wonder than to observe this keenly?

There must be no feeling of revenge, of unkindness, of bitterness against anyone in the heart. When such a feeling comes, one must say: this is rust coming into my heart. When all such feelings are cleared off the heart, it becomes like a mirror. A mirror without rust reflects all that is before it; then everything divine is reflected in the heart.

The heart aflame becomes the torch on the path of the lover, which lightens his way that leads him to his destination. The pleasures of life are blinding, it is love alone that clears the rust from the heart, the mirror of the soul. Hazrat Inyat Khan

In the name of Allah, the Beneficent, the Merciful

And We sent not as Our messengers before thee other than men whom We inspired. (21:7 Quran)

We gave them not bodies that would not eat food, nor were they immortals. (21:8 Quran)

Then We fulfilled the promise unto them. So We delivered them and whom We would, and We destroyed the prodigals. (21:9 Quran)

Now We have revealed unto you a Scripture wherein is your Reminder. Have ye then no sense? (21:10 Quran)

We appointed immortality for no mortal before thee. What if thou diest, can they be immortal? (21:34 Quran)

Every soul must taste of death, and We try you with evil and with good, for ordeal. And unto Us ye will be returned. (21:35 Quran)

Say, O Muhammad, unto mankind: I warn you only by the Inspiration. But the deaf hear not the call when they are warned. (21:45 Quran)

And We verily gave Moses and Aaron the criterion of right and wrong, and a light and a Reminder for those who keep from evil. (21:48 Quran)

And We verily gave Abraham of old his proper course, and We were Aware of him. (21:51 Quran)

And unto Lot We gave knowledge and judgment, and We delivered him from the community that did abominations. Lo, they were folk of evil, lewd. (21:74 Quran)

And We brought him in unto Our mercy. Lo, he was of the righteous. (21:75 Quran)

And Noah, when he cried of old, We heard his prayer and saved him and his household from great affliction. (21:76 Quran)

And David and Solomon, when they gave judgment concerning the field, when people's sheep had strayed, and browsed therein by night, and We were witness to their judgment. (21:78 Quran)

And We made Solomon to understand the case, and unto each of them We gave judgment and knowledge. And We subdued the hills and the birds to hymn His praise along with David. We were the doers thereof. (21:79 Quran)

And We taught him making garments of mail to protect you in your daring. Are ye then thankful? (21:80 Quran)

And unto Solomon We subdued the wind in its raging. It set by his command toward the land which We had blessed. And of everything We are aware. (21:81 Quran)

And of the evil ones subdued We unto him, some who dived for pearls for him and did other work, and We were warders unto them. (21:82 Quran)

And Job when he cried unto his Lord, saying: Lo, adversity afflicteth me, and Thou are Most Merciful of all who show mercy. (21:83 Quran)

Then We heard his prayer and removed that adversity from which he suffered, and We gave him his household that he had lost and the kids thereof along with them, a mercy from our store, and a remembrance for the worshippers. (21:84 Quran)

And mention Ishmael and Idris and Dhu'l Kilfl. All were of the steadfast. (21:85 Quran)

And We brought them in unto Our mercy. Lo, they are among the righteous. (21:86 Quran)

And Zachariah when he cried unto his Lord: My Lord! Leave me not childless, though Thou art the best of inheritors. (21:89 Quran)

Then We heard his prayer, and bestowed upon him John, and adjusted his wife to bear a child for him. Lo, they used to vie one with the other in good deeds, and they cried unto Us in longing and in fear, and were submissive unto Us. (21:90 Quran)

And she who was chaste, therefore We breathed into her something of Our spirit and made her and her son a token for all peoples. (21:91 Quran)

Lo, this, your religion, is one religion, and I am your Lord, so worship Me. (21:92 Quran)

And they have broken their religion into fragments among them, yet all are returning unto Us. (21:93 Quran)

Then whoso doeth good works and is a believer, there will be no rejection of his effort. Lo, We record it for him. (21:94 Quran)

And verily We have written in the Scripture, after the Reminder: My righteous slaves will inherit the earth. (21:105 Quran)

Lo, there is a plain statement for folk who are devout. (21:106 Quran)

We sent thee not save as a mercy for the peoples. (21:107 Quran)

The wise man, by studying nature, enters into unity through its variety, and realizes the personality of God by sacrificing his own.

It may be said that the personality of a man is quite comprehensible, since his actions exhibit him as a single individual, whereas God's personality has no clear identification of its own. The answer is, that variety covers unity.

Hidden things are manifested by their opposites, but as God has no opposite He remains hidden. God's light has no opposite in the range of creation whereby it may be manifested to view. (Jalaluddin Rumi)

The wise man by studying nature enters into the unity through its variety, and realizes the personality of God by sacrificing his own. 'He who knows himself knows Allah' (Islamic Saying). 'The Kingdom of God is within you' (Bible). 'Self-knowledge is the real wisdom' (Vedanta).

Life starts by distinguishing between the two; life starts us in this way. If we did not distinguish between the two and we arrived at that conception of unity of which I have spoken, we would be missing a great deal in life. It is after distinguishing these that, without becoming congested, we may come to the idea of unity which raises us above it all. For instance, when a person says, 'I will not look at the fault of another' and closes his eyes, he has missed a great deal. But the one who has seen it and risen above it has really closed his eyes; he is the person who deserves to close his eyes from the other side.

The purpose of our life on earth is to come and see all the distinctions and all the differences, but not to be congested by them and so to be thrown downwards. We should go on rising above them all, at the same time experiencing them all. For instance a man may say, 'I have never thought about anyone who has done me any good, and I have never considered any harm that has ever come to me from anyone; I have always had just that one idea before me and after that idea I kept going'. He may be advanced, he may be spiritual, he may be pious, and yet he has missed a great deal. But the one who has received all the good that has come to him with grateful thanks and felt it, and who has also felt the harm done to him and forgiven and pardoned it, he is the one who has seen the world and is going beyond with success. *Hazrat Inayat Khan*

Surah Twenty-Two

Al Hajj

The pain of love is the dynamite that breaks up the heart, even if it be as hard as a rock.

The effect of love is pain. The love that has no pain is no love. The lover who has not gone through the agonies of love is not a lover, he claims love falsely. Rumi describes six signs of the lover: deep sigh, mild expression, moist eyes, eating little, speaking little, sleeping little, which all show the sign of pain in love. Hafiz says, 'All bliss in my life has been the outcome of unceasing tears and continual sighs through the heart of night.'

The sorrow of the lover is continual, in the presence and in the absence of the beloved: in the presence for fear of the absence, and in absence in longing for the presence. According to the mystical view the pain of love is the dynamite that breaks up the heart, even if it be as hard as a rock. When this hardness that covers the light within is broken through, the streams of all bliss come forth as springs from the mountains. Hazrat Inayat Khan

In the name of Allah, the Beneficent, the Merciful

O mankind! If you are in doubt concerning the Resurrection, then lo! We have created you from dust, then from a drop of seed, then from a clot, then from a little lump of flesh, shapely and shapeless, that We may make it clear for you. And We cause what We will to remain in the wombs for an appointed time, and afterward We bring you forth as infants, then give you growth that ye attain your full strength. And among you there is he who dieth young, and among you there is he who is brought back to the most abject time of life so that, after knowledge, he knoweth naught. And thou Muhammad seest the earth barren, but when We send down water thereon, it doth thrill and swell and put forth every lovely kind of growth. (22:5 Quran)

This is because Allah, He is the Truth. Lo, He quickeneth the dead, and lo, He is able to do all things. (22:6 Quran)

And because the Hour will come, there is no doubt thereof, and because Allah will raise those who are in the graves. (22:7 Quran)

And among mankind is he who disputeth concerning Allah without knowledge or guidance or a Scripture giving light. (22:8 Quran)

Lo, those who believe this Revelation and those who are Jews, and the Sabaeans and the Christians and the Magians and the idolaters—Lo, Allah will decide between them on the Day of Resurrection. Lo, Allah is witness over all things. (22:17 Quran)

Lo, Allah will cause those who believe and do good works to enter Garden underneath which rivers flow, wherein they will be allowed armlets of gold, and pearls, and their raiment therein will be of silk. (22:23 Quran)

They are guided unto gentle speech, they are guided unto the path of the Glorious One. (22:24 Quran)

Lo, those who disbelieve and bar men from the way of Allah and from the Inviolable Place of Worship, which We have appointed for mankind together, the dwellers therein and the nomad. Whosoever seeketh wrongful partiality therein, him, We shall cause to taste a painful doom. (22:25 Quran)

And remember when We prepared for Abraham the place of the Holy House, saying: Ascribe thou no thing as partner unto Me, and purify My House for those who bow and make prostration. (22:26 Quran)

And proclaim unto mankind the Pilgrimage. They will come unto thee on foot and on every lean camel. They will come from every deep ravine. (22:27 Quran)

That they may witness things that are benefit to them, and mention the name of Allah on appointed days over the beast of cattle that He hath bestowed upon them. Then eat thereof and feed therewith the poor unfortunate. (22:28 Quran)

Then let them make an end of their unkemptness and pay their vow and go around the ancient House (22:29 Quran)

And for every nation have We appointed a ritual, that they may mention the name of Allah over the beast of cattle that He hath given them for food. And your God is One God, therefore surrender unto Him. And give good tidings, O Muhammad, to the humble. (22:34 Quran)

Whose hearts fear when Allah is mentioned, and patient of whatever may befall them, and those who establish worship and who spend of that We have bestowed on them. (22:35 Quran)

And the camels! We have appointed them among the ceremonies of Allah. Therein ye have much good. So mention the name of Allah over them when they are drawn up in lines. Then when their flanks fall dead, eat thereof and feed the beggar and the suppliant. Thus have We made them subject unto you, that haply ye may give thanks. (22:36 Quran)

Their flesh and their blood reach not Allah, but the devotion from you reacheth Him. Thus have We made them subject unto you that ye may magnify Allah that He hath guided you. And give good tidings, O Muhammad, to the good. (22:37 Quran)

Lo, Allah defendeth those who are true. Lo, Allah loveth not each treacherous ingrate. (22:38 Quran)

Sanction is given unto those who fight because they have been wronged. And Allah is indeed Able to give them victory. (22:39 Quran)

Those who have been driven from their homes unjustly only because they said: Our Lord is Allah—For had it not been for Allah's repelling some men by means of others, cloisters and churches and oratories and mosques, wherein the name of Allah is oft mentioned, would assuredly have been pulled down. Verily Allah helpeth one who helpeth Him. Lo, Allah is strong, Almighty. (22:40 Quran)

Say: O mankind! I am only a plain warner unto you. (22:49 Quran)

Those who believe and do good works, for them is a pardon and rich provision. (22:50 Quran)

Never sent We a messenger or a Prophet before thee, but when He recited the message, Satan proposed opposition in respect of that which he recited thereof. But Allah abolisheth that which Satan proposeth. Then Allah establisheth His revelations. Allah is Wise, Knower. (22:52 Quran)

Hast thou not seen how Allah hath made all that is in the earth subservient unto you? And the ship runneth upon the sea by His command, and He holdeth back the heaven from falling on the earth unless by His leave. Lo, Allah is, for mankind, full of Pity, Merciful. (22:65 Quran)

And He it is Who gave you life, then He will cause you to die, and then will give you life again. Lo, man is verily an ingrate. (22:66 Quran)

Unto each nation have We given sacred rites which they are to perform, so let them not dispute with thee of the matter, but summon thou unto thy Lord. Lo, thou indeed thou followest right guidance. (22:67 Quran)

And they wrangle with thee. Say: Allah is well aware of what ye do. (22:68 Quran)

Allah will judge between you on the Day of Resurrection concerning that wherein ye used to differ. (22:69 Quran)

And strive for Allah with the endeavor which is His right. He hath chosen you and hath not laid upon you in religion any hardship, the faith of your father Abraham is yours. He hath named you Muslims of old time and in this Scripture that the messenger may be a witness against you, and that ye may be a witness against mankind. So establish worship, pay the poor-due, and hold fast to Allah. He is your Protecting Friend. A blessed Patron and a blessed Helper! (22:78 Quran)

Whoever knows the mystery of vibrations indeed knows all things.

All planes of existence consist of vibrations, from the finest to the grossest kind; the vibrations of each plane have come from a higher one, and have become grosser. Whoever knows the mystery of vibrations, he indeed knows all things. From the scientific standpoint, spirit and matter are quite different from each other, but according to the philosophical point of view they are one. Spirit and matter are different, just as water is different from snow; yet again they are not different, for snow is nothing other than water. When spiritual vibrations become more dense they turn into matter, and when material vibrations become finer they develop into spirit.

All existing things we see or hear, which we perceive, vibrate. If it were not for vibration, the precious stones would not show us their color and their brilliance; it is vibration which makes the tree grow, the fruit ripen, and the flowers bloom. Our existence is also according to the law of vibrations, not only the existence of our physical body but also our thoughts and feelings. When we begin to see life from this point of view it will appear that birth and death are only our conceptions of life, that there is no such thing as death and that all is living. It only changes from one form to the other, subject to the law of vibrations.

The inward and essential part of every being is composed of fine vibrations, and the external part is formed of gross ones. The finer part we call spirit and the grosser matter, the former being less subject to change and destruction and the latter more so.

The standard of right and wrong, the conception of good and evil, and the idea of sin and virtue are understood differently by the people of different races, nations, and religions; therefore it is difficult to discern the law governing these opposites. It becomes clear, however, by understanding the law of vibrations. Everything and being on the surface of existence seem separate from one another, but in every plane beneath the surface they approach nearer to each other, and in the innermost plane they all become one. Every disturbance therefore, caused to the peace of the smallest part of existence on the surface, inwardly affects the whole. Thus any thought, speech or action that disturbs peace is wrong, evil, and a sin; if it brings about peace it is right, good, and a virtue. Life being like a dome, its nature is also dome-like. Disturbance of the slightest part of life disturbs the whole and returns as a curse upon the person who caused it; any peace produced on the surface comforts the whole, and thence returns as peace to the producer. *Hazrat Inayat Khan.*

Surah Twenty-Three

Al Muminun
The first sign of the realization of truth is tolerance.

A soul shows the proof of its evolution in the degree of the tolerance it shows. The life in the lower creation shows the lack of tolerance. The tendency of fighting with one another, which one sees among beasts and birds, shows the reason at the back of it that intolerance is born in their nature. But when a soul has evolved still more, tolerance becomes the natural thing for him. Because the highly evolved soul then begins to realize 'Another person is not separate from me, but the other person is myself. The separation is on the surface of life, but in the depth of life I and the other person are one.' Therefore tolerance is not learned fully by trying to follow it as a good principle. It is learned by having the love of God, by attaining the knowledge of self, and by understanding the truth of life.

A Sufi tries to keep harmony in his surroundings, the harmony which demands many sacrifices. It makes one endure what one is not willing to endure, it makes one overlook what one is not inclined to overlook, it makes one tolerate what one is not accustomed to tolerate, and it makes one forgive and forget what one would never have forgotten if it were not for the sake of harmony. But at whatever cost harmony is attained, it is a good bargain. For harmony is the secret of happiness, and in absence of this a person living in palaces and rolling in gold can be most unhappy.

The first step to the attainment of the truth cannot be taught in books, or be imparted by a teacher. It must come spontaneously, namely through the love for truth. The next step is to search for it; the third step is the actual attainment. How can one attain? In order to attain truth one must make one's own life truthful. Passing from the state of natural man, through the state of being a lover of truth and a seeker after truth, one begins to express truth. One begins to understand what the great teachers have taught. Then one becomes tolerant to the various religions. Nothing seems strange any more. Nothing surprises. For now one begins to know the innermost nature of man; one sees the cause behind every action. Therefore tolerance and forgiveness and understanding of others come naturally. The person who knows the truth is the most tolerant. It is the knower of truth who is forgiving; it is the knower of truth who understands another person's point of view. It is the knower of truth who does not readily voice his opinion, for he has respect for the opinions of others.

When man gains insight into himself, he also gains insight into the hearts of others. All this desire for learning occult or mystical powers or psychic powers now disappears, because he begins to see all this power in one truth—loving truth, seeking truth, looking for truth, and living the truthful life. That it is which opens all doors. Hazrat Inayat Khan

In the name of Allah, the Beneficent, the Merciful
Successful indeed are the believers. (23:1 Quran)
Who are humble in their prayers. (23:2 Quran)
And who shun vain conversation. (23:3 Quran)
And who are payers of the poor-due. (23:4 Quran)
And who guard their modesty. (23:5 Quran)
Verily, We created man from a product of wet earth. (23:12 Quran)
Then placed him as a drop of seed in a safe lodging. (23:13 Quran)
Then fashioned We the drop a clot, then fashioned We the clot in a lump, then fashioned We the little lump bones, then clothed the bones with flesh, and then produced it as another creation. So blessed be Allah, the Best of Creators! (23:14 Quran)
And lo, after that ye surely die. (23:15 Quran)
Then lo, on the Day of Resurrection ye are raised again. (23:16 Quran)
And We have created above you seven paths, and We are never unmindful of creation. (23:17 Quran)

And We send down from the sky water in measure, and We give it lodging in the earth and lo! We are able to withdraw it. (23:18 Quran)

Then We produce for you therewith gardens of grapes and date-palms, wherein is much fruit for you and whereof ye eat. (23:19 Quran)

And a tree that springeth forth from Mount Sinai that groweth oil and relish for the eaters. (23:20 Quran)

And lo, in the cattle there is verily a lesson for you. We give you to drink of that which is in their bellies, and many uses have ye in them, and of them do ye eat. (23:21 Quran)

And on them and on the ship ye are carried. (23:22 Quran)

And We verily sent Noah unto his folk, and he said: O my people, serve Allah! Ye have no other God save Him. Will ye not ward off evil? (23:23 Quran)

And We verily gave Moses the Scripture that haply they may go aright. (23:49 Quran)

And We made the son of Mary and his mother a portent, and We gave them refuge on a height, a place of flocks and water-springs. (23:50 Quran)

O ye messengers! Eat of the good things, and do right. Lo, I am Aware of what ye do. ((23:51 Quran)

And lo, this religion is one religion, and I am your Lord, so keep your duty unto Me. (23:52 Quran)

But they mankind have broken their religion among them into sects, and each sect rejoicing in its tenets. (23: 53 Quran)

Now Allah be exalted, the True King? There is no God save Him, the Lord of the Throne of Grace. (23:116 Quran)

And O Muhammad, say: My Lord! Forgive and have mercy, for Thou art best of all who show mercy. (23:118 Quran)

There is one Teacher, God Himself; we are all His pupils.

According to the Sufi point of view there is only one teacher, and that teacher is God Himself. No man can teach another man. All one can do for another is to give him one's own experience in order to help him to be successful. For instance if a person happens to know a road, he can tell another man that it is the road which leads to the place he wishes to find. The work of the spiritual teacher is like the work of Cupid. The work of Cupid is to bring two souls together. And so is the work of the spiritual teacher: to bring together the soul and God. But what is taught to the one who seeks after truth? Nothing is taught. He is only shown how he should learn from God. For no man can ever teach spirituality. It is God alone who teaches it. And how is it learned? When these ears which are open outwardly are closed to the outside world and focused upon the heart within, then instead of hearing all that comes from the outer life one begins to hear the words within. Thus if one were to define what meditation is, that also is an attitude: the right attitude towards God. The attitude should first be to seek God within. And, after seeking God within, then to see God outside.

If truth is to be attained, it is only when truth itself has begun to speak, which happens in revelation. Truth reveals itself; therefore, the Persian word for both God and truth is Khuda, which means self-revealing, thus uniting God with truth. One cannot explain either of these words. The only help the mystic can give is by indicating how to arrive at this revelation. No one can teach or learn this, one has to learn it oneself. The teacher is only there to guide one towards this revelation. There is only one teacher, and that teacher is God. The great masters of the world were the greatest pupils, and they each knew how to become a pupil. *Hazrat Inayat Khan*

'**There is One Master, the Guiding Spirit of all Souls, Who constantly leads His followers towards the light.**'

To the Sufi therefore there is only one Teacher, however differently He may be named at different periods of history, and He comes constantly to awaken humanity from the slumber of this life of illusion, and to guide man onwards towards divine perfection. As the Sufi progresses in this view he recognizes his Master not only in the holy ones, but in the wise, in the foolish, in the saint and in the sinner, and has never allowed the Master who is One alone, and the only One who can be and who ever will be, to disappear from his sight.

The Persian word for Master is Murshid. The Sufi recognizes the Murshid in all beings of the world, and is ready to learn from young and old, educated and uneducated, rich and poor, without questioning from whom he learns. Then he begins to see the light of Risalat, the torch of truth which shines before him in every being and thing in the universe, thus he sees Rasul, his Divine Message Bearer, a living identity before him. Thus the Sufi sees the vision of God, the worshipped deity, in His immanence, manifest in nature, and life now becomes for him a perfect revelation both within and without. *Hazrat Inyat Khan*

Surah Twenty-Four

An Nur

He who is filled with the knowledge of names and forms has no capacity for the knowledge of God.

A man filled with earthly knowledge — and what he calls learning is often only the knowledge of names and forms — has no capacity for the knowledge of truth or God. It is the innocent and pure soul who has a capacity for learning. When a person comes to take a lesson on any subject, and he brings his own knowledge with him, the teacher has little to teach him, for the doors of his heart are not open. His heart that should be empty in order to receive knowledge is occupied by the knowledge that he already had acquired.

Intellect is the knowledge of names and forms, their character and nature, gathered from the external world. It shows in an infant from birth, when he begins to be curious about all he sees; then, by storing in his mind the various forms and figures he sees he recognizes them as an addition to his knowledge of variety. Man thus gathers the knowledge of numberless forms of the whole world in his mind and holds them and calls that 'learning'. This becomes his world, although it neither gives him a sense of unchanging comfort, nor does he thereby gain an everlasting peace.

Wisdom is contrary to the above-named knowledge. It is the knowledge which is illumined by the light within; it comes with the maturity of the soul, and opens up the sight to the similarity of all things and beings, as well as the unity in names and forms. The wise man penetrates the spirit of all things; he sees the human in the male and female, and the racial origin which unites nations. He sees the human in all people and the divine immanence in all things in the universe, until the vision of the whole being becomes to him the vision of the One Alone, the most beautiful and beloved God.

Every soul yearns for knowledge, that knowledge which will give exaltation. But the soul cannot be satisfied by the knowledge one gathers from books, by learning, or by the study of outside things. For instance the knowledge of science, the knowledge of art, are outside knowledge. They give one a kind of strength, a kind of satisfaction, but this does not last. It is another knowledge that the soul is really seeking. The soul cannot be satisfied unless it finds that knowledge, but that knowledge does not come by learning names and forms.

We must enrich ourselves with thought, with that happiness which is spiritual happiness, with that peace which belongs to our soul, with that liberty, that freedom, for which our soul longs; and attain to that higher knowledge which breaks all the fetters of life and raises our consciousness to look at life from a different point of view. Once a person has realized this opportunity he has fulfilled the purpose of Life.

Hazrat Inayat Khan

In the name of Allah, the Beneficent, the Merciful

And those who accuse honorable women, but bring not four witnesses, scourge those men with eighty stripes and never afterward accept their testimony—They indeed are evil-doers. (24:4 Quran)

Save those who afterward repent and make amends. For such, lo, Allah is Merciful, Forgiving. (24:5 Quran)

As for those who accuse their wives but have no witnesses accept themselves, let the testimony of one of them be four testimonies, swearing by Allah that he is of those who speak the truth. (24:6 Quran)

And yet a fifth, invoking the curse of Allah on himself if he is of those who lie. (24:7 Quran)

And it shall avert the punishment from her if she bear witness before Allah four times that the thing he saith is indeed false. (24:8 Quran)

And a fifth time that the wrath of Allah be upon her if he speaketh truth. (24:9 Quran)

And had it not been for the grace of Allah and His mercy unto you, and the Allah is Wise, Clement, ye had been undone. (24:10 Quran)

O ye who believe! Enter not houses other than your own without first announcing your presence, and invoking peace upon the folk thereof. That is better for you, that ye may be heedful. (24:27 Quran)

Allah is the Light of the heavens and the earth. The similitude of His light is as a niche wherein is a lamp. The lamp is in a glass. The glass is as it were a glittering star. This lamp is kindled from a blessed tree, an olive neither of the East, nor of the West, whose oil would almost glow forth of itself though no fire touched it. Light upon light. Allah guideth unto His light whom He will. And Allah speaketh to mankind in allegories, for Allah is Knower of all things. (24:35 Quran)

This lamp is found in houses which Allah hath allowed to be exalted and that His name shall be remembered therein. Therein do offer praise to Him as morn and evening. (24:36 Quran)

They only are true believers who believe in Allah and His messenger, and when they are with him on some common errand, go not away until they have asked leave of him. Lo, those who ask leave of thee, those are they who believe in Allah and His messenger. So, if they ask thy leave for some affair of theirs, give leave to whom thou wilt of them, and ask for them forgiveness of Allah. Lo, Allah is Merciful, Forgiving. (24:62 Quran)

All earthly knowledge is as a cloud covering the Sun

Truth is the very self of man. Truth is the divine element in man. Truth is every soul's seeking. Therefore as soon as the clouds of illusion are scattered, that which man now begins to see is nothing but the truth which has been there all the time. He finds that the truth was never absent; it was only covered by clouds of illusion.

Man brings unhappiness upon himself by holding in his hands the clouds of bad impressions, which fall as a shadow upon his soul. Once a person is able to clear from his mind, by whatever process, the undesirable impressions, a new power begins to spring from his heart. This opens a way before him to accomplish all he wishes, attracting to him all he requires, clearing his path of all obstacles, and making his atmosphere clear, for him to live and move and to accomplish all he wishes to accomplish.

As there are times when the sun becomes covered by clouds, so there are times when the God-ideal becomes covered by materialism. But if for a moment the cloud covers the sun, that does not mean that the sun is lost; and so the God-ideal may seemed to have disappeared in the reign of materialism, yet God is there just the same. We find that during the past few years all over the world we have come to a phase when the God-ideal has seemed entirely forgotten. It does not mean that the Churches have disappeared, it does not mean that God does not exist, but that a light that was once there has been covered and has ceased to illuminate us.

Now the time has come that humanity, after its contemplation on material gain, must contemplate on another gain. Material gains are taken away in a moment's time and leave man in his grave alone without any of them. This does not mean that the knowledge of the world is useless, but the knowledge of the world does not suffice the whole purpose of life. There is only one thing from which true satisfaction can come, and that is the knowledge of the deeper side of life, the knowledge of the source and goal of all things.

It is the receptivity of our heart and the passivity of our mind, it is the eagerness, the thirst and hunger after truth. It is the direction of our whole life to that Ideal from who all light and truth come, that alone can bring us truth and the knowledge of God. All knowledge of the earth is as clouds covering the sun. It is the breaking of these clouds and clearness of the sky, or in other words the purity of heart, which gives the capacity for the knowledge of God. *Hazrat Inyat Khan*

Surah Twenty-Five

Al Furqan
It is wise to see all things, and yet to turn our eyes from all that should be overlooked.

It is to the great disadvantage of the fault-finding man that he wishes to find fault with all he sees, for if he is not able to throw away immediately the undesirable impression received, which is not always so easy, he begins in due time to reproduce what he has received. If man only knew what harm is brought to one's being by letting any undesirable impression enter the heart, he also would adopt the above-mentioned policy of the wise, to overlook.

The aim of the Sufi, therefore, is to see and yet not be interested. Those who trouble about others' thoughts and interest themselves in others' actions most often lose their time and blunt their inner sight. Those who go farther, their moral is to overlook all they see on their way, as their mind is fixed on the goal. The best thing is to see and rise above, never to halt on the way, and it is this attitude that, if constantly practiced, will lead man safely to his soul's desired goal.

There is a tendency which manifests itself and grows in a person who is advancing spiritually, and that tendency is overlooking. At times this tendency might appear as negligence, but in reality negligence is not necessarily overlooking. Negligence is most often not looking. Overlooking may be called in other words rising beyond these things: one has to rise in order to overlook; the one who stands beneath life could not overlook, even if he wanted to. Overlooking is a manner of graciousness; it is looking and at the same time not looking. It is seeing and not taking notice of what is seen. It is being hurt or harmed or disturbed by something and yet not minding it. It is an attribute of nobleness of nature. It is the sign of souls who are tuned to a higher key.

Whenever we see that goodness is lacking, we may add to it from our own heart and so complete the nobility of human nature. This is done by patience, tolerance, kindness, forgiveness. The lover of goodness loves every little sign of goodness. He overlooks the faults and fills up the gaps by pouring out love and supplying that which is lacking. This is real nobility of soul. Hazrat Inayat Khan

In the name of Allah, the Beneficent, the Merciful

Blessed is He Who hath revealed unto His slave the criterion of right and wrong, that he may be a warner to the peoples. (25:1 Quran)

Say unto them, O Muhammad: He Who knoweth the secret of the heavens and the earth hath revealed it. Lo, He is ever Merciful, Forgiving. (25:6 Quran)

And the messenger saith: O my Lord! Lo, mine own folk make this Quran of no account. (25:30 Quran)

Even so We have appointed every Prophet an opponent from among the guilty, but Allah sufficeth for a Guide and Helper. (25:31 Quran)

And He it is Who maketh night a covering for you, and sleep repose, and maketh day a resurrection. (25:47 Quran)

And He is it Who sendeth the Winds, glad tidings heralding His mercy, and We send down purifying water from the sky. (25:48 Quran)

That We may give life thereby to a dead land, and We give many beasts and men that We have created to drink thereof. (25:49 Quran)

And He it is Who hath created man from water and hath appointed for him kindred by blood and kindred by marriage, for thy Lord is ever Powerful. (25:54 Quran)

And We have sent thee, O Muhammad, only as a bearer of good tidings and a warner. (25:56 Quran)

And trust thou in the Living One Who dieth not, and hymn His praise. He sufficeth as the Knower of the bondmen's sins. (25:58 Quran)

Who created the heavens and the earth and all that is between them in six Days, then He mounted the Throne. The Beneficent! Ask anyone informed concerning Him. (25:59 Quran)

And when it is said unto them: Adore the Beneficent! They say: what is the Beneficent? Are we to adore whatever thou Muhammad biddest us? And it increaseth aversion in them. (25:60 Quran)

Blessed be He Who hath placed in the heaven mansions of the stars, and hath placed therein a great lamp and a moon giving light! (25:61 Quran)

And He it is Who hath appointed night and day in succession, for him who desireth to remember, or desireth thankfulness. (25:62 Quran)

The faithful slaves of the Beneficent are they who walk upon the earth modestly, and when the foolish ones address them answer: Peace. (25:63 Quran)

And who say: Our Lord! Vouchsafe us comfort of our wives and of our offspring and make us patterns for all those who ward off evil. (25:74 Quran)

They will be awarded the high place for as much as they were steadfast and they will meet therein with welcome and the word of peace. (25:75 Quran)

Abiding there forever. Happy is it as abode and station! (25:76 Quran)

Man is closer to God than the fishes are to the ocean.

One day Inayat was praying on the roof of the house, offering his prayers and he thought to himself that there had not been an answer yet to all the prayers he had offered to God and he did not know where God was to hear his prayers and he could not reconcile himself to going on praying to the God whom he knew not. He went fearlessly to his father and said: "I do not think I will continue my prayers any longer, for it does not fit in with my reason. I do not know how I can go on praying to a God I do not know." His father, taken aback, did not become cross lest he might turn Inayat's beliefs sour by forcing them upon him without satisfying his reason and he was glad on the other hand to see that, although it was irreverent on the child's part, yet it was frank, and he knew that the lad really hungered after Truth and was ready to learn now, what many could not learn in their whole life.

He said to him: "God is in you and you are in God. As the bubble is in the ocean and the bubble is a part of the ocean and yet not separate from the ocean. For a moment it has appeared as a bubble, then it will return to that from which it has risen. So is the relation between man and God. The Prophet has said that God is closer to you than the jugular vein, which in reality means that your own body is farther from you than God is. If this be rightly interpreted, it will mean that God is the very depth of your own being." This moment to Inayat was his very great initiation, as if a switch had turned in him, and from that moment onward his whole life Inayat busied himself, and his whole being became engaged in witnessing in life what he knew and believed, by this one great Truth.

The innermost being of man is the real being of God; man is always linked with God. If he could only realize it, it is by finding harmony in his own soul that he finds communion with God. All meditation and contemplation are taught with this purpose: to harmonize one's innermost being with God, so that He is seeing, hearing, thinking through us, and our being is a ray of His light. In that way we are even closer to God than the fishes are to the ocean in which they have their being.

Many think that spiritual attainment can only be achieved by great labor. It is not so; labor is necessary for material attainment, but for spiritual attainment what one needs is a seeking soul like that of Moses. Moses falling upon the ground may be interpreted as the Cross, which means, 'I am not; Thou art.' In order to be, one must pass through a stage of being nothing. In Sufi terms this is called Fana, when one thinks, 'I am not what I had always thought myself to be.' This is the true self-denial, which the Hindus called Layam, and the Buddhists annihilation. It is the annihilation of the false self which gives rise to the true self; once this is done, from that moment man approaches closer and closer to God, until he stands face to face with his divine ideal, with which he can communicate at every moment of his life. *Hazrat Inayat Khan*

Surah Twenty-Six

Ash Shuara
Truth alone can succeed; falsehood is a waste of time and loss of energy.

Falsehood, whatever its apparent success, has its limitations and its end. For at every step the false person will feel falseness; and with every step a person takes towards falsehood, he will feel his feet growing heavier and heavier when he encounters the truth, while those who walk towards the truth will feel their feet becoming lighter with every step they take.

Truth is the divine element in man. Truth is every soul's seeking. Therefore as soon as the clouds of illusion are scattered, that which man now begins to see is nothing but the truth which has been there all the time. He finds that the truth was never absent; it was only covered by clouds of illusion.

By changing his own nature, by making himself more truthful, he disperses the clouds of falsehood within and without, and begins to see life as it really is both inwardly and outwardly. From this time onwards, the meaning of religion becomes clear. One begins to understand what the great teachers have taught. Then one becomes tolerant to the various religions. Nothing seems strange any more. Nothing surprises. For now one begins to know the innermost nature of man; one sees the cause behind every action.

People speak about truth and falsehood, but once the mystic has reached the truth, all is truth to him; then everything is a phenomenon of truth, a picture of truth. For instance, a person looking at a picture may distinguish light and shade, but another instead of speaking of light and shade, will say, 'This is a portrait of so and so, it is a very good picture, exactly like him.' Truth is like this; and so to a mystic the whole of life is a picture of the divine Beloved. Hazrat Inayat Khan

In the name of Allah, the Beneficent, the Merciful

And lo, thy Lord! He is indeed the Mighty, the Merciful. (26:9 Quran)

And lo, thy Lord! He is indeed the Mighty, the Merciful. (26:175 Quran)

The dweller in the woods of Midian denied the messengers of Allah. (26:176 Quran)

When Shueyb said unto them: Will you not ward off evil? (26:177 Quran)

Lo! I am a faithful messenger unto you. (26:178 Quran)

So keep your duty to Allah and obey me. (26:179 Quran)

And I ask of you no wage for it, my wage is concern only of the Lord of the Wolds. (26:180 Quran)

Give full measure, and be not one of those who give less than the due. (26:181 Quran)

And weigh with the true balance. (26:182 Quran)

Wrong not mankind in their goods, and do not evil, making mischief, in the earth. (26:183 Quran)

And keep your duty unto Him Who created you and the generations of the men of the old. (26:184 Quran)

And lo, thy Lord! He is indeed the Mighty, the Merciful. (26:191 Quran)

And lo, it is a revelation of the Lord of the Worlds. (26:192 Quran)

Which the True Spirit has brought down. (26:193 Quran)

Upon thy heart that thou mayest be one of the warners. (26:194 Quran)

In plain Arabic speech. (26:195 Quran)

And lo, it is in the Scriptures of the men of old. (26:196 Quran)

Is it not a token for them that the doctors of Children of Israel know it? (26:197 Quran)

And lower thy wing in kindness unto those believers who follow thee. (26:215 Quran)

And if thy kinfolk disobey thee, say: Lo, I am innocent of what they do. (26:216 Quran)

And put thy trust in the Mighty, the Merciful. (26:217 Quran)

Who seeth thee when thou standeth up to pray? (26:218 Quran)

And seeth thine abasement among those who fall prostrate in worship. (26:219 Quran)

Lo! He, only He, is the Hearer, the Knower. (26:220 Quran)

Verily, he is victorious who has conquered himself.

Our greatest enemy is our self. All weakness, all ignorance keeps us from the truth of our being, from all the virtues hidden in us and all perfection hidden in our souls. The first self we realize is the false self. Unless the soul is born again it will not see the kingdom of heaven. The soul is born into the false self; it is blind. In the true self the soul opens its eyes. Unless the false self is fought with, the true self cannot be realized.

The soul is a bird of paradise, a free dweller in the heavens. Its first prison is the mind, then the body. In these it becomes not only limited, but also captive. The whole endeavor of a Sufi in life is to liberate the soul from its captivity, which he does by conquering both mind and body.

If a man has control over himself, he will smile and be patient even if he is exposed to rages a thousand times. He will just wait. He who has spiritual control has great control; but he who has it not can control neither spiritual nor physical events. He cannot control his own sons and daughters, for he never listens to himself first. If he listened to himself, not only persons but even objects would listen to him.

There is a poem by the great Persian poet Iraqi in which he tells, 'When I went to the gate of the divine Beloved and knocked at the door, a voice came and said — Who art thou?' When he had told, 'I am so and so', the answer came. 'There is no place for anyone else in this abode. Go back to whence thou hast come'. He turned back and then, after a long time, after having gone through the process of the cross and of crucifixion, he again went there — with the spirit of selflessness. He knocked at the door; the word came, 'Who art thou? ', and he said, 'Thyself alone, for no one else exists save Thee'. And God said, 'Enter into this abode for now it belongs to thee'. It is such selflessness, to the extent that the thought of self is not there, it is being dead to the self, which is the recognition of God. *Hazrat Inayat Khan*

Life is an opportunity given to satisfy the hunger and thirst of the soul.

And what is life? Life is an opportunity. To the optimistic person the opportunity is a promise, and for the pessimistic person this opportunity is lost. It is not that the Creator makes man lose it, but it is man who withdraws himself from the possibility of seizing the opportunity.

If there is something that can be accomplished today, we need not wait for it to be accomplished tomorrow. For life is an opportunity, and desire has the greatest power, and perfection is the promise of the soul. We seek perfection, because perfection is the ultimate aim and the goal of creation. The source of all things is perfect. Our source is perfect, our goal is perfect. And therefore every atom of the universe is working towards perfection, and sooner or later it must arrive at perfection consciously. If it were not so, you would not have read in the Bible, 'Be ye perfect as your Father in heaven is perfect.'

Kabir, the great poet of India says, 'Life is a field and you are born to cultivate it. And if you know how to cultivate this field you can produce anything you like. All the need of your life can be produced in this field. All that your soul yearns after and all you need is to be got from the field, if you know how to cultivate it and how to reap the fruit.' But if this opportunity is only studied in order to make the best of life by taking all that one can take and by being more comfortable, that is not satisfying. We must enrich ourselves with thought, with that happiness which is spiritual happiness, with that peace which belongs to our soul, with that liberty, that freedom, for which our soul longs; and attain to that higher knowledge which breaks all the fetters of life and raises our consciousness to look at life from a different point of view. Once a person has realized this opportunity he has fulfilled the purpose of Life. *Hazrat Inayat Khan*

Surah Twenty-Seven

An Naml

Man forms his future by his actions; his every good or bad action spreads its vibrations and becomes known throughout the universe.

According to the ideas of the mystics the world in which we make our life is an Akasha, and Akasha means capacity. It is pictured by them as a dome; and whatever is spoken in it has its echo. Therefore no one can do, say, or think anything for one moment which will become non-existent. It is recorded; and that record is creative. It is not only what one does, says, or thinks that is recorded in the memory or in the atmosphere, but that record also creates at every moment, so that every line and letter of it becomes the seed or the germ that produces a similar effect.

The law of cause and effect is as definite in its results in the realm of speech and thought as in the physical world. Man forms his future by his actions. His every good or bad action spreads its vibrations and becomes known throughout the universe. The more spiritual a man is, the stronger and clearer are the vibrations of his actions, which spread over the world and weave his future.

Wherever a person goes there he takes his influence, thereby creating harmony or in-harmony in the atmosphere. As a person who is drunken feels most delighted to see another person also drunken in the same way as he, and enjoys his company and offers him a drink, so the inharmonious person creates in-harmony, and so the harmonious person spreads the vibrations of harmony, tuning the whole atmosphere to the pitch of his soul. Hazrat Inayat Khan

In the name of Allah, the Beneficent, the Merciful

Lo, as for thee, Muhammad, thou verily receives the Quran from the presence of One Wise, Aware. (27:6 Quran)

Remember when Moses said unto his household: Lo, I spy afar of a fire, I will bring you tidings thence, or bring to you a borrowed flame that ye may warm yourselves. (27:7 Quran)

But when he reached it, he was called, saying: Blessed is whosoever is in the fire and whosoever is round about it! And glorified be Allah, the Lord of the Worlds! (27:8 Quran)

O Moses, Lo! It is I Allah, the Mighty, the Wise. (27:9 Quran)

And throw down thy staff! But when he saw it writhing as it were a demon, he turned to flee headlong, but it was said unto him: O Moses, fear not! The emissaries fear not in My presence. (27:10 Quran))

Save him who hath done wrong and afterward hath changed evil for good. And lo, I am Merciful, Forgiving. (27:11 Quran)

And We verily gave knowledge unto David and Solomon, and they said: Praise be to Allah, Who hath preferred us above many of His believing slaves! (27:15 Quran)

And Solomon was David's heir. And he said: O mankind! Lo, we have been taught the language of birds, and have been given abundance of all things. This surely is evident favor. (27:16 Quran)

Say, O Muhammad: None in the heavens and the earth knoweth the Unseen save Allah, and they know not when they will be raised again. (27:65 Quran)

Say unto them, O Muhammad: Travel in the land and see the nature of the sequel for the guilty! (27:69 Quran)

And grieve thou not for them, nor be in distress because what they plot against thee. (27:70 Quran)

And they say: When will this promise be fulfilled, if ye are truthful? (27:71 Quran)

Say: it may be that a part of that which ye would hasten on is close behind you. (27:72 Quran)

Lo, thy Lord is full of bounty for mankind, but most of them do not give thanks. (27:73 Quran)

Lo, thy Lord knoweth surely all that their bosoms hide, and all that they proclaim. (27:74 Quran)

And there is nothing hidden in the heaven or the earth, but it is in a clear Record. (27:75 Quran)

Lo, this Quran narrateth unto the Children of Israel most of that concerning which they differ. (27:76 Quran)

And lo, it is a guidance and mercy for believers. (27:77 Quran)

Lo, thy Lord will judge between them of His wisdom, and He is the Mighty, the Wise. (27:78 Quran)

Therefore, O Muhammad, put thy trust in Allah, for thou standest on the plain Truth. (27:79 Quran)

Say: I Muhammad am commanded only to serve the Lord of the land which He hath hallowed, and unto Whom all things belong. And I am commanded to be of those who surrender unto Him. (27:91 Quran)

And to recite the Quran. And whoso goeth right, goeth right only for the good of his own soul, and as for him who goeth astray—unto him say: Lo, I am only a warner. (27:92 Quran)

And say: Praise be to Allah Who will show you His portents so that ye shall know them. And thy Lord is not unaware of what ye mortals do. (27:93 Quran)

The universe is like a dome; it vibrates to that which you say in it, and answers the same back to you; so also is the law of action we reap what we sow.

Everything and being on the surface of existence seem separate from one another, but in every plane beneath the surface they approach nearer to each other, and in the innermost plane they all become one. Every disturbance therefore, caused to the peace of the smallest part of existence on the surface, inwardly affects the soul. Thus any thought, speech or action that disturbs peace is wrong, evil, and a sin; if it brings about peace it is right, good, and a virtue.

The picture itself inspires the painter. As it progresses he sees that in a certain place there ought to be a different color. This is not right; that is not right, and so on. And as he looks at the picture, he sees its faults, and so he alters it here and there. So it is with each life. As we sow, so we reap. All that we do, we see in its reaction, and the reaction changes our life. The painter sees he must finish the picture differently, and so our actions tell us whether we ought to act differently. *Hazrat Inayat Khan*

Surah Twenty-Eight

Al Qasas

Concentration and contemplation are great things; but no contemplation is greater than the life we have about us every day.

As one goes further in the soul's unfoldment one finally arrives at the stage of revelation. Life begins to reveal itself, the whole of life, each soul becomes communicative — not only living beings but each thing. They say that the twelve apostles knew all languages. It does not mean that they knew English, French and Italian, but that they knew every soul's language, as every soul has its own separate language. They began to perceive vibrations and so every evolved soul will feel the vibrations of every other soul, and every condition, every soul, every object in the world will reveal its nature and character to him. Sadi, the Persian poet, has said, 'Once a soul has begun to read, every leaf of the tree becomes as a page of the sacred book of life'.

From the moment man's eyes open and he begins to read the book of nature he begins to live; and he continues to live forever. Hazrat Inayat Khan

In the name of Allah, the Beneficent, the Merciful

These are revelations of the Scripture that maketh plain. (28:2 Quran)

We narrate unto thee somewhat of the story of Moses and Pharaoh with truth, for folk who believe. (28:3 Quran)

Lo, Pharaoh exalted himself in the earth and made its people castes. A tribe among them he oppressed, killing their sons and sparing their women. Lo, he was of those who work corruption. (28:4 Quran)

And We desired to show favor unto those who were oppressed in the earth, and to make them examples and to make them the inheritors. (28:5 Quran)

And to establish them in the earth, and to show Pharaoh and Haman and their hosts that which they feared for them. (28:6 Quran)

And We inspired the mother of Moses, saying: Suckle him and when thou fearest for him, then cast him into the river and fear not nor grieve. Lo, We shall bring him back unto thee and shall make him one of Our messengers. (28:7 Quran)

And the family of Pharaoh took him up, that he might become for them an enemy and a sorrow. Lo, Pharaoh and Haman and their hosts were ever sinning. (28:8 Quran)

And the wife of Pharaoh said: He will be a consolation for me and for thee. Kill him not. Peradventure he may be of use to us, or we may choose him for a son. And they perceived not. (28:9 Quran)

And the heart of mother of Moses became void, and she would have betrayed him if We had not fortified her heart, that she might be of the believers. (28:10 Quran)

And she said unto his sister: Trace him. So she observed him from afar, and they perceived not. (28:11 Quran)

And We had before forbidden foster mothers for him, so she said: Shall I show you a household who will rear him for you and take care of him? (28:12 Quran)

So We restored him to his mother that she might be comforted and not grieve, and that she might know that the promise of Allah is true. But most of them know not. (28:13 Quran)

And when he reached his full strength and was ripe, We gave him wisdom and knowledge. Thus do We reward the good. (28:14 Quran)

And thou, Muhammad, was not on the western side of the Mount when We expounded unto Moses the commandment, and thou wast not amongst thou present. (28:44 Quran)

But We brought forth generations, and their lives dragged on for them. And thou wast not a dweller in Midian, reciting unto them Our revelations, but We kept sending messengers to men. (28:45 Quran)

And thou wast not beside the Mount when We did call, but the knowledge of it is a mercy from thy Lord that thou mayest warn a folk unto whom no warner came before thee, that haply they may give heed. (28:46 Quran)

Otherwise, if disaster should afflict them because that which their own hands have sent before them, they might say: Our Lord! Why sentest Thou no messenger unto us, that we might have followed Thy revelations and been of the believers? (28:47 Quran)

But when come unto them the Truth from Our presence, they said: Why is he not given the like of what was given unto Moses? Did they not disbelieve in that which was given unto Moses of old? They say: Two magics that support each other, and they say: Lo, in both we are disbelievers. (28:48 Quran)

Say unto them, O Muhammad: Then bring a Scripture from the presence of Allah that giveth clear guidance than these two that I may follow it, if ye are truthful. (28:49 Quran)

And now verily We have caused the word to reach them, that haply they may give heed. (28:51 Quran)

Those unto whom We gave the Scripture before it, they believe in it. (28:52 Quran)

And when it is recited unto them, they say: We believe in it. Lo, it is the truth from our Lord. Lo, even before it we were of those who surrender unto Him. (28:53 Quran)

These will be given their reward twice over, because they are steadfast and repel evil with good, and spend of that wherewith We have provided them. (28:54 Quran)

And when they hear vanity they withdraw from it and say: Unto us our works and unto you your works. Peace be unto you! We desire not the ignorant. (28:55 Quran)

Lo, thou, O Muhammad guidest not whom thou lovest, but Allah guideth whom He will. And He is the best aware of those who walk aright. (28:56 Quran)

But seek the abode of the Hereafter in that which Allah hath given thee and neglect not thy portion of the world, and be thou kind even as Allah hath been kind to thee, and seek not corruption in the earth. Lo, Allah loveth not corrupters. (28:77 Quran)

Wisdom is intelligence in its pure essence, which is not necessarily dependent upon the knowledge of names and forms.

The knowledge which is learned by knowing names and forms in the outside world belongs to the intellect; but there is another source of knowledge, and that source of knowledge is within oneself.

The words 'within oneself' might confuse some people. They might think 'within oneself' means inside one's body; but that is because man is ignorant of himself. Man has a very poor idea of himself, and this keeps him in ignorance of his real self. If man only knew how large, how wide, how deep, how high is his being, he would think, act, and feel differently; but with all his width, depth, and height, if man is not conscious of them he is as small as he thinks himself to be.

The essence of milk is butter, the essence of the flower is honey, the essence of grapes is wine, and the essence of life is wisdom. Wisdom is not necessarily a knowledge of names and forms; wisdom is the sum total of that knowledge which one gains both from within and without.

Intellectual knowledge has much to do with the brain, while wisdom comes from within the heart. In wisdom both head and heart work. One may call the brain the seat of the intellect, and the heart the throne of wisdom; but they are not actually located in the brain or in the heart. Wisdom may be called spiritual knowledge but the best definition of wisdom would be perfect knowledge, the knowledge of life within and without. How does one pursue the wisdom which is within? By first realizing that intuition exists within oneself.

It is not meant by this that everyone should become a kind of super-being. It is not meant at all that people should be able to perform wonders or miracles; it is only intended that they should live a fuller life and become real human beings, in order to bring about better conditions in the world. What do we want? We want human beings. It is not necessary that everyone should become religious, or exceedingly pious, or too good to live. We want wise men in business, in politics, in education, in all walks of life; those who do not live only on the surface and those who do not believe only in matter, but who see life both within and without. It is such souls who will produce beauty; it is such souls who will harmonize the world, who will bring about the conditions we need today. *Hazrat Inayat Khan*

Surah Twenty-Nine

Al Ankabut
We start our lives trying to be teachers; it is very hard to learn to be a pupil.

The principal teaching of Sufism is that of learning to become a pupil, for it is the pupil who has a chance of becoming a teacher, and once a person considers that he is a teacher, his responsiveness is gone. The greatest teachers of the world have been the greatest pupils.

We often start our lives as teachers, and then it is hard to become a pupil. From childhood on we start to teach our parents. There are seldom souls who have more inclination for pupilship than for teaching, and there are many whose only difficulty in life is that they are teachers already. Man thinks that perhaps his reading or study of different religions and doctrines has qualified him and made him capable to understand the truth and to have the knowledge of God, but he forgets that there is only one teacher, and that is God Himself. We all are pupils, and what we can do in life is to qualify ourselves to become true pupils.

It should be remembered that all the great teachers of humanity, such as Jesus Christ, Buddha, Muhammad and Zarathustra, have been great pupils; they have learned from the innocent child, they have learned from everyone, from every person that came near them. They have learned from every situation and every condition of the world. They have understood and they have learned. It is the desire to learn continually that makes one a teacher, and not the desire to become a teacher. As soon as a person thinks, 'I am something of a teacher,' he has lost ground. For there is only one teacher: God alone is the Teacher, and all others are His pupils. We all learn from life what life teaches us. When a soul begins to think that he has learned all he had to learn and that now he is a teacher, he is very much mistaken. The greatest teachers of humanity have learned from humanity more than they have taught. Hazrat Inayat Khan

In the name of Allah, the Beneficent, the Merciful

And whosoever striveth, striveth only for himself, for, lo, Allah is altogether Independent of His creatures. (29:6 Quran)

And as for those who believe and do good works. We shall remit from them their evil deeds and shall repay them the best that they did. (29:7 Quran)

And as for those who believe and do good works, We verily shall make them enter in among the righteous. (29:9 Quran)

And argue not with the People of the Scripture unless it be in a way that is better, save with such of them as do wrong and say: We believe in that which hath been revealed unto us and revealed unto you. Our God and your God is One, and unto Him We surrender. (29:46 Quran)

In like manner We revealed unto thee the Scripture, and those unto whom We gave the Scripture aforetime will believe therein. And none deny our revelations save the disbelievers. (29:47 Quran)

And thou O Muhammad was not a reader of any scripture before it, nor didst thou write it with thy right hand, for them might those have doubted, who follow falsehood. (29:48 Quran)

Every soul will taste of death. Then unto Us ye will be returned. (29:57 Quran)

Those who believe and do good works, them, verily We shall house in lofty dwellings of the Garden underneath which rivers flow. There they will dwell secure. How sweet the garden of the toilers. (29:58 Quran)

Who persevere and put their trust in their Lord. (29:59 Quran)

And how many an animal there is that beareth not its own provision. Allah provideth for it and for you. He is the Hearer, the Knower. (29:60 Quran)

And if thou wert to ask them: Who created the heavens and the earth, and constrained the sun and the moon to their appointed work? They would say: Allah. How then are they turned away? (29:61 Quran)

As for those who strive in Us, We surely guide them to Our paths, and lo, Allah is with the good. (29:69 Quran)

As one can see when the eyes are open, so one can understand when the heart is open.

Every name and every form speaks constantly, constantly makes signs for you to hear, for you to respond to, for you to interpret, that you may become a friend of God. The whole purpose of your life is to make yourself ready to understand what God is, what your fellow man is, what the nature of man is, what life is.

Now coming to a still greater secret of life I want to answer the question: how can we grow to read and understand the message that life speaks through all its names and forms? The answer is that, as by the opening of the eyes you can see things, so by the opening of the heart you can understand things. As long as the heart is closed you cannot understand things. The secret is that, when the ears and eyes of the heart are open, all planes of the world are open, all names are open, all secrets, and all mysteries are unfolded.

Everything becomes spiritual once this door of the chamber of the heart is open. If a man is a musician, then his music is celestial. If he is a poet, then his poetry is spiritual. If he is an artist, then his art is a spiritual work. Whatever he may do in life that divine spirit manifests. He need not be a religious person, he need not be a philosopher, and he need not be a mystic. It is simply that what was hidden in him and thereby was keeping his life incomplete begins to manifest to view, and that makes his life perfect. *Hazrat Inayat Khan.*

Surah Thirty

Ar Rum

Among a million believers in God there is scarcely one who makes God a reality.

If only we could recognize the inner voice, we would see that the different scriptures all contain words spoken by one and the same voice. Some hear the voice, others only hear the words, just as in nature some see only the branches and others the roots of the tree; but all these different scriptures and ways of worship and of contemplating God are given for one purpose: the realization of unity. In unity resides the happiness and illumination of man, and his guidance in life. We all know unity by name, but most of us think of it as uniformity. The Vedanta for thousands of years in all its prayers and mantras voiced this central theme: unity, the oneness of all. The Qur'an with all its warnings expresses in one essential Sura the Being of God: that not only in the unseen, but in all that is seen there is one underlying current; and the Bible says that we live and move and have our being in God.

Of all the millions of believers in God perhaps only one makes God a reality, and that is because the picture man makes of God is as limited as himself. The knowledge of God is beyond man's reason. Man only perceives things he is capable of perceiving. He cannot raise his imagination above what he is used to, and he cannot reach beyond his imagination to where the being of God is.

Among millions of believers in God, there is hardly one who makes God a reality. To so many He is an imagination, to many He is in a mosque, a church, or a temple. Many wonder if God is really God. Many others think God is goodness, He is a personality separate from us, He is most high, most pure, most beautiful, but He is separate and difficult to reach. Many think that as it takes so long to reach this planet or that, God must be further away still. The purpose of one's whole life is to make God a reality. If you will seek for good in everything, you will always find it, for God is in all things, and still more He is in all beings. Seek Him in all souls, good and bad, wise and foolish, attractive or unattractive, for in the depth of each there is God. He is all around and about us at every moment, we are living His life, we are breathing His breath, and yet we are ignorant of the perfection of beauty which unites and inspires every soul. Hazrat Inayat Khan

In the name of Allah, the Beneficent, the Merciful

In Allah's help to victory. He helpeth to victory whom He will. He is the Mighty, the Merciful. (30:5 Quran)

It is a promise of Allah. Allah faileth not His promise, but most of mankind know not. (30:6 Quran)

Allah produceth creation, then He reproduceth it, then unto Him ye will be returned. (30:11 Quran)

He bringeth forth the living from the dead, and He bringeth forth the dead from the living, and He reviveth the earth after her death. And even so ye will be brought forth. (30:19 Quran)

And of His signs is this: He created you of dust, and behold, you human beings, ranging widely! (30:20 Quran)

And of His signs is this: He created for you helpmates from yourselves that ye might find rest in them, and He ordained between you love and mercy. Lo, here indeed are portents for folk who reflect. (30:21 Quran)

And of His signs is the creation of the heavens and the earth, and the difference of your colors and languages. Lo, herein indeed are portents for men of knowledge. (30:22 Quran)

And of His signs is your slumber by night and by day, and your seeking of His bounty. Lo, herein are portents for folk who heed. (30:23 Quran)

And of His signs is this: He showeth you the lightning for a fear and for a hope, and sendeth down water from the sky, and thereby quickeneth the earth after her death. Lo, therein indeed are portents for folk who understand. (30:24 Quran)

And of His signs is this: The heavens and the earth stand fast by His command, and afterward, when He calleth you, lo, from the earth ye will emerge. (30:25 Quran)

Unto Him belongeth whosoever is in the heavens and in the earth. All are obedient unto Him. (30:26 Quran)

He it is Who produceth creation, then reproduceth it, and it is easier for Him. He is the Sublime Similitude in the heavens and in the earth. He is the Mighty, the Wise. (30:27 Quran)

So set thy purpose, O Muhammad, for religion as a man by nature upright—the nature framed of Allah, in which He hath created man.

There is no altering the laws of Allah's creation. This is the right religion, but most men know not. (30:30 Quran)

And when We cause mankind to taste of mercy they rejoice therein; but if an evil thing befall them as the consequence of their own deeds, lo, they are in despair! (30:36 Quran)

So give to the kinsmen his due, and to the needy and to the wayfarer. This is best for those who seek Allah's countenance. And such are they who are successful. (30:38 Quran)

And of His signs is this: He sendeth herald winds to make you taste His mercy, and the ships may sail at His command, and that ye may seek His favor, and that haply ye may be thankful. (30:46 Quran)

Verily We sent before thee, Muhammad, messengers to their own folk. They brought them clear proofs of Allah's Sovereignty. Then We took vengeance upon those who were guilty in regard to them. To help believers is incumbent upon Us. (30:47 Quran)

Look therefore at the prints of Allah's mercy in creation: How He quickeneth the earth after her death. Lo, He verily is the quickener of Dead and He is able to do all things. (30:50 Quran)

Allah is He Who shaped you out of weakness, then appointed after weakness strength, then after strength, appointed weakness and grey hair. He createth what He will. He is the Knower, the Mighty. (30:54 Quran)

So have patience, Muhammad. Allah's promise is the very truth, and let not those who have no certainty make thee impatient. (30:60 Quran)

'God is love' — three words which open up an unending realm for the thinker who desires to probe the depths of the secret of life.

Every kind of power lies in this one thing which we call by the simple name: love. Charity, generosity, kindness, affection, endurance, tolerance, and patience—all these words are different aspects of one; they are different names of only one thing: love. Whether it is said, 'God is love,' or whatever name is given to it, all the names are the names of God; and yet every form of love, every name for love, has its own peculiar scope, has a peculiarity of its own. Love as kindness is one thing, love as tolerance is another, love as generosity is another, love as patience another; and yet from beginning to end it is just love.

When we look at this subject from a mystic's point of view, we see that love has two aspects. Love in itself, and the shadow of love fallen on the earth. The former is heavenly the latter is earthly. The former develops self-abnegation in a person; the latter makes him more selfish than he was before. Virtues such as tolerance, mercy, forgiveness and compassion rise of themselves in the heart which is awakened to love.

How beautiful are the words of the Prophet: 'The shrine of God is the heart of man.' How true that is! Is God to be found in a mosque, or temple, or church, or in any place where people sing hymns and offer their prayers? Can He be found where there is no love? He is not to be found in the houses that men have built for worship. These are only schools for children, and their playgrounds. Children like playing with toys, and yet they are preparing themselves for something else. When man has come to know the real beauty of God, he will find that it dwells only in one place: in the heart of man. God is love, and He is found in the heart of man.

Love, whether it is human or divine is considered to be sacred, in the view of the mystics, philosophers, and thinkers. That it is possible to regard it thus is shown by the fact that in its root it is beyond both the human and the divine. As it is written in the Bible, 'God is Love', three words which open up an unending realm for the thinker who desires to probe the depth of the secret of love. In ordinary life, we make this word mean affection for our surroundings, for our relatives or our beloved, but when we think deeply about it, we see that from start to finish it represents the power underlying the power of all activities and all intelligences. *Hazrat Inayat Khan*

Surah Thirty-One

Luqman
As the light of the sun helps the plant to grow, so the divine Spirit helps the soul towards its perfection.

The Spirit of Guidance is a plant that grows and blossoms when it meets with response and care; and when it is watered by the rainfall of divine inspiration it blooms in the light of the divine sun. The Spirit of Guidance is the light of God, which may be likened to a lantern that the farmer carries when walking on the farm in the darkness of night. It is like a searchlight, which shows up any object upon which it is thrown; and so when the light of the Spirit of Guidance is thrown upon any aspect of life, man receives a keen insight into it. In the Spirit of Guidance one finds a living God active in the heart of every person.

The purpose of life is that we grow towards perfection; from the greatest limitation we grow towards perfection. Its beauty is in acquiring wisdom, in living at the cost of all our failures, our mistakes. It is all worthwhile, and it all accomplishes the purpose of our coming to the earth.

What is necessary today is to find the first and last religion, to come to the message of Christ, to divine wisdom, so that we may recognize wisdom in all its different forms, in whatever form it has been given to humanity. It does not matter if it is Buddhism, Islam, Judaism, Zoroastrianism, Hinduism. It is one wisdom, that call of the Spirit, which awakens man to rise above limitation and to reach perfection. Hazrat Inayat Khan

In the name of Allah, the Beneficent, the Merciful

These are revelations of the wise Scripture. (31:2 Quran)

A guidance and a mercy for the good. (31:3 Quran)

Those who establish worship and pay the poor-due and have sure faith in the Hereafter. (31:4 Quran)

Such have guidance from their Lord. Such are the successful. (31:5 Quran)

Lo, those who believe and do good works, for them are gardens of delight. (31:8 Quran)

Wherein they will abide. It is a promise of Allah in truth. He is the Mighty, the Wise. (31:9 Quran)

And verily We gave Luqman wisdom, saying: Give thanks unto Allah, and whosoever giveth thanks, he giveth thanks for the good of his soul. And whosoever refuseth—Lo, Allah is Absolute, Owner of Praise. (31:12 Quran)

O my dear son! Establish worship and enjoin kindness and forbid iniquity, and persevere whatever may befall thee. Lo, that is of the steadfast heart of things. (31:17 Quran)

Turn not thy cheek in scorn toward folk, nor walk with pertness in the land. Lo, Allah loveth not each braggart, boaster. (31:18 Quran)

Be modest in thy bearing and subdue thy voice. Lo, the harshest of all voices is the voice of the ass. (31:19 Quran)

See ye not how Allah hath made serviceable unto you whatsoever is in the skies and whatsoever is in the earth and hath loaded you with His favors both within and without? Yet of mankind is he who disputeth concerning Allah, without knowledge or guidance or a Scripture giving light. (31:20 Quran)

Whosoever surrendereth his purpose to Allah while doing good, he verily hath grasped the firm hand-hold. Unto Allah belongeth the sequel of all things. (31:22 Quran)

And whosoever disbelieveth, let not his disbelief afflict thee, O Muhammad. Unto Us is their return and We shall tell them what they did. Lo, Allah is aware of what is in the breasts of men. (31:23 Quran)

If thou shouldst ask them: Who created the heavens and the earth? They would answer: Allah. Say: Praise be to Allah! But most of them know not. (31:25 Quran)

Unto Allah belongeth whatsoever is in the heavens and the earth. Lo, Allah! He the Absolute, the Owner of Praise. (31:26 Quran)

And if all the trees in the earth were pens, and the sea, with seven more seas to help it were ink, the words of Allah could not be exhausted. Lo, Allah is Mighty, Wise. (31:27 Quran)

Your creation and your raising from the dead are only as the creation and the raising of a single soul. Lo, Allah is Hearer, Knower. (31:28 Quran)

Hast thou not seen how Allah causeth the night to pass into the day, and causeth the day to pass into the night, and hath subdued the sun and the moon to do their work, each running into an appointed term, and that Allah is informed of what ye do? (31:29 Quran)

Hast thou not seen how the ship glides on the sea by Allah's grace, that He may show you of His wonders? Lo, therein indeed are portents for every steadfast, grateful heart. (31:31 Quran)

Lo, Allah! With Him is the knowledge of the Hour. He sendeth down the rain, and knoweth that which is in the wombs. No soul knoweth what it will earn tomorrow, and no soul knoweth in what land it will die. Lo, Allah is Knower, Aware. (31:34 Quran)

The ideal of God is a bridge connecting the limited life with the unlimited; whosoever travels over this bridge passes safely from the limited to the unlimited life.

There is a side in man's being—call it spirit—which remains unsatisfied with all that one has attained in one's lifetime. The satisfaction of the spirit, which is the deepest being of man, lies only in the pursuit of the ideal. With all progress that humanity makes, idealism neglected will show at each step towards progress a great lack, and nothing can substitute that lack. If there is anything that fills the gap, if there is anything that makes a bridge between God and man, it is the ideal.

An ideal is something to hope for and to hold on to, and in the absence of an ideal hope has nothing to look forward to. It is the lack of idealism which accounts for the present degeneration of humanity in spite of all the progress it has made in other directions. There are many kinds of ideals: principles, virtues, objects of devotion; but the greatest and highest of all ideals is the God-ideal. And when this God-ideal upon which all other ideals are based is lost, then the very notion of ideal is ignored. Man needs many things in life, but his greatest need is an ideal.

If a man is standing on a staircase and remains on the first step, he may be a believer but he is not going up. Thus there are many believers who have a certain conception of God, but they are standing there without moving, while perhaps a person who has no conception of God at all may be moving. There are thousands of people who pronounce the name of God many times during the day, but who are perhaps most wretched. The reason is that they have not yet discovered the purpose of the God-ideal. It is not merely belief; belief is only the first step. God is the key to truth, God is the stepping-stone to self-realization, and God is the bridge which unites the outer life with the inner life, bringing about perfection. It is by understanding this that the secret of the God-ideal is to be realized.

The God-ideal is so tremendous that men can never comprehend it fully, therefore the best method adopted by the wise is to allow every man to make his own God. In this way he forms whatever conception he is capable of forming. He makes Him King of the heavens and of the earth; he makes Him judge, greater than all judges; he makes Him Almighty, having all power; he makes Him the possessor of all grace and glory; he makes Him the beloved God, merciful and compassionate; he recognizes in Him providence, support, and protection; and in Him he recognizes all perfection. This ideal becomes a stepping-stone to the higher knowledge of God.

In reality the ideal of God is a bridge connecting the limited life with the unlimited. Whoever goes over this bridge passes safely from the limited to the unlimited life. The bridge may be taken away, it is true, and one may yet swim across the chasm; but one may be drowned too. The ideal of God is a safe bridge, which takes you safely to the goal.

Hazrat Inayat Khan

Surah Thirty-Two

As Sajdah

The great teachers of humanity become streams of love.

Forgiveness is a stream of love which washes away all impurities wherever it flows. By keeping this spring of love, which is in the heart of man, running, man is able to forgive, however great the fault of his fellow man may seem. One who cannot forgive closes his heart. The sign of spirituality is that there is nothing you cannot forgive, there is no fault you cannot forget.

The great personalities who have descended on earth from time to time to awaken in man that love, which is his divine inheritance, have always found an echo in innocent souls rather than in great intellects. Man often confuses wisdom with cleverness, but a man can be clever and not wise, and by cleverness a person may strive and strive, and yet not reach God. It is a stream, the stream of love, which leads towards God. Law has no power to stand before love; the stream of love sweeps it away. When the woman accused by everyone was brought before Christ, what arose from the heart of the master? The law? No, it was love in the form of mercy and compassion.

In correcting a mureed of his faults it is not the intellect that is of much use. It is the pouring out of the stream of love which can wash away the stains; closing one's eyes to their faults, forgiving them, and yet correcting them with all tolerance, gentleness, and humility; making before them all things natural, nothing too horrible, but showing them the picture of a better life and thus drawing them toward that which is ideal and beautiful. When the teacher finds that the mureed is wrong he will not tell him that he is wrong, but will show him what is right.

The great teachers and prophets, and the inspirers of humanity of all times have not become what they were by their miracles or wonder-workings; these belong to other people. The main thing that could be seen in them was their loving manner. One may ask: How to cultivate the heart quality? There is only one way: to become selfless at each step one takes forward on this path, for what prevents one from cultivating the loving quality is the thought of self. The more we think of our self the less we think of others.

There is no greater magnetic power than love. Its magnetic power is very great. It changes a person's voice, his heart, his manner, his form, his movement, his activity, everything becomes changed. What a difference between water and rock; that smoothness and that liquid state of being, the rise and fall of the surface of the water compared with the rigidity of the rock! The great teachers of humanity become streams of love. It is the first sign of the sage or holy man that he himself becomes love. His voice, his feeling, his presence, everything makes one realize that there is something open in him which we do not find in everybody; this something is his deep love. Hazrat Inayat Khan

In the name of Allah, the Beneficent, the Merciful

The revelation of the Scripture whereof there is no doubt is from the Lord of the Worlds. (32:2 Quran)

Or they say: He hath invented it? Nay, but it is the truth from thy Lord, that thou mayest warn a folk to whom no warner came before thee, that haply they may walk aright. (32:3 Quran)

Allah it is Who created the heavens and the earth, and that which is between them, in six days. Then He mounted the throne. Ye have not, beside Him, a protecting friend or mediator. Will ye not then remember? (32:4 Quran)

He directeth the ordinance from the heavens unto the earth, then it ascendeth unto Him in a Day, whereof the measure is thousand years of that ye reckon. (32:5 Quran)

Such is the Knower of the invisible and the visible, the Mighty, the Merciful. (32:6 Quran)

Who made all things good which He created, and He began the creation of man from clay. (32:7 Quran)

But as for those who believe and do good works, for them are the Gardens of Retreat—a welcome in reward for what they used to do. (32:19 Quran)

Lo, thy Lord will judge between them on the Day of Resurrection concerning that wherein they used to differ. (32:25 Quran)

It is the surface of the sea that makes waves and roaring breakers; the depth is silent.

The bubbles are to be found on the surface of the sea. The depth of the sea is free from bubbles. The commotion is to be seen on the surface, the depth of the sea is still. The mind is the commotion of that something that is within us, that something which we call heart. The happiness, knowledge, pleasure and love that is stored in our innermost being is in our profound depth. Changing emotions and passions, dreams, ever-rising thoughts and imaginations, all belong to the surface, as the bubbles belong to the surface of the sea.

To attain peace, what one has to do is to seek that rhythm which is in the depth of our being. It is just like the sea: the surface of the sea is ever moving; the depth of the sea is still. And so it is with our life. If our life is thrown into the sea of activity, it is on the surface. We still live in the profound depths, in that peace. But the thing is to become conscious of that peace which can be found within ourselves. It is this which can bring us the answer to all our problems. If not, when we want to solve one problem, there is another difficult problem coming. There is no end to our problems. There is no end to the difficulties of the outer life. And if we get excited over them, we shall never be able to solve them. Some think, 'We might wait. Perhaps the conditions will become better. We shall see then what to do.' But when will the conditions become better? They will become still worse! Whether the conditions become better or worse, the first thing is to seek the kingdom of God within ourselves, in which there is our peace. As soon as we have found that, we have found our support, we have found our self. And in spite of all the activity and movement on the surface, we shall be able to keep that peace undisturbed if only we hold it fast by becoming conscious of it.

Spiritual knowledge is nothing but this: that there is a constant longing in the heart of man to have something of its origin, to experience something of its original state, the state of peace and joy which has been disturbed, and yet is sought after throughout its whole life, and never can cease to be sought after until the real source has at length been realized. What was it in the wilderness that gave peace and joy? What was it that came to us in the forest, the solitude? In either case it was nothing else but the depth of our own life, which is silent like the depths of the great sea, so silent and still. It is the surface of the sea that makes waves and roaring breakers; the depth is silent. So the depth of our own being is silent also.

And this all-pervading, unbroken, inseparable, unlimited, ever-present omnipotent silence unites with our silence like the meeting of flames. Something goes out from the depths of our being to receive something from there, which comes to meet us; our eyes cannot see and our ears cannot hear and our mind cannot perceive because it is beyond mind, thought, and comprehension. It is the meeting of the soul and the Spirit. *Hazrat Inayat Khan*

Surah Thirty-Three

Al Ahzab

Things are worthwhile when we seek them; only then do we know their value.

Very often people ask, 'How long has one to go on the spiritual path?' There is no limit to the length of this path, and yet if one is ready, it does not need a long time. It is a moment and one is there. How true it is, what the wise of past ages said to their followers, 'Do not go directly into the temple; first walk around it fifty times!' The meaning was, first get tired and then enter. Then you value it. One values something for which one makes an effort.

The adept values his object of attaining the inner life more than anything else in life. As long as he does not really value it, so long he remains unable to attain it. That is the first condition: that man should value the inner life more than anything else in the world, more than wealth, power, position, rank, or anything else. It does not mean that in this world he should not pursue the things he needs. It means he should value most something which is really worthwhile.

The next thing is that when one begins to value something one thinks it is worthwhile giving time to it. For in the modern world it is said that time is money, and money today means the most valuable thing. So if a person gives his precious time to what he considers most worthwhile, more so than anything else in the world, then that is certainly the next step towards the inner life.

There are really two journeys. There is the journey from the goal to the life in the world, and there is the journey from the life in the world to the goal. And both journeys are natural. As it is natural to go forth from the eternal goal, so it is natural to go from the changing life to the life which is unchangeable.

Which is the most desirable thing in life, to seek for the goal or to dwell in this changing life? The answer is that every person's desire is according to his evolution. That for which he is ready is desirable for him. Milk is a desirable food for the infant, other foods for the grown-up person. Every stage in life has its own appropriate and desirable things. The desire to attain to a goal must be there before reaching it; when he does not feel the desire, it is not necessary for a man to seek it. All things are worthwhile when we seek after them; then only do we appreciate their value; then only are we happy to have them. Hazrat Inayat Khan

In the name of Allah, the Beneficent, the Merciful

And put thy trust in Allah, for Allah is sufficient as Trustee. (33:3 Quran)

Allah hath not assigned unto any man two hearts within his body, nor hath he made your wives whom ye declare to be your mothers, your mothers, nor hath he made those whom ye claim be your sons, your sons. This is but a saying of your mouths. But Allah sayeth the truth and He showeth the way. (33:4 Quran)

Proclaim their real parentage. That will be more equitable in the sight of Allah. And if ye know not their fathers, then they are your brethren in faith, and your clients. And there is no sin for you in the mistakes that ye make unintentionally, but what your heart purpose that will be a sin for you. Allah is Merciful, Forgiving. (33:5 Quran)

The Prophet is closer to the believers than their selves, and his wives are as their mothers. And the owner of kinship are closer one to another on the ordinance of Allah than other believers and fugitives who fled from Mecca, except that ye should do kindness to your friends. This is written in the book of nature. (33:6 Quran)

And when We exacted a covenant from the Prophets, and from thee, O Muhammad, and from Noah and Abraham and Moses and Jesus son of Mary. We took from them a solemn covenant. (33:7 Quran)

That Allah may reward the true men for their truth, and punish the hypocrites if He will, or relent toward them if He will. Lo, Allah is Merciful, Forgiving. (33:24 Quran)

Lo, men who surrender unto Allah, and women who surrender, and men who believe, and women who believe, and men who obey and women who obey, and men who speak the truth, and women who speak the truth, and men who persevere in righteousness and women who persevere, and men who are humble and women who are humble, and men who give alms and women who give alms, and men who fast and women who fast, and men who guard their modesty and women who guard their modesty, and men who remember Allah much and women who remember—Allah hath prepared for them a vast reward and forgiveness. (33:35 Quran)

O ye who believe! Remember Allah with much remembrance. (33:41 Quran)

And glorify Him early and later. (33:42 Quran)

He it is who blesseth you, and His angels bless you and He may bring you forth from darkness unto light, and He is merciful to the believers. (33:43 Quran)

Their salutation of the day when they shall meet Him will be: Peace. And He hath prepared for them a goodly recompense. (33:44 Quran)

O Prophet! Lo, We have sent thee as a witness and a bringer of good tidings and a warner. (33:45 Quran)

And as a summoner unto Allah by His permission, and as a lamp that giveth light. (33:46 Quran)

And announce unto the believers the good tidings that they will have great bounty from Allah. (33:47 Quran)

O ye who believe! If ye wed believing women and divorce them before ye have touched them, then there is no period that ye should reckon. But content them and release them handsomely. (33:49 Quran)

Thou canst defer whom thou wilt of them and receive unto thee whom thou wilt, and whomsoever thou desirest of those whom thou hast set aside temporarily, it is no sin for thee to receive her again, that is better, that they may be comforted and not grieve, and may all be pleased with what thou givest them. Allah knoweth what is in your hearts, O men, and Allah is Clement, Forgiving. (33:51 Quran)

O ye who believe! Be not as those who slandered Moses, but Allah proved his innocence of what they alleged, and he was well esteemed in Allah's sight. (33:69 Quran)

O ye who believe! Guard your duty to Allah, and speak words straight to the point. (33:70 Quran)

He will adjust your works for you and will forgive you your sins. Whosoever obeyeth Allah and His messenger, he verily hath gained a signal victory. (33:71 Quran)

He who wants to understand, will understand.

In India it is considered a great sin to awaken anyone who is asleep. If a man is asleep, do not wake him; let him sleep; it is the time for him to sleep; it will not do to wake him before his time. Thus a mystic understands also that a person who is taking his time to wake up must not be awakened to give him the mystic's idea. It would be a sin, because he is not prepared to understand it, and his beliefs would be shaken. Let him go on thinking God is in Benares; let him think He is in the temple of Buddha; let him think He is in heaven; let him think He is in the seventh heaven above the sky. It is the beginning; he will evolve in time and arrive at the same stage. The rest he is having just now is good for him. The awakening comes, all in its good time.

This explains what is meant by saying that Sufism is a religious philosophy; the philosophy is clothed with religion, that it may not break the ideals and faiths and beliefs of those who are beginning their journey towards the goal. Externally: the religion, inwardly: the philosophy. The one who wants to understand will understand. 'He who has ears to hear, let him hear.'

In whatever form, life expresses its meaning, if only man is able to understand it. The one who does not understand this will not understand life's meaning. His inner sense is closed; it is just like being deaf. In the same way his sense of communication with things has become dull, he does not understand them. But if a person does not hear he may not say that life is not speaking. In the same way, if a person cannot sense the meaning of life, he may not say that life has no meaning. The word is everywhere, and the word is continually speaking.

A mystic removes the barrier that stands between himself and another person by trying to look at life not only from his own point of view, but also from the point of view of another. All disputes and disagreements arise from people's misunderstanding of each other. Mostly, people misunderstand each other because they have their fixed points of view and are not willing to move from them. If we are willing to understand, then understanding is within our reach. Very often, however, we are not willing to understand, and that is why we do not understand. Mankind suffers from a sort of stubbornness. A man goes against what he thinks is coming from another person. Yet, everything he has learned has come from others, he has not learned one word from himself. All the same, he calls it his argument, his idea, and his view, although it is no such thing. He has always taken it from somewhere. It is by accepting this fact that a mystic understands all, and it is this which makes him a friend of all. *Hazrat Inayat Khan*

Surah Thirty-Four

Saba
Man is the picture of the reflection of his imagination; he is as large or as small as he thinks himself.

All works of art and music and poetry come from imagination, for imagination is the free flow of mind, when the mind is allowed to work by itself and bring out the beauty and harmony it contains. But when it is restricted by a certain principle or rule, then it does not work freely. No one has believed in God, no one has loved God, and no one has reached the presence of God who has not been helped by his imagination.

Then there is the person who has imagination which is strengthened by faith. He not only prays to God, but he prays before God, in the presence of God. Once imagination has helped a man to bring the presence of God before him, God is awakened in his own heart. Then before he utters a word, it is heard by God. When he is praying in a room, he is not alone. He is there with God. Then to him God is not in the highest heaven but close to him, before him, in him. Then to him heaven is on earth and earth is heaven. No one is then so living, so intelligible as

God; and all names and forms disappear before Him. Then every word of prayer he utters is a living word. It not only brings blessing to him, but to all those around him.

When one invokes the names of God, one forgets his limitations and impresses his soul with the thought of the Unlimited, which brings him to the ideal of limitlessness. This is the secret of life's attainment.

Man is the picture or reflection of his imagination. He is as large as he thinks himself, as great as he thinks himself, as small as he thinks himself to be. If he thinks he is incapable, he remains incapable; if he thinks himself foolish, he will be foolish and will remain foolish; if he thinks himself wise, he will be wise and become wiser every moment; if he thinks himself mighty, he will be mighty. Those who have proved themselves to be the greatest warriors, where did their might come from? It was from their thought, their feeling; 'I am mighty.' The idea of might was impressed on their soul, and the soul became might. The poet had poetry impressed on his soul, and so the soul became a poet. Whatever is impressed on man's soul, with that the soul becomes endowed, and that the soul will become. Hazrat Inayat Khan

In the name of Allah, the Beneficent, the Merciful

Praise be to Allah, unto Whom belongeth whatsoever is in the heavens and whatsoever is in the earth. His is the praise in the Hereafter, and He is the Wise, the Aware. (34:1 Quran)

He knoweth that which goeth down into the earth and that which cometh forth from it, and that which descendeth from the heaven and that which ascendeth into it. He is the Merciful, the Forgiving. (34:2 Quran)

Those who have been given knowledge see that what is revealed unto thee from thy Lord is the truth and lendeth unto the path of the Mighty, the Owner of Praise. (34:6 Quran)

And assuredly We gave David grace from Us, saying: O ye hills and birds, echo his psalms of Praise! And We made the iron supple unto him. (34:10 Quran)

Saying: Make thou long coats of mail and measure the links thereof. And do ye right. Lo, I am Seer of what ye do. (34:11 Quran)

There was indeed a sign for Sheba in their dwelling place. Two gardens on the right hand and the left as who should say: Eat of the provisions of your Lord and render thanks to Him. A fair and an indulgent Lord. (34:15 Quran)

And We have not sent thee, O Muhammad, save as a bringer of good tidings and a warner unto all mankind, but most of mankind know not. (34:28 Quran)

And they say: When is the promise to be fulfilled if ye are truthful? (34:29 Quran)

Say, O Muhammad: Yours is the promise of a Day which ye cannot postpone nor hasten by an hour. (34:30 Quran)

Say, O Muhammad: Lo, my Lord enlargeth the provision for whom He will and narroweth it for whom He will. But most mankind know not. (34:36 Quran)

And it is not your wealth nor your children that will bring you near unto Us, but he who believeth and doeth good, draweth near. As for such, theirs will be twofold reward for what they did, and they will dwell secure in lofty halls. (34:37 Quran)

Say: Whatever reward I might have asked of you is yours. My reward is the affair of Allah only. He is Witness over all things. (34:47 Quran)

Say: Lo, my Lord hurleth the truth. He is the Knower of Things Hidden. (34:48 Quran)

Say: the truth has come, and falsehood showeth not its face and will not return. (34:49 Quran)

Say: If I err, I err only to my own loss, and if I am rightly guided it is because of that which my Lord hath revealed unto me. Lo, He is Hearer, Nigh. (34:50 Quran)

Our success or failure depends upon the harmony or disharmony of our individual will with the Divine Will.

It is the Divine Will that is manifested throughout the whole universe, which has created the whole universe; and it is part of the divine will that manifests itself through us. Everything we do in life is governed and directed by that power. Now coming to the question of the will of man as opposed to the will of God: which is which? We understand the difference when we perceive that the nature of will power differs only according to whether it exists in its fullness, or whether it is limited. The will power in its fullness is divine power; the will power in its limited state is the individual will.

Resignation is a quality of the saintly souls. It is bitter in taste but sweet in result. Whatever a man's power and position in life may be, he has always to meet with a more powerful will, in whatever form it may manifest. In truth this is the divine will. By opposing the divine will one may break oneself; but by resigning oneself to the divine will one opens up a way.

We come to understand that there are two aspects of will working through all things in life. One is the individual will, the other the divine will. When a person goes against the divine will, naturally his human will fails and he finds difficulties, because he is swimming against the tide. The moment a person works in consonance, in harmony with the divine will, things become smooth.

Sometimes things are accomplished without the least effort. When it is the divine will it is like something floating on water; it advances without effort. Problems and actions may be achieved in a moment then, whilst at other times the smallest problem cannot be solved without great difficulty. One finds that some persons are very clever and experienced in industrial work or in politics; and they have striven very hard to attain their goal, and yet have accomplished nothing; they are always a failure. And there are others who take up a thing, and without much effort, without much worry on their part they complete it and attain their goal.

All this is accounted for by harmony with the divine will. Everyone experiences such a thing at some time or other. When things are in harmony with the divine will, everything is there; we just glance towards a thing and it is found, as in the saying, 'Word spoken, action done.' When we strive with all the material in our hands and yet cannot achieve our desire that is when the matter is contrary to the divine will. Our success or failure all depends upon the harmony or disharmony of our individual will with the divine will. Contentment and perfect resignation open up a harmonious feeling and bring the divine will into harmony with our own. Our blessing now becomes a divine blessing, our words divine words, our atmosphere a divine atmosphere, although we seem to be limited beings; for our will becomes absorbed into the whole, and so our will becomes the will of God. *Hazrat Inayat Khan*

Surah Thirty-Five

Al Malaikah

When a man looks at the ocean, he can only see that part of it which comes within his range of vision; so it is with the truth.

As there is water in the depths of the earth, so there is truth at the bottom of all things, false or true. In some places, one has to dig deep; in other places, only a short distance; that is the only difference. But there is no place where there is no water. One may have to dig very, very deep in order to get it; but in the depths of the earth, there is water, and in the depths of all this falsehood that is on the surface, there is truth. If we are really seeking for the truth, we shall always find it.

Man with his learning becomes so proud that he thinks there is nothing else worthy of attention. He does not know that there is a perfection of wisdom before which he is not even like a drop in the ocean. Man looks at the surface of the ocean, yet he is so small that he cannot even be compared with one of its drops, limited as he is in intellect and knowledge. He seeks to find out about the whole of creation, whereas those who have touched it have bowed before God, forgetting their limited selves. After that God remained with them and spoke through them. These are the only beings who have been able to give any truth to the world.

When we consider the mystics and thinkers who look at life from a spiritual point of view, they all agree, be they Yogis, Sufis, Buddhists, or Christians—it does not matter which. When they arrive at a certain stage of understanding they all agree, they all have the same experiences, they all have the same realization to which they come in spite of all differences of form: those who look at the surface see variations, but those who look below the surface see one and the same truth hidden beneath all religions, which have been given at different times by different masters. Naturally, therefore, the method of expression is different, but when one comes to the essence it is all one and the same, and those who are spiritually evolved come to the conclusion that they do not differ one from the other in their belief.

All beliefs are simply degrees of clearness of vision. All are part of one ocean of truth. The more this is realized the easier it is to see the true relationship between all beliefs, and the wider does the vision of the one great ocean become. Limitations and boundaries are inevitable in human life; forms and conventions are natural and necessary; but they none the less separate humanity. It is the wise who can meet one another beyond these boundaries. *Hazrat Inayat Khan*

In the name of Allah, the Beneficent, the Merciful

Praise be to Allah, the Creator of the heavens and the earth, who appointeth the angels messengers having wings two or three and four. He multiplieth the creation what He will. Lo, Allah is able to do all things. (35:1 Quran)

That which Allah openeth unto mankind of mercy none can withhold it, and that which He withholdeth none can release thereafter. He is the Mighty, the Wise. (35:2 Quran

O mankind! Remember Allah's grace toward you! Is there any creator other than Allah who provideth for you from the sky and the earth? There is no God save Him. Wither then are you turned? (35:3 Quran)

And if they deny thee, O Muhammad, messengers of Allah were denied before thee. Unto Allah all things are brought back. (35:4 Quran)

Allah created you from dust, then from a little fluid, then he made you pairs, the male and female. No female beareth or bringeth forth save with His knowledge. And no one groweth old who groweth old, nor is aught lessened of the life, but it is recorded in a book. Lo, that is easy for Allah. (35:11 Quran)

And no burdened soul can bear another's burden, and if one heavy laden crieth for help with his Lord, naught of it be lifted even though he unto whom he crieth be of kin. Thou warnest only those who fear their Lord in secret, and have established worship. He who groweth in goodness groweth only for himself, he cannot by his merit redeem others. Unto Allah is journeying. (35:18 Quran)

The blind man is not equal with the seer. (35:19 Quran)

Nor is darkness tantamount to light. (35:20 Quran)

Nor is the shadow equal with the sun's full heat. (35:21 Quran)

Nor are the living equal with the dead. Lo, Allah maketh whom He will to hear. Thou canst not reach those who are in the graves. (35:22 Quran)

Thou are but a warner. (35:23 Quran)

Lo! We have sent thee with the Truth, a bearer of glad tidings and a warner, and there is not a nation but a warner hath passed among them. (35:24 Quran)

And if they deny thee, those before them also denied. Their messengers came unto them with clear proofs of Allah's sovereignty, and with the Psalms and the Scripture giving light. (35:25 Quran)

Hast thou not seen how Allah causeth water to fall from the sky, and we produce therewith fruit of divers hues, and among the hills are streaks red and white, of divers hues and others raven black. (35:27 Quran)

And if men and beasts and cattle, in like manner, divers hues? The erudite among his bondmen fear Allah alone. Lo, Allah is Mighty, Forgiving. (35:28 Quran)

Lo, those who read the Scripture of Allah, and establish worship, and spend of that which We have bestowed on them secretly and openly, they look forward to imperishable gain. (35:29 Quran)

That He will pay them their wages and increase them of His grace. Lo, He is Forgiving, Responsive. (35:30 Quran)

And that which We inspire in thee of the Scripture, it is the Truth confirming that which We revealed before it. Lo, Allah is indeed Observer, Seer of His slaves. (35:31 Quran)

Then We gave the Scripture as inheritance unto those whom We elected of our bondmen. But of them are some who wrong themselves and of them are some who outstrip others through good deeds, by Allah's leave. That is the great favor! (35:32 Quran)

Gardens of Eden! They enter, them wearing armlets of gold and pearl and their raiment therein is silk. (35:33 Quran)

And they say: Praise be to Allah who hath put grief away from us. Lo! Lord is Forgiving, Bountiful! (35:34 Quran)

Who, of His grace, hath installed us in the mansion of eternity, where toil toucheth us not, nor can weariness affect us. (35:35 Quran)

It does not matter in what way a person offers his respect and his reverence to the deity he worships; it matters only how sincere he is in his offering.

The forms of worship of all the different religions are necessarily different. It depends upon what one is accustomed to, what is akin to one's nature. One cannot make a common rule and say that this form is wrong and that form is right. One person will perhaps feel more exaltation in a form of worship which includes some art. It stimulates his emotional nature. Music, pictures, perfumes, colors, and light, all these have an effect upon such a person. Another can concentrate better if there is nothing in the place of worship to catch his attention. It is all a matter of temperament. It is not wrong to prefer the one or the other. The Sufi sees the variety of forms as different ideals. He does not attach importance to the outer expression. If there is a sincere spirit behind it, if a person has a feeling for worship, it does not matter what form of worship it is.

In what manner prayer be offered matters little if only the sentiment be right. The orthodox world has fought with each other, each claiming that, "Our manner of prayer is the best. Our church is the best. Our temple is the best. Our sermon is the best. The others are astray;" not knowing that in the house of God it is not asked, "To which church do you belong? To which temple do you belong?" but it is asked, "How sincere were you in your prayer?"

Nature teaches every soul to worship God in some way or other, and often provides that which is suitable for each. Those who want one law to govern all have lost sight of the spirit of their own religion. And it is in people who have not yet learned their own religion that such ideas are commonly found. Did they but know their own religion, how tolerant they would become, and how free from any grudge against the religion of others!

So it is too with the manner of worship. It does not matter in what way a person offers his respect and his reverence to the deity he worships. It only matters how sincere he is in his offering. In one house of God we find that people do not wear hats; in Hindustan, Persia, and Arabia they put on turbans to go to the mosque. That is their custom. It makes no difference whether one person prays standing, another sitting, another kneeling, another prostrating himself, another in company with other people and another alone. All that matters is that the heart of the worshipper is pure, that the mind is connected with God, that there is sincerity and earnestness. *Hazrat Inayat Khan*

Surah Thirty-Six

Ya Sin

To give sympathy is sovereignty, to desire it from others is captivity.

Although sometimes it gives a tender sensation in the heart to say, 'Oh, how poorly I am', and it is soothing to hear from someone, 'Oh, I am so sorry you are not well', yet I should think that one would prefer if another thing were said in sympathy, namely, 'I am so happy to see you are so well'. In order to create that tender sensation one need not be ill. What is needed is to be thankful. We can never be too thankful.

The first lesson given to man was to be grateful for his daily bread, because that was the greatest necessity of his life. Now that has become so simple and life has changed so much that man forgets to be thankful. He even thinks, 'Why should I give thanks?' He forgets that behind his own personality he covers God. His own toil seems more to him than the toil of every atom of nature that is preparing blessings for him.

Self-pity is the worst poverty; it is the source of all unhappiness and blinds man to all he should be thankful for. The constantly complaining habit and the tendency to demand sympathy from others bring the greatest thorn into man's life: he becomes dependent upon the sympathy of others. The best thing is to give sympathy. *Hazrat Inayat Khan*

In the name of Allah, the Beneficent, the Merciful

Ya Sin. By the wise Quran. Lo, thou art of those sent. On a straight path. A revelation of the Mighty, the Merciful. (36: 1-5 Quran)

This day no soul is wronged in aught, nor are ye requited aught save what ye used to do. (36:53 Quran)

Lo, those who merit paradise this day are happily employed. (36:54 Quran)

They and their wives, in pleasant shade, on thrones reclining. (36:55 Quran)

Theirs the fruit of their good deeds and theirs all that they ask. (36:56 Quran)

The word from a Merciful Lord for them is: Peace! (36:57 Quran)

And We have not taught Muhammad poetry, nor is it meet for him. This is naught else than a Reminder and a Lecture making plain. 36: 68 Quran)

Have they not seen how We have created for them of Our handiwork the cattle, so that they are their owners. (36:70 Quran)

And have subdued them unto them, so that some of them they have for riding, some for food. (36:71 Quran)

Benefits and divers drinks have they from them. Will they not then give thanks? (36:72 Quran)

So let not their speech grieve thee, O Muhammad. Lo, We know what they conceal and what they proclaim. (36:75 Quran)

The wave realizes "I am the sea", and by falling into the sea prostrates itself before its God.

Prayer has been taught by all religions in different forms: by bowing, by prostrations, by recitation or chant. As soon as man begins to feel the immanence of God in nature, he begins to prostrate himself before that

Being, calling his limited self, helpless before Him, bowing before Him, worshipping Him.

Therein lies the whole of religion. The mystic's prayer is to that beauty, and his work is to forget the self, to lose himself like a bubble in the water. The wave realizes, 'I am the sea', and by falling into the sea prostrates itself before its God. As it is said, 'Be ye perfect, even as your Father which is in heaven is perfect'.

The Sufi recognizes the knowledge of self as the essence of all religions; he traces it in every religion, he sees the same truth in each, and therefore he regards all as one. Hence he can realize the saying of Jesus; 'I and my Father are one.' The difference between creature and Creator remains on his lips, not in his soul. This is what is meant by union with God. It is in reality the dissolving of the false self in the knowledge of the true self, which is divine, eternal, and all pervading. *Hazrat Inayat Khan*

Surah Thirty-Seven

As Saffat
Life is a misery for the man absorbed in himself.

The more living the heart, the more sensitive it is; but that which causes sensitiveness is the love-element in the heart, and love is God. The person whose heart is not sensitive is without feeling; his heart is not living, it is dead. In that case the divine Spirit is buried in his heart. A person who is always concerned with his own feelings is so absorbed in himself that he has no time to think of another. His whole attention is taken up with his own feelings. He pities himself, he worries about his own pain, and is never open to sympathize with others. He who takes notice of the feelings of another person with whom he comes in contact, practices the first essential moral of Sufism.

A person who, alone, has seen something beautiful, who has heard something harmonious, who has tasted something delicious, who has smelt something fragrant, may have enjoyed it, but not completely. The complete joy is in sharing one's joy with others. For the selfish one who enjoys himself and does not care for others, whether he enjoys things of the earth or things of heaven, his enjoyment is not complete.

When a person is absorbed in himself, he has no time for character-building, because he has no time to think of others: then there is no other. But when he forgets himself, he has time to look here and there, to collect what is good and beautiful, and to add it naturally to his character. So the character is built. One need not make an effort to build it, one has only to forget oneself.

Every step in evolution makes life more valuable. The more evolved you are, the more priceless is every moment; it becomes an opportunity for you to do good to others, to serve others, to give love to others, to be gentle to others, to give your sympathy to souls who are longing and hungering for it. Life is miserable when a person is absorbed in himself; as soon as he forgets himself he is happy. The more he thinks of himself, his own affairs, work and interests, the less he knows the meaning of life. When a person looks at another he cannot at the same time look at himself. Illness, disappointments and hardships matter very little when one can look at them from a higher standpoint. *Hazrat Inayat Khan*

In the name of Allah, the Beneficent, the Merciful

Peace be unto Noah among the peoples! (37:79 Quran)

Lo! Thus We reward the good. (37:80 Quran)

Lo! He is one of Our believing slaves. (37:81 Quran)

Peace be unto Abraham! (37:109 Quran)

Thus do We reward the good. (37:110 Quran)

Lo! He is one of Our believing slaves. (37:111 Quran)

And We gave him tidings of the birth of Isaac, a Prophet of the righteous. (37:112 Quran)

And We blessed him and Isaac. And of their seed are some who do good, and some who plainly wrong themselves. (37:113 Quran)

And We verily gave grace unto Moses and Aaron! (37:114 Quran)

And saved them from their people from the great distress. (37:115 Quran)

And helped them so that they became the victors. (37: 116 Quran)

And We gave them the clear Scripture. (37:117 Quran)

And showed them the right path. (37:118 Quran)

And We left for them among the later folk the salutation. (37:119 Quran)

Peace be unto Moses and Aaron! (37:120 Quran)

Lo! Thus We reward the good. (37:121 Quran)

Sympathy is the root of religion, and so long as the spirit of sympathy is living in your heart, you have the light of religion.

Those great souls who have brought the message of God to humanity from time to time, like Buddha, Krishna, Jesus Christ, Moses, Abraham or Zarathustra, were well known as most learned men. But whatever they learned, they learned from the love principle. What they knew was compassion, forgiveness, sympathy, tolerance, the attitude of appreciation, the opening of the heart to humanity.

Sympathy is something more than love and affection, for it is the knowledge of a certain suffering which moves the living heart to sympathy. That person is living whose heart is living, and that heart is living which has wakened to sympathy. The heart void of sympathy is worse than a rock. The feeling of sympathy must be within, it need not manifest purely as sympathy but as an action to better the condition of the one with whom one has sympathy. There are many attributes found in the human heart which are called divine, but among them there is no greater and better attribute than sympathy, by which man shows in human form God manifested.

In a popular English song there is a beautiful line, which says, 'The light of a whole life dies when love is done.' That living thing in the heart is love. It may come forth as kindness, as friendship, as sympathy, as tolerance, as forgiveness, but in whatever form this living water rises from the heart, it proves the heart to be a divine spring. And when once this spring is open and is rising, then everything that a man does in action, in word, or in feeling is all religion; that man becomes truly religious.

A great poet has said in Hindi, 'Sympathy is the root of religion, and so long as the spirit of sympathy is living in your heart, it is illuminated with the light of religion'. This means that religion and morals can be summed up in one thing and that is sympathy, which in the words of Christ, as interpreted in the Bible, is charity. All beautiful qualities as tolerance, forgiveness, gentleness, consideration, reverence and the desire to serve—all these come from sympathy. Another poet has said in Urdu that it was for sympathy that man was created, and the day when man discovers this special attribute in himself, he is shown his first lesson of how life should be lived. *Hazrat Inayat Khan*

Surah Thirty-Eight

Sad
When one praises the beauty of God, one's soul is filled with bliss.

The only secret of attaining happiness is to learn how to appreciate our privileges in life. If we cultivate that sense of appreciation we shall be thankful, we shall be contented and every moment we shall offer our thanks to God, for His gifts are many and enormous. When we do not see them it is because our wants cover our eyes from seeing all with which we are blessed by Providence. No meditation, no study, nothing can help in that direction, except one thing, and that is to keep our eyes open to appreciate every little privilege in life, to admire every glimpse of beauty that comes before us, being thankful for every little love, kindness or affection shown to us by young or old, rich or poor, wise or foolish. In this way, continually developing the faculty of appreciating life and devoting it to thanksgiving, we arrive at a bliss which no words can explain, a bliss which is beyond imagination: the bliss that we find ourselves having already entered the kingdom of God.

The two important things in life are the praise of God and the pursuit of God. The praise of God is important, and it gives bliss in life, but it is not the real attainment. The all-important work in life is the attainment of God. God cannot be explained. Any attempt to do this always ends in failure. The knowledge of Him can only be attained in the silence and in solitude, and how to do this cannot be explained better than in the words of the Urdu poet Zahir, 'He who attaineth best the peace of God, his very self must lose.' Hazrat Inayat Khan

In the name of Allah, the Beneficent, the Merciful

Shall We treat those who believe and do good works as those who spread corruption in the earth, or shall We treat the pious as the wicked? (38:29 Quran)

This is a Scripture that We have revealed unto thee full of blessing, and they may ponder upon its revelations, and that men of understanding may reflect. (38:30 Quran)

And We bestowed on David, Solomon. How excellent a slave! Lo, he was ever turning in repentance toward Allah. (38:31 Quran)

And verily We tried Solomon, and We put upon his throne a mere body. Then did he repent. (38:35 Quran)

He said: My Lord! Forgive me and bestow on me sovereignty such as shall not belong to any after me. Lo! Thou art the Bestower. (38:36 Quran)

So We made the wind subservient unto him, setting fair by his command withersoever he intended. (38:37 Quran)

And the unruly, every builder and the diver made We subservient. (38:38 Quran)

And others linked together in chains. (38:39 Quran)

Saying: This is Our gift, so bestow thou, or withhold, without reckoning. (38:40 Quran)

And lo, he hath favor with Us, and a happy journey's end. (38:41 Quran)

And make mention, O Muhammad, of Our bondman Job, when he cried unto his Lord, saying: Lo, the devil doth afflict me with distress and torment. (38:42 Quran)

And it was said unto him: Strike the ground with thy foot. This spring is a cool bath and a refreshing drink. (38:43 Quran)

And We bestowed on him again his household and therewith the like thereof, a mercy from Us, and a memorial for men of understanding. (38:44 Quran)

And it was said unto him: Take in thine hand a branch and smite therewith, and break not thine oath. Lo, We found him steadfast, how excellent a slave! Lo, he was ever turning in repentance to his Lord. (38:45 Quran)

And make mention of our bondmen, Abraham, Isaac and Jacob, men of parts and vision. (38:46 Quran)

Lo! We purified them with a pure thought, remembrance of the Home of the Hereafter. (38:47 Quran)

Lo! In Our sight they are verily of the elect, the excellent. (38:48 Quran)

And make mention of Ishmael and Elisha and Dhul-Kifl. All are of the chosen. (38:49 Quran)

This is a reminder. And lo! For those who ward off evil is a happy journey's end. (38:50 Quran)

Garden of Eden, whereof the gates are opened for them. (38:51 Quran)

Wherein, reclining, they call for plenteous fruit and cool drink that is therein. (38:52 Quran)

Say unto them, O Muhammad, I am only a warner, and there is no God save Allah, the One, the Absolute. (38:66 Quran)

Lord of the heavens and the earth and all that is between them, the Mighty, the Pardoning. (38:67 Quran)

Say: it is tremendous tidings. (38:68 Quran)

Whence ye turn away! (38:69 Quran)

I had no knowledge of the Highest Chiefs when they disputed. (38:70 Quran)

It is revealed unto me only that I may be a plain warner. (38:71 Quran)

Say, O Muhammad, unto mankind: I ask you of no fee for this, and I am no impostor. (38:87 Quran)

Lo, it is naught else but a reminder for all peoples. (38:88 Quran)

And ye will come in time to know the truth thereof. (38:89 Quran)

Even to utter the name of God is a blessing that can fill the soul with light and joy and happiness as nothing else can do.

In the East, religion is sown in the heart of the child from birth, no matter to what religion he may belong. The invocation of the name of God becomes a daily custom, which he consciously or unconsciously repeats in sorrow as well as in joy. 'bismillah' — In the name of Allah, or 'al-hamdulillah' — Praise be to Allah, or 'Allahu akbar' — God is great, and 'ya Allah' — O God; such expressions as these are used at the beginning and the end, as well as in the midst of every ordinary conversation. This attunes the believer and even attracts the unbeliever to the thought of God, which in the end leads the seeker to self-realization and the peace of God.

A thousand people may say the same prayer; but one person's prayer said with such faith and belief is equal to the prayers of a thousand people, because that prayer is not mechanical. Man is mechanical and he generally says his prayers mechanically too. If he is genuine and if he has faith and belief and devotion, all he says has an effect; and that effect will perform miracles. When he invokes the names of God man forgets his limitations and impresses his soul with the thought of the Unlimited, which brings him to the ideal of limitlessness. This is the secret of life's attainment.

The mystic on the spiritual path perseveres in wiping out this false ego as much as he can, by meditation, by concentration, by prayer, by study, by everything that he does. His one aim is to wipe out so much that one day reality, which is always there buried under the false ego, may manifest.

By calling on the Name of God, in the form of prayer, or in zikr, or in any other form, what the mystic does is to awaken the spirit of the real ego, in order that it may manifest. It is just like a spring that rises up out of the rock and that, as soon as the water has gained power and strength, breaks even through stone and becomes a stream. So it is with the divine spark in man. Through concentration, through meditation, it breaks out and manifests; and where it manifests, it washes away the stains of the false ego and turns into a greater and greater stream. This in turn becomes the source of comfort, consolation, healing and happiness for all who come into contact with that spirit. *Hazrat Inayat Khan*

Surah Thirty-Nine

Az Zumar

We can never sufficiently humble our limited self before limitless perfection.

I have seen with my own eyes souls who have attained saintliness and who have reached to great perfection; and yet such a soul will stand before an idol of stone with another, with a fellow man, and worship, not letting him know that he is in any way more advanced than other men, keeping himself in a humble guise, not making any pretense that he has gone further in his spiritual evolution. The further such souls go, the more humble they become; the greater the mystery they have realized, the less they speak about it.

The first aspect of prayer is giving thanks to God for all the numberless blessings that are bestowed upon us at every moment of the day and night, and of which we are mostly unconscious. The second aspect of prayer is laying our shortcomings before the unlimited perfection of the divine Being, and asking His forgiveness. This makes man conscious of his smallness, of his limitation, and therefore makes him humble before his God. And, by humbling himself before God man does not lose any virtue. God alone has the right to demand complete humility.

There is a beautiful story told of the King Akbar that when he was grieving with an almost ungovernable grief over the death of his mother, his ministers and friends tried to comfort him by influence and power. Akbar replied, "Yes, that is true, and that only makes my grief greater; for while I have everyone to bow before me, to give way to me, to salute me and obey me, my mother was the one person before whom I could humble myself; and I cannot tell you how great a joy that was to me."

Think, then, of the far greater joy of humbling one's self before the Father-Mother God on Whose Love one can always depend. A spark only of love expresses itself in the human father and mother; the Whole of Love in God. In whatever manner a man humbles himself it can never be enough to express the humility of the limited self before Limitless Perfection. *Hazrat Inayat Khan*

In the name of Allah, the Beneficent, the Merciful

He hath created the heavens and the earth with truth. He maketh night to succeed day, and He maketh day to succeed night, and He commandeth the sun and the moon to give service, each running on for an appointed term. Is He not the Mighty, the Forgiver? (39:5 Quran)

If ye are thankless, yet Allah is Independent of you, though He is not pleased with thanklessness for his bondmen, and if ye are thankful He is pleased therewith with you. No laden soul will bear another's load. Then unto your Lord is your return, and He will tell you what ye used to do. Lo, He knoweth what's in the breasts of men. (39:7 Quran)

Say: O Muhammad who believe! Observe your duty to your Lord. For those who do good in this world there is good, and Allah's earth is spacious. Verily the steadfast will be paid their wages without stint. (39:10 Quran)

Say, O Muhammad: Lo, I am commanded to worship Allah, making religion pure for Him only. (39:11 Quran)

And I am commanded to be the first of those who surrender unto Him. (39:12 Quran)

And verily We have coined for mankind in this Quran all kinds of similitudes that haply they may reflect. (39:27 Quran)

A lecture in Arabic, containing no crookedness that haply they may ward off evil. (39:28 Quran)

Allah coineth a similitude: A man in relation to whom are several part-owners, quarrelling, and a man belonging wholly to one man. Are the two equal in similitude? Praise be to Allah! But most of them know not. (39:29 Quran)

Lo, We have revealed unto thee, Muhammad, the Scripture for mankind with truth. Then whosoever goeth right it is for his soul, and whosoever strayeth, strayeth only to its hurt. And thou art not a warder over them. (39:41 Quran)

Say: O My slaves who have been prodigal to their own hurt. Despair not of the mercy of Allah, Who forgiveth all sins. Lo, He is the Merciful, the Forgiving. (39:53 Quran)

And those who keep their duty to their Lord are given unto the Garden in troops, till when they reach it, and the gates thereof are opened, and the warders thereof say unto them: Peace be unto you! Ye are good, so enter ye the Garden of delight, to dwell therein. (39:73 Quran)

They say: Praise be to Allah, Who hath fulfilled His promise unto us and hath made us inherit the land, sojourning in the Garden where we will! So bounteous is the wage of the workers. (39:74 Quran)

And thou, O Muhammad, seest the angels thronging round the Throne, hymning the praises of their Lord. And they are judged right. And it is said: Praise be to Allah, the Lord of the Worlds! (39:75 Quran)

The secret of happiness is hidden under the cover of spiritual knowledge.

The soul in Sanskrit, in the terms of the Vedanta, is called Atman which means happiness or bliss itself. It is not that happiness belongs to the soul; it is that the soul itself is happiness. Today we often confuse happiness with pleasure; but pleasure is only an illusion, a shadow of happiness; and in this delusion man may pass his whole life, seeking after pleasure and never finding satisfaction. Do you think that if these people gained their desires they would be happy? If they possessed all, would that suffice? No, they would still find some excuse for unhappiness; all these excuses are only like covers over a man's eyes, for deep within is the yearning for the true happiness which none of these things can give. He who is really happy is happy everywhere, in a palace or in a cottage, in riches or in poverty, for he has discovered the fountain of happiness which is situated in his own heart. As long as a person has not found that fountain, nothing will give him real happiness.

A Marathi poet has said, 'O mind, my restless mind, my mind with its thoughts of a thousand things which it supposes will make it happy, saying, 'If I had that, I should be happy; if I had this, I should feel life was not wasted.' O, my mind, will you tell me who in this world is happy?' The mind says, 'if I had the wealth which I see others have, I should be happy.' But are these others happy? They in their turn say they would be, if they had something still higher!

The secret of happiness is hidden under the veil of spiritual knowledge. And spiritual knowledge is nothing but this: that there is a constant longing in the heart of man to have something of its origin, to experience something of its original state, the state of peace and joy which has been disturbed, and yet is sought after throughout its whole life, and never can cease to be sought after until the real source has at length been realized. It is only those who are blessed by perceiving the origin and source of all things who awaken to the fact that the real inclination of every life is to attain to something which cannot be touched or comprehended or understood. The hidden blessing of this knowledge is the first step to perfection. Once awake to this fact, man sees there is something in life that will make him really happy and give him his heart's desire. He can say, 'Though there are many things in life which I need for the moment, and for which I shall certainly work, yet there is only that one thing, around which life centers, that will satisfy me: the spiritual attainment, the religious attainment, or, as one may even call it, the attainment of God.' Such a one has found the key to all happiness, and has found that all the things he needs will be reached because he has the key to all. 'Seek, and ye shall find: knock, and it shall be opened unto you. Seek first the kingdom of God, and all these things shall be added unto you.' This kingdom of God is the silent life; the life inseparable, eternal, self-sufficient, and all-powerful. This is the life of the wise, whatever be the name given to it; this is the life which the wise contemplate. It is the face of this life that they long to see; it is the ocean of this life that they long to swim in; as it is written: 'In Him we live and have our being.'

These are the ones who are really happy, who are above all unhappiness, above death and the destruction of life. *Hazrat Inayat Khan*

Surah Forty

Al Mumin
The soul is first born into the false self, it is blind; in the true self the soul opens its eyes.

Our greatest enemy is our self. All weakness, all ignorance keeps us from the truth of our being, from all the virtues hidden in us and all perfection hidden in our souls. The first self we realize is the false self. Unless the soul is born again it will not see the kingdom of heaven. The soul is born into the false self; it is blind. In the true self the soul opens its eyes. Unless the false self is fought with, the true self cannot be realized.

The lions could not harm Daniel because of the harmony of his will with the universal Will. The lions represent the destructive elements in the human mind. They represent wars, disappointments, rivalries, jealousies, envy, passions, and so forth, in different horrible guises. Our ego is the lion of lions, and if this is conquered, then these external lions—different egos around us—are conquered also, and wherever we go, with anyone, whether foolish or wise, good or bad, we now have peace.

The work of the spiritual man is to forget his false self and so to realize the true self which is God, and this true self not only in him, but in his neighbor also. *Hazrat Inayat Khan*

In the name of Allah, the Beneficent, the Merciful

The revelation of the Scripture is from Allah, the Mighty, the Knower. (40:2 Quran)

The Forgiver of sin, the Acceptor of repentance, the Stern in punishment, the Bountiful. There is no God save Him. Unto Him is the journeying. (40:3 Quran)

Whoso doeth an ill deed, he will be repaid the like thereof, while whoso doeth right, whether male or female and is a believer, all such will enter the Garden, where they will be nourished without stint. (40:40 Quran)

And We verily gave Moses the guidance, and We caused the Children of Israel to inherit the Scripture. (40:53 Quran)

A guide and a reminder for men of understanding. (40:54 Quran)

Then have patience, O Muhammad. Lo, the promise of Allah is true. And ask forgiveness of thy sin, and hymn the praise of thy Lord at full of night and in the early hours. (40:55 Quran)

Lo, those who wrangle concerning the revelations of Allah without a warrant having come unto them, there is naught else in their breasts save pride which they will never attain. So take thou refuge in Allah. Lo, He only He is the Hearer, the Seer. (40:56 Quran)

Assuredly the creation of the heavens and the earth is greater than the creation of mankind, but most of mankind know not. (40:57 Quran)

And the blind man and the seer are not equal, neither are those who believe and do good works equal with the evil-doer. Little do ye reflect! (40:58 Quran)

Allah it is Who appointed for you the earth for a dwelling place and the sky for a canopy, and fashioned you and perfected your shapes, and hath provided you with good things. Such is Allah, your Lord. Then blessed be Allah, the Lord of the Worlds! (40:64 Quran)

He is the Living One. There is no God save Him. So pray unto Him, making religion pure for Him. Praise be to Allah, the Lord of the Worlds! (40:65 Quran)

He it is Who created you from dust, then from a drop of seed, then from a clot, then bringeth you forth as a child. Then ordaineth that ye attain full strength and afterward ye become old men—though some among you die before—and that ye reach an appointed term, that haply ye may understand. (40:67 Quran)

He it is who quickeneth and giveth death. When He ordaineth a thing. He saith unto it only: Be! And it is. (40:68 Quran)

Then have patience, O Muhammad. Lo, the promise of Allah is true. And whether We let thee see a part of that which We promise them, or whether We cause thee to die, still unto us they will be brought back. (40:77 Quran)

Verily We sent messengers before thee, among them those of whom We have told thee, and some of whom We have not told thee, and it was not given to any messenger that he should bring a portent save by Allah's leave, but when Allah's commandment cometh, the cause is judged aright, and the followers of vanity will then be lost. (40:78 Quran)

Allah it is Who hath appointed for you cattle that ye may ride on some of them, and eat some. (40:79 Quran)

Many benefits ye have from them—and that ye may satisfy by their means a need that is in your breasts, and may be borne upon them as upon the ship. (40:80 Quran)

Knowledge without love is lifeless.

The loveless heart may have all the religion and all the knowledge, yet it is dead. As the Bible says, "God is love." God is in the heart of each person, and the heart of each person is the highest heaven. When that heart is closed by the absence of love, then God is closed. When this heart is open, God is open, and one is alive from that time.

When the heart is not empty, in other words, when there is no scope in the heart, there is no place for love. Rumi, the great poet of Persia, explains this idea more clearly. He says the pains and sorrows the soul experiences through life are like holes made in a reed flute, and it is by making these holes that a player makes the flute out of a reed. This means that the heart of man is first a reed and the sufferings and pains it goes through make it a flute which can then be used by God as the instrument for the music that He constantly wishes to produce. But as every reed is not a flute, so every heart is not His instrument. As the reed can be made into a flute, so the human heart can be turned into an instrument, and can be offered to the God of love. It is the human heart which becomes the harp of the angels. It is the human heart which is known as the lute of Orpheus. It was on the model of the heart of man that the first instrument of music was made, and no earthly instrument can produce that music which the heart produces, raising the mortal soul to immortality. It is the knowledge of the head and the love of the heart that together fully express the divine message. It is by keen observation that man acquires knowledge. Knowledge without love is lifeless.

In love abides all knowledge. It is mankind's love and interest in things that in time reveals their secret, and then man knows how to develop, control, and utilize them. No one can know anybody, however much he may profess to know, except the lover, because in the absence of love the inner eyes are blind. Only the outer eyes are open, which are merely the spectacles of the inner eyes. If the sight is not keen, of what use are the spectacles? It is for this reason that we admire all those whom we love, and are blind to the good qualities of those whom we do not love. It is not always that these deserve our neglect, but our eyes, without love, cannot see their goodness. Those whom we love may have bad points too, but as love sees beauty, so we see that alone in them. Intelligence itself in its next step towards manifestation is love. When the light of love has been lit, the heart becomes transparent, so that the intelligence of the soul can see through it. But until the heart is kindled by the flame of love, the intelligence, which is constantly yearning to experience life on the surface, is groping in the dark. *Hazrat Inayat Khan*

Surah Forty-One

Fusilat
Until the heart is empty, it cannot receive the knowledge of God.

When a person comes to take a lesson on any subject, and he brings his own knowledge with him, the teacher has little to teach him, for the doors of his heart are not open. His heart that should be empty in order to receive knowledge is occupied by the knowledge that he already had acquired.

It is not solid wood that can become a flute, but the empty reed. It is the perfection of that passiveness in the heart of the messenger which gives scope for the message from above; for the messenger is the reed, the instrument. The difference between his life and the life of the average man is that the latter is full of self. It is the blessed soul whose heart is empty of self, who is filled with the light of God.

The Sufi, therefore, takes the path of being nothing instead of being something. It is this feeling of nothingness which turns the human heart into an empty cup into which the wine of immortality is poured. It is this state of bliss which every truth-seeking soul yearns to attain. It is easy to be a learned person, and it is not very difficult to be wise. It is within one's reach to become good. And it is not an impossible achievement to be pious or spiritual. But if there is an attainment greater and higher than all these things, it is to be nothing.

All the great saints and sages, the great ones who have liberated humanity, have been as innocent as children and at the same time wiser, much more so, than the worldly-wise. And what makes it so? What gives them this balance? It is repose with passiveness. When they stand before God, they stand with their heart as an empty cup; when they stand before God to learn, they unlearn all things the world has taught them; when they stand before God, their ego, their self, their life, is no more before them. They do not think of themselves in that moment with any desire to be fulfilled, with any motive to be accomplished, with any expression of their own; but as empty cups, that God may fill their being. Hazrat Inayat Khan

In the name of Allah, the Beneficent, the Merciful

Lo! As for those who believe and do good works, for them is a reward enduring. (41:8 Quran)

Lo, those who say: Our Lord is Allah, and afterward are upright, the angels descend upon them, saying: Fear not, nor grieve, but hear good tidings of the paradise which ye are promised. (41:30 Quran)

We are your protecting friends in the life of the world and in the Hereafter. There ye shall have all that your souls desire, and there ye shall have for all for which ye pray. (41:31 Quran)

A gift of welcome from the Merciful, the Forgiving. (41:32 Quran)

And who is better in speech than him who prayeth unto his Lord and doth right, and saith: Lo! I am of those who surrender unto Him. (41:33 Quran)

The good deed and evil deed are not alike. Repel the evil deed with one which is better, then lo, he, between whom and thee there was enmity will become as though he was a bosom friend. (41:34 Quran)

But none is granted save those who are steadfast, and none is granted it save the owner of great happiness. (41:35 Quran)

And if a whisper from the devil reach thee, O Muhammad, then seek refuge in Allah. Lo! He is the Hearer, the Knower. (41:36 Quran)

And of His portents is this: that thou seest the earth lowly, but when We send down water thereon it thrilleth and groweth. Lo! He who quickeneth it is verily the quickener of the dead. Lo! He is able to do all things. (41:39 Quran)

Lo! Those who distort Our revelations are not hid from Us. Is it he who is hurled into the fire better or he who cometh secure on the Day of Resurrection? Do what ye will. Lo! He is the Seer of what ye do. (41:40 Quran)

Naught is said unto thee, Muhammad, save what was said unto the messengers before thee. Lo! Thy Lord is owner of Forgiveness, and owner also of punishment. (41:43 Quran)

Whoso doeth right it is for his soul, and whoso doeth wrong it is against it. And thy Lord is not at all tyrant to His slaves. (41:46 Quran)

To make God a reality is the real object of worship.

The first and principle thing in the inner life is to establish a relationship with God, making God the object with which we relate ourselves, such as the Creator, Sustainer, Forgiver, Judge, Friend, Father, Mother, and Beloved. In every relationship we must place God before us, and become conscious of that relationship so that it will no more remain an imagination.

The work of the inner life is to make God a reality, so that He is no more an imagination; that this relationship that man has with God may seem more real than any other relationship in the world; and when this happens, then all relationships, however near and dear, become less binding. But at the same time, a person does not thus become cold; he becomes more loving. It is the godless man who is cold, impressed by the selfishness and lovelessness of the world, because he partakes of those conditions in which he lives. But the one who is in love with God, the one who has established his relationship with God, his love becomes living.

To him all things appeal, everything unfolds itself, and it is beauty to his eyes, because God is all-pervading, in all names and all forms; therefore his Beloved is never absent. How happy therefore is the one whose Beloved is never absent, because the whole tragedy of life is the absence of the beloved; and to one whose Beloved is always there, when he has closed his eyes the Beloved is within, and when he has opened his eyes the Beloved is without. His every sense perceives the Beloved; his eyes see Him, his ears hear His voice. When a person arrives at this realization he, so to speak, lives in the presence of God; then to him the different forms and beliefs, faiths and communities do not count. To him God is all-in-all; to him God is everywhere. If he goes to the Christian church, or to the synagogue, to the Buddhist temple, to the Hindu shrine, or to the mosque of the Muslim, there is God. In the wilderness, in the forest, in the crowd, everywhere he sees God.

Of all the millions of believers in God perhaps only one makes God a reality, and that is because the picture man makes of God is as limited as himself. The knowledge of God is beyond man's reason. Man only perceives things he is capable of perceiving. He cannot raise his imagination above what he is used to, and he cannot reach beyond his imagination to where the being of God is. The secret of God is hidden in the knowledge of unity. True life cannot be ours until unity is achieved. It is the work of religion to promote the spirit of unity, in the knowledge and love of God to whom all devotion belongs. Man often seeks for psychic, occult, and magnetic powers. This is not the purpose of religion; these developments come of themselves. Where there is life and love, there is magnetism; love itself is the healing power and the remedy for all pain. All occult powers belong to the divine life, but man should live a natural life and realize the nature of God. The only studies which are worth accomplishing are those which lead to the realization of God, and of unity first with God and then with the self, and so with all. It is not necessary for us to be told that we have progressed; we ourselves will know when our hearts go forward; and by loving, forgiving, and serving, our whole life becomes one single vision of the sublime beauty of God.

One might say, 'How can one love God? God whom one does not know, does not see?' But the one who says this wants to take the second step instead of the first. He must first make God a reality, and then God will make him the truth. This stage is so beautiful. It makes the personality so tender and gentle. It gives such patience to the worshipper of God; and together with this gentleness and patience he becomes so powerful and strong that there is nothing that he will not face courageously: illness, difficulties, loss of money, opposition — there is nothing that he is afraid of. With all his gentleness and tenderness, inwardly he becomes strong. If a friend comes to meet him, to the Sufi it is God who is coming to meet him. If a beggar is asking for a penny, it is God whom the Sufi recognizes in that form. If a wretched man is suffering misery, he sees also in this the existence of God. Only, the difference is that in some he sees God unconscious, in others he sees God conscious. All those who love him, who hate him, who like or dislike him, who look upon him with admiration or contempt, he looks at with the eyes of the worshipper of God, who sees his Beloved in all aspects.
Hazrat Inayat Khan

Surah Forty-Two

Ash Shura

Every passion, every emotion has its effect upon the mind, and every change of mind, however slight, has its effect upon man's body.

Different conditions and the changes that take place in the world have their effect upon the mind, and the different conditions of the mind have their effect upon the body. As bodily illness makes man irritable, confused and exhausted in mind, so different conditions of the mind cause health or illness in the body. The link between the body and the mind is the breath, a link through which the influences of the body and the mind are exchanged and work upon one another.

Every passion, every emotion has its effect upon the mind; and every change of mind, however slight, has its effect upon a man's body. One man is perhaps striving all day to earn his own bread so that he may live in a comfortable manner. Another is always worrying about how to maintain himself and his children. Another is thinking, 'What can I do to save my fellow man from his trouble?' If we compare these people, in order to see who is the greatest, we see that he is greatest whose ideal is greatest.

When we consider that great heroes of the past and present, those whom we admire and to whom we look with hope for right guidance, we shall find that what has made them great has been the greatness of their ideal. The lower the ideal, the less the efforts. The higher the ideal, the greater the life. If we use all our intelligence and strength and wisdom to accomplish some little thing, it is only a waste of life. To consider what great things one can accomplish, to seek to do those things which will be most useful and valuable to others, that is the ideal life. Come to the mystic, then, and sit with him when you are tired of all these other remedies that you have employed in vain; come and take a glass of wine with him. The mystic wine is the inner absorption, which removes all the worries and anxieties and troubles and cares of the physical and mental plane. All these are now done away with forever. It is the mystic who is at rest. It is he who experiences that happiness which others do not experience. It is he who teaches the way to attain that peace and happiness which are the original heritage of man's soul. *Hazrat Inayat Khan*

In the name of Allah, the Beneficent, the Merciful

Thus Allah the Mighty, the Knower inspireth thee, Muhammad, as He inspired those before thee. (42:3 Quran)

Unto Him belongeth all that is in the heavens and all that is in the earth, and He is the Sublime, the Tremendous. (42:4 Quran)

Almost might the heavens above be rent asunder while the angels hymn the praise of their Lord ask forgiveness for those on earth. Lo! Allah is the Forgiver, the Merciful. (42:5 Quran)

Or have they chosen protecting friends beside Him? But Allah, He alone is the Protecting Friend. He quickeneth the dead, and He is able to do all things. (42:9 Quran)

And whatsoever ye differ, the verdict therein belongeth to Allah. Such is my Lord, in Whom I put my trust, and unto Whom I turn. (42:10 Quran)

The Creator of the heavens and the earth. He hath made for you pairs of yourselves, and of the cattle also pairs, whereby He multiplieth you. Naught is as His likeness, and He is the Hearer, the Seer. (42:11 Quran)

His are the keys of the heavens and the earth. He enlargeth providence for whom He will and straiteneth it for whom He will. Lo! He is the Knower of all things. (42:12 Quran)

He hath ordained for you that religion which He commanded unto Noah and that which We inspire in thee, Muhammad, and that which We recommended unto Abraham and Moses and Jesus, saying: Establish the religion, and be not divided therein. Dreadful for the idolatrous is that unto which thou callest them. Allah chooseth for himself whom He will, and guideth unto Himself him who turneth toward Him. (42:13 Quran)

And they were not divided until after the knowledge came unto them, through rivalry among themselves, and had it not been for a Word that had already gone forth from thy Lord for an appointed term, it surely had been judged between them. And those who were made to inherit the Scripture after them are verily in hopeless doubt concerning it. (42:14 Quran)

Unto this them summon, O Muhammad. And be thou upright as thou art commanded, and follow not their lusts, but say: I believe in whatever Scripture Allah hath sent down, and I am commanded to be just among you. Allah is our Lord and your Lord. Unto us our works and unto you your works, no argument between us and you. Allah will bring us together, and unto Him is the journeying. (42:15 Quran)

Allah is gracious unto His slaves. He provideth for whom He will. And He is the Strong, the Mighty. (42:19 Quran)

This it is which Allah announceth unto His bondmen who believe and do good works. Say, O Muhammad, unto mankind: I ask of you no fee therefor, save lovingkindness among kinsfolk. And whoso scoreth a good deed We add unto its good for him. Lo! Allah is Forgiving, Responsive. (42:23 Quran)

And He it is Who sendeth down the saving rain after they have despaired, and spreadeth out His mercy. He is the Protecting Friend, the Praiseworthy. (42:28 Quran)

Whatever of misfortune striketh you, it is what your right hands have earned. And He forgiveth much. (42:30 Quran)

Ye cannot escape in the earth, for beside Allah ye have no protecting friend nor any helper. (42:31 Quran)

And of His portents are the ships, like banners on the sea. (42:32 Quran)

If He will He calmeth the wind so that they keep still on its surface — Lo! Herein verily are signs for every steadfast, grateful heart. (42:33 Quran)

The way of blame is only against those who oppress mankind, and wrongfully rebel in the earth. For such there is a painful doom. (42:42 Quran)

And verily whoso is patient and forgiveth—lo, that verily is of the steadfast heart of things. (42:43 Quran)

And it was not vouchsafed to any mortal that Allah should speak to him unless it be by revelation, or from behind a veil, or that He sendeth a messenger to reveal what He will by His leave. Lo! He is Wise, Exalted. (42:51 Quran)

And thus We have inspired in thee, Muhammad, a Spirit of Our command. Thou knewest not what the Scripture was, nor what the Faith. But We have made it a light whereby We guide whom We will of Our bondmen. And lo, thou verily dost guide unto a right path. (42:52 Quran)

The path of Allah, unto Whom belongeth whatsoever is in the heavens and whatsoever is in the earth. Do not all things reach Allah at last? (42:53 Quran)

Sleep is comfortable, but awakening is interesting.

There are some who are content with a belief taught at home or in church. They are contented, and they may just as well rest in that stage of realization where they are contented until another impulse is born in their hearts to rise higher. The Sufi does not force his belief or his thoughts upon such souls.

The awakened soul sees all of the doings of adults as the doings of the children of one father. He looks upon them as the Father would look upon all human beings on the earth, without thinking that they are German or English or French. They are all equally dear to him. He looks upon all full of forgiveness, not only upon those who deserve it, but also upon the others, for he understands the reason behind it all. By seeing good in everybody and in everything, he begins to develop that divine light that expands itself, illuminating the greater part of life and revealing it as a scene of divine sublimity.

The mystic develops a wider outlook on life, and this wider outlook changes his actions. He develops a point of view that may be called a divine point of view. Then he rises to the state in which he feels that all that is done to him comes from God, and when he himself does right or wrong, he feels that he does right or wrong to God. To arrive at such a stage is true religion. There can be no better religion than this, the true religion of God on earth. This is the point of view that makes a person God-like and divine. He is resigned when badly treated, but for his own shortcomings, he will take himself to task, for all his actions are directed towards God.

A person whose soul has awakened becomes awake to everything he sees and hears. Compared to that person everyone else seems to be with open eyes and yet not to see, to be with open ears and yet not to hear. There are many with open ears, but there is rarely one who hears, and there are many with open eyes, but there is hardly one who sees. The moment the soul has awakened, music makes an appeal to it. Poetry touches it. Words move it. Art has an influence upon it. It no longer is a sleeping soul, it is awake and it begins to enjoy life to a fuller extent. It is this awakening of the soul which is mentioned in the Bible, 'Unless the soul is born again it will not enter the kingdom of heaven'. Being born again means that the soul is awakened after having come on earth, and entering the kingdom of heaven means that this world, the same kingdom in which we are standing just now, turns into heaven as soon as the point of view has changed.

Is it not interesting and most wonderful to think that the same earth we walk on is earth to one person and heaven to another? And it is still more interesting to notice that it is we who change it; we change it from earth into heaven, or we change it otherwise. This change comes not by study, nor by anything else, but only by the changing of our point of view. *Hazrat Inayat Khan*

Surah Forty-Three

Az Zukhruf
Every moment has its special message.

Every step in evolution makes life more valuable. The more evolved you are, the more priceless is every moment; it becomes an opportunity for you to do good to others, to serve others, to give love to others, to be gentle to others, to give your sympathy to souls who are longing and hungering for it. Life is miserable when a person is absorbed in himself; as soon as he forgets himself he is happy. The more he thinks of himself, his own affairs, work and interests, the less he knows the meaning of life.

If we only understood that every moment in life, every day, every month, and every year, has its particular blessing; if we only knew life's opportunity! But the greatest opportunity that one can realize in life is to accomplish that purpose for which man was sent on earth. And if he has lost that opportunity, then whatever he may have accomplished in the world, whether he has gathered wealth, possesses much property, or has made a great name for himself, he will not be satisfied. Once man's eyes are opened and he begins to look at the world, he will find there is a greater opportunity than he had ever thought before.

Man is as poor as he is, as limited as he is, as troubled as he is; yet there is nothing in this world which could not be accomplished by man if he only knew what thought can do. It is ignorance which keeps him from what he ought to accomplish. Man should know how to operate his thought, how to accomplish certain things, how to focus his mind on the object that should be accomplished. If he does not know then he has not made use of his mind but has lived like a machine. If man knew the power of feeling, and realized that the power of feeling can reach anywhere and penetrate anything, he could achieve whatever he might wish. Every man is a captive in some form or other; his life is limited in some form or other; but one could get above this limitation by realizing the latent power and inspiration of the soul. *Hazrat Inayat Khan*

In the name of Allah, the Beneficent, the Merciful

By the Scripture which maketh plain. (43::2 Quran)

Lo! We have appointed a lecture in Arabic that haply ye may understand. (43:3 Quran)

When Jesus came with clear proofs of Allah's sovereignty, he said: I have come unto you with wisdom, and to make plain some of that concerning which ye differ. So keep your duty to Allah and obey me. (43:63 Quran)

Lo! Allah, He is my Lord and your Lord. So worship Him. This is a right path. (43:64 Quran)

Ye who believed Our revelations and were self-surrendered. (43:69 Quran)

Enter the Garden, ye and your wives, to be made glad. (43:70 Quran)

Therein are brought round for them trays of gold and goblets, and therein is all that souls desire and eyes find sweet. And ye are immortal therein. (43:71 Quran)

This is the Garden which ye are made to inherit because of what ye used to do. (43:72 Quran)

Therein for you is fruit in plenty whence to eat. (43:73 Quran)

And He it is Who in the heaven is God, and in the earth God. He is the Wise, the Knower. (43:84 Quran)

And blessed be He unto Whom belongeth the Sovereignty of the heavens and the earth and all that is between them, and with Whom is knowledge of the Hour, and unto Whom ye will be returned. (43:85 Quran)

And if thou ask them who created them, they will surely say, Allah. How then are they turned away? (43:87 Quran)

And he saith: O my Lord! Lo, those are a folk who believe not. (43:88 Quran)

Then bear with them, O Muhammad, and say: Peace. But they will come to know. (43:89 Quran)

When souls meet each other, what truth they can exchange! It is uttered in silence, yet always surely reaches its goal.

Truth comes to man's soul, and yet truth is not the exclusive property of creed, caste, or race. We are all the children of God, the Father-Mother Spirit of all that exists. And we ought to have such a feeling of brotherhood that we exchange helpful thoughts with one another all the time. We can take love and guidance from one another. Speech is not as great a help as contact; but the privilege of meeting one another is great. When souls meet, what truth they can exchange! It is uttered in silence, yet surely always reaches its goal.

In everyday life we are confronted with a thousand troubles that we are not always evolved enough to meet, and then only silence can help us. For if there is any religion, if there is any practice of religion, it is to have regard for the pleasure of God by regarding the pleasure of man. The essence of religion is to understand. And this religion we cannot live without having power over the word, without having realized the power of silence. There are so very many occasions when we repent after hurting friends, which could have been avoided if there had been control over our words. Silence is the shield of the ignorant and the protection of the wise. For the ignorant does not prove his ignorance if he keeps silent, and the wise man does not throw pearls before swine if he knows the worth of silence.

What gives power over words? What gives the power that can be attained by silence? The answer is: it is will-power which gives the control over words; it is silence which gives one the power of silence. It is restlessness when a person speaks too much. The more words are used to express an idea, the less powerful they become. It is a great pity that man so often thinks of saving pennies and never thinks of sparing words. It is like saving pebbles and throwing away pearls. An Indian poet says, 'Pearl-shell, what gives you your precious contents? Silence; for years my lips were closed.'

For a moment it is a struggle with oneself; it is controlling an impulse; but afterwards the same thing becomes a power.

Every race and every creed has its principles of right and wrong, but there is one fundamental principle of religion in which all creeds and all people can meet, and that is to see beauty in attitude, in action, in thought, and in feeling. There is no action with a stamp on it saying that it is right or wrong, but what we think wrong or wicked is really that which our mind sees as such because it is without beauty. All the great ones who have come into the world from time to time to awaken humanity to a greater truth, what did they bring? They brought beauty. It is not what they taught, it is what they were themselves. Words seem inadequate to express either goodness or beauty. One can speak of it in a thousand words, and yet one will never be able to express it. For it is something which is beyond words, and the soul alone can understand it. And the one who will always follow the rule of beauty in his life, in every little thing he does, will always succeed. *Hazrat Inayat Khan*

Surah Forty-Four

Ad Dukhan

The aim of the mystic is to keep near to the idea of unity, and to find out where we unite.

When people say that they distinguish between right and wrong by their results, even then they cannot be sure if in the punishment there was not a reward, or in the reward a punishment. What does this show us? It shows us that life is a puzzle of duality. The pairs of opposites keep us in an illusion and make us think, 'This is this, and that is that'. At the same time by throwing a greater light upon things we shall find in the end that they are quite different from what we had thought.

Seeing the nature and character of life the Sufi says that it is not very important to distinguish between two opposites. What is most important is to recognize that One which is hiding behind it all. Naturally after realizing life the Sufi climbs the ladder which leads him to unity, to the idea of unity which comes through the synthesis of life, by seeing One in all things, in all beings. Whatever a man desires, that desire informs us of the state of mind he is in, and those who understand the mind well, know the mind of another simply by studying the desires and tendencies of his life. Love of a rose, a lily, a jasmine, of sweet, sour, salt, or savory things, expresses the particular tendency of a person's mind, the mood he is in. Modern education omits the study of the truth which teaches us that unity comes from nature's variety, whereas the sole aim of the mystic is to keep near to the idea of unity and to find out where we unite.

There is an Arabic saying, 'If you wish to know God, you must know yourself.' How little man knows while he is in the intoxication of individualism! He thinks, 'I am a separate being; you are another; there is no connection between you and me, and we all have our own joys and free will.' Did man but know it, his life is dependent not only on the objects and things that keep the body alive, but also on the activity of a thousand minds in a day. Who then can say, 'I am an individual, independent and free, I can think as I wish, and I can do what I wish? We are connected with one another. Our lives are tied together, and there is a link in which we can see one current running through all. There are many globes and lamps, and yet one current is running through all. The mystic seeks to realize this constantly and to impress it on his mind in whatever he may see. What, for him, are the waves of the sea? Are they not the sea itself? *Hazrat Inayat Khan*

In the name of Allah, the Beneficent, the Merciful

By the Scripture that maketh plain. (44:2 Quran)

Lo! We revealed it on a blessed night—Lo! We are ever warning. (44:3 Quran)

Whereon every wise command is made clear. (44:4 Quran)

As a command from Our presence—Lo! We are ever sending. (44:5 Quran)

A mercy from thy Lord! Lo! He is the Hearer, the Knower. (44:6 Quran)

Lord of the heavens and the earth and all that is between them, if ye would be sure. (44:7 Quran)

There is no God save him. He quickeneth and giveth death, your Lord and Lord of your forefathers. (44:8 Quran)

Assuredly the day of Decision is the term for all of them. (44:40 Quran)

A day when friend can in naught avail friend, nor can they be helped. (44:41 Quran)

Save him on whom Allah hath mercy. Lo! He is the Mighty, the Merciful. (44:42 Quran)

And We have made this Scripture easy in thy language only that they may heed. (44:58 Quran)

Wait then, O Muhammad, Lo! They too are waiting. (44:59 Quran)

According to his evolution, man knows truth.

Every person's desire is according to his evolution. That for which he is ready is desirable for him. Milk is a desirable food for the infant, other foods for the grown-up person. Every stage in life has its own appropriate and desirable things.

When one realizes the ultimate truth, one comes to understand that one single underlying current to which all the different religions, philosophies and faiths are attached. These are all only different expressions of the same truth, and it is the absence of that knowledge which causes all to be divided into so many different sects and religions.

In India there is a well-known story exemplifying this fact: that some blind men were very anxious to see an elephant. So a kind man one day took them to see one. There, standing by its side, he said, "Now, here is the elephant, see what you can make of it." Each one tried to make out by touch what the elephant looked like, and afterwards when they met together they began to discuss its appearance. One said, "It looks like the big pillar of a palace," another said, "It looks like a fan." And so they differed and discussed amongst one another, then they quarreled so much as to come to a hand-to-hand fight. Each one said, "I have seen it, I know what it is; I have touched it." Then the man who took them to the elephant came and said, "You are every one of you right, but you have each seen only a part of the elephant."

So it is with the religions. A person says, "This religion is the one, this doctrine is the only one, this truth is the only truth possible." That shows a lack of knowledge of the ultimate truth. As soon as one comes to the realization of the depth of truth, one begins to discern that it is the same truth which the great ones have tried to express in words. They could not put it fully into words. They have done their best to help humanity to evolve and reach to a point at which it is able to understand what can never be explained in words.

Somebody can be praised by one and hated by another, and ten people may all have a different idea of the same person, because each understands him according to his state of evolution. Each sees that person according to his own point of view, each looks at him through his own eyes, and therefore the same person is different to each being. In the mind of one the person is a sinner, in the mind of another he is a saint. The same person who is considered gentle and good by one is considered the opposite by another. If this can be so in connection with a living being, it is equally possible that various ideas of the deity should be formed in each heart, and that each soul should mold his own deity according to his own evolution and according to his way of idealizing and understanding. Therefore the deity of every heart is different and is as that person has imagined; but the God of every soul is one and the same, whatever people imagine. It is the same God that they all imagine, but their imaginations are different and it is the lack of understanding of this that has caused the differences in religion. *Hazrat Inayat Khan*

Surah Forty-Five

Al Jathiyah

To learn the lesson of how to live is more important than any psychic or occult learning.

The hustle and bustle of life leaves a man very little time to think of his general condition. The only news he receives is from the newspapers, and so he depends upon the papers for his ideas; and the intoxication of life leaves him very little time to think about the real meaning of life. When he looks around him and considers the condition of the nations today, he finds that in spite of all the progress, there is an increase in ill-feeling between them. Friendship only exists for self-interest. A nation only thinks about its own interest whether it has to deal with friend or enemy.

What is needed today is an education that will teach humanity to feel the essence of its religion in everyday life. Man is not put upon this earth to be an angel. He need not be praying in church all day long, nor go into the wilderness. He needs only to better understand life. He must learn to set apart a certain time in the day to think about his own life and doings. He must ask himself, 'Have I done an honest deed today? Have I proved myself worthy in that place, in that capacity?' In this way, he can make his everyday life a prayer.

The need of the world today is not learning, but how to become considerate towards one another. To try and find out in what way happiness can be brought about, and in this way to realize that peace which is the longing of every soul and to impart it to others, thereby attaining our life's goal, the sublimity of life.

To learn the lesson of how to live is more important than any psychic or occult learning. Every day we think we have learned the lesson, but if we had the world would have become a heaven for us now. We may seek the higher knowledge or the higher things, but the very smallest thing, the control of all the creatures of the mind, which seems as nothing compared with the higher knowledge, once learnt and acted upon is greater than all. Man's selfishness shows itself in wanting to get the better of his fellow man. If we developed humanity we should do differently. We should be satisfied with a slice of bread if there were another in need, but as it is, it happens that even when we are fed ourselves, we do not wish anyone else to share the food. The human heart can only be really satisfied by knowing that the other person is happy. True pleasure lies in the sharing of joy with another. From the day that we realize this we begin to act as human beings; hitherto we have not done so even though we have human forms.

Sages have always repented of all things that make them animal. It is human beings that repent; the animals are pleased with everything that they do. The Bible says, 'Repent, for the kingdom of God is at hand.' This has to be done all day long. Once one has realized it, the kingdom of God is at hand. *Hazrat Inayat Khan*

In the name of Allah, the Beneficent, the Merciful

Tell those who believe to forgive those who hope not for the days of Allah, in order that He may requite folk what they used to earn. (45:14 Quran)

Whoso doeth right, it is for his soul, and whoso doeth wrong, it is against it. And afterward unto your Lord ye will be brought back. (45:15 Quran)

And verily We gave the Children of Israel the Scripture and the Command and the Prophethood, and provided them with good things and favored them above all peoples. (45:16 Quran)

And gave them plain commandments. And they differed not until after the knowledge came unto them, through rivalry among themselves. Lo! Thy Lord will judge between them on the Day of Resurrection concerning that wherein they used to differ. (45:17 Quran)

And now have We set thee, O Muhammad, on a clear road of Our commandment, so follow it, and follow not the whims of those who know not. (45:18 Quran)

Lo! They can avail thee naught against Allah. And lo, as for the wrongdoers some of them are friends of others, and Allah is the Friend of those who ward off evil. (45:19 Quran)

This is a clear indication for mankind, and a guidance and a mercy for a folk whose faith is sure. (45:20 Quran)

This Our book pronounceth against you with truth. Lo! We have caused all that ye did to be recorded. (45:29 Quran)

Then as for those who believed and did good works, their Lord will bring them unto His mercy. That is the evident triumph. (45:30 Quran)

All gains, whether material, spiritual, moral or mystical, are in answer to one's own character.

It is easy to help children, but it is most difficult to help the grown-up. One may change snow into water and water into ice, but to try to change a character is the most difficult thing one can ever imagine. Therefore, it is usually vain to try. But what one can do is to build one's own character; that is in one's own hands. Only, what people are most occupied with is the character of someone else; they are always thinking of the other but they never want to change themselves.

The seer, therefore, teaches that all the things that we desire and think beautiful, we ought to produce within ourselves instead of expecting them from others. What a task that is! What great self-sufficiency there would be if every country always itself produced that which it seeks from others; what an independent life it would be to produce within ourselves what we expect to obtain from others! Instead of depending on them for something we ourselves can give them, we should experience the joy of giving, the joy of being kind to others. What joy and freedom we should ourselves find in being kind to another. However natural it may be to have someone love and admire us, are we not dependent? The wife is dependent of her husband's love; the friend is dependent on the friend's love. But in the other case we would be free and independent; for our joy would lie in the love itself, and not in the person.

We should enjoy life by doing kindness to others. Receiving kindness from others only makes the recipient expect more. He keeps saying, 'He is doing this for his own benefit; he is not considering me; he is blaming me; he did not help me; he did not deal fairly with me.' His life becomes full of grudges because he expects from everybody all the good that he wants, and he does not know that he ought to have it all in himself; that he should become independent. Therein lies the secret of character. If a person thinks that God is all, but the whole world is vile, he does not worship God, for God is all and God is beautiful. 'God is beautiful and he loves beauty,' the Prophet said. And as His being is in us, we are supposed to love beauty also. What is beauty? Not only the external beauty, but the beauty of personality, the beauty of character, that is the real beauty. If we did not worship it, we should not admire it in other people. We cannot appreciate anything without beauty of character.

All gains, whether material, spiritual, moral, or mystical, are the outcome of one's own character; and if we have gained nothing, it is only by reason of our own character. *Hazrat Inayat Khan*

Surah Forty-Six

Al Ahqaf
The truth need not be veiled, for it veils itself from the eyes of the ignorant.

The soul, absorbed in its child-like fancies in things that it values and to which it gives importance, and in the beings to which it attaches itself, blinds itself by the veils of its illusion. Thus it covers with a thousand veils its own truth from its own eyes.

Truth is vaster than any frame we can make to put it in. Besides, no matter what frame we make for truth to be presented in, an un-awakened soul will never see it, but will only see the frame.

With still another step further there comes the realization which may be called revelation. When the soul is tuned to that state, then the eyes and the ears of the heart are open to see and hear the word that comes from all sides. In point of fact every atom of this world, either in heaven or earth speaks and speaks aloud. It is the deaf ears of the heart and the closed eyes of the soul which prevent man from seeing and hearing it. There is a verse of a Hindustani poet which says:

> O' self, it is not the fault of the divine Beloved
> that you do not see Him, that you do not hear Him.
> He is continually before you and He is continually speaking to you.
> If you do not hear it and if you do not see it, it is your own fault.

It is for this purpose that every soul has been created and it is in the fulfillment of this that man fulfills the object of God. When the spark that is to be found in every heart, the spark that may be called the divine spark in man, is blown upon and the flame arises, the whole life becomes illuminated and man hears and sees and knows, and he understands.

We may ask ourselves, 'Who is another?' Then we realize that in the true sense of being there is but One. When the veil of ignorance is raised there is no longer any 'I' and 'you', but only the One exists. This is the teaching of the Bible and of all scriptures. *Hazrat Inayat Khan*

In the name of Allah, the Beneficent, the Merciful

And when our clear revelations are recited unto them, those who disbelieve say of the Truth when it reacheth them: This is mere magic. (46:7 Quran)

Or they say: He hath invented it? Say, O Muhammad, if I have invented it, still ye have no power to support me against Allah. He is best aware of what ye may say among yourselves concerning it. He sufficeth for a witness between me and you. And He is the Merciful, the Forgiving. (46:8 Quran)

Say: I am no new thing among the messengers of Allah, nor know I what will be done with me or with you. I do but follow that which is inspired in me, and I am but a plain warner. (46:9 Quran)

Bethink you: If it is from Allah and ye disbelieve therein, and a witness of the Children of Israel hath already testified to the like thereof and hath believed, and ye are too proud, what plight is yours? Lo, Allah guideth not wrongdoing folk. (46:10 Quran)

And those who disbelieve say of those who believe: If it had been any good, they would not have been before us in attaining it. And since they will not be guided by it, they say: This is an ancient lie. (46:11 Quran)

When before it there was the Scripture of Moses, an example and a mercy, and this is a confirming Scripture in the Arabic language, that it may warn those who do wrong, and bring good tidings for the righteous. (46:12 Quran)

Lo! Those who say: Our Lord is Allah, and thereafter walk aright, there shall be no fear come upon them, neither shall they grieve. (46:13 Quran)

Such are the rightful owners of the Garden, immortal therein, as a reward for what they used to do. (46:14 Quran)

And We have commanded unto man kindness toward parents. His mother beareth him with reluctance, and bringeth him forth with reluctance, and the bearing of him and the weaning of him is thirty months, till, when he attaineth full strength and reacheth forty years, he saith: My Lord! Arouse me that I may give thanks for the favor wherewith Thou hast favored me and my parents, and that I may do right acceptable unto Thee. And be gracious unto me in the matter of my seed. Lo! I have turned unto Thee repentant, and lo, I am of those who surrender unto Thee. (46:15 Quran)

Those are they from whom We accept the best of what they do, and overlook their evil deeds. They are among the owners of the Garden. This is the true promise which they were promised in the world. (46:16 Quran)

You can have all good things—wealth, friends, kindness, love to give and love to receive—once you have learned not to be blinded by them, learned to escape from disappointment, and from repugnance at the idea that things are not as you want them to be.

Do not expect much from friends. Why must they be as you want them to be? They are not made by you. They are as they are. You must try to be for them what they expect you to be. It matters little if your friend proves to you to be a friend. What matters is, if you prove to be a friend.

However evolved we may be with our education and experience, yet what are we really seeking? Things from which we cannot derive any lasting gain. From these false things we gain the experience that the things to which we have hitherto attached importance and which we have valued are things that do not last. We learn at length that it would be wise to remember that all these objects and ideals and aspirations which we have in life should be judged according to whether they are dependable or not, lasting or not.

After we have perceived the truth that this or that is not to be depended upon, we find that it is not necessary to renounce them all, to give up everything in life. We can be in the crowd just as well as in seclusion in the wilderness. We can have all good things, wealth, friends, kindness, love to give and love to take once we have learned not to be blinded by them, learned to escape from disappointment, learned to escape from repugnance at the idea that the things are not as we would want them to be. A man can still attend to business, he may attain wealth, he can carry out all those things, but now his eyes are wide open; before, they were blind. This is the teaching of life.

It is not the actual literal renunciation which counts, it is the personal abandonment of belief in the importance of transient things. If there is such a thing as saintly renunciation, it is renouncing small gains for better gains; not for no gains, but seeing with open eyes what is better and what is inferior. Even if the choice has to lie between two momentary gains, one of these would always be found to be more real and lasting; that is the one that should be followed for the time. When we take the torch of wisdom to show us our path through life, we will end by realizing what is really profitable in life and what is not. *Hazrat Inayat Khan*

Surah Forty-Seven

Muhammad

No man should allow his mind to be a vehicle for others to use; he who does not direct his own mind lacks mastery.

Our minds need to be dusted and swept just as much as our houses, and this we do by meditation and concentration, which wipe away all wrong impressions. We must be masters of our own minds as well as our houses, and not allow them to be like a furniture warehouse with all the furniture mixed up together. We must direct where everything is to be placed, so that complete order may reign therein.

The more the mind is allowed to go on without purpose, the more likely it is to become a vehicle or machine which all manner of influences around it of other human beings or spirit obsessions will employ instead of its owner. If the user of that mind is a sensible person, then it may perhaps act properly, but otherwise the work of the mind is wasted. In any case it would not be a fulfillment of the purpose of his life. This purpose is to learn mastery, not to be a vehicle for others to use. He who does not direct his own mind lacks mastery.

Man is his mind, is the product of his mind, and is also the controller of the activity of mind. If he does not control his mind, he is not a master but a slave. It lies with his own mind whether he shall be master, or whether he shall be slave. He is slave when he neglects to be master; he is master if he cares to be master. A man with a perfectly stilled, comforted, and rested mind will at once raise up another who is going through distress, or restlessness, or pain, or ill-temper, or worry, or anxiety. The very presence of one whose mind is stilled gives such hope, such inspiration, such sympathy, such power and life. All the heavenly properties flow so smoothly and freely from the person whose mind is stilled that his words, his voice, his presence, all react upon the mind of others; and as he stills his mind, so his very presence becomes healing. Hazrat Inayat Khan

In the name of Allah, the Beneficent, the Merciful

While as for those who walk aright, He addeth to their guidance, and giveth them their protection against evil. (47:17 Quran)

So know, O Muhammad, that there is no God save Allah, and ask forgiveness for thy sin and for believing men and believing women. Allah knoweth both your place of turmoil and your place of rest. (47:19 Quran)

Or do those in whose hearts is a disease deem that Allah will not bring to light their secret hates? (47:29 Quran)

And if We would. We would show unto thee, Muhammad, so that thou shouldst know them surely by their marks. And thou shalt know them by the burden of their talk. And Allah knoweth your deeds. (47:30 Quran)

So do not falter, and cry out for peace when ye will be the uppermost, and Allah is with you, and He will not grudge the reward of your actions. (47:35 Quran)

The life of the world is but a sport and a pastime. And if ye believe and ward off evil, He will give you your wages, and will not ask of you your worldly wealth. (47:36 Quran)

A study of life is the greatest of all religions, and there is no greater or more interesting study.

There are two ways in which we may attain control over our activity. The first is confidence in the power of our own will; to know that if we have failed today, tomorrow we will not do so. The second is to have our eyes wide open, and to watch keenly our activity in all aspects of life. It is in the dark that we fall, but in the light we can see where we are going.

So it is in life: we should have our eyes wide open to see where we walk. We should study life, and seek to know why we say a thing, and why we act as we do. We have failed perhaps hitherto because we have not been wide awake. We have fallen, and felt sorry, and have forgotten all about it, and perhaps may have fallen again. This is because we have not studied life. A study of life is the greatest of all religions, and there is no greater and more interesting study. Those who have mastered all grades of activity, they above all experience life in all its aspects. They are like swimmers in the sea who float on the water of life and do not sink.

If we only knew how much the study of life can tell us! One could go into the British Museum and read every book in the building, and yet not obtain satisfaction. It is not study, it is not research, it is not inquiry which gives this knowledge; it is actually going through the experiences of life, witnessing life in its different aspects and in its different phases or spheres; that is what reveals the ideal of life. Look not on life as a person would watch a play on the stage. Rather look upon it as a student who is learning at college.

It is not a passing show; it is not a place of amusement in which to fool our life away. It is a place for study, in which every sorrow, every heartbreak brings a precious lesson. It is a place in which to learn by one's own suffering, by the study of the suffering of others; to learn from the people who have been kind to us as well as from the people who have been unkind. It is a place in which all experiences, be they disappointments, struggles, and pains, or joys, pleasures, and comforts, contribute to the understanding of what life is, and the realization what it is. Then do we awake to the religion of nature, which is the only religion. And the more we understand it, the greater our life becomes, and the more of a blessing will our life be for others. *Hazrat Inayat Khan*

Surah Forty-Eight

Al Fath
He who can quicken the feeling of another to joy or to gratitude, by that much he adds to his own life.

Each one has his circle of influence, large or small; within his sphere so many souls and minds are involved; with his rise, they rise; with his fall, they fall. The size of a man's sphere corresponds with the extent of his sympathy, or we may say, with the size of his heart. His sympathy holds his sphere together. As his heart grows, his sphere grows; as his sympathy is withdrawn or lessened, so his sphere breaks up and scatters. If he harms those who live and move within his sphere, those dependent upon him or upon his affection, he of necessity harms himself. His house or his palace or his cottage, his satisfaction or his disgust in his environment is the creation of his own thought. Acting upon his thoughts, and also part of his own thoughts, are the thoughts of those near to him; others depress him and destroy him, or they encourage and support him, in proportion as he repels those around him by his coldness, or attracts them by his sympathy.

Each individual composes the music of his own life. If he injures another, he brings disharmony. When his sphere is disturbed, he is disturbed himself, and there is a discord in the melody of his life. If he can quicken the feeling of another to joy or to gratitude, by that much he adds to his own life; he becomes himself by that much more alive. Whether conscious of it or not, his thought is affected for the better by the joy or gratitude of another, and his power and vitality increase thereby, and the music of his life grows more in harmony. *Hazrat Inayat Khan*

In the name of Allah, the Beneficent, the Merciful

Lo! We have given thee, O Muhammad, a signal victory. (48:1 Quran)

That Allah may forgive thee of thy sin that which is past and that which is to come, and may perfect His favor unto thee, and may guide thee on a right path. (48:2 Quran)

And Allah may help thee with strong help. (48:3 Quran)

He it is Who sent down peace of reassurance into the hearts of the believers that they might add faith unto their faith. Allah's are the hosts of the heavens and the earth, and Allah is ever Wise, Knower. (48:4 Quran)

That He may bring the believing men and the believing women into Gardens underneath which rivers flow, wherein they will abide, and may remit from them their evil deeds. That, in the sight of Allah, is the supreme triumph. (48:5 Quran)

Allah's are the hosts of the heavens and the earth, and Allah is ever Wise, Mighty. (48:7 Quran)

Lo! We have sent thee, O Muhammad, as a witness and a bearer of good tidings and a warner. (48:8 Quran)

That ye mankind may believe in Allah and His messenger, and may honor Him at early dawn and at the close of day. (48:9 Quran)

Lo! Those who swear allegiance unto thee, Muhammad, swear allegiance only unto Allah. The hand of Allah is above their hands. So, whosoever breaketh his oath, breaketh it only to his soul's hurt, while whosoever keepeth his covenant with Allah, on him will He bestow immense reward. (48:10 Quran)

Those of the wandering Arabs who were left behind to tell thee: Our possessions and our households occupied us, so ask forgiveness for us! They speak with their tongues that which is not in their hearts, say: Who can avail you aught against Allah, if he intend you hurt, or intend your profit? Nay, but Allah is ever Aware of what ye do. (48:11 Quran)

And Allah's is the Sovereignty of the heavens and the earth. He forgiveth whom He will, and punisheth whom He will. And Allah is ever Merciful, Forgiving. (48:14 Quran)

And He it is Who hath withheld men's hands from you, and hath withheld your hands from them, in the valley of Mecca, after He made you victors over them. Allah is seer of what ye do. (48:24 Quran)

When those who disbelieve had set up in their hearts zealotry, the zealotry of the Age of Ignorance, then Allah sent down His peace of reassurance upon His messenger and upon the believers and imposed on them the word of self-restraint, for they were worthy of it and meet for it. And Allah is aware of all things. (48:26 Quran)

Allah hath fulfilled the vision for His messenger in very truth. Ye shall indeed enter the Inviolable Place of Worship, if Allah will secure, having your hair shaven and cut, not fearing. But He knoweth that which ye know not, and hath given you a near victory beforehand. (48:27 Quran)

He it is Who hath sent His messenger with the guidance and the religion of truth, that He may cause it to prevail over all religion. And Allah sufficeth as a witness. (48:28 Quran)

Muhammad is the messenger of Allah. And those with him are hard against the disbelievers and merciful among themselves. Thou, O Muhammad, seest them bowing and falling prostrate in worship, seeking bounty from Allah and His acceptance. The mark of them is on their foreheads from the traces of prostration. Such is their likeness in the Torah and their likeness in the Gospel—like as sown corn that sendeth forth its shoot and strengtheneth it and riseth from upon its stalk, delighting the sowers—that He may enrage the disbelievers with the sight of them. Allah hath promised, unto each of them as believe and do good works, forgiveness and immense reward. (48:29 Quran)

Praise cannot exist without blame; it has no existence without its opposite.

There is a pair of opposites in all things, and in each there exists the spirit of the opposite: in man the quality of woman, in woman the spirit of man, in the sun the form of the moon, in the moon the light of the sun. The closer one approaches reality, the nearer one arrives at unity.

Life is differentiated by the pairs of opposites.

Praise cannot exist without blame, for nothing has existence without its opposite, just as pleasure cannot exist without pain. No one can be great and not small; no one can be loved and not hated. There is no one who is hated by all and not loved by some-one; there is always someone to love him. If one would realize that the world of God, His splendor and magnificence, are to be seen in the wise and the foolish, in the good and the bad, then one would think tolerantly and reverently of all mankind

How does the Sufi struggle? He struggles with power, with understanding, with open eyes, and with patience. He does not look at the loss; what is lost is lost. He does not think of the pain of yesterday; yesterday is gone for him. Only if a memory is pleasant does he keep it before him, for it is helpful on his way. He takes both the admiration and the hatred coming from around him with smiles; he believes that both these things form a rhythm within the rhythm of a certain music; there is one and two, the strong accent and the weak accent. Praise cannot be without blame, nor can blame be without praise. He keeps the torch of wisdom before him, because he believes that the present is the echo of the past, and that the future will be the reflection of the present. It is not sufficient to think only of the present moment; one should also think where it comes from and where it goes. Every thought that comes to his mind, every impulse, every word he speaks, is to him like a seed, a seed which falls in this soil of life, and takes root. And in this way he finds that nothing is lost; every good deed, every little act of kindness, of love, done to anybody, will someday rise as a plant and bear fruit.

Hazrat Inayat Khan

Surah Forty-Nine

Al Jujarat

Riches and power may vanish because they are outside ourselves; only that which is within can we call our own.

Where is man's wealth? It is in his knowledge. If his wealth is only in the bank and not in his knowledge he does not really possess it. It is in the bank. All desirable and great things, values and titles, position and possession, where are they? Outside? No, because outside is only that which one knows by the knowledge one has within. Therefore the real possession is not without but within. It is the self within, it is the heart which must be developed, the heart which must be in its natural rhythm and at its proper pitch. When it is tuned to its natural rhythm and pitch, then it can accomplish the purpose for which it is made.

The claim to be kind and sympathetic is like a drop of water saying, 'I am water,' but which, on seeing the ocean, realizes its nothingness. In the same way, when man has looked on perfection, he realizes his shortcomings. It is then that the veil is raised from before his eyes and his sight becomes keen. He then asks himself, 'What can I do that I may awaken this love and sympathy in my heart?' The Sufi begins by realizing that he is dead and blind, and he understands that all goodness as well as all that is bad comes from within. Riches and power may vanish because they are outside of us, but only that which is within can we call our own. In order to awaken love and sympathy in our hearts, sacrifices must be made. We must forget our own troubles in order to sympathize with the troubles of others. *Hazrat Inayat Khan*

In the name of Allah, the Beneficent, the Merciful

O ye who believe! Lift not up your voices above the voice of the Prophet, nor shout when speaking to him as ye shout one to another, lest your works be rendered vain while ye perceive not. (49:2 Quran)

Lo! They who subdue their voices in the presence of the messenger of Allah, those are they whose hearts Allah hath proven unto righteousness. Theirs will be forgiveness and immense reward. (49:3 Quran)

And if they had had patience till thou comest forth unto them, it had been better for them. And Allah is Merciful, Forgiving. (49:5 Quran)

And if two parties of believers fall to fighting, then make peace between them. And if one party of them doeth wrong to the other, fight ye that which doeth wrong till it return to the ordinance of Allah, then, if it return, make peace between them justly, and act equitably. Lo! Allah loveth the equitable. (49:9 Quran)

The believers are naught else than brothers. Therefore make peace between your brethren and observe your duty to Allah, that haply ye may obtain mercy. (49:10 Quran)

O ye who believe! Let not a folk deride a folk who may be better than they are, nor let women deride women who may be better than they are, neither defame one another, nor insult one another by nickname. Bad is the name of lewdness after faith. And whoso turneth not in repentance, such are evil doers. (49:11 Quran)

O ye who believe! Shun much suspicion, for, lo, some suspicion is a crime. And spy not, neither backbite one another. Would one of you love to eat the flesh of the dead brother? Ye abhor that, so abhor the other! And keep your duty to Allah. Lo! Allah is Merciful, Relenting. (49:12 Quran)

O mankind! Lo! We have created you male and female, and have made you tribes and nations that ye may know one another. Lo! The noblest of you, in the sight of Allah, is the best in conduct. Lo! Allah is Aware, Knower. (49:13 Quran)

The wandering Arabs say: we believe. Say unto them, O Muhammad: ye believe not, rather say 'we submit', for the faith hath not yet entered into your hearts. Yet, if ye obey Allah and His messenger, He will not withhold from you aught of the reward of your deeds. Lo! Allah is Merciful, Forgiving. (49:14 Quran)

Unity in realization is far greater than unity in variety.

What keeps the soul in perplexity is the threefold aspect of manifestation, and as long as the soul remains puzzled by this, it cannot arrive at the knowledge of the One. These three aspects are the seer, sight, and the seen; the knower, knowledge, and the known. In point of fact these are three aspects of life. One aspect is the person who sees; the second aspect is the sight, or the eyes, by the help of which he sees; and the third aspect is that which he sees. That is why one cannot readily accept the idea that what one sees is the same as oneself, nor can one believe for a moment that the medium by which one sees is oneself, for these three aspects seem to be separate and to be looking at one another's faces, as the first person, second person, and third person of Brahma.

When this riddle is solved by the realization that the three are one, then the purpose of the God-ideal is fulfilled. For then the three veils which cover the One are lifted, then they no longer remain three, and then they are found to be One, the Only Being. As Abdul Karim al Jili, the fifteenth-century mystic, says, 'If you believe in one God, you are right; if you believe in two Gods, that is true; but if you believe in three Gods, that is right also, for the nature of unity is realized by variety.'

Man's thought has a great power. And when he comes to the realization that everything comes from one source and that everything is developing towards one goal, he begins to see that the source and the goal are God. Then the world of variety is no longer variety to him but unity; it is one.

The power is in unity, but is lost in variety. Thus, for instance, if we hold a thing in our hand, we can hold it with strength, because all five fingers have united to hold the object. But if we try to lift it by one finger, this one finger may drop it, even though the finger belongs to the same hand. In all aspects of life unity is power. All religions show that power is in unity. This is the secret of philosophy.

There are two aspects of unity: firstly, the unity of variety; secondly, unity realizing itself. One is earthly, the other is heavenly. One cannot serve two masters. Unity is the only source of happiness. Unity in realization is far greater than unity in variety.

'When two hearts unite, they can break even mountains.' As two fuse in love, the more does intuition grow, the more does one understand whether the other is happy, or pleased, or displeased, whatever distance may separate them. This is nothing but just the unity of the one person with the other. It is clairvoyance. The mother knows the condition of her son at the battlefront. She can see him in her dreams. Hearts, which are united in love, perceive the state of mind of the loved ones. They do not have to study mysticism or concentration, for they have natural concentration. The mother does not pretend to meditate; love teaches her more meditation than a person who pretends to study it can attain.
Hazrat Inayat Khan

Surah Fifty

Qaf
Rest of mind is as necessary as rest of body, and yet we always keep the former in action.

Imagine, after having toiled for the whole day, how much the body stands in need of rest; how much more then must the mind stand in need of rest! The mind works much faster than the body. Naturally the mind is much more tired than the body. And not every person knows how to rest his mind and therefore the mind never has a rest. And then what happens after a while is that the mind becomes feeble. It loses memory, the power of action. It loses reason. The worst effects are mostly brought about by not giving the mind proper repose. If such infirmities as doubt and fear happen to enter the mind, then a person becomes restless, he can never find rest. For at night the mind continues on the track of the same impressions. Simple as it seems to be, very few know the resting of the mind and how wonderful it is in itself. And what power, what inspiration, comes as a reaction from it, and what peace one experiences by it, and how it helps the body and mind! The spirit is renewed once the mind has had its rest.

The first step towards the resting of the mind is the relaxation of the body. If one is able to relax one's muscular and nervous system at will, then the mind is automatically refreshed. Besides that, one must be able to cast away anxiety, worries, doubts, and fears by the power of will, putting oneself in a restful state. This will be accomplished by the help of proper breathing.

We usually rest our body at will whenever circumstances allow us to; we recline on a couch or in an armchair after coming back from the office or work and at night we rest and go to sleep; but when do we give the mind a rest? Rest for the mind is as necessary as rest for the body, and yet we always keep the mind in action. It is constantly at work even if our body is resting.

All this shows the great practical need for the mind to be at rest, for the mind to be stilled. Those who make it a principle that work is always an advisable thing are one-sided. Balance lies in perceiving that work and rest are equally necessary for good health, both physical and mental.

The work of the body is sometimes kept under a man's control, but he does not keep the work of the mind under his control. This is not because he cannot do so; it is because he never thinks about it. *Hazrat Inayat Khan*

In the name of Allah, the Beneficent, the Merciful

Qaf. By the glorious Quran. (50:1 Quran)

Nay, but they marvel that a warner of their own hath come unto them, and the disbelievers say: this is a strange thing. (50:2 Quran)

When we are dead and have become dust, shall we be brought back again? That would be a far return. (50:3 Quran)

We know which the earth taketh of them, and with Us is the recording Book. (50:4 Quran)

Nay, but they have denied the truth when it came unto them, therefore they are now in troubled case. (50:5 Quran)

Have they not then observed the sky above them, how We constructed it and beautified it, and how there are no rifts therein? (50:6 Quran)

And the earth We have spread out, and have flung firm hills therein, and have caused of every lovely kind to grow thereon. (50:7 Quran)

A vision and a reminder for every penitent slave. (50:8 Quran)

And We send down from the sky blessed water whereby We give growth unto gardens and the grain of crops. (50:9 Quran)

And lofty date-palms with ranged cluster. (50:10 Quran)

Provisions made for men and therewith We quicken a dead land. Even so will be the resurrection of the dead. (50:11 Quran)

We verily created man and We know what his soul whispereth to him, and We are nearer to him than his jugular vein. (50:16 Quran)

Who feareth the Beneficent in secret and cometh with a contrite heart. (50:33 Quran)

Enter it in peace. This is the day of immortality. (50:34 Quran)

There they have all that they desire, and there is more with Us. (50:35 Quran)

We are best aware of what they say, and thou, O Muhammad, are in no wise a compeller over them. But warn by the Quran him who feareth My threat. (50:45 Quran)

Those who have given deep thoughts to the world are those who have controlled the activity of their minds.

He is thoughtful whose mind is directed by his will, whose mind fulfills his intentions, whose mind is under the control of his intention. Only those who have controlled the activity of their minds have given deep thoughts to the world. Those whose minds are working mechanically like a machine, or just reflecting the activity of those around them, may appear to be living beings, but the mystic would say differently; for it is not till a person has gained mastery over his mind, till he is above this activity, that he is a ruling power, a true person.

When we think about it, we find that all the things that are accomplished in this world are accomplished by the power of mind. Whatever man creates in science, in art, in phenomena or wonder making, in poetry, in music, in pictures, in everything that he brings into being, is all achieved by the power of mind.

Mastery lies not merely in stilling the mind, but in directing it towards whatever point we desire, in allowing it to be active as far as we wish, in using it to fulfill our purpose, in causing it to be still when we want to still it. He who has come to this has created his heaven within himself; he has no need to wait for a heaven in the hereafter, for he has produced it within his own mind now.

People pursue spirituality with their brain: that is where they are mistaken. Spirituality is attained through the heart. What do I mean by the heart? Is it the nervous center in the midst of the breast, the small piece of flesh that doctors call the heart? No, the definition of the heart is that it is the depth of the mind, the mind being the surface of the heart. That in us which feels is the heart, that which thinks is the mind. It is the same thing which thinks and feels, but the direction is different: feeling comes from the depth, thought from the surface. When thought is not linked with feeling it is just like a plant rising up from the earth, the root of which has not gone deep. A thought without feeling is a powerless thought; it is just like a plant without a deep root. A tree the root of which has gone deep into the earth is stronger, more reliable, and so the thought deeply rooted in the heart has greater power. *Hazrat Inayat Khan*

Surah Fifty-One

Adh Dhariyat

He who depends upon his eyes for sight, his ears for hearing and his mouth for speech, he is still dead.

It is the soul that sees, but we attribute sight and hearing to the eyes and ears. In absence of the soul neither the body nor the mind can see. When a person is dead the eyes are there, but they cannot see; the ears are there, but they cannot hear. When the eyes are closed, do you think that the soul sees nothing? It sees. When the ears are closed, do you think that the soul hears nothing? It hears.

If we depend on our eyes for sight, and our ears for hearing, and our mouth for speech, we are still dead. But we sometimes experience in life that which we see without eyes, hear without ears, and express without speech. If we have once seen without eyes, does it not show that we can see without eyes? Can we not see in a dream without eyes? Therefore, the faculty of seeing and hearing is in us. But, as we always depend on the physical body, on the physical eyes and ears, we become helpless and subject to death.

The teaching of immortality is to awaken. We must rise above the physical and material conditions if we are to live at all. We must aim at being independent of physical sight and hearing. We know that if we really want to understand a thing, we close our eyes because we can see it better. If we are thinking in this manner, it means that we are listening to some thought coming from some other plane. At such a time we want to cut off and stop outward sound or sight. All the meditations and concentrations of the mystics, as well as their dreams, are their journeys to the inner planes. It is necessary, if the soul has the desire to know the past, the present, and the future, to satisfy its desire by a contemplative life. The more tired and exhausted the mind, the more is meditation needed.

Sages, such as St. Francis, have spoken with rocks, birds, and animals, not as we talk, but by means of an insight into things. And every object expressed itself to them, speaking to them about its past, its present, and its future. The seer will see all in his consciousness, and wherever he casts his glance, he will see still more clearly. Hazrat Inayat Khan

In the name of Allah, the Beneficent, the Merciful

Lo! Those who keep from evil will dwell amid gardens and water-springs (51:15 Quran)

Taking that which their Lord giveth them, for lo, aforetime they were doers of good. (51:16 Quran)

They used to sleep but little of the night. (51:17 Quran)

And ere the dawning of each day would seek forgiveness. (51:18 Quran)

And in their wealth the beggar and the outcast had due share. (51:19 Quran)

And in the earth are portents for those whose faith is sure. (51:20 Quran)

And also in yourself. Can ye then not see? (51:21 Quran)

And in the heavens in your providence and that which ye are promised. (51:22 Quran)

And by the Lord of the heavens and the earth, it is the truth, even as it is true that ye speak. (51:23 Quran)

Hath the story of Abraham's honored guests reached thee, O Muhammad? (51:24 Quran)

When they came unto him and said: Peace! He answered, Peace! And thought: folk unknown to me. (51:25 Quran)

Then he went apart unto his housefolk so that they brought a fatted calf. (51:26 Quran)

And he set it before them, saying: will you not eat? (51:27 Quran)

Then he conceived a fear of them. They said: fear not, and gave him tidings of the birth of a wise son. (51:28 Quran)

Then his wife came forward, making moan, and smote her face, and cried: a barren old woman! (51:29 Quran)

They said: even so with thy Lord. Lo! He is the Wise, the Knower. (51:30 Quran)

The afterlife is like a gramophone; man's mind brings the records; if they are harsh, the instrument produces harsh notes, if beautiful then it will sing beautiful songs. It will produce the same records that man has experienced in this life.

There is a story of a murshid and a mureed. The mureed said, 'O, Teacher, I should like to see heaven.' The teacher said, 'Yes, this is the way you should meditate in order to see heaven.' So the mureed went and did so; but the vision of heaven which he had was not as described in the scriptures, a place where one enjoys nothing but comfort and luxury, milk and honey, marble halls and white robes, beautiful gems and jewels, garlands of flowers, and the waving of palms. He could not see any of these, and he asked himself, 'Has the murshid perhaps shown me a wrong heaven, or have the prophets given a wrong message in the scriptures?'

So he went back to his teacher saying, 'Now I should like to see hell.' The murshid said, 'Yes, this is the way you should meditate in order to see hell.' And then the mureed did this, and he saw in a trance that there was certainly such a place, but there was no fire or snakes or serpents or thorns or tortures or imps or flames such as have been described to people throughout the ages. So he could not understand whether his vision was right or wrong; and he went back to the teacher, and said, 'I have seen in this way: I have not seen in heaven the things that are promised, nor have I seen in hell the things which are foretold as being there.' 'O,' the teacher said, 'all the things promised for the hereafter you will have to take there from here. They are not kept ready for you; you will have to bring them with you. If you take sorrows with you, you will find them there; if you take hatred, you will find it there. Your mind is like a gramophone record, and if you use a harsh voice, the instrument produces a harsh note; if beautiful words and tones, it will sing beautiful words and tones. It will produce the same record that you have experienced in life. Indeed you have not to wait till after death in order to experience it; you are experiencing it even now.'

Everything is reproduced before us now, if we would only listen to it and perceive it. Every good or bad word or deed is reproduced before us, though it seems as in a dream.

If we watched life keenly, we should see how true this is. Joy, sorrow, love, all depend on our thought, on the activity of our mind. If we are depressed, if we are in despair, it is still the work of our mind; our mind has prepared that for us. If we are joyful and happy, and all things are pleasant, that also has been prepared for us by our mind. *Hazrat Inayat Khan*

Surah Fifty-Two

At Tur

We cover our spirit under our body, our light under a bushel; we never allow the spirit to become conscious of itself.

The life one recognizes is only the mortal aspect of life. Very few have ever seen or been conscious of the immortal aspect at all. Once one has realized life that which one has hitherto called life is found to be only a glimpse or shadow of the real life that is beyond comprehension. To understand it one will have to raise one's light high from under the cover that is hiding it like a bushel. This cover is man's mind and body; it is a cover that keeps the light active on the world of things and beings. 'Do not keep your light under a bushel' means that we are not to keep the consciousness absorbed in the study of the external world, and in its pleasures and enjoyments.

We cover our spirit under our body. We cover our light under a bushel. We never allow the spirit to become conscious of itself. When the soul is illuminated it will desire to find some other soul illuminated in like manner, and will find great joy and bliss in its society. Such a one will surely find others who are on the verge of illumination. Even a drunkard will find others to drink with. And so it is mystically. A very little light can be turned into a flame, and that flame into a very big flame.

Why is it better to become a mystic than to remain a drunkard? As a matter of fact a drunkard will never be satisfied. The mystic will look for what Omar Khayyam calls wine, the wine of the Christ, after drinking which no one will ever thirst. He will always seek the wine whose intoxication never wears off. It is the only wine: the intoxication of the divine love.

According to the belief of a Sufi the heart is the shrine of God, and when the doors of the shrine are closed it is just like a light being hidden under a bushel. God is Love. If He is love He does not stay in the heavens. His earthly body is the heart of man. Hazrat Inayat Khan

In the name of Allah, the Beneficent, the Merciful

Lo! Those who keep their duty dwell in gardens and delight. (52:17 Quran)

Happy because of what their Lord hath given them, and because their Lord hath warded off from them the torment of hell-fire. (52:18 Quran)

And it is said unto them: eat and drink in health as a reward for what ye used to do. (52:19 Quran)

Reclining on ranged couches. And We wed them unto fair ones with wide, lovely eyes. (52:20 Quran)

And they who believe and whose seed follow them in faith. We cause their seed to join them there, and We deprive them of naught of their life's work. Every man is a pledge for that which he hath earned. (52:21 Quran)

And We provide them with fruit and meat such as they desire. (52:22 Quran)

There they pass from hand to hand a cup wherein is neither vanity nor cause of sin. (52:23 Quran)

And they go round, waiting on them manservants of their own, as they were hidden pearls. (52:24 Quran)

And some of them draw near unto others, questioning. (52:25 Quran)

Saying: Lo! Of old, we were with our families, we were ever anxious. (52:26 Quran)

But Allah hath been gracious unto us and hath preserved us from the breath of Fire. (52:27 Quran)

Lo! We used to pray unto Him of old. Lo! He is the Benign, the Merciful. (52:28 Quran)

Therefore warn men, O Muhammad. By the grace of Allah thou art neither madman, nor soothsayer. (52:29 Quran)

The Belief in God ~ Hazrat Inayat Khan

It is the spirit of all souls which is personified in all ages as God. There are periods when this spirit is materialized in the faith of humanity and worshiped as God, the Sovereign and the Lord of both the worlds, as Judge, Sustainer and Forgiver; but there are periods when this realization has become less in humanity, when mankind has become absorbed in the life of the world more than in the spiritual ideal. Therefore the belief in God comes to humanity like tides in the sea. Every now and then it appears on the surface mostly with a Divine Message given as an answer to the cry of humanity at a certain period. So in the life of individuals at times the belief in God comes as tides in the sea, with an impulse to worship, to serve God, to search for God, to love God and to long for God-communication. The more the material life of the world is before one's eyes the more the spiritual impulse is closed. The spiritual impulse therefore follows times of sorrow and of disappointment through life.

The belief in God is natural, but in life both art and nature are necessary. So God Who exists independent of our making Him, must be made by us for our own comprehension. To make God intelligible first man must make his God. It is on this principle that the idea of many gods and the custom of idol worship was based in the ancient religions of the world. God cannot be two. The God of each is the God of all, but in order to comprehend that God we each have to make our own God. Some of us seek justice, we can seek for God Who is just. Some of us look for beauty, we must find it in the God of beauty. Some of us seek for love, we must find it in the God of mercy and compassion. Some of us wish for strength and power, we must find it in the God Almighty. The seeking of every soul in this world is different, distinct and peculiar to himself, and he can best attain to it by finding the object of his search in God.

Those who out of their materialistic view cannot believe in the God-ideal lose a great deal in their lives. That ideal which is the highest and best ideal, the only ideal worth loving, worth worshiping, worth longing for, worth sacrificing all one has, and worth depending upon during the daylight and through the darkness of night, is God; and he who has God in his life has all he needs; he who has not God, he, having all things of this mortal world, is lonely, he is in the wilderness even if he be in the midst of the crowd. The journey of the Sufi, therefore, is to God. It is Divine Knowledge which he seeks, it is the realization of God consciousness which is his goal.

Surah Fifty-Three

An Najm

When we devote ourselves to the thought of God, all illumination and revelation is ours.

The whole aim of the Sufi is, by thought of God, to cover his imperfect self even from his own eyes, and that moment when God is before him and not his own self, is the moment of perfect bliss to him.

The Sufi realizes the truth of his being, and his whole life becomes an attitude of prayer, in spite of his free thought and his rising above good and bad, right and wrong. When a person loves, he may be in the crowd, and yet be unaware of those around him, being absorbed in the thought of the beloved. And so it is with the love of God. He who loves God may be in the crowd, yet, being in the thought of God he is in seclusion. To such a person the crowd makes no difference. Sadi says, 'Prayer is the expansion of the limited being to the unlimited, the drawing closer of the soul to God.' Those who realize the truth of their being, they recognize their God ideal in all of His creation. They see their divine Beloved in all manifestations, in every name and form.

The ultimate freedom of the soul is gained by concentration, by meditation, by contemplation, and realization. What concentration is needed for the freedom of the soul? The concentration on that object which is prescribed by one's spiritual teacher, that by the thought of that particular object one may be able to forget oneself for a moment. And then what contemplation is necessary? The contemplation that 'this, my limited self, is no longer myself but God's own instrument, God's temple, which is made in order that the Name of God be glorified'. What meditation is required? The meditation on the thought of God, the Being of God, forgetting absolutely one's limited self. And the realization is this, that then whatever voice comes to one is God's voice, every guidance is God's guidance, every impulse is divine impulse, every action is done by God. It is in this way that the soul is made free, and in the freedom of the soul lies the purpose of life.

Is not God enough for our souls, and is He not sufficient to inspire us and to illuminate our wills and guide our souls? Is He any less of a friend here or in the spirit life? He is the great well-wisher. In Him mercy is complete. He is the Soul of all souls. When we devote ourselves to the thought of Him, all illumination and revelation are ours. Hazrat Inayat Khan

In the name of Allah, the Beneficent, the Merciful

By the star when it setteth. (53:1 Quran)

Your comrade erreth not, nor is deceived (53:2 Quran)

Nor doeth he speak of his own desire. (53:3 Quran)

It is naught save an inspiration that is inspired (53:4 Quran)

Which one of might powers hath taught him? (53:5 Quran)

One vigorous, and he grew clear to view. (53:6 Quran)

When he was on the uppermost horizon. (53:7 Quran)

Then he drew nigh and came down. (53:8 Quran)

Till he was distant two bows' length or even nearest. (53:9 Quran)

And He revealed unto His slave that which He revealed. (53:10 Quran)

The heart lied not in seeing what it saw. (53: 11 Quran)

Will ye then dispute with him concerning what he seeth? (53:12 Quran)

And verily he saw him yet another time. (53:13 Quran)

By the Lote-tree of the utmost boundary. (53:14 Quran)

Nigh unto which is the Garden of Abode. (53:15 Quran)

When that which shroudeth did enshroud the Lote-tree. (53:16 Quran)

The eye turned not aside nor yet was overbold. (53:17 Quran)

Verily he saw one of the greater revelations of his Lord. (53:18 Quran)

Those who avoid enormities of sin and abomination, save the unwilled offences—for them, lo, thy Lord is of vast mercy. He is best aware of you from the time when He created you from the earth, and when ye were hidden in the bellies of your mothers. Therefore ascribe not purity unto yourselves. He is best aware of him who wardeth off evil. (53:32 Quran)

The mystic desires what Omar Khayyam calls wine; the wine of Christ, after drinking which, no one will ever thirst.

There are many ideas which intoxicate man, many feelings there are which act upon the soul as wine, but there is no stronger wine than the wine of selflessness. It is a might and it is a pride that no worldly rank can give. To become something is a limitation, whatever one may become. Even if a person were to be called the king of the world, he would still not be emperor of the universe. If he were the master of earth, he would still be the slave of Heaven. It is the person who is no one, who is no one and yet all. The Sufi, therefore, takes the path of being nothing instead of being something. It is this feeling of nothingness which turns the human heart into an empty cup into which the wine of immortality is poured. It is this state of bliss which every truth-seeking soul yearns to attain.

Wine is symbolical of the soul's evolution. Wine comes from the annihilation of grapes, immortality comes from the annihilation of self. I drink the wine of Thy divine presence and lose myself in its intoxication.

There is a wine which the mystic drinks, and that wine is ecstasy. A wine so powerful that the presence of the mystic becomes as wine for everyone who comes into his presence. That intoxication is the love which manifests in the human heart. What does it matter, once a mystic has drunk that wine, whether he is sitting amongst the rocks in the wilderness, or in a palace? It is all the same. The palace does not deprive him of the mystic's pleasures, and neither does the rock take them away. He has found the kingdom of God on earth, about which Jesus Christ said, 'Seek ye first the kingdom of God, and all these things shall be added unto you.' *Hazrat Inyat Khan*

Surah Fifty-Four

Al Qamr

God-communication is the best communication that true spiritualism can teach us.

The most profound inspiration comes always from the divine mind, and to God alone the credit is due. Even if an inspiration comes through the mind of a person living on earth or through a soul who has passed on to the other side, it still has come from God, for all knowledge and wisdom belong to God.

It is a fault on the part of mankind to attribute inspiration to some limited being who is nothing but a shadow covering God. When a person believes that an old Egyptian comes from the other side to inspire him or that an American Indian comes to lead him on his way, he builds a wall between himself and God. Instead of receiving directly from the source that is perfect and all sufficient, he is picturing his limited idea, making it a screen between himself and God.

Is not God enough for our souls, and is He not sufficient to inspire us and to illuminate our wills and guide our souls? Is he any less of a friend here or in the spirit life? He is the great well-wisher. In Him mercy is complete. He is the Soul of all souls. When we devote ourselves to the thought of Him, all illumination and revelation are ours. God-communication is the best communication that true spiritualism can teach us.

Thus the ultimate purpose, for which the soul is seeking every moment of our life, is our spiritual purpose. And you may ask how to attain to that purpose. The answer is that what you are seeking for is within yourself. Instead of looking outside, you must look within. The way to proceed to accomplish this is for some moments to suspend all your senses such as sight, hearing, smell, touch, in order to put a screen before the outside life. And by concentration and by developing that meditative quality you will sooner or later get in touch with the inner Self which is more communicative, which speaks more loudly than all the noises of this world. And this gives joy, creates peace, and produces in you a self-sufficient spirit, a spirit of independence, of true liberty. The moment you get in touch with your Self you are in communion with God. It is in this way, if God-communication is sought rightly, that spirituality is attained. Hazrat Inayat Khan

In the name of Allah, the Beneficent, the Merciful

The hour drew nigh and the moon was rent in twain. (54: 1 Quran)

And if they behold a portent they turn away and say: Prolonged illusion. (54:2 Quran)

They denied the Truth and followed their own lusts. Yet everything will come to a decision. (54:3 Quran)

And surely there hath come unto them news, whereof the purport should deter. (54: 4 Quran)

Effective wisdom, but warnings avail not. (54:5 Quran)

And in truth We have made the Quran easy to remember, but is there any that remembered? (54:22 Quran)

And every small and great thing is recorded. (54:53 Quran)

Lo! The righteous will dwell among gardens and rivers. (54:54 Quran)

Firmly established in the favor of a Mighty King. (54:55 Quran)

Religion 1 ~ Hazrat Inayat Khan

In the ancient Sanskrit language the word for religion is Dharma, which means duty. Now, there are two things in the world, one of which we may describe as free choice of action and the other as duty. Everybody follows either the way of free choice or the way of duty. As an example we may think of the child which sees the fire, and wants to touch it, and does so. This action will show a certain disagreeable result which teaches the child a certain thing. This teaching might also have come to the child as a warning from the parents, telling the child that the result of the action would be burning. The child might thus refrain from doing a certain action for the reason that it accepted the warning of the parents before burning its hand.

Every child is born in life a pupil, one who is willing to learn and willing to believe. It is certain that if one had not been born a believer one would never have learned the language of one's country, because if anyone had tried to teach the words and one had refused to accept the teaching as true, one would never have learned the names and character of things. For instance, if it were said, 'This is water,' and one had not believed it, and had thought, 'It is fruit.' Then one would never really have known what water was and what fruit. Child is born with the tendency to believe and learn what it is taught.

The divine life has a certain capability to give life, and it gives this life as teaching to the children of earth, and this teaching is called Dharma, religion. Religions are many and different from one another, but only in form, for water is one and the same element, and formless, only it takes the shape of the channel which holds it and which it uses for its accommodation; and so the name water is changed into river, lake, sea, stream, pond, etc. So it is with religion; the essential truth is one, but the aspects are different. Those who fight about external forms will always fight, those who recognize the inner truth will not disagree, and thus will be able to harmonize the people of all religions.

Dharma has been given from time to time to the world, at times quietly, and sometimes with a loud voice; but it is a continual outpouring of the inner knowledge, of life, and of divine blessing. Those who stick to their old forms, closing their eyes from the inner truth, paralyze their Dharma by holding on to an old form, while refusing the present stream that is sent. As life is the cause of activity, so such persons lose their activity; they remain where they are and are as dead. And when man has been thus paralyzed and shut out from further spiritual progress, he clings to outer forms which are not progressing. There was a time when the message was given while the people were wanting a messenger to come. During the time of Jesus Christ there were thousands and millions waiting for a messenger to come from above. The Master came, and did his service, and went away. Some realized then, and some are still waiting. But the One Who claimed to be Alpha and Omega is never absent; sometimes he appears on the surface, sometimes he is reserving himself.

When directed by the new spiritual inspiration law, morals, education, and all departments of life come to new life; but if the spiritual current is lacking, then there is no further progress in the forms of life. People mostly think that the spiritual message must be something concrete and definite in the way of doctrines or principles; but that is a human tendency and does not belong to the divine nature, which is unlimited and life itself. The divine message is the answer to the cry of souls, individually and collectively; the divine message is life, and it is light. The sun does not teach anything, but in its light we learn to know all things. The sun does not cultivate the ground nor does it sow seed, but it helps the plant to grow, to flower, and to bear fruit.

The Sufi Message, in its utter infancy, strikes the note of the day, and promises the fulfillment of that purpose for which, now and then, the blessing from above descends, for spreading love and peace on earth and among men.

Surah Fifty-Five

Ar Rahman

Our limited self is a wall separating us from the Self of God.

In order to reach spiritual perfection the first thing is to destroy this false self. First this delusion must be destroyed. And this is done by the ways taught by the great teachers, ways of concentration and meditation, by the power of which one forgets oneself and removes one's consciousness from oneself, in other words rises from one's limited being. In this way a person effaces himself from his own consciousness, and places God in his consciousness instead of his limited self. And it is in this way that he arrives at that perfection which every soul is seeking.

Real justice cannot be perceived until the veil of selfishness has been removed from his eyes. The least spark of selfishness will prevent man from being just; he will continue to have a partial interest, because he will be looking after his own interest. Whatever furthers his own interests, he will call his right and his justice.

The prophets and the holy ones have all recognized the justice of God as the only real justice. What is the nature of the justice of God? It cannot be read in scripture; it cannot be learned from a book; it can only be learned from the Self within after selfishness has been removed. Our limited self is like a wall separating us from the Self of God. God is as far away from us as that wall is thick. Hazrat Inayat Khan

In the name of Allah, the Beneficent, the Merciful

He created man of clay like the potter's. (55:14 Quran)

And Jinn did He create of smokeless fire. (55:15 Quran)

Lord of the two Easts and Lord of the two Wests. (55:17 Quran)

He hath loosed the two seas, they meet. (55:19 Quran)

There is a barrier between them. They encroach not one upon the other. (55:20 Quran)

There cometh forth from both of them the pearl and the coral stone. (55:22 Quran)

His are the ships displayed upon the sea, like banners. (55:24 Quran)

Everyone that is thereon will pass away. (55:26 Quran)

There remaineth but the countenance of thy Lord of Might and Glory. (55:27 Quran)

But for him who feareth the standing before the Lord there are two gardens. (55:46 Quran)

Wherein are two fountains flowing. (55:50 Quran)

Wherein is every kind of fruit in pairs. (55:52 Quran)

Reclining upon couches, lined with silk brocade, the fruit of both gardens near to hand. (55:54 Quran)

Which is it, of the favors of your Lord that ye deny? (55:55 Quran)

Blessed be the name of thy Lord, Mighty and Glorious. (55:78 Quran)

The Manner of Prayer ~ Hazrat Inayat Khan

There are three kinds among those who are in the habit of offering prayer.

There is one who by praying fulfills a certain duty which he considers as one among all the duties of life. He does not know to whom he is praying, he thinks to some God. If he is in the congregation he, of necessity, feels obliged to do as the others do. He is like one among the sheep who goes on, he does not know where and why. Prayer to him is something that he must do because he is put in a situation where he cannot help it. In order to fall in with the custom of the family or community, and in order to respect those around him, he does it as everybody else. His prayer is mechanical, and if it makes any effect it is very little.

And the second kind of person who offers his prayers is the one who offers the prayers because he is told to do so and yet is confused if there is any God, if his prayers are really heard. He may be praying and at the same time confusion may be going on in his mind; 'Am I doing right or wrong?' If he is a busy man he might think 'Am I giving my time to something really profitable, or am I wasting it? I see no one before me, I hear no answer to my prayer.' He does it because he was told by someone to do it or because it might bring him some good. His prayer is a prayer in the dark. The heart which must be opened to God is covered by his own doubt, and if he prayed in this way for a thousand years it is never heard. It is this kind of soul who in the end loses his faith, especially when he meets with a disappointment, and he prays, and if his prayer is not answered that puts an end to his belief.

Then there is a third person who has imagination which is strengthened by faith. He does not only pray to God but he prays before God, in the presence of God. Once the imagination has helped man to bring the presence of God before him, God in his own heart is wakened. Then before he utters a word it is heard by God. When he is praying in a room he is not alone, he is there with God. Then God to him is not in the highest Heaven but next to him, before him, in him. Then Heaven to him is on earth and the earth for him is Heaven. No one to him is then so living as God, so intelligible as God, and the names and forms before him, all are covered under Him. Then every word of prayer he says, it is a living word. It does not only bring him blessing, but blessings to all those around him. It is this manner of prayer which only is the right way of prayer, and by this manner the object that is to be fulfilled by prayer is accomplished.

Surah Fifty-Six

Al Waqiab

The wisdom and justice of God are within us, and yet they are far away, hidden by the veil of the limited self.

Whenever wars have occurred, whenever there has been bloodshed in the world, whenever there have been revolutions and upheavals in life, all the various disasters that have taken place are due to these same causes: on the one side man's selfishness, and on the other his lack of understanding of the law of nature and the law of happiness.

Our limited self is like a wall separating us from the Self of God. God is as far away from us as that wall is thick. The wisdom and justice of God are within us, and yet they are far away under the covering of the veil of the limited self. Whoever has arrived at that realization of the nature of God's justice is able to see all things in a different way from others. His whole outlook on life becomes different.

Man has now become cold, ignorant, and blind to the law that life depends on the happiness of those with whom we live. The whole of life is one. In all these different names and manifestations life is one. The true thought is, 'If my wife is not happy, if my children, my neighbors, my servants are not happy, how can I ever be happy?' An insult given to someone will one day return. How simple it is. Yet how difficult for man to understand! It is simple to him who observes life keenly. It is difficult to him who is absorbed in himself. Hazrat Inayat Khan

In the name of Allah, the Beneficent, the Merciful

And foremost in the race, the foremost in the race. (56:10 Quran)

Those are they who will be brought nigh. (56:11 Quran)

In gardens of delight. (56:12 Quran)

A multitude of those of old. (56:13 Quran)

And a few of those of late time. (56:14 Quran)

On lined couches. (56:15 Quran)

Reclining therein face to face. (56:16 Quran)

There wait on them immortal youths. (56:17 Quran)

With bowls and ewers and a cup from a pure spring. (56:18 Quran)

Wherefrom they get no aching of the head nor any madness. (56:19 Quran)

And fruit that they prefer. (56:20 Quran)

And flesh of fowls that they desire. (56:21 Quran)

And there are fair ones with wide, lovely eyes. (56:22 Quran)

Like unto hidden pearls. (56:23 Quran)

Reward for what they used to do. (56:24 Quran)

There hear they no vain speaking nor recrimination. (56:25 Quran)

Naught but the saying: Peace, and again, Peace. (56:26 Quran)

Therefore, O Muhammad, praise the name of thy Lord, the Tremendous. (56:96 Quran)

The Present Need of the World ~ Hazrat Inayat Khan

If one truly observes the present condition of humanity, no one with sense will deny the fact that the world today needs the Religion. Why I say the religion and not a religion, is because there are many religions existing today called a religion, but what is needed today is the religion. And now coming to the question what the religion must be. Must it be a new religion? If it were a new religion, it could not be called the religion; then it would be like many religions. I call the religion that religion which one can see by rising above the sects and differences which divide men; and by understanding the religion, we shall understand all religions which may be called a religion.

I do not mean that all the religions are not religion; they are the notes, there is the music, and that music is the religion. Every religion strikes a note, a note which strikes the demand of humanity in a certain epoch. But at the same time, the source of every note is the same music which manifests, when the notes are arranged together. In this way I want to explain that all the different religions are the different notes and when they are arranged together they make music. You may ask why at each epoch all the music was not given; only a single note? In answer I say, there are times in the life of an infant when a rattle is sufficient, for the violin another time in life comes. During the time of the Chaldeans, Arabs, Romans, Greeks, different religious ideals were brought. To the few music was brought, to the many only a note. This shows this music has always existed, only that man in general was not ready to grasp it, and so was given only one note. But the consequence was that the person who was given the C note and another the G note, they fought together; each saying 'the note given to us is the right note'; and there have always existed souls who have said 'G is right', and others who said 'C is right'; all are right notes, and when they are mixed together then there is music.

This shows that there is an outer substance of religion which is the form, and the inner essence which is wisdom. When wisdom has blessed the soul, then the soul has heard the divine music. And the words of Christ I am Alpha and Omega, what do they mean.' That it was only when He came as Jesus' No, that music belongs to Alpha and Omega, and First and the Last. Those who tuned their hearts to listen to music, who elevated their souls high enough, they heard this divine music. But those who played with their rattle, their unique note they disputed one with the other; they would have refused a violin; they were not ready for it, they would not have known how to use it.

Today the world is starved more for religion than ever before; and what is the reason? The reason is that some simple souls, attached to the faith of their ancestors held their faith with esteem, considering religion necessary in life; but many souls, with intelligence and reason and understanding of life, rebelled against religion, as the child when grown up throws away his rattle, he is no longer interested in it. So today the condition is that religion remains in the hands of those who have kept it in its outer form out of devotion and loyalty to their ancestor's faith; and those who are, so to speak, grown up in mind and spirit, and want something better, they can find nothing. Their souls hunger for music, and when they ask for music they are given a rattle, and they throw away the rattle and say they do not care for music, and yet there is the inner yearning for music, the soul's music, and without it their life becomes empty. How few recognize this fact, and fewer still will admit it.

The psychological condition of humanity has become such that a person with intelligence refuses the music; he does not want the music, he wants something, but he calls it by another name. I will tell you my own experience in the Western world. Traveling for ten years I have come in contact with people of intelligence, thinkers, people of science; and in them I have seen the greatest yearning for that religion's spirit; they are longing every moment of their life for it, for they find with all their education and science there is some space empty in themselves and they want it filled but at the same time if you speak of religion they say 'No, no, speak of something else, we do not want religion'. This means they know only the rattle part of religion and not the violin part. They do not think such a thing exists which can be different from a rattle and yet there is a perplexity in themselves, a spiritual craving that is not answered even by all their learned and scientific pursuits.

Now, therefore, what is needed today in this world is a reconciliation between the religious man and the one who runs away from religion. But what can we do when we see even in the Christian religion so many sects, one opposing another; and besides the Christian the Muslim religion, the Buddhist, Jewish and many others, each considering their own and thinking the others not worth thinking about? Now to me these different religions are like different organs of the body, cut apart and thrown asunder. Therefore to me personally it seems as if one arm of the same person were cut off and rising to fight the other; both are arms of the same person, and when this person is complete; when all these parts are brought together then there is the religion.

Then what is the effort of the Sufi Order? To make a new religion? No, it is to bring together the different organs of the one body which is meant to be united and not thrown apart. Now you may ask what is our method? How do we work to bring about a reconciliation? By realizing for ourselves that the essence of all religion is one and that essence is Wisdom; and considering that Wisdom to be our religion, whatever be our own form. The Sufi Order has persons belonging to many different faiths among its members. Do you think they have given up their own religion? No. On the contrary they are firmer in their own faith by understanding the faith of others. From the narrow point of view fault may be found because they do not hate, mistrust and criticize the religion of others. They have respect for the Scripture that millions of people have held as sacred, though those scriptures do not belong to their own religion. They desire to study and appreciate other's scriptures, and so to find out that all Wisdom comes from the one Source; the Wisdom of the East and of the West.

Surah Fifty-Seven

Al Hadid
He who is looking for a reward is smaller than his reward; he who has renounced a thing has risen above it.

When doing a kindness to others the first thing that must be considered is that it should be unselfish, and not for the sake of appreciation or a reward. He who does good and waits for a reward is a laborer of good; but he who does good and disregards it is the master of good.

Life consists of a continual struggle for gain, of whatever kind it may be. Gain seems to be the purpose of life. But by a still deeper insight into the subject one sees that every gain a person has in view limits him to a certain extent to that gain, directs his activities into a certain channel, and forms the line of his fate. At the same time it deprives him of a still greater or a better gain and of the freedom of activity which might perhaps accomplish something still better. It is for this reason that renunciation is practiced by the Sufis; for with every willing renunciation a person proceeds a step towards a higher goal. No renunciation is ever fruitless. The one who is looking for a gain is smaller than his gain; the one who has renounced a thing has risen above it.

Renunciation is not a thing that can be learned or taught. It comes by itself as the soul develops; when the soul begins to see the true value of things. All that is valuable to others, a seer soul begins to see otherwise. This shows that all things that we see as precious or not precious, their value is according to the way we look at them. For one person, the renunciation of a penny is too much; for another that of all he has is nothing. It depends on how we look at things. All things one renounces in life, one rises above. Man is a slave of the thing which he has not renounced; of things that he has renounced he becomes king. This whole world can become a kingdom in his hand if a person has renounced it. But renunciation depends upon the evolution of the soul. One who has not evolved spiritually cannot well renounce. Hazrat Inayat Khan

In the name of Allah, the Beneficent, the Merciful

His is the sovereignty of the heavens and the earth. He quickeneth and He giveth death, and He is able to do all things. (57:2 Quran)

He is the First and the Last, and the Outward and the Inward, and He is Knower of all things. (57:3 Quran)

He it is Who sendeth down clear revelations unto His slave, that He may bring you forth from darkness unto light. And lo, for you, Allah is Full of Pity, Merciful. (57:9 Quran)

On the day when thou, Muhammad, wilt see the believers, men and women, their light shining forth before them and on their right hands, and wilt hear it said unto them: Glad news for you this day: Gardens underneath which rivers flow, wherein ye are immortal. That is the supreme triumph. (57:12 Quran)

Lo, those who give alms, both men and women, and lend unto Allah a goodly loan, it will be doubled for them, and theirs will be a rich reward. (57:18 Quran)

Know that the life of the world is only play, and idle talk, and pageantry, and boasting among you, and rivalry in respect of wealth and children. As the likeness of vegetation after rain, whereof the growth is pleasing to the husbandman, but afterward it drieth up and thou seest it turning yellow, then it becometh straw. And in the Hereafter there is grievous punishment and also forgiveness from Allah and His good pleasure, wherein the life of the world is but matter of illusion. (57:20 Quran)

Race one with another for forgiveness from your Lord and a Garden whereof the breadth is as the breadth of heavens and the earth, which is in store for those who believe in Allah and His messenger. Such is the bounty of Allah which He bestoweth upon whom He will, and Allah is of infinite bounty. (57:21 Quran)

Naught of the disaster befalleth in the earth or in yourselves, but it is in a Book before We bring it into being—lo, that is easy for Allah. (57:22 Quran)

That ye grieve not for the sake of that which hath escaped you, nor yet exult because of that which hath been given. Allah loveth not all prideful boasters. (57:23 Quran)

Who hoard and who enjoin upon the people avarice. And whosoever turneth away, still Allah is the Absolute, the Owner of Praise. (57:24 Quran)

We verily sent our messengers with clear proofs, and revealed with them the Scripture and the Balance, that mankind may observe right measure. And He revealed iron wherein is mighty power and many uses for mankind, and that Allah may know him who helpeth Him and His messengers, though unseen. Lo, Allah is Strong, Almighty. (57:25 Quran)

And We verity sent Noah and Abraham and placed the Prophethood and the Scripture among their seed, and among them there is he who goeth right, but many of them are evil-livers. (57:26 Quran)

Then We caused our messengers to follow in their footsteps, and We caused Jesus, Son of Mary, to follow, and gave him the Gospel, and placed compassion and mercy in the hearts of those who followed him. But monasticism they invented—We ordained it not for them—only seeking Allah's pleasure, and they observed it not with right observance. So We give those of them who believe their reward, but many of them are evil-livers. (57:27 Quran)

O ye who believe! Be mindful of your duty to Allah and put faith in His messenger. He will give you twofold of His mercy and will appoint for you a light wherein ye shall walk, and will forgive you. Allah is Forgiving, Merciful. (57:28 Quran)

That the People of the Scripture may know that they control naught of the bounty of Allah, but that the bounty is in Allah's hand to give to whom He will. And Allah is of infinite bounty. (57:29 Quran)

The poverty of one who has renounced is real riches compared with the riches of one who holds them fast.

The saints and sages and prophets all had to go through this test and trial, and in proportion to the greatness of their renunciation, so great have these souls become. Renunciation is the sign of heroes, it is the merit of saints, it is the character of the masters, and it is the virtue of the prophets. It is as Fariduddin Attar, the great Persian poet, says, 'Renounce the good of the world, renounce the good of heaven, renounce your highest ideal, and then renounce your renunciation.'

He who wants anything becomes smaller than the thing he wants; he who gives away anything is greater than the thing he gives. Therefore, to a mystic each act of renunciation becomes a step towards perfection.

Forced renunciation, whether forced by morality, religion, law, convention, or formality, is not necessarily renunciation. The real spirit of renunciation is willingness; and willing renunciation comes when one has risen above the thing one renounces.

Every step towards progress and ascent is a step of renunciation. The poverty of the one who has renounced is real riches compared with the riches of the one who holds them fast. One could be rich in wealth and poverty-stricken in reality; and one can be penniless and yet richer than the rich of the world. The final victory in the battle of life for every soul is when he has abandoned, which means when he has risen above, what once he valued most. Such is the case with all things of the world; they seem important or precious when we need them or when we do not understand them; as soon as the veil which keeps man from understanding is lifted, then they are nothing. *Hazrat Inayat Khan*

Surah Fifty-Eight

Al Mujadilah
Love for God is the expansion of the heart, and all actions that come from the lover of God are virtues; they cannot be otherwise.

The Sufi establishes his relationship with God as the relationship between him and the Beloved. His worship of God is the expansion of the heart. His love for all beings and for every being is his love for God. He cannot find anyone to love except God, because he sees God in all. If his love is shown in devotion to parents, to wife, to children if it is shown to neighbors, to a friend or in tolerating enemies, the Sufi considers this as an action of his love towards God. In this way he fulfills in his life the teaching of the Bible, ' We live and move and have our being in God.'

Jesus Christ not only told us to love our friends, but also, he went as far as to say we should love our enemies; and the Sufi treads the same path. He considers his charity of heart towards his fellow man to be love for God; and in showing love to everyone, he feels he is giving his love to God.

Love for God is the expansion of the heart, and all actions that come from the lover of God are virtues; they cannot be otherwise. There is a different outlook on life when the love of God has filled a man's heart. The lover of God will not hate anyone; for he knows that by doing so he will hate the Creator by hating His creation. He cannot be insincere, he cannot be unfaithful; for he will think that to be faithful and sincere to mankind is to be faithful and sincere to God. You can always trust the lover of God, however impractical or however lacking in cleverness he may appear to be, for simply to hold strongly in mind the thought of God purifies the soul. Hazrat Inayat Khan

In the name of Allah, the Beneficent, the Merciful

Allah hath heard the saying of her that disputeth with thee, Muhammad, concerning her husband, and complaineth unto Allah. And Allah heareth your colloquy. Lo! Allah is Hearer, Knower. (58:1 Quran)

Such of you as put away your wives by saying they are their mothers. They are not their mothers, none are their mothers except those who gave them birth—they indeed utter an ill world and a lie. And lo, Allah is Merciful, Forgiving. (58:2 Quran)

O ye who believe when you conspire together, conspire not together for crime and wrongdoing and disobedience toward the messenger, but conspire together for piety and righteousness, and keep your duty toward Allah, unto whom ye will be gathered. (58:9 Quran)

Lo! Conspiracy is only of the devil, that he may vex those who believe, but he can harm them not at all unless by Allah's leave. In Allah let believers put their trust. (58:10 Quran)

O ye who believe when it is said, Make room in assemblies, then make room. Allah will make way for you hereafter. And when it is said, Come up higher, go up higher. Allah will exalt those who believe among you, and those who have knowledge, to high ranks. Allah is informed of what ye do. (58:11 Quran)

O ye who believe when you hold conference with the messenger, offer an alms before your conference. That is better and purer for you. But if ye cannot find the wherewithal, then lo, Allah is Merciful, Forgiving. (58:12 Quran)

Fear ye to offer alms before your conference? Then when ye do it not and Allah hath forgiven you, establish worship and pay the poor-due and obey Allah and His messenger. And Allah is Aware of what ye do. (58:13 Quran)

Thy Will be Done, on Earth as it is in Heaven ~ Hazrat Inayat Khan

In the prayer of the Christian church there is a sentence: Thy Will be done, on earth as it is in Heaven. This gives a great key to metaphysics. It gives a hint to the seer—that His Will, which is easily done in Heaven, has difficulty in being done on earth. And who stands against His Will? Man. And where lies the Will of God? In the inner most being of man. And what stands as an obstacle? The surface of the heart of man; and this means struggle in man himself. In him there is the will of God and in him there is the obstacle. In the sphere within him, there is the will of God, as in Heaven; and where there is the obstacle to it, there is the earth.

By this prayer man is prepared to remove the obstacle which stands before the will of God. Now how can we distinguish between these two aspects of will: the will of God and the obstacle, which is the will of man? It is easy for a person with clear mind and open heart to distinguish, if he only knew the secret of it. For to that which is the will of God his whole being responds and in doing His will his whole being becomes satisfied. When it is his will then only one side of his being is perhaps satisfied for a certain time and there comes a conflict in himself. He himself finds fault with his idea or action. He himself feels dissatisfied with his own being. The wider the scope in which he sees his idea or his action the more dissatisfied he will become.

When in this manner, by the ray of intelligence, one sees life, one begins to distinguish between his will and the will of God. The kingdom of God, which is in Heaven, then comes on earth. It does not mean that it disappears from Heaven, but it only means that not only Heaven remains as a kingdom of Heaven, but even earth becomes a kingdom of Heaven. The purpose behind all this creation is that Heaven may be realized on the earth. And if one did not realize it on earth, he cannot realize it in Heaven.

One may ask, 'What do I mean by Heaven?' Heaven is that place where all is the choice of man and everything moves at his command. Heaven is the natural condition of life. When on earth life becomes so entangled that it loses its original harmony, Heaven ceases to exist and the motive of the soul is to gain in life the kingdom of Heaven which the soul has lost. Nothing does one attain in life which will give that satisfaction which can only be attained by bringing Heaven on earth.

Surah Fifty-Nine

Al Hashr
God is the ideal that raises mankind to the utmost height of perfection.

An ideal is something to hope for and hold on to, and in the absence of an ideal hope has nothing to look forward to. It is the lack of idealism which accounts for the present degeneration of humanity in spite of all the progress it has made in other directions. There are many kinds of ideals: principles, virtues, objects of devotion; but the greatest and highest of all ideals is the God-ideal. And when this God-ideal upon which all other ideals are based is lost, then the very notion of ideal is ignored. Man needs many things in life, but his greatest need is an ideal.

God is the ideal that raises mankind to the utmost reach of perfection. As man considers and judges his dealings with man in his conscience, so the real worshipper of God considers his dealings with God. If he has helped anybody, if he has been kind to anybody, if he has made sacrifices for anybody, he does not look for appreciation or return for his doing so to the people to whom he has done good; for he considers that he has done it for God, and therefore, his account is with God, not with those with whom he has dealt. He does not care even if instead of praising they blame him; for in any case he has done it for God, who is the best judge and the knower of all things.

There is no ideal that can raise the moral standard higher than the God-ideal, although love is the root of all and God is the fruit of this. Love's expansion and love's culmination and love's progress all depend upon the God-ideal. How much a man fears his friend, his neighbor, when he does something that might offend him whom he loves, whom he respects; and yet how narrow is his goodness when it is only for one person or for certain people! Imagine if he had the same consideration for God, then he would be considerate everywhere and in dealing with all people; as in a verse of a Sufi which says, 'Everywhere I go I find Thy sacred dwelling-place; and whichever side I look I see Thy beautiful face, my Beloved.' Hazrat Inayat Khan

In the name of Allah, the Beneficent, the Merciful

And those who came into the faith after them say: Our Lord! Forgive us and our brethren who were before us in faith, and place not in our hearts any rancor toward those who believe. Our Lord! Thou art full of Pity, Merciful. (59:10 Quran)

O ye who believe! Observe your duty to Allah. And let every soul look to that which it sendeth on before for the morrow. And observe your duty to Allah. Lo! Allah is informed of what ye do. (59:18 Quran)

If We had caused this Quran to descend upon a mountain, thou O Muhammad verily hadst seen it humbled, rent asunder by the fear of Allah. Such similitudes We coin for mankind that haply they may reflect. (59:21 Quran)

He is Allah than whom there is no God, the Knower of the visible and the invisible. He is the Merciful, the Beneficent. (59:22 Quran)

He is Allah than whom there is no other God, the Sovereign Lord, the Holy One, Peace, the Keeper of Faith, the Guardian of the Majestic, the Compeller, the Superb. Glorified be Allah from all that they ascribe as partner unto him. (59:23 Quran)

He is the Allah, the Creator, the Shaper out of naught, the Fashioner. His are the most beautiful names. All that is in the heavens and the earth glorifieth Him, and He is the Wise, the Mighty. (59:24 Quran)

Religion 11 ~ Hazrat Inayat Khan

Is a certain religion an important thing or is living it an important thing?

Perhaps a person belongs to the best religion there is in the world, he does not live it, but belongs to it. He says that he is a Muslim, or a Christian, or a Jew. He is sure it is the best religion, but at the same time he does not care to live it, he just belongs to it, and thinks that belonging to a certain religion that is an accepted religion is all that is needed. And people of all different religions have made it appear so, owing to their enthusiasm and forced by their mission in life; for they have made facilities for those who belong to their particular religion, saying that by the very fact of their belonging to that particular religion they will be saved on the Day of Judgment, while the others with all their good actions will not be saved, because they do not belong to that particular religion. This is a man-made idea, not God-made.

God is not the Father of one sect, God is the Father of the whole world and all are entitled to be called his children, whether worthy or unworthy. And in fact it is man's attitude toward God and truth which can bring him closer to God, which is the ideal of every soul. And if this attitude is not developed, then whatever a man's religion be, he has failed to live it. Therefore what is important in life is to try and live the religion to which one belongs or that one esteems, or that one believes to be one's religion.

But one must always know that religion has a body and has a soul. But whatever body of religion you may touch you touch the soul, but if you touch the soul you touch all its bodies, which are like its organs. And all the organs constitute one body, which is the body of the religion, the religion which is the religion of Alpha and Omega, which was and which is and which will always be. Therefore the dispute, 'I am right and you are wrong,' in the path of religion is not necessary. We do not know what is in the heart of man. If outwardly he seems to be a Jew, a Christian, a Muslim, or a Buddhist, we are not the judge of his religion, for every soul has a religion peculiar to itself, and no one else is entitled to judge its religion.

There may be a person in a very humble garb, without any appearance of belief in God or of piety or orthodoxy, and he may have a religion hidden in his heart which not everybody can understand. And there may be a person who is highly evolved and his outward conduct, which alone manifests to people's view, may appear to be altogether contrary to their own way of looking at things, and they may accuse him of being a materialist or an unbeliever, or someone who is far from God and truth. And yet we do not know; sometimes appearances are merely illusions; behind them there may be the deepest religious devotion, the highest ideal, hidden, of which we know very little.

For the Sufi, therefore, the best thing is to respect man, his belief, whatever it may be, his ideal, whatever it may be, his way of looking at life, even if it be quite different from our own way of looking at it. It is this spirit of tolerance that, when developed, will bring about the brotherhood which is the essence of religion and the want of the day. The idea, 'You are different and I am different; your religion is different and my religion is different; your belief is different and my belief is different,' that will not unite, that will only divide humanity.

Surah Sixty

Al Mumatahanah

He is wise who treats an acquaintance as a friend, and he is foolish who treats a friend as an acquaintance, and he is impossible who treats friends and acquaintances as strangers; you cannot help him.

Friendship as the average person understands it is perhaps little more than acquaintance; but in reality it is more sacred than any other connection in the world. To a sincere person, entering into friendship is like entering the gates of heaven; and a visit to his friend is a pilgrimage to a true loving friend.

When, in friendship, a thought arises, 'I will love you as you love me,' or, 'I will do to you as you do to me,' this takes away all the virtue of the friendship, because it is a commercial attitude, prevalent everywhere in the commercial world: everything is done for a return, and measure is given for measure. One ought to look upon acquaintanceship as the sowing of the seed of friendship, not as a situation forced upon one; for those who turn their backs on a man and look at him with contempt also do that to God. To think, 'That person is perhaps of no value; that person is of no importance,' is impractical, besides being unkind. As all things have their use, both flowers and thorns, both sweet and bitter, so all men are of some use; what position, what class, what race, what caste they belong to makes no difference.

Friendship with good and bad, with wise and foolish, with high and low, is equally beneficial, whether to yourself or to the other. What does it matter if another be benefited by your friendship, since you would like to be benefited by someone else's friendship? Hazrat Inayat Khan

In the name of Allah, the Beneficent, the Merciful

Verily you have in them a goodly pattern for everyone who looketh to Allah and the Last Day. And whosoever may turn away, lo, still Allah, He is the Absolute, the Owner of Praise. (60:6 Quran)

It maybe that Allah will ordain love between you and those of them with whom ye are at enmity. Allah is Mighty, and Allah is Merciful, Forgiving. (60:7 Quran)

Allah forbiddeth you not those who warred not against you on account of religion and drove you not out from your homes, that ye should show them kindness and deal justly with them. Lo, Allah loveth the just dealers. (60:8 Quran)

Prayer 1 ~ Hazrat Inayat Khan

If we can only know the joy of asking pardon even of our fellow man, when we realize we are in fault, however little it may be! And when we ask the Father of all to forgive our fault, joy, beauty, happiness, spring up in the heart in a way unknown until it is experienced. And then to think we can ask pardon of him Whose love is unlimited, while our errors are numberless and our ignorance limitless! Think of the joy of asking forgiveness from God! Every moment of our life, if we can see wisely, contains some fault or error, and asking pardon is just like purifying the heart and washing it white. Only think of the joy of humbling yourself before God!

And the blessing one can receive by prayer becomes a thousand-fold greater when that blessing is received by some few who are united in the same thought and are praying together.

Surah Sixty-One

As Saff

Insight into life is the real religion, which alone can help men to understand life.

Say to yourself. 'My ideal, my religion, my desire is to please my Lord before whom I bow my head. So when I am before anyone, I am before my Lord, my God. I must take care always to be considerate and thoughtful, lest I hurt my God.' That is the real religion. If you take care not to hurt a loved one, a friend, but do not mind hurting a servant, or wicked or foolish person that will not be real religion. Love will recognize the ideal of love, the divine ideal, in every heart, and will refrain from using words which will make others unhappy; words expressing pride, thoughtless words, sarcastic words, any word which will disturb a person's peace of mind, or hurt his sensibilities.

Good deeds, kindness, forgiveness, tolerance, acts of love, none of these are ever lost, and some day they will return to us. Even if the recipient appears ungrateful or heedless, it is all the same. There is no need to be disappointed even if he proves to be unworthy of our kindness and our love. When we realize that all life is one life, we discover that it is to that life that we give our love and kindness and mercy. Then it is bound to return to us, if not today, perhaps next week. If not next week, perhaps next year. If not here, then somewhere where we never expected it could possibly come. 'Thou shalt find it after many days.'

Though there may still be time to awaken to a true understanding of these things, it is often too late by the time that sufferings, troubles, and misery have come to the individual or to the multitude. If someone has so far failed to understand them before they actually came, perhaps he will never understand. When there is some little pain or he feels bad in himself, he may think he has some illness. But if he does not think about it, if he takes no notice of it, something worse may come. And so it has been with the world. The worst evil that has ever been should show man that it is now time to awaken and understand that it is not a study of national or social problems, not a study of religious questions that will bring an everlasting peace; but it is the insight into life which is the real religion and which alone can help man to understand life. Hazrat Inayat Khan

In the name of Allah, the Beneficent, the Merciful

And when Jesus son of Mary said: O Children of Israel! Lo, I am the messenger of Allah unto you, confirming that which was revealed before me in the Torah, and bringing good tidings of a messenger who cometh after me, whose name is the Praised One. Yet when he hath come unto them with clear proofs, they say: This is mere magic. (61:6 Quran)

And who doth greater wrong than he who inventeth a lie against Allah when he is summoned unto Al-Islam. And Allah guideth not wrongdoing folk. (61:7 Quran)

Fain would they put out the light of Allah with their mouths, but Allah will perfect his light however much the disbelievers are averse. (61:8 Quran)

Ye should believe in Allah and His messenger, and should strive for the cause of Allah with your wealth and your lives. That is better for you, if ye did but know. (61:11 Quran)

He will forgive you your sins and bring you into Gardens underneath which rivers flow, and pleasant dwellings in Gardens of Eden. That is the supreme triumph. (61:12 Quran)

And He will give you another blessing which ye love: help from Allah and present victory. Give good tidings, O Muhammad, to Believers. (61:13 Quran)

O ye who believe! Be Allah's helpers, even as Jesus son of Mary said unto the disciples: Who are my helpers for Allah? They said: We are Allah's helpers. And a party of the Children of Israel believed, while a party disbelieved. Then We strengthened those who believed against their foe, and they became the uppermost. (61:14 Quran)

Prayer 11 ~ Hazrat Inayat Khan

Often mankind thinks, 'Since God is the knower of the heart of every man what does it matter if prayer is recited and gesture or action made?

Would it not be sufficient if one sat in silence and thought of God?' And the answer is that it is according to the extent of your consciousness of prayer that your prayer reaches God.

If your body is silent and only your mind working, part of your being is praying and part is not, for you are constituted of both mind and body. Therefore, when the mind is praying the body must pray too, to make it complete. In reality God is within you, and as He is within you, you are the instrument of God and through you God experiences the external world and you are the best instrument of conveying yourself to God. Therefore, your thought, action and word makes prayer complete.

Then there is another idea. The next question is, when God already knows what we want what is good for us, what we need, why should we ask Him for it? He knows it. For this in the first place I would quote Christ's words: 'Knock, and it shall be opened unto you; ask, and ye shall receive.' In other words God knows your need, He knows what you want, but your want becomes clear when it is expressed not by the mind, or the body only but by your whole being. That is the secret.

Surah Sixty-Two

Al Jumah
The realization that the whole life must be "give and take" is the realization of the spiritual truth and the fact of true democracy; not until this spirit is formed in the individual can the whole world be elevated to the higher grade.

A child should know the moral of give and take; it must know that it should give to others what it wishes to receive from them. The great fault of humanity today is that everyone seeks to get the better of others, by which one is often caught in one's own net.

The mystic learns that life is give and take. It is not only that one receives what one gives, but also one gives what one receives. In this way the mystic begins to see the balance of life. He realizes that life is a balance, and if the gain or loss, the joy or pain of one outweighs that of another, it is for the moment, but in time it all sums up in a balance, and without balance there is no existence possible.

Real spiritual democracy we see in Jesus Christ. According to their law, some of the theologians and Pharisees wished to accuse the people who had sinned, but he told them to let him who had never sinned throw the first stone. That was the outlook of democracy. In that, Christ suggested that human nature was everywhere. However humble and low a person may be in occupation and evolution, we are none the less interdependent and require his help and service as he needs ours. However much wealth or power or rank we possess, we still depend upon the humblest and poorest person in the world. The realization that the whole of life must be give and take, is the realization of the spiritual truth and the fact of true democracy. Not until this spirit is formed in the individual himself can the whole world be raised to a higher grade of evolution. Hazrat Inayat Khan

In the name of Allah, the Beneficent, the Merciful

He it is Who hath sent among the unlettered ones a messenger of their own, to recite unto them His revelations and to make them grow, and to teach them the Scripture and Wisdom, though heretofore they were indeed in error manifest. (62:2 Quran)

Along with others of them who have not yet joined them. He is the Mighty, the Wise. (62:3 Quran)

This is the bounty of Allah, which He giveth unto whom He will. Allah is of infinite bounty. (62:4 Quran)

Say unto them, O Muhammad. Lo, the death from which ye shrink will surely meet you, and afterward you will be returned unto the Knower of the visible and the invisible and He will tell you what ye used to do. (62:8 Quran)

O ye who believe when the call is heard for the prayer of the day of congregation, hasten unto remembrance of Allah and leave your trading. That is better for you if ye did but know. (62:9 Quran)

And when the prayer is ended, then disperse in the land and seek of Allah's bounty, and remember Allah much, that ye may be successful. (62:10 Quran)

But when they spy some merchandise or pastime they break away to it, and leave thee standing. Say: that which Allah hath is better than pastime, and merchandise, and Allah is the best of providers. (62:11 Quran)

The Prophet ~ Hazrat Inayat Khan

The Prophet is the manifestation of the same spirit who can rightfully be called Alpha and Omega in its fullest expression, although the spirit of Alpha and Omega is in all beings, in a loving mother, in a kind father, in an innocent child, in a helpful friend, in an inspiring teacher. The Prophet is a mystic and greater than a mystic; the Prophet is a philosopher and greater than a philosopher; the prophet is a poet and greater than a poet, the Prophet is a teacher and greater than a teacher, the Prophet is a seer and greater than a seer. Why greater? Because he has a duty to perform, together with the blessing that he brings upon earth.

In the terms of the Eastern people the prophet is termed Paghambar. There are also two other names, Nabi and Rasul; and although each of these names is expressive of the prophet, yet each name is significant of a certain attribute of the prophet, also each of those words denotes a certain degree of his evolution. Paghambar verbally means the message bearer, and this word is used for the Holy Ones who from time to time brought a divine message to a certain community, nation or race, whenever there was need of wakening a certain people.

The Paghambar has worked as an alarm to warn people of the coming dangers; the Paghambar has brought reforms to improve the condition of his people. Nabi is the prophet who is not only for a certain section of humanity. Although he may live and move only in a limited region of the world, yet what he brings has its bearing upon the whole humanity. It may not be fulfilled in his lifetime, but a day of the fulfillment comes some time, even if it be in some centuries that all he brought reaches the whole humanity. Rasul is a term which denotes a degree advanced, where the prophet has not only brought a message to the world, but fulfilled his task during his lifetime, through all tests and trials that a prophet is meant to meet in life.

The prophet is an interpreter of the divine law in human tongue. He is an ambassador of the spiritual hierarchy, for he represents to humanity the illuminated souls who are known and unknown to the world, who are hidden and manifest, who are in the world or on the other side of the world. The prophet is an initiate, and initiator, for he is an answer to the cry of humanity of individuals and of the collectivity, the one who sympathizes with those in pain, guides those in darkness, harmonizes those who are in conflict and brings peace to the world, which always when excited with its activity of centuries loses its equilibrium.

The prophet can never tell the ultimate truth, which only his soul knows and no words can explain. His mission is therefore to design and paint and make the picture of the truth in words that may be intelligible to mankind. The bare truth not every man can see. If he can see he needs no more teaching. The prophet, so to speak, listens to the words of God in the language of God, and he interprets the same words in the human tongue. He speaks to every man in his own language, he converses with every man, standing on his own plane. Therefore he has little chance to disagree, unless there were someone who wanted disagreement and nothing else; there he cannot help.

Besides the words which even an intellectual person can speak, the prophet brings the love and the light which is the food of every soul. The very presence of the prophet may make a person see things differently, and yet he may not know that it was because of the prophet. He may only think that that which was not clear to him, or for a moment seemed different to him is now right and clear. For the prophet is a living light, a light which is greater in power than the sun, for the light of the sun can only make things clear to the eyes, but the light that the prophet brings to the world makes the heart see all that the eyes are not capable of seeing. The prophet brings love, the love of God, the Father and Mother of the whole humanity, a love that is life itself. No words nor actions can express that love. The presence of the prophet, his very being, speaks of it, if only the heart had ears to listen. Verily, to the believer all is right, and to the unbeliever all is wrong.

The principal work of the prophet is to glorify the Name of God and to raise humanity from the denseness of the earth, to open the doors of the human heart to the divine beauty which is everywhere manifested and to illuminate souls which are groping in darkness for years. The prophet brings the message of the day, a reform for that particular period in which he is born. A claim of a prophet is nothing to the real prophet. The being of the prophet, the work of the prophet, and the fulfillment of his task is itself the proof of prophethood.

Surah Sixty-Three

Al Munafiqun

The perfect life is following one's own ideal, not in checking those of others; leave everyone to follow his own ideal.

Religion in the East is not made into a thing apart from one's life, as in the West where business, profession, and other things on the one side of life, and going to church one day in the week on the other side, together constitute religion, with a prayer before going to rest. But, strictly speaking, life is religion. When one has that ideal before one with whatever occupation one is concerned, business, industry, domestic life, or whatever it is, one carries it out, trying to be worthy of it, that is religion.

We, with our narrowness of faith or belief, accuse others of belonging to another religion, another chapel or church. We say, 'This temple is better, that faith is better.' The whole world has kept on fighting and devastating itself just because it cannot understand that each form of religion is peculiar to itself. Therefore, the ideal life is in following one's own ideal. It is not in checking other people's ideals. If a certain thing is ones ideal that does not mean that another person will agree that it is best to offer prayers ten times a day. He may be doing better by following his religion in his shop than by going to a mosque and offering up a prayer twenty times a day. Perhaps somebody with that ideal cannot see that the other person's way is an ideal also. Leave everyone to follow his own ideal.

We see now that it is all a matter of his ideal whether a man differs from his neighbor, whether he is heavenly or earthly, as high as the Devas, the heavenly beings, or as low as the demons. His ideal makes him as high as the one, or as low as the demons. The greatness of man lies in the greatness of his ideal. *Hazrat Inayat Khan*

In the name of Allah, the Beneficent, the Merciful

And when it is said unto them: Come. The messenger of Allah will ask forgiveness for you, they avert their faces and thou seest them turning away, disdainful. (63:5 Quran)

They it is who say: Spend not on behalf of those who dwell with Allah's messenger that they may disperse and go away from you, when Allah's are the treasures of the heavens and the earth, but the hypocrites comprehend not. (63:7 Quran)

They say: Surely, if we return to Al-Madinah the mightier will soon drive out the weaker, when might belongeth to Allah and His messenger and the believers, but the hypocrites know not. (63:8 Quran)

O ye who believe! Let not your wealth, nor your children distract you from remembrance of Allah. Those who do so, they are the losers. (63:9 Quran)

And spend of that wherewith We have provided you before death cometh unto one of you and he saith: My Lord! If only thou wouldst reprieve me for a little while, then I would give alms and be among the righteous. (63:10 Quran)

How the Wise Make Life in the World ~ Hazrat Inayat Khan

It is not easy to learn, and after learning, to practice, how to make life in the world with harmony and peace. The desire of every person in the world is to possess all he wants, whether it belongs to him or whether it belongs to anybody else. He wants all things to last, if they are any use to him, he wants all those dear and near to him should abide close to him; all he doesn't wish to see must be exiled from the town, and at the same time even the whole nature must work to suit him, the cold must not be more than he wants, the heat must not exceed his desire, the rain must obey him, pain must not approach near. There must not be anything difficult in life and all things and people must be perfect in the perfection of God; everybody must act in life as he wishes them to, he alone must be the engineer and all others his machines. They must have all the endurance he demands, of them, at the same time all must be as sensitive as he wants them to be. No one should move against his desire, nor even a bird must fly in the sky, nor even a leaf must make a flutter — all under his command, he alone must live and all others must live, but under him. This attitude I have not spoken of someone in the world, but every individual. The world is a place where every individual wishes to be the king, so many kings and only one kingdom, and the whole tragedy of life is accounted for by this.

The wise out of wisdom, make life easy. But among the wise there are two categories, one is the Master, the other is the Saint. The attitude of both in life is quite contrary. The attitude of the Saint is to feel sympathy for the others and to see the difficulties of the situation in life of others as of himself, and to sacrifice his wants for the need of others, realizing that he knows that life is difficult, and those who are void of wisdom have still more difficulties as they know not how to surmount the difficulties of life. Out of his love, mercy and compassion he thus sacrifices his life to the service of his fellow man by making life easy for them.

In the first place he sees the worst enemy of his fellow man in himself, knowing that the nature of every ego is hostile, and by being resigned to the will of his fellow man, by sacrificing his life's advantages for his brother, he feels he has given his fellow man some relief that he could give him on his part. By practicing this moral through life at every step that a wise man takes, he becomes a source of happiness to all he meets and with whom he comes in contact in life, and his spirit becomes deepened in saintliness. The spirit of a saint results in being tuned to the whole universe, he is in tune with the climates, with the weather, with nature, with animals, birds, he becomes in tune with the trees and plants, in tune with all atmospheres, with all human beings of various natures, because he becomes the keynote to the whole universe. All harmonize with him, the virtuous souls, the wicked souls, angels and devils, all become in tune. He becomes in harmony with every object, with every element, with those who have passed from this earth he is in tune, those in the atmosphere he is in tune with them and in tune with those who live on earth. The moral of a saint is very difficult, but the spirit of the saint is a benediction to himself and blessing to others.

Then there is the way of the Master which is quite opposite. He conquers himself, he battles with life, he is in war with destiny he invades all that seems wrong to him, he finds the key to the secrets unknown to him, he instead of being resigned to all conditions, all things, all people, turns them to the shape that he wishes and molds as he likes the personalities which come in touch with him. He tunes personalities in the tune which would suit his orchestration. He has command over objects, He produces effects in objects which naturally are not there. He can even rise to a state where he can command nature, and the spiritual hierarchy is made of the masters. For the world is ruled, it is governed, although outward governments are different, inward government is the spiritual hierarchy. In the East such ones are called Wali, whose thought, whose feeling, whose glance, whose impulse can move the universe.

And yet neither of them, Saint or Master, comes to claim before the world, 'Look at me—I am a Saint' 'I am a Master' 'I can do this' or 'I am such a virtuous person' or 'a good person.' They keep themselves in humble guise, one like everybody in the world. It is not a claim, it is an action which proves the Master. And yet what do they care if the world acclaims them as a Saint or as a Master? What benefit is it to them? It is only a benefit to the one who is false, because he is glad to be something he is not; he who is all, he does not wish that everybody should recognize him as such. A person with his riches knows that he is rich, he need not put on fifty rings to tell everybody how rich he is, but the one who puts on fifty rings is seldom rich. There is a beautiful simile known in India that it is the empty vessel that makes the noise, when it is filled with water it makes no noise. In short, sincerity is the principal thing to attain in life. What little is gained sincerely and held unassumingly is worth much more than a greater gain void of sincerity, for it is a hill of sand, once the storm will come and blow it away. Verily, truth is the treasure that every soul is seeking.

Surah Sixty-Four

At Taghibun
Every man's desire is according to his evolution; that which he is ready for, is the desirable thing for him.

Which is the most desirable thing in life, to seek for the goal or to dwell in this changing life? The answer is that every person's desire is according to his evolution. That for which he is ready is desirable for him. Milk is a desirable food for the infant, other foods for the grown-up person. Every stage in life has its own appropriate and desirable things. The desire to attain to a goal must be there before reaching it; when he does not feel the desire, it is not necessary for a man to seek it.

Two of the principal sources of pleasure in the physical world are good food and bodily comfort, yet one single beautiful thought or one charming mental image may provide more pleasure and joy than all the beauty there is in the whole physical world. So we can see that when we raise the intelligence from the physical plane, and then even higher, we will come to a state of realization where we see that life is not really limited at all; that it too is unlimited. It is when our experience is confined to the lower phases of existence that we find that our life is limited. Herein lies the whole tragedy of life. Hazrat Inayat Khan

In the name of Allah, the Beneficent, the Merciful

The day when He shall gather you unto the Day of Assembling that will be a day of mutual disillusion. And whoso believeth in Allah and doth right. He will remit from him his evil deeds and will bring him into gardens underneath which rivers flow, therein to abide forever. That is the supreme triumph. (64:9 Quran)

No calamity befalleth save by Allah's leave. And whoso believeth in Allah, He guideth his heart. And Allah is Knower of all things. (64:11 Quran)

Obey Allah and obey His messenger, but if ye turn away, then the duty of Our messenger is only to convey the message plainly. (64:12 Quran)

Allah! There is no God save Him. In Allah therefore, let believers put their trust. (64:13 Quran)

O ye who believe! Lo, among your wives and your children there are enemies for you, therefore beware of them. But if ye efface and overlook and forgive, then lo, Allah is Forgiving, Merciful. (64:14 Quran)

Your wealth and your children are only a temptation, whereas Allah! With him is an immense reward. (64:15 Quran)

So keep your duty to Allah as best as you can, and listen and obey, and spend, that is better for your souls. And whoso is saved from his own greed, such are the successful. (64:16 Quran)

If ye lend unto Allah a goodly loan, He will double it for you and will forgive you, for Allah is Clement, Responsive. (64:17 Quran)

Knower of the visible and the invisible, the Wise, the Mighty. (64:18 Quran)

Master, Saint and Prophet ~ Hazrat Inayat Khan

There are two distinct paths opposite to each other, those of the Master and of the Saint. The path of the Master is a path of war, war with outer influences which prevent one from making one's way through life. The path of the Saint is also a path of battle, but it is a battle with oneself. No doubt in the path of the Master also battle with oneself is necessary, for if one did not fight with oneself one would not be able to make his way through life. But the path of the saint is a constant battle with the self, for the nature of the world is such that from the good person more good is asked; from a kind person more kindness is demanded; from a person who is patient more patience is expected; from a person who is gentle more gentleness is asked. There is no end to the world's demands: all one gives to the world, and more is asked; and always do right, and it is always wrong. Therefore there is no end to the battle in both the paths that the wise take and it is the warrior in life's path who in the end becomes victorious. Those who have not that power remain wandering about in the same place.

The work of the Master is to comfort individuals and comfort the world; the work of the Master is to keep away all disasters that might come about, caused by the in-harmony of the nature of individuals and of the collectivity; the work of the Master is to help the feeble, but right the weak and just, when he is in a situation where he is opposed by a powerful enemy. The work of the Saint is to console the wretched, to take under the wings of mercy and compassion those left alone in life, to bless the souls that come in their way.

But there is a third path of the wise in which there is a balance of the spirit of the Master and of the Saint. This line is called Kamal, or perfect or balanced, and it is on this line that the destiny of the Prophet leads him. For the Prophet's work is more difficult and complicated than that of the Master and of the Saint. To the souls who ask from him that compassion which they would ask from a Saint, he gives it; to those who ask of him that power, that strength which is necessary to be able to stand through the sweeping waves of life, the Prophet gives that. But besides, the Prophet is the Message-bearer; the Prophet is the master and a servant at the same time; the Prophet is a teacher and at the same time a pupil for there is a great deal that he must learn from his experience through life, not in order to make himself capable to receive the Message, but in order to make himself efficient enough to give the Message. For God speaks to the Prophet in His divine tongue, and the Prophet interprets it in his turn in the language of men, making it intelligible to them, and trying to put the finest ideas in the gross terms of worldly language. Therefore all is not given that the Prophet comes to give to the world in words, but all that cannot be given in words is given without words. It is given through the atmosphere; it is given by the presence; it is given by the great affection that gushes forth from his heart; it is given in his kind glance; and it is given in his benediction. And yet the most is given in silence that no earthly sense can perceive. The difference between human language and divine word is this that a human word is a pebble; it exists, but there is nothing further; the divine word is a living word, just like a grain of corn. One grain of corn is not one grain; in reality, it is hundreds and thousands. In the grain there is an essence which is always multiplying and which will show the perfection in itself.

Surah Sixty-Five

At Talaq
Discussion is for those who say, "What I say is right, and what you say is wrong." A sage never says such a thing hence, there is no discussion.

Once I was with a sage whom many people went to see. He pleased them all, and he was not fond of disputing or discussing, because to a sage there is nothing to discuss. Discussion is for those who say, 'What I say is right, and what you say is wrong.' A sage never says such a thing;

hence there is no discussion. But the world is always fighting and discussing and disputing.

Many would come and try to dispute with him, but he did his best to avoid dispute. I was very fond of listening to his way of dealing with inquirers. My friends wanted to discuss what the ideal life is. He said, 'Whatever you think it is.' But my friends were not satisfied with this. They wanted a discussion. They answered, 'Do you think this worldly life, with so many responsibilities, with strife from morning to evening, can be the ideal life?' He said, 'Yes.' They asked, 'Do you not think that the life you lead, retirement and seclusion, is the ideal life?' He answered, 'Yes.' They said, 'But how can we give up our present life, our responsibilities to our children, our occupations, and all these things that take up so much time. How can we leave that life in order to follow your ideal life?' He said, 'Do not leave it.'

They went on, 'But, if we do not leave it, how can we get on in the spiritual life?' Then the sage asked, 'What do you mean by the spiritual life?' 'We mean by spiritual life a life like yours,' they answered. He said, 'If you think my life is a spiritual life, be like me. If you think your life is a spiritual life, keep to it. It is not possible to say which life is best. If you think your worldly strife brings you happiness, just keep to it. If you think my life gives you happiness, give up your own. Whatever makes you happy and makes you think you are doing right, do it from that moment, and see what the result is. If it gives you more happiness, go on regardless of what others say. If it gives you happiness, if you are satisfied while doing it, while reaping its effect, then it is all right. Go on with it, and you will always be blessed.'

People discuss dogmas, beliefs, and moral principles, as they know them. But there comes a time in a man's life when he has touched truth of which he cannot speak in words; and at that time all dispute, discussion, argument ends. Hazrat Inayat Khan

In the name of Allah, the Beneficent, the Merciful

O Prophet! When ye men put away women, put them away for their legal period, and reckon the period, and keep your duty to Allah, your Lord! Expel not them from their houses unless they commit open immorality. Such are the limits imposed by Allah, and whoso transgresseth Allah's limits, he verily wrongeth his soul. Thou knowest not, it may be that Allah will afterward bring some new thing to pass. (65:1 Quran)

Then, when they have reached their term, take them back in kindness or part from them in kindness and call to witness two just men among you, and keep your testimony upright for Allah. Whoso believeth in Allah and the Last Day is exhorted to act thus. And whosoever keepeth his duty to Allah, Allah will appoint a way out for him. (65:2 Quran)

And will provide for him from a quarter whence he hath no expectation. And whosoever putteth his trust in Allah, He will suffice him. Lo, Allah bringeth His command to pass. Allah hath set a measure for all things. (65:3 Quran)

And for such of your women who as despair of menstruation, if ye doubt, then period of waiting shall be three months, along with those who have it not. And for those with child, their period shall be till they bring forth their burden. And whosoever keepeth their duty to Allah, He maketh his course easy for him. (65:4 Quran)

That is the commandment of Allah which He revealeth unto you. And whoso keepeth his duty to Allah, He will remit from him his evil deeds and magnify reward for him. (65:5 Quran)

Lodge them where ye dwell according to your wealth, and harass them not so as to straiten life for them. And if they are with child, then spend for them till they bring forth their burden. Then if they give suck for you, give them their due payment and consult together in kindness, but if ye make difficulties for one another, then let some other woman give suck for him the father of the child. (65:6 Quran)

Let him who hath abundance spend of his abundance, and he whose provision is measured, let him spend of that which Allah hath given him. Allah asketh naught of any soul save that which he hath given it. (65:7 Quran)

Degrees in the Spiritual Hierarchy ~ Hazrat Inayat Khan

There are seven grades recognized by the Sufis of those in the spiritual hierarchy, Pir, Buzurg, Wali, ghaus, Qutb, Nabi, Rasul. These are the degrees which come from the inner initiations, the inner initiations to which one becomes entitled on having the outer initiations which are necessary. It is beyond words to express what inner initiation means and in what form it is given. Those to whom the inner initiation is unknown may explain it as a dream or as a vision, but in reality it is something higher and greater than that. I can only explain it by saying that the definite changes which take place during one's journey through the spiritual path are initiations, and it is these initiations which include man in the spiritual hierarchy.

In the life of a Saint or a Master there are five degrees known, and the two last degrees the Progress of the Saint and of the Master is silent. But in the life of a Prophet these seven degrees manifest to view. For a Saint or a Master there is one facility, that he can do his work by avoiding the notice of the world. But the life of the Prophet necessitates his coming into the world, and thus as he progresses from grade to grade through his life, he cannot very well cover himself, however much he may want to, from the gaze of the world, though the sage of every category, saint, master or Prophet, and every degree always prefers not being known to the world, and as he progresses so that desire increases more. But it is not only out of modesty or humbleness, but also for the protection of the spiritual ideal which is developed in him, for it attracts dangers of all sorts by being exposed to the common gaze.

All beauty is veiled by nature, and the higher the beauty the more it is covered. And that makes it easy for a wise person find out the difference between a true Prophet and a false Prophet, for one beats his drums and the other tries to keep in the background, if only his work in the world would let him keep back. It is his efforts in accomplishing something that bring him to the notice of the world. However, his longing is to be unknown, for the one who really deserves being known is God alone.

Surah Sixty-Six

At Tahrim
Tolerance does not come by learning, but by insight; by understanding that each one should be allowed to travel along the path which is suited to his temperament.

The Sufi looks on all with tolerance, and knows that there is a path for everyone. The path of the lover is for him, the path of the one seeking for wealth is for him, the seeker after paradise is following his path, and it is all a journey. It is simply that there are four different routes by which the journey is made. The Sufi sees the same goal at the end of each; the lover has to meet the seeker after wealth, and both have to meet the one who has done his duty. Therefore at the end of their journey there is a place where they can meet. What does it matter if one does not go by a certain path? Let each choose the way that belongs to his own temperament and tendency. Therefore the Sufi does not worry. He gives no preference to one or the other. He sees the journey of life being made along one or other of these roads. The saying of Buddha, 'Forgive all', comes true. Forgiveness does not come by learning, it comes by understanding that a person should be allowed to travel along that path which is suited to his temperament. As long as he is journeying with open eyes, let him journey.

The great thing is that one should journey with one single desire. There should be the single desire: whether to love a beloved, to collect wealth, or to do some good for the world of humanity, or to attain paradise. There should be the desire to journey to the goal. So many do not know which the goal is or what it is. One thinks wealth is the goal, another paradise, another the beloved. They do not see that there is still a further goal. They are naturally prompted by the desire to get to the goal, and yet they are not conscious of the further goal.

Hazrat Inayat Khan

In the name of Allah, the Beneficent, the Merciful

O Prophet! Why bannest thou that which Allah hath made lawful for thee, seeking to please thy wives? And Allah is Merciful, Forgiving. (66:1 Quran)

Allah hath made lawful for you Muslims absolution of your oaths of such a kind, and Allah is your Protector. He is the Wise, the Knower. (66:2 Quran)

When the Prophet confided a fact unto one of his wives and when she afterward divulged it and Allah apprised him thereof, he made known to her part thereof and passed over part. And when he told it her she said: who hath told thee? He said: The Knower, the Aware hath told me. (66:3 Quran)

If ye twain turn unto Allah repentant, ye may have cause to do so, for your hearts desired the ban, and if ye aid one another against him, Muhammad, then lo, Allah, even He, is his Protecting Friend and Gabriel and the righteous among the believers, and furthermore the angels are his helpers. (66:4 Quran)

And Mary, daughter of Imran, whose body was chaste, therefore We breathed therein something of Our Spirit. And she put faith in the words of her Lord and His Scriptures and was of the obedient. (66:12 Quran)

The Message of Christ ~ Hazrat Inayat Khan

The words of Christ in the Bible are: 'I am Alpha and Omega', which means 'I am First and Last'. Would this then mean 'I came on earth only when I was called Jesus, I gave the message and went, and then never came again?' If that were the meaning of 'I am Alpha and Omega', it would have no meaning. Really the meaning is, 'I was, am and shall be'.

Now about the question that arises in the enquiring mind: Who may this Alpha and Omega be? What he was before Jesus Christ? What would he be like after the time of Jesus Christ?' For those who put the water of the Ocean in a pitcher that water is from the Ocean, but really the Ocean is the Ocean. For those of the different creeds who have different forms of worship and dogmas and say 'This is the teaching of Christ.' Yes it is true, but it is not all the teaching of Christ. It is as true as to say, 'This is the ocean', if one brought water from the ocean in a pitcher; it is true, but there is an ocean. This shows that a shield called Jesus Christ brought the message. It was the shield that was Jesus. This is the secret of that Alpha and Omega spirit of Christ.

If one can only see that spirit hidden behind different shields one would be constantly in the vision of Christ. In the smile of the innocent child, there is Christ, in the warmth of the mother's heart for her child Christ is hidden. In that unselfish, self-sacrificing love of the father, there Christ shows himself. In the kindly attitude of a friend you can see the spirit of Christ. What is there which has beauty, tenderness, gentleness, which has not the spirit of Christ? From those who keep Christ away from them he is far, but in reality they have covered their eyes themselves. It is not the fault of Christ, it is their own fault, not that of Christ who speaks in the whisper of the wise people of all centuries, who speaks aloud in the voice of the prophet, the Warner who comes now and then; the same coming sometimes, sometimes hiding himself, the same always. Man's doubt and skepticism prevent his seeing him. When Christ came in the form of Jesus those who saw him did not recognize him.

If you analyze what he said, what he taught was very simple. It was not elaborate words and theories, there was not any great literary skill. What was it? It was, where the arrow came from. The word was an arrow from the depth of his being. In the Bible it is often said that revelation came with a fiery tongue. What does it mean? If the heart is burning the flame comes in a word.

Where is God? God is in the Heart of man. When it is the voice of God that rises in the heart of man it is a divine word. The words of Christ are a tongue of fire that pierces the heart of man.

In the East the Christ attribute is called Mansumiat, innocence. It takes a different point of view from the ordinary one to see the value and power of innocence. Every person when born on earth is born an innocent soul. He gets the experience of the world and becomes worldly.

Surah Sixty-Seven

Al Mulk
So long as a man has a longing to obtain any particular object, he cannot go further than that object.

As a man's ideal is, so is his state of evolution. The man who is only interested in himself is very narrow and limited, whereas the man who has expanded his interests to his family and surroundings is greater; while he who expands them still further to his nation is yet greater, and he who extends them to the world at large is the greatest. But in all these cases a man is limited. The highest ideal of man is to realize the unlimited, the immortal Self within. There is no need for any higher ideal, for when man holds this ideal in his vision, he expands and becomes all he wants to be, and in time he attains to that peace which is the longing of every soul.

There is a constant desire of the soul to find its own nature. Until it finds it, it is always looking for something, though what it does not know. Is it not true of every individual in this world that, whatever may be his desire, as long as he has not attained it he is unhappy, and eager and anxious to achieve it? He is longing and suffering and doing all he can to attain it; but when he has succeeded, he does not feel happy. At once a new desire arises; if he has a thousand he wants a million; if he has done one duty there is another, and after that another. So it is with love affairs; so it is with paradise. He will never feel contented and satisfied, because fundamentally it is not the desire that he is really concerned with. Though he crosses the boundary wall of the desire he finds himself again with a new desire. And this itself proves the fact that there is really only one fundamental desire underlying all others: the desire for spiritual perfection.

Motive limits one to certain kinds of accomplishment; and it does not allow one to accomplish anything beyond the scope of that particular motive. As long as a person has the desire to attain to something with a particular motive, he cannot go further. That is why the sages have said, 'Rise above the earthly motives. Accomplish all you wish to accomplish in life, whatever be the motive, and then that itself will lead you to a stage from which you can rise above them, and above the earthly desires of the body'. Hazrat Inayat Khan

In the name of Allah, the Beneficent, the Merciful

Blessed is He in Whose hand is the Sovereignty, and He is able to do all things. (67:1 Quran)

Who hath created life and death that He may try you, which of you is best in conduct, and He is the Mighty, the Forgiving. (67:2 Quran)

Who hath created seven heavens in harmony. Thou Muhammad canst see no fault in the Beneficent One's creation, then look again: Canst thou see any rifts? (67:3 Quran)

Then look again and yet again, thy sight will return unto thee weakened and made dim. (67:4 Quran)

Lo, those who fear their Lord in secret, theirs will be a forgiveness and a great reward. (67:12 Quran)

Say unto them, O Muhammad: He it is Who gave you being, and hath assigned unto you ears and eyes and hearts. Small thanks give ye! (67:23 Quran)

Say: He it is Who multiplieth you in the earth, and unto Whom ye will be gathered. (67:24 Quran)

And they say: When will this promise be fulfilled, if ye are truthful? (67:25 Quran)

Say: The knowledge is with Allah only, and I am but a plain warner.
(67:26 Quran)

The Message of Unity ~ Hazrat Inayat Khan

Beloved ones of God, my subject for this evening is the Sufi Message. The word message itself conveys a different meaning from that of an intellectual philosophy. There are two ideas prevailing in the world, the one is that man has evolved through years and centuries, and the other idea is that as Solomon has said, there is nothing new under the sun. And that explains to us the divine truth has always been and always will be the same. No one can improve upon it and nobody can give a new Message.

It is the Divine Tongue which at times has spoken louder, and at times in a whisper and it is the consciousness of the Divine Spirit which made Christ say 'I am Alpha and Omega.' Those who limit Christ to the historic period of the life of the Prophet of Nazareth, surely limit the message, in spite of His open declaration that He is the First and the Last. Also Christ said: 'I have not come to give a new law but I have come to fulfill the law'; which means, that no new religion has ever been given, although the world has taken it so.

Man divides, God unites humanity. Man's pleasure is in thinking and feeling 'I am different from you' 'You are different from me' by nationality, by race, in creed or religion. The animals do that. But as man evolves his first tendency is to unite, to become one. Did Jesus Christ come to form an exclusive community to be named Christian or Buddha to found a creed called Buddhism? Or was it Muhammad's ideal to form a community called Muslim? On the contrary the Prophet warned His disciples that they should not attach His name to His message, but that it should be called Islam—the message of peace.

Not one of the Masters came with the thought of forming an exclusive community or to give a certain religion. They came with the same message from one and the same God. Whether the message was in Sanskrit, Zen or Arabic, it had one and the same meaning. The difference between religions is external, the inner meaning of all is one.

If only man had understood this the world would have avoided many wars, for war has mostly been caused by religion. Religion given to the world is to establish peace and harmony! What a pity that from the same source should come war and disaster!

Surah Sixty-Eight

Al Qalam

Every man's path is for himself; let him accomplish his own desires that he may thus be able to rise above them to the eternal goal.

The sages have said, 'Rise above the earthly motives. Accomplish all you wish to accomplish in life, whatever be the motive, and then that itself will lead you to a stage from which you can rise above them, and above the earthly desires of the body'. They have never said, 'Stop, and go into the jungle, and see life from our point of view'. Everybody's path is for himself. Let everyone achieve the fulfillment of his own desires so as to be able to rise above them to the eternal goal.

All our experiences are nothing but preparation for something else. Nothing that belongs to this world, however precious, must hinder one's path of progress. For every step in the direction to that spiritual gain must be the aim of every soul. Every belief and every experience for a wise person is a step of a staircase. He has taken this step, there is another step for him to take. The steps of the staircase are not made for one to stand there. They are just made for one to pass, to go further. Because life is progress. Where there is no progress there is no life. Hazrat Inayat Khan

In the name of Allah, the Beneficent, the Merciful

Nun. By the pen and that which they write therewith. (68:1 Quran)

Thou art not, for thy Lord's favor unto thee, a madman. (68:2 Quran)

And lo, thine verily will be a reward unfailing. (68:3 Quran)

And lo, thou art of a tremendous nature. (68:4 Quran)

And thou wilt see and they will see. (68:5 Quran)

Which of you is the demented. (68:6 Quran)

Lo, thy Lord is best aware of him who strayeth from his way, and He is best aware of those who walk aright. (68:7 Quran)

Lo, for those who keep from evil are gardens of bliss with their Lord. (68:34 Quran)

The Coming World Religion (1) ~ Hazrat Inayat Khan

There are many prophecies and several beliefs on this subject, but in this lecture I have no desire to make any prophecy on the subject. I only wish to explain what religion means. The present religion or the coming religion, or the past religion, is for those who divide the truth, which is one, into many. In point of fact what was is, and what is will be. Was this idea not supported by Jesus Christ, who said: 'I have not come to give a new law, I have come to fulfill the law? If Jesus Christ said this, who else can come out and say: 'I give you a new religion?' There cannot be a new religion; one could as well say, 'I wish to teach you a new wisdom.' There cannot be a new wisdom; wisdom is the same, which was and is and always will be.

There arises a question in the heart of the enquirers, 'Then what is this variety of religions which has engaged humanity for years in conflict with one another, so that most of the wars and battles were fought in the cause of religion?' This only shows the childish character of human nature. The religion which was given and is given, wherever it is given, the religion which was given for unity, for harmony, for brotherhood was used by the childish human nature to fight and to dispute and to engage themselves in battles for years and years. And the most amusing thing for a thoughtful person is to think and to see how they have given in the past history, a most sacred character to war, to battle, and called it sacred war, or holy war.

And the same tendency of making war with one another which began in their religion, persisted in the time of materialism; the same tendency turned into war between nations. And at the same time the differences and distinctions which existed between the different faiths and beliefs still exist and that prejudice and that difference and the bigotry which existed between nations still exist in a smaller or greater degree. What does it show? It shows that the meaning of true religion has not been understood by the majority. And therefore that mission that religion had to fulfill in connection with humanity still remains to be fulfilled. And it is at that fulfillment that Jesus Christ has hinted: 'I have come to fulfill the law, not to give a new law.'

For instance, a person who has a great devotion, a great love and attachment for his friends, is speaking about friendship in high words and he is saying what a sacred thing it is to become friends. But then there is another one who says: 'Oh, I know your friend, what he is; he is no better than anybody else.' The answer to this idea is given by Majnun in the story told by the ancients, where someone said to Majnun, 'Laila, your beloved, is not as beautiful as you think.' He said, 'My Laila must be seen with my eyes. If you wish to see how beautiful Laila is, you must borrow my eyes.' Therefore if you wish to regard the object of devotion of whatever faith, of whatever community, of whatever people, you will have to borrow their eyes, you will have to borrow their heart. There is no use in disputing over the points of history, over each tradition in history; they are made by prejudice. Devotion is a matter of heart and is made by the devotee.

Surah Sixty-Nine

Al Haqqah

The control of self means the control of everything.

Self-control is the most necessary thing to be learned; a person may have great spirituality, illumination and piety, but in the absence of self-control this is nothing. Self-control also is the way of happiness and peace. No thought or feeling should arise without our will. When we have gained mastery over the self, we have mastery over all things. Self-control is an attribute which distinguishes man from the animal; both have their appetites and passions, but it is man alone who can control them.

The control of the self means the control of everything. What does it mean when we see a person fail time after time, or another person succeed time after time? It is just a matter of holding the reins of our affairs in our hands. When there is no rein there is failure. Failure means that there has been lack of self-control, whether it is a failure in affairs or in health. Illness always comes when a person has lost the control of the self. It is because this is the main theme of metaphysics that Hatha Yoga has been considered of the greatest value. All the miracles and all the wonders that have ever been known in this world have been done by those who have been able to control themselves by abstinence, and therefore to control life. However much was said upon this subject, it would still not express it. To begin with a person is puzzled by it, and he wonders whether he should believe it or not. That is why in the East the adepts never speak of their experiences in the spiritual life. They only tell their disciples to lead it and practice for years. 'That will make it clear to you', they say. Hazrat Inayat Khan

In the name of Allah, the Beneficent, the Merciful

But say! I swear by all that ye see. (69:38 Quran)

And all that ye see not. (69:39 Quran)

That it is indeed the speech of an illustrious messenger. (69:40 Quran)

It is not a poet's speech—little is it that ye believe! (69:41 Quran)

Nor diviner's speech—little is it that ye remember! (69:42 Quran)

It is a revelation from the Lord of the Worlds. (69:43 Quran)

And if he had invented false sayings concerning Us. (69:44 Quran)

We assuredly had taken him by the right hand. (69:45 Quran)

And then severed his life-artery. (69:46 Quran)

And not one of you could have held Us off from him. (69:47 Quran)

And lo, it is a warrant unto those who ward off evil. (69:48 Quran)

And lo, We know that some among you will deny it. (69:49 Quran)

And lo, it is indeed an anguish for the disbelievers. (69:50 Quran)

And lo, it is absolute truth. (69: 51 Quran)
So glorify the name of thy Tremendous Lord. (69:52 Quran)

The Coming World Religion (continued) ~ Hazrat Inayat Khan

When a person is thoughtful, when a person is considerate, when a person feels the obligations that he has towards his fellow man, towards his friend, towards his father or mother, or in whatever relation he stands to man; it is something living, it is something like water which gives the sense of the living soul; the soul is not dead. It is this living soul which really makes a person alive. And the person who is not conscious of this, this tenderness, this sacredness of life, he lives, but the soul is in the grave. You do not need to ask that man what his religion is, what his belief is, for he is living it, life itself is his religion and this is the true religion. The man conscious of honor, the man who has the sense of shame, who has the feeling of sincerity, whose sympathy, whose devotion is alive, that man is living, that man is religious.

And it is this religion which has been the religion of the past and which will be the religion of the future. And religion, if ever it was taught by Christ or any other great ones, was to awaken in man that sense which is awakened when this religion is living.

It does not matter in which house you go and pray, for every moment of your life then is religion. Then it is not a religion in which you believe, but it is a religion which you live.

What is the Message of Sufism? Sufism is the Message of digging out that water like life which has been buried by the impressions of this material life. There is an English phrase: 'A lost soul.' The soul is not lost, the soul is buried, when it is dug then the divine life springs out like a spring of water. And the question is': 'What is digging? What does one dig in oneself?' Is it not true, is it not said in the scriptures that God is love? Then where is God to be found? Is He to be found in the seventh heaven, or is He to be found in the heart of man? He is to be found in the heart of man which is his shrine.

If there is any coming religion, a new religion to come, it will be this religion, the religion of the heart. After all the suffering that has been caused to humanity by the recent war, man is beginning to open his eyes. And as the time will pass he will open his eyes to know and understand that the true religion is in opening the heart, in widening the outlook and in living the religion which is one religion.

Surah Seventy

Al Miraj

'God is love'; when love is awakened in the heart, God is awakened there.

Life's light is love; and when the heart is empty of love, a man is living and yet not living; from a spiritual point of view he is dead. When the heart is asleep, he is as though dead in this life, for one can only love through the heart. But love does not mean give and take. That is only a trade; it's selfishness. To give sixpence and receive a shilling is not love. Love is when one loves for the sake of love, when one cannot help but love, cannot do anything but love. Then one is not forced to love; there is no virtue in that. One does not love because another does. It is simply there. It cannot be helped. It is the only thing that makes a person alive. If a person loves one and hates another, what can he know of love? Can you love one person fully if at the same time you cannot bestow a kind glance on some other person? Can you say you love one person fully when you cannot bear him to be loved by someone else as well? Can you hate a person when love is sprinkled like water in your heart? Love is like the water of the Ganges. It is itself a purification. As the Bible says, 'God is love'. When love is awakened in the heart, God is awakened there. When a man has journeyed, he reaches the goal as soon as his heart has reached love.

The Sufi says, 'The Kaaba, the divine place, paradise, is the heart of the human being'. That is why he has respect for every heart. Every heart is his Kaaba, his shrine. The human heart is the place toward which he bows, for in this heart is God.

Some object to Christ being called divine; but if divinity is not sought in man, then in what shall we seek God? Can divinity be found in the tree, in the plant, in the stone? Yes indeed, God is in all; but at the same time, it is in man that divinity is awakened, that God is awakened, that God can be seen. *Hazrat Inayat Khan*

In the name of Allah, the Beneficent, the Merciful

And those who preserve their chastity. (70:29 Quran)

Save with their wives and those whom their right hands possess, for thus they are not blameworthy. (70:30 Quran)

But whoso seeketh more than that, those are they who are transgressors. (70:31 Quran)

And those who keep their pledges and their covenant. (70:32 Quran)

And those who stand by their testimony. (70:33 Quran)

And those who are attentive at their worship. (70:34 Quran)

These will dwell in gardens, honored. (70:35 Quran)

The Purpose of All Beings ~ Hazrat Inayat Khan

In the first place we must see whether it is an affair of individuals, or a work that can be done collectively. To see the truth as a whole is beyond the power of the generality. The ordinary point of view of life would be like that of a man in a forest who would see into the horses running about, one to the north, another to the south. If one can see the purpose behind things every little coincidence in life proves this, that man very often thinks about his free will, and sees a kind of freedom and pride in what he calls free will, and the more deeply he thinks about it, the more he finds that, 'man proposes and God disposes.' Man, individually and collectively, tries to get all that is best in life, all happiness, wealth, comfort, power, all that seems to him worthwhile, and if free will really existed, everyone would have these things.

Yes, there seems to be free will, man feels it, because it springs from his heart, and as long as he understands that it is his own impulse that has come to manifestation, he cannot understand the real meaning of free will. But the more one studies life, and the deeper one sees into life, the more one sees that all things adjust themselves. And perhaps it would confuse many, and would seem exaggeration if I said, as any mystic would say, that all is truth, and that truth is all, of course it is a deep question, and difficult to be understood by an explanation, unless one rises above the generality, and looks at life from another point of view. Sadi, the great poet of Persia said that each soul is created for a special purpose and that to fulfill this purpose a light is in his heart. This may confuse many, of course. Some may say, 'If I am created for a certain purpose what is the use of progress? Why not stay where I am since it is my destiny?' One can help others to understand, but one cannot make them understand.

If someone thinks he is a chair, or a table, he will remain such, but if he thinks he is a living being, he will feel that action is the object of life, and that everything adjusts itself to that, and that every part is made for a purpose, as for instance the parts of a table or a chair. And if we think of life and the whole world, and see into it deeply we shall find that we live and move, and have our being for a certain purpose. A person may say it is the idea of a fatalist that everything must go through to its destiny. It is not the idea of a fatalist, it is the idea of a seer, of a mystic. Because the fatalist makes human beings as chairs and tables, the mystic makes even chairs and tables living beings.

Jalaluddin Rumi says, 'The fire and the water and the earth and the air are as dead things to every person, but before God they are His living servants who work according to His command.' *Mathnawi I, 838*

The fatalist makes the living dead, and the mystic makes things into living beings.

Now coming to the point of view of the subject, what is after all the purpose of life? No doubt when we take an individual there is a separate purpose in his life, and when we take the multitude we see that there is a common purpose, and looking at the whole we can see that there is a purpose for the whole of humanity. Every purpose, whether for an individual or collectively, has a certain value, but the purpose of all beings is beyond value, and when every individual is engaged in a certain purpose, and a group of individuals also, the whole is also accomplishing a purpose, and this is under a direction, which is called a Hierarchy.

Surah Seventy-One

Noah
All the disharmony of the world caused by religious differences is the result of man's failure to understand that religion is One, truth is One, God is One; how can there be two religions?

God is one, the Truth is one. How can there be two religions? There is one religion, the only religion. Yes, we are living in different lands, but under one sky. So, we have many churches, but one God; many scriptures, but one wisdom; many souls, but one spirit, the only Spirit of God.

The one Spirit of life is given different names, the sacred names. We more easily recognize the [Spirit of life] by the particular name to which we are accustomed. So far we are right, but the mistake we make, and it is to our loss, is to ignore or deny the same truth because it is given to us in another form and under another name. We limit it. We say the truth existed only in that period when certain teachers came to the world, and that after that it stopped. But the spirit of illumination can never stop as long as life goes on. Illumination has continued from the beginning, and will always continue until the manifestation ends; so long will the spirit of illumination continue to spread out its rays.

We accept some forms and ignore others. It is the natural tendency of mankind. It is this that accounts for so many religions. Even if a person cannot see things in this light, he can at least be tolerant of other people's religions. He can respect the religion because he sees others respect it, even if he himself has no respect for its teacher. After all, spirituality means respect, advancement. Man shows his evolution according to his respect, his consideration, his thoughtfulness. If we could only develop that faculty in our mind, it would not matter not believing or recognizing the Spirit of Guidance shown in different human forms. If we held our own teacher or master in the greatest esteem it would do a great deal of spiritual good. The disharmony of the world is usually caused by religious differences, as were the wars of ancient times. The differences are caused by men failing to understand that religion is one, truth is one, and God is one. How can there be two religions? Hazrat Inayat Khan

In the name of Allah, the Beneficent, the Merciful

Lo, We sent Noah unto his people, saying: Warn thy people ere the painful doom come unto them. (71:1 Quran)

He said: O my people! Lo, I am a plain warner unto you. (71:2 Quran)

Bidding you: Serve Allah and keep your duty unto Him and obey me. (71:3 Quran)

That He may forgive you somewhat of your sins and respite you to an appointed term. Lo, the term of Allah, when it cometh, cannot be delayed, if ye but knew. (71:4 Quran)

He said: My Lord! Lo, I have called unto my people night and day. (71:5 Quran)

But all my calling doth but add to their repugnance. (71:6 Quran)

And, lo, whenever I call unto them that: Thou mayest pardon them, they thrust their fingers in their ears and cover themselves with their garments and persist in their refusal and magnify themselves in pride. (71:7 Quran)

And lo, I have called unto them aloud. (71:8 Quran)

And lo, I have made public proclamation unto them, and I have appealed to them in private. (71:9 Quran)

And I have said: Seek pardon of your Lord. Lo, He was ever Forgiving. (71:10 Quran)

He will let loose the sky for you in plenteous rain. (71:11 Quran)

And will help with wealth and sons, and will assign unto you Gardens and will assign unto you rivers. (71:12 Quran)

Abraham ~ Hazrat Inayat Khan

Abraham, whose name seems to come from the Sanskrit root Brahma, which means the creator, was the father of four great religions of the world. For it is from his descendants, who were called Beni Israel, that came Judaism, Christianity, and Islam, besides Zoroastrianism.

Abraham was the first to bring the knowledge of mysticism from Egypt, where he was initiated in the most ancient order of esotericism. And the place, which, on his return, he chose to establish as a center, with the idea that some place must be the world center, was Mecca, whither not only in the age of Islam did people make pilgrimage, but at all times the sacred center of Mecca was held in esteem by the pious who lived before Muhammad. The family of Jesus Christ is traced in the ancient tradition from the family of Isaac, and Muhammad came from the family of Ishmael.

The prophecies of Abraham have always been living words, though various people made their different interpretations according to their own ideas, but to the mind of the seer the prophecies of Abraham have a very deep meaning.

With his great knowledge of esotericism, he has been a great patriarch among his people. He was interested in everybody's trouble and difficulty. He was thrown in the midst of worldly responsibilities, to learn all that he has learned from it, and then to teach his knowledge and experience to those who looked to him for the bread of knowledge. No doubt, the stories of the ancient times very often strike our modern ears as most childish. But it is the way they were told, and by the people that they were told, that makes a great difference. In the first place, there was such a scarcity of lettered people in those days, therefore the stories were told by the unlettered, and certainly they must have improvised upon every legend they told, and pictured it according to the artistic development of their particular age. Nevertheless, truth is there, if we only knew how to lift the veil.

One story of the life of Abraham has been the source of great argument in the East, which is the sacrifice of Isaac. It is not only an argument in the Past, but alarming to a western mind. They can put a thousand questions, to give a proper reason and justification to such an act. But at the same time, if we looked from the ideal point of view, no sacrifice for a beloved ideal can be too great. There are numberless souls whose dear ones, their beloved mates, husbands or sons, have been sacrificed in this recent war. They could do nothing else, they had to surrender their will to the ideal of the nation, and offer the sacrifice for the cause of the nation, without thinking for one moment that it was unusual.

Surah Seventy-Two

Al Jinn

The use of friendship for a selfish motive is like mixing bitter poison with the sweet rose-syrup.

A friendship used to carry out one's aims and objects in life through the love and kindness of a friend is only business. The unselfish friend is the pure one, and it is such a friendship that will last; but a selfish friendship will vanish.

The use of friendship for a selfish motive is like mixing bitter poison with sweet rose-syrup; and it is necessary to be ready, without the least hesitation, to serve a friend attentively, in every capacity of life, not expecting for one moment any thanks or return from him.

In the name of Allah, the Beneficent, the Merciful

And among us there are righteous folk and among us there are far from that. We are sects having different rules. (72:11 Quran)

And we know that we cannot escape from Allah in the earth, nor can we escape by flight. (72:12 Quran)

And when we heard the guidance, we believed therein, and whoso believeth in his Lord, he feareth neither loss, nor oppression. (72:13 Quran)

Say: Lo, I control not hurt nor benefit for you. (72:21 Quran)

Say: Lo, none can protect me from Allah, nor can I find any refuge beside Him. (72:22 Quran)

Say O Muhammad unto the disbelievers: I know not whether that which ye are promised is nigh, or if my Lord hath set a distant term for it. (72:25 Quran)

He is the Knower of the Unseen, and He revealeth unto none His secret. (72:26 Quran)

Save unto every messenger whom He hath chosen, and then He maketh a guard to go before him and a guard behind him. (72:27 Quran)

That He may know that they have indeed conveyed the messages of their Lord. He surroundeth all their doings, and He keepeth current of all things. (72:28 Quran)

Muhammad ~ Hazrat Inayat Khan

Muhammad is the one among the prophets the account of whose life is to be found in history. Born of the family of Ishmael, Muhammad had in him the prophetic heritage and before him that purpose to be fulfilled the prophecy of which had been made by Abraham, in the Old Testament. The prophet became an orphan in his childhood, and had known what it is in the world to be without the tender care of the mother and without the protection of the father when a child. And this experience was the first preparation for the child who was born to sympathize in the pain of others. He showed traces of the sense of responsibility in his boyhood, when looking after his cows. A cowherd came and said 'I will look after your herd, and you may go to the town and enjoy yourself. And then you must take charge of my cows and I will go there for some time.' Young Muhammad said, 'No, I will take charge of your herd. You may go, but I will not leave my charge.' The same principle he showed through his life.

As a youth Muhammad traveled with his uncle, who went to Syria on a business trip; and he knew the shortcomings of human nature, which have a large scope to play their role in the world of business, he knew what profit means, what loss means, what both mean in the end. This gave him a wider outlook on life, where he saw how one is eager to profit by the loss of another, the human beings live in this world no better than the large and small fishes in the water, who live upon one another.

When the time came to defend the country against a powerful enemy, young Muhammad stood shoulder to shoulder with the young men of his land, to defend his people in their most terrible strife. His sincerity in friendship, and honesty in his dealings endeared him to all those far and near who called him by the name Amin, which means trusty, or trustworthy. His marriage with Khadija showed him a man of devotion, a man of affection, an honorable man as a husband, as a father and as a citizen of the town he lived in.

Then came the time of contemplation, that time of the fulfillment of that promise which his soul had brought in the world. There came moments when life began to seem sad, with all the beauty and comfort it could offer. He then sought refuge from that depression in the solitude. Sometimes for hours, sometimes for days, for weeks sitting in the mountains of Ghar-i Hira, he tried to see if there was anything else to be seen. He tried to hear if there was anything to be heard, he tried to know if there was anything to be known.

Patient as Muhammad was, he continued in the path of the search after truth. In the end he began to hear a word of inner guidance, 'Cry on the Sacred Name of Thy Lord,' and as he began to follow that advice, he found the re-echo of the word his heart repeated in all things of nature; as if the wind repeated the same name as he did, the sky, the earth, the moon, and the planets, all said the same that he was saying. When once in tune with the infinite, realizing his soul one within and without, the call came that, 'Thou art the man, go forward into the world and carry out Our command, glorify the name of God, unite them who are separated, waken those who are asleep, and harmonize one with the other, as in this is the happiness of man.'

Often Khadija found Muhammad had covered himself with a mantle that he might not see himself, trembling at the sight of the responsibility that was thrown on him. But she kept telling him, 'You are the man, a man so kind and true, so sincere and devoted, forgiving and serving. It is your part of work to perform; fear not, you are destined to it by the Almighty, trust in His great power, in the end success will be yours.':

The day when Muhammad gave his Message, to his surprise not only the enemies, but the friends who were near and dear to the prophet turned against, would not listen to a new gospel taught. Through the insults and the harm and injury they caused him and those who listened to him he still continued, in spite of being exiled from home three times, and proved in the end, as every real prophet must prove, that truth alone is the conqueror, and to truth belongs all victory.

Surah Seventy-Three

Al Muzammil

Man's bodily appetites take him away from his heart's desires; his heart's desires keep him away from the abode of his soul.

There are two parts in man. One part is his external self, which the soul has borrowed from the earth; and the other part is his real self, which belongs to his Source. In other words an individual is a combination of spirit and matter, a current which runs from above and attracts to it the earth from below, shaping it in order to make it a vehicle. The human body is nothing but a vehicle of the soul which has come from above and has taken the human body as its abode. Thus an individual has two aspects of being: one is the soul, the other is the body. Whether he is in the forest or amidst the world's strife, the soul of man is always capable of rising to the greatest heights, if only he wishes to attain to them. Man does not need to trouble about what is lacking outside, for in reality all is within himself.

The soul cannot see itself; it sees what is round it, it sees that in which it functions; and so it enjoys the comforts of the shell which is around it, and experiences the pains and discomforts which belong to the shell. And in this way it becomes an exile from the land of its birth, which is the Being of God, which is divine Spirit; and it seeks consciously or unconsciously once again the peace and happiness of home. God therefore is not the goal but the abode of the soul, its real self, its true being.

Plato wrote that we live in a shadow world, where we confuse the shadow of ourselves with reality. This is the Nafs, the false ego, which stands in the light before God, causing, so to speak, a spiritual eclipse. The Nafs turns us from the One to the many, enticing us with the things of this world. Then man attaches himself to one thing after another, which brings, at best, momentary satisfaction. Through his spiritual practices the Sufi learns to chain the Nafs, to perceive that it is only a shadow of reality; and finding the sun of truth within his being, looking upon it, one is no longer aware of the shadow. Then the Nafs is not destroyed, but harnessed. The whole of man's being is attuned to God and everything within him serves God. Hazrat Inayat Khan

In the name of Allah, the Beneficent, the Merciful

Oh thou wrapped up in thy raiment. (73:1 Quran)
Keep vigil the night long, save a little. 73:2 Quran)
A half thereof, or abate a little thereof. (73:3 Quran)
Or add a little thereto—and chant the Quran in measure. (73:4 Quran)
For We shall charge thee with a word of weight. (73:5 Quran)

Lo, thy Lord knoweth how thou keepest vigil sometimes nearly two-thirds of the night, or sometimes half or a third thereof, as do a party of those with thee. Allah measureth the night and the day. He knoweth that ye count it not, and turneth unto you in mercy. Recite, then, of the Quran that which is easy for you. He knoweth that there are sick folk among you, while others travel in the land in search of Allah's bounty, and others still are fighting for the cause of Allah. So recite of it that which is easy for you and establish worship and pay poor-due, and so lend unto Allah a goodly loan. Whatsoever good ye send before you for your souls, ye will surely find it with Allah, better and greater in the recompense. And seek forgiveness of Allah. Lo, Allah is Merciful, Forgiving. (73:20 Quran)

The God-Ideal (1) ~ Hazrat Inayat Khan

God and the God-Ideal may be explained as the sun and the light. And as there come times when the sun becomes covered by clouds so there come times when the God-Ideal becomes covered by materialism. But if the cloud for a moment covers the sun that does not mean that the sun is lost to you; and so if in the reign of materialism the God-Ideal seems to have disappeared yet God is there all the same. The condition of the world is just like the ever-rising and falling waves. Sometimes it seems to rise and sometimes to fall, but with every rising and falling wave the sea is the same; and so with all its changes life is the same.

The most dreadful nightmare the world has ever seen has just passed away; and although that wave, that nightmare, seems to be gone its effect is still here, and the effect that is left is worse than the cause, for prejudice is worse than bloodshed. And when man thirsts for the blood of his fellow man how can we say that there is light? If a man can eat joyfully at his table when his neighbor is dying of hunger, where is the light? That is the condition of humanity today. And what is the cause? It is because the Light, the God-Ideal, is not there, I was once amused by a very simple answer from a maid, when somebody came to the door and knocked, and the maid was not free to go at once but took her time; and when at last she came the man was very cross and said: 'Why did you not open the door quickly?' And then I asked the maid: What do you think was the reason for the person's being cross?' and she said with her innocent expression, 'Because there is no God with him.'

Friends, the word of Christ is that God is Love and if God is Love then we, every one of us, can prove God in us by expressing God in our life. Yes, according to the external customs of the different religions, one goes to church, one to the mosque, one to the synagogue, one to the temple of Buddha; but the inner church is neither in the mosque, nor in the synagogue, but in the heart of man, where God abides and which is the habitation of Christ. With this divine element lighted in man's heart he will go to the house of prayer and then his prayer will be heard.

There is a well-known story in India that girl was crossing a place where a Muslim was performing his prayers; and the law is that one should not cross where a person is praying. When the girl returned, the man said to her: 'How insolent! Do you know what sin you have done?' 'What did I do?' said the girl. And the man said that no one was allowed to cross.' 'I did not mean any harm,' said the girl,' but tell me, what do you mean by praying?' 'For me, prayer is thinking of God', said the man. 'Oh! She said, but I was going to see my young man, and I was thinking of him and I did not see you; and if you were thinking of God, how did you see me?'

Surah Seventy-Four

Al Mudath-Thir
Words are but the shadows of thought and feelings.

Although the elements may be called earth, water, fire, air and ether, this must not be taken literally. Their nature and character, according to the mystics, are different. But, as words are few, one cannot give other names to these elements, although in Sanskrit we have distinctive words for them. 'Ether' is not ether in the scientific sense; it is capacity. 'Water' is not water as we understand it in everyday language; it is liquidity. 'Fire' is understood differently; it means glow or heat, dryness, radiance, all that is living. All of these words suggest something more than is ordinarily meant by them. Every activity of the outer world is a kind of reaction. In other words, a shadow of the activity which is behind it and which we do not see.

A world of idea is hidden in a word. Think, therefore, how interesting life must become for the one who can see behind every word that is spoken to him its length, breadth, height, and depth. He is an engineer of the human mind. He then does not know only what is spoken to him, but he knows what is meant by it. By knowing words you do not know the language; what you know is the outside language, the inner language is known by knowing the language of ideas. So the language of ideas cannot be heard by the ears alone, the hearing of the heart must be open for it. Hazrat Inayat Khan

In the name of Allah, the Beneficent, the Merciful

O thou enveloped in thy cloak. Arise and warn. Thy Lord magnify. Thy raiment purify. Pollution shun. And show not favor, seeking worldly gain. (74:1-6 Quran)

Nay, by the Moon. And the night when it withdraweth. And the dawn when it shineth forth. (74:32-34 Quran)

Lo, this is one of the greatest portents. (74:35 Quran)

And a warning unto men. (74:36 Quran)

Unto him of you who will advance or hang back. (74:37 Quran)

Every soul is a pledge for its own deeds. (74:38 Quran)

Save those who will stand on the right hand. (74:39 Quran)

And they will not heed unless Allah willeth it. He is the fount of fear. He is the fount of Mercy. (74:56 Quran)

The God Ideal (2) ~ Hazrat Inayat Khan

Man has a respect for his mother or father or husband or wife or for his superiors, but they have limited personalities; where then shall he give most respect? Only to one being; to God. Man can love another human being, but by the very fact of his loving another human being, he has no scope; to express all the love that is there, you must love the unlimited God. One admires all that is beautiful, beautiful in color, tone or form, but all that is beautiful has its limitations; but when one rises above limitations, there is that perfection which is God alone.

But many people say, 'Yes, the perfection of all things, of love, harmony and beauty is God; but where is the personality of God? And it is this difficulty which some feel, when at loss to find something to adore or worship, different from all they see. In all ages men have, perhaps, worshipped idols, or the sun, or fire, or some other form as God, because they were not able to see further than their eyes could see. Of course it is easy to criticize anyone or to look at anyone with contempt, but really that shows that every soul has a desire for someone to admire, to adore, and to worship.

Although there can be no trace of the personality of God to be found on the surface, yet one can see that there is a source from which all personality comes, and a goal to which all must return. And if there is one source, what a great personality that one Source must be! It cannot be learnt by great intellect, or even not by the study of metaphysics, or comparative religion, but only understood by a pure and innocent heart full of love.

The great personalities who have descended on earth, from time to time, to awaken in man that Love which is his divine inheritance, found echo in innocent souls rather than in great intellects. Man often confuses wisdom with cleverness and cleverness with wisdom. But these two are different; man can be wise and can be clever and man can be clever and not wise; and by cleverness a person will strive and strive, and will not reach there. It is a stream, the stream of love, which leads towards God.

There is a story that a king was traveling and hunting in the woods, and the king was hungry, and stopped at the house of a peasant who treated him very kindly. When the king was leaving this peasant he was so touched with his kindness that, without telling him he was a king, he said to him. 'Take this ring and if ever you are in trouble, come to me in the city and I will see what I can do for you.' After a time there was a famine and the peasant was in great trouble, and his wife and child were dying, and he set out to come and see this man. Of course, when he showed the ring, he was brought to the king and when he entered the room, he saw the king busy in prayer, and when the king came near to him, he said, 'What were you doing?' 'Praying for peace and love and happiness among my subjects.' 'So there is a greater than you, to whom you must go for what you seek? Then I will go to him, who is greater, and on whom even your destiny depends.' He would accept no help, and at last the king had to send what was needed quietly to his home, first saying that no one must tell him that it came from the king. The idea is that it is not only belief but faith which is necessary. Belief is a thing, but faith is a living being.

Surah Seventy-Five

Al Qiyamah

The more elevated the soul, the broader the outlook.

Attitude is the principle thing in life. It is not the conditions in life which change life for us, but mostly it is our attitude toward life and its conditions upon which depends our happiness or unhappiness. The attitude becomes high and broad when one looks at life from a higher point of view. When the point of view is not high, the range of man's sight becomes limited; man becomes narrow in his outlook on life, and in his feelings, thought, speech and action the same is expressed. Why is God pointed out on high, toward the sky? Why not toward the earth, for God is everywhere? The reason is that within the range of God's sight the whole universe stands as a little grain of corn, as to one that flies in the balloon and looks down from high the whole city comes within the range of his sight, when he stands on earth he sees no further than the four walls which keep the whole world covered from his sight.

What does it mean to become spiritual, or godly? It means to have a higher view of life, to look at life from a higher point of view. It is the high point of view in life which ennobles the soul.

The eyes of the man who neglects his duty to his fellow men, absorbed in life's intoxication, will certainly become dazzled and his mind exhausted before the presence of God. It does not mean that any soul will be deprived of the divine vision, it only means that the soul who has not learned to open his eyes wide enough will have his eyes closed before the vision of God. All virtues come from a wide outlook on life, all understanding comes from the keen observation of life. Nobility of soul, therefore, is signified in the broad attitude that man takes in life. Hazrat Inayat Khan

In the name of Allah, the Beneficent, the Merciful

Nay I swear by the day of Resurrection. (75:1 Quran)

Nay I swear by the accusing soul that this Scripture is true. (75:2 Quran)

Thinketh man that We shall not assemble his bones? (75:3 Quran)

Yea, verily. Yea, We are able to restore his very fingers. (75:4 Quran)

But man would fain deny what is before him. (75:5 Quran)

Was he not a drop of fluid which gushed forth? (75:37 Quran)

Then he became a clot, then Allah shaped and fashioned. (75:38 Quran)

And made of him a pair, the male and female. (75:39 Quran)

Is not He who doth so able to bring the dead to life? (75:40 Quran)

Moses ~ Hazrat Inayat Khan

Moses, the most shining Prophet of the Old Testament gave to the world the divine Law, the Ten Commandments, which in reality was the interpretation of the divine Law that he perceived, expressed in the words of those who stood before him at that time of the world's civilization. It is interesting to notice the Sufi saying which comes from the ages, which says: 'Be the followers of love, and forget all distinction,' for in this path of spiritual attainment to claim that 'I am so and so' is meaningless. Moses was found by the river side by a Princess, who knew not what family he came from, or who was his Father and Mother. Only the name of God came to the mind of every thoughtful inquirer as to the Father and Mother of Moses.

When people compare the teachings of different religions, and readily form their opinions upon them, they are often mistaken; it is premature to make such distinctions. There comes a stage in the evolution of an illuminated soul who begins to see the law hidden behind nature, the true psychology. To him the whole life reveals the secrets of its nature and character, and when he gives an interpretation of these secrets to others, they become limited, for they take the color of his own personality, and the form of the thought of those to whom the message is given. The story of Moses as told by Sufis is most interesting and helpful to the traveler on the path Moses has been the favorite character of the poets of Arabia and Persia, and in the poems of the Persian Sufis, Moses is often mentioned as Krishna is mentioned in the poetry of the Hindus.

Moses was walking in the wilderness looking for some fire, he saw from a distance a smoke rising on the top of a mountain, so he climbed to the top of the mountain, in order to find that fire. But on arriving at the top of the mountain, he saw a glimpse of the lighting which was so powerful, that it went throughout his whole being. Moses fell down unconscious on the ground, and when he recovered his senses he found himself with illumination. From that time the Mount Sinai was the place where he often went and communicated with God. The story is very enlightening when one can think that it is possible that all the illumination that is desired can come to a soul in a moment.

Many think that spiritual attainment can be achieved by a great labor; no, labor is necessary for material attainment, for spiritual attainment what one needs is the seeking soul like that of Moses. Moses falling down upon the ground may be interpreted as the Cross, which means: 'I am not, THOU art.' In order to be, one must pass a stage of being nothing. In the Sufi terms it is called fana. When one thinks 'I am not' (what I had always thought myself to be.) This is the true self-denial which the Hindus called laya, and in Buddhism the term annihilation. It is the annihilation of the false self which gives rise to the true self: once this is done, from that moment man approaches closer and closer to God, and stands face to face with his divine ideal, with whom he can communicate at every moment of his life.

The law of God is endless, as limitless as God himself, and once the eye of the seeker penetrates through the veil that hangs before him, hiding from his eyes the real law of life, the mystery of the whole life manifests to him, and happiness and peace becomes his own, for they are the birthright of every soul.

Surah Seventy-Six

Al Insan

The secret of a friend should be kept as one's own secret; the fault of a friend one should hide as one's own fault.

A very important thing in character-building is to become conscious of one's relationship, obligation, and duty to each person in the world, and not to mix that link and connection which is established between oneself and another with a third person. One must consider that everything that is entrusted to one by any person in life is one's trust, and one must know that to prove true to the confidence of any person in the world is one's sacred obligation. In this manner a harmonious connection is established with everyone; and it is this harmony which attunes the soul to the infinite.

To keep the secret of our friend, our acquaintance, even of someone with whom for a time one has been vexed, is the most sacred obligation. The one who thus realizes his religion would never consider it right to tell another of any harm or hurt he has received from his friend. It is in this way that self-denial is learned; not always by fasting and retiring into the wilderness. The one who knows what the relation of friendship is between one soul and another, the tenderness of that connection, its delicacy, its beauty, and its sacredness, that one can enjoy life in its fullness, for he is living; and in this manner he must someday communicate with God. For it is the same bridge that connects two souls in the world, which, once built, becomes the path to God. Hazrat Inayat Khan

In the name of Allah, the Beneficent, the Merciful

And feed with food the needy wretch, the orphan and the prisoner, for love of Him. (76:8 Quran)

Saying: We feed you, for the sake of Allah only. We wish for no reward nor thanks from you. (76:9 Quran)

Lo, we fear from our Lord a day of frowning and of fate. (76:10 Quran)

Therefore Allah hath warded off from them the evil of that day, and hath made them find joy and brightness. (76:11 Quran)

And hath awarded them for all that they endured, a Garden and a silk attire. (76:12 Quran)

Reclining therein upon couches, they will find there neither heat of a sun nor bitter cold. (76:13 Quran)

The shade thereof is close upon them and the clustered fruits thereof bow down. (76:14 Quran)

Goblets of silver are brought round for them, and beakers as of glass. (76:15 Quran)

Bright as glass but made of silver, which they themselves have measured to the measure of their deeds. (76:16 Quran)

There are they watered with a cup whereof the mixture is of Zanjabil. The water of a spring therein named Salsabil. (76:17-18 Quran)

There serve them youths of everlasting youth, whom when thou seest, thou wouldst take for scattered pearls. (76:19 Quran)

When thou seest, thou wilt see there bliss and high estate. (76:20 Quran)

Their raiment will be fine green silk and gold embroidery. Bracelets of silver they will wear. Their Lord will slake their thirst with a pure drink. (76:21 Quran)

And it will be said unto them: Lo, this is a reward for you. Your endeavor upon earth hath found acceptance. (76:22 Quran)

Lo, We, even We, have revealed unto thee the Quran, a revelation. (76:23 Quran)

What is Religion? ~ Hazrat Inayat Khan

What is religion? Religion is a lesson, a lesson which teaches the manner of living aright and reaching the object for which we are born. This religion has come time after time to the world, through those who have brought the Message of God to the world. Those who came with this Message of religion, they have given it in diverse forms, in accordance with the evolution of the people, at that particular time, but religion was one and the same. There never has been any other religion than one, for God is one, Truth is one, and so the religion is one. If there is any difference, it is the difference of form, not of the soul. It is the same water, the pure water, perhaps filled in several pitchers. One pitcher is made in India, the other in China, the other in Arabia, perhaps the other in the Western world. It is like a stream which comes through the fountain and falls in various streams, but it is one and the same stream, in its stem.

The real understanding of religion is not in disputing over the diversity of the forms, saying. 'Your religion is worse and my religion is better.' The true religion is in recognizing that one life in all. There are different candles here on the altar, each candle named by a different teacher and religion, but it is one and the same light.

What then does this service teach us? This service teaches us: one light and different lamps. It is not the lamps that are to be taken first to the mind. No, it is the one light that should be taken to heart. It is this religion of unification which Jesus Christ came to teach. The teaching of Moses, and the efforts of Muhammad, they were all towards this one object. All that Buddha has taught, all that Krishna has said, this all sums up in one thing, and that is: it is one Light that is the Divine Light, and it is the guidance that comes from that Light that becomes the path for humanity to tread upon. The Sufi Movement, though in its infancy, is destined to serve God and humanity in this direction. The Sufi Message is the re-echo of the same Divine Message which has always come, and will always enlighten humanity.

Surah Seventy-Seven

Al Mursalat

Forbearance, patience and tolerance are the only conditions which keep two individual hearts united.

Love teaches the lover patience, forbearance, gentleness, because he thinks, 'My beloved will be displeased; I will be as gentle as possible in my action and in my movements'. These thoughts are a correction to the lover. With every such thought that passes in the life of the lover he corrects himself. Hope is the only thing in life which keeps us alive, because it feeds on love. Patience is fed by love. We can never have patience with anybody without love. How valuable is patience! As it is said in the Quran, 'Allah loves the patient'.

Sacrifice is needed in love to give all there is—wealth, possessions, body, heart, and soul. There remains no 'I', only 'you', until the 'you' becomes the 'I'. Where there is love there is patience, where there is no patience there is no love.

The idea of sacrifice has always existed in some form or other, in every religion. Sometimes it has been taught as giving up one's possessions for the love of a higher ideal, which means that when man claims to love his high ideal and yet is not willing to give up something he possesses for it, then there is doubt about his devotion. But sacrifice of a possession is the first step; the next one is self-sacrifice, which was the inner note of the religion of Jesus Christ. Charity, generosity, even tolerance and forbearance, are a kind of sacrifice, and every sacrifice in life, in whatever form, means a step towards the goal of every soul.

To be today friendly and tomorrow unfriendly cannot for one moment be called friendship; the value of friendship is in its constancy. Forbearance, patience, and tolerance are the only conditions which keep two individual hearts united. Hazrat Inayat Khan

In the name of Allah, the Beneficent, the Merciful

By the emissary winds sent one after another. (77:1 Quran)

By the raging hurricanes. (77:2 Quran)

By those which cause earth's vegetation to revive. (77:3 Quran)

By those who winnow with a winnowing. (77:4 Quran)

By those who bring down the Reminder. (77:5 Quran)

To excuse or to warn. (77:6 Quran)

Surely that which ye are promised will befall. (77:7 Quran)

So when the stars are put out. (77:8 Quran)

And when the sky is riven asunder. (77:9 Quran)

And when the mountains are blown away. (77:10 Quran)

And when the messengers are brought unto their time appointed. (77:11 Quran)

For what day is the time appointed. (77:12 Quran)

For the Day of Decision. (77:13 Quran)

The Religion of All Prophets (3) ~ Hazrat Inayat Khan

Religion has its place in the world, whatever be the condition. From the beginning of civilization there has been some religion or other followed by people. Of course, whenever a new religion came the old religion was routed out. But what was routed out? Was it the religion or the corruption that was routed out? The truth is the truth, religion is religion. That religion can never be routed out. That religion which is the need of human soul; that religion has always been and will always be.

It is only the outer form, its outer dogmas, which have perhaps been corrupted at times, which did not answer the purpose of humanity at that stage of evolution. And not understanding that, man has very often revolted against religion, not knowing that it was the revolt against corruption, not against religion. Now the world as we find it today, it seems that it is again in a revolt against religion. And revolt is like an intoxication. People do not know, when they are in revolt, whether they do right or wrong. When a person is cross with his friend, by seeing the defects or the faults of the friend he forgets his merits.

Therefore man today, intoxicated in a revolt against religion — which means against corruption revolts also, ignorantly, against God, or form, or prayer, or anything which appears to him religious. But if you ask his soul, if you asked the deepest of his being you will find that there is some place for religion. And what has this revolt brought about in the Western world just now? It has brought about a condition where it has become the fashion to be an atheist. There are people who wish to mention the name of God, and yet they are afraid whether it will be against the fashion, the custom of the day.

It is just as in the past — an atheist in the past would not dare to say that he did not believe; he had to respect the custom. The outcome of this condition is that man is absorbed in material gain, and the spiritual gain and heavenly inspirations are away out of his sight.

The Sufi movement is intended to play its part at the present moment in this condition of the world. And, however small and infantile it has a wide horizon and a vast field of work before it. Its work is to bring to the world that religion which has always been the religion of humanity. That nature's religion: to respect one another's belief, one another's scripture, and one another's teacher. It is not, therefore, only a church, it is a school where we learn to respect the religions of all the people in the world and their scriptures, and to pay our homage to the teachers that they have esteemed the most. This was the object of all the great prophets, and it is at the present moment that this object, held by all prophets, is being fulfilled. And in this way with us is the blessing, inspiration and the power of all souls who have for ages come in this world and wakened humanity towards that goal which is the longing of every soul.

Surah Seventy-Eight

An Naba
We blame others for our sorrows and misfortunes, not perceiving that we ourselves are the creators of our world.

Externally we are a single being, but internally we are a world. As vast as is the world around us, so vast is the world within. Asif says, 'The limitation of the sky and land cannot be compared with man's heart. If man's heart be wide, there is nothing wider than this.' All can be accommodated in it; heaven earth, sun, moon, all are reflected in it. It becomes itself the whole. This world becomes as one chooses to make it. If man only knew that! But since he does not know that, the world is not heaven, but has become its opposite. We blame others for our sorrows and misfortunes, not perceiving that we ourselves are the creators of our world; that our world has an influence upon our life within as well as upon our life without.

One learns to understand that there is a world in one's self, that in one's mind there is a source of happiness and unhappiness, the source of health and illness, the source of light and darkness, and that it can be awakened, either mechanically or at will, if only one knew how to do it. Then one does not blame his ill fortune nor complain of his fellow man. He becomes more tolerant, more joyful, and more loving toward his neighbor, because he knows the cause of every thought and action, and he sees it all as the effect of a certain cause. Hazrat Inayat Khan

In the name of Allah, the Beneficent, the Merciful
Have We not made earth an expanse. (78: 6 Quran)
And the high hills bulwark? (78:7 Quran)
And We have created you in pairs. (78:8 Quran)
And have appointed your sleep for repose. (78:9 Quran)
And have appointed the night as a cloak. (78:10 Quran)
And have appointed the day for livelihood. (78:11 Quran)
And We have built above you seven strong heavens. (78:12 Quran)
And have appointed a dazzling lamp. (78:13 Quran)
And have sent down from the rainy clouds abundant water. (78:14 Quran)
Thereby to produce plant and grain. (78:15 Quran)

And gardens of thick foliage. (78:16 Quran)

The Idea of Sacredness ~ Hazrat Inayat Khan

The feeling of sacredness comes from that profound depth of the heart which may be called the divine chamber; and therefore it is the religious feeling which is to be valued rather than the outward form. People have called, in all ages, those who did not worship in the same form as themselves heathen or pagan, and this hatred has caused all the wars and disagreements between the religions of the world. However high, beautiful or wonderful the religious form may be, if there is no sincerity of the heart it is nothing. Therefore the true religion is that sentiment which is to be found in the deepest depth of our being. And when once that sentiment has become real one naturally begins to respect of the same sentiment in another person.

I have very often seen the sign of the true religious person. A person who is truly religious, if he sees another person, to whatever religion he belongs, occupied in his way of worship, he respects him, because he feels the same feeling in his heart. It is just like the language of the mother—that the sentiment that a mother has for her child, she may go to the North pole and see a mother from quite a different part of the land, but she will know her feelings—she may not know the language. Therefore religion is the religious sentiment, sacred sentiment, religion is not a form. And if this sentiment is there, then one respects that sentiment in every form it may be.

It is to learn this, to understand this idea that the Sufi Movement has this Universal Worship; that in this Universal Worship, whatever form a person has, it does not matter; as long as he believes in God, he may come together with other human beings, without thinking his belief in this or that. This worship does not take away anyone from his own way; it only presents before everyone his own scripture. In this service one begins to train oneself to love one's own religion and tolerate the religions of the other.

At this time when the world is divided into so many sections, one working against another, it is most necessary that humanity must at least unite in God. For whatever difference there may be among human beings, before God there is no difference. He is the father of all humanity, and we all go before Him as His children. This Universal Worship reminds us of this, and this Universal Worship prepares us to sympathize with one another and to be blessed by all forms of wisdom which have come to us by different great Teachers of humanity. There is one God and there is one truth, so in reality there cannot be many religions, there is only one religion. And it is by the realization of this truth that we shall be truly benefited by what is called religion.

Surah Seventy-Nine

An Naziat

Nobody appears inferior to us when our heart is kindled with kindness and our eyes are open to the vision of God.

We are so situated in life that whatever position we may occupy we are never independent, we are never self-sufficient. Therefore, every individual depends upon others for help, and others depend upon him for help; only the position of the person who is one among many who receive help becomes lower in the eyes of those who count themselves among the few who can help.

This makes every person a master as well as a servant. Yet everyone, in the intoxication of his mastership, forgets his place as a servant, and looks upon the one who helps him as his servant. The wise, whose feelings are awakened, think on this question deeply, and do their best to avoid every possibility of giving even an idea to a servant of his servant-ship, far less insulting him in any way or hurting his feelings. We are all equal, and if we have helpers to serve us in life we ought to feel humble and most thankful for the privilege, instead of making the position of the servant humble. One cannot commit a greater sin than hurting the feelings of the one who serves us and depends upon our help. Once the Prophet heard his grandson call a servant by his name. On hearing this he at once said to his grandson, 'No, child, that is not the right way of addressing elders. You ought to call him 'uncle.' It does not matter if he serves us, we are all servants of one another, and we are equal in the sight of God.'

There is a verse of Mahmud-i Ghaznavi: 'The Emperor Mahmud, who had thousands of slaves to wait on his call, became the slave of his slaves when love gushed forth from his heart.' Nobody appears inferior to us when our heart is kindled with kindness and our eyes are open to the vision of God.

As Christ teaches, 'Whosoever shall compel thee to go a mile, go with him twain.' What does all this teach us? It is all a lesson in sympathy for one's fellow man, to teach us to share in his troubles, in his despair. For whoever really experiences this joy of life, finds that it becomes so great that it fills his heart and his soul. It does not matter if he has fewer comforts or an inferior position than many in this world, because the light of his kindness, of his sympathy, of the love that is growing, the virtue that is springing up in his heart, all fill the soul with light. There is nothing now that he lacks in life, for he has become the king of it. Hazrat Inayat Khan

In the name of Allah, the Beneficent, the Merciful

But as for him who feared to stand before his Lord and restrained his soul from lust. (79:40 Quran)

Lo! The Garden will be his home. (79:41 Quran)

They ask thee of the Hour: when will it come to port? (79:42 Quran)

Why ask they? What hast thou to tell thereof? (79:43 Quran)

Unto thy Lord belongeth knowledge of the term thereof. (79:44 Quran)

Thou art but a warner unto him who feareth it. (79:45 Quran)

On the day when they behold it, it will be as if they had but tarried for an evening or the morn thereof. (79:46 Quran)

Attaining the Inner Life Through Religion ~ Hazrat Inayat Khan

Very often people divide the esoteric, or the inner, part of life from the exoteric, or the outer, form of religion. But to divide them in a conception is possible, to divide them in reality is as separating the head from the body. As head linked with body makes the form complete, so religion with inner life makes the spiritual ideal perfect. Nevertheless the thoughtful and wise of all ages, with their philosophical minds, with their scientific tendencies, with their intellectual strife, often thought of separating religion from the inner life.

But if they are separated, it is just like bread without butter, it is like milk without sugar, it is like food without salt. But there has been a reason why this tendency has come very often, especially among the thoughtful people. The reason is that it is natural that such a tendency should come: when the body becomes a corpse and life leaves the body, even the dear ones, those who loved the person begin to think:' As soon as possible we should clear away this body for the one whom they loved is gone from it, the body is left as a corpse. And so when the inner life, which is just like a breath in the body of religion, departs from it, then the religion becomes like a corpse, then the most faithful adherents begin to feel that it is a corpse.

In all ages and in all periods of history we shall trace this, that there has been a limit of years for a religion. During that the religion prospered and it gave benefit to humanity. Why? Because it had the breath in it, it had the spiritual aspect in it. But when that inner life departed it was left like a corpse. Still the faithful kept it, but those with intelligence could not keep it any longer. Still there is a necessity: as the rain falls year after year, and gives to the earth a new life, a new sustenance, so it has been necessary then that the new Message of spiritual upliftment should come.

Whenever it came people have fought against it, not knowing that it is the same true breath, soul of religion that has come again, not knowing the secret of religion.

Was it not the desire of Muhammad, was it not the wish of Jesus Christ, was it not the task of Moses, was it not the wish of Krishna, or of Buddha, that wisdom in all its aspects may be understood, that all those who have sacrificed their lives and energies in service for man, that the service may be fulfilled and humanity blessed and benefited by what they brought? Was it not the wish of Rama that all the men of the world should come together in understanding that there is only one religion? The evolution of man today has allowed us, and we must be thankful that we can gather together even some few souls who can tolerate such an idea, and be patient, and try to understand that behind all religion there is one, that there can only be one Truth, that there is only one Truth, that we are willing to listen to the words of all the great souls, who have come perhaps thousands of years before us, and what is left of them is in their words, we can see the glimpses of their feelings in their words. Why should we not be benefited by them?

The Universal Worship, therefore, is the religion of the future, which brings to humanity the ideal of unification of religion. The ideal of getting above the sectarianism, the limitedness of communities, of groups. And we must remember that any effort made by political or social efforts will not be complete unless the uniting in God, the only Source in which humanity must unite, is held fast in Truth.

Surah Eighty

Abasa
Selfishness keeps man blind through life.

Christ's teaching that man should be kind and charitable, and that of all other teachers who showed humanity the right path, seems to differ from what one sees from the practical point of view which is called common sense; yet according to uncommon sense, in other words super-sense, it is perfectly practical. If you wish to be charitable, think of the comfort of another; if you wish to be happy, think of the happiness of your fellow men; if you wish to be treated well, treat others well; if you wish that people should be just and fair to you, first be so yourself to set an example.

Man's greatest enemy is his ego which manifests itself in selfishness. Even in his doing good, in his kind actions, selfishness is sometimes at work. When he does good with the thought that one day it may return to him and that he may share in the good, he sells his pearls for a price. A kind action, a thought of sympathy, of generosity, is too precious to trade with. One should give and, while giving, close the eyes. Man should remember to do every little action, every little kindness, and every act of generosity with his whole heart, without the desire of getting anything in return making a trade out of it. The satisfaction must be in doing it and in nothing else.

Every step in evolution makes life more valuable. The more evolved you are, the more priceless is every moment; it becomes an opportunity for you to do good to others, to serve others, to give love to others, to be gentle to others, to give your sympathy to souls who are longing and hungering for it. Life is miserable when a person is absorbed in himself; as soon as he forgets himself he is happy.

Tulsidas, the Hindu poet, says that the essence of religion is kindness. Those who are inclined to do kindness in life must not discriminate among the people around them, between those to whom they must be kind and those to whom they need not be kind. However kind and good a person may be to those he likes, to those he wishes to be kind to, he cannot for this be called kind by nature; real kindness is that which gushes out from the heart to the worthy and to the unworthy. Man is the outcome of the development of the whole of creation; therefore the ego, which makes one selfish, is developed in him more than in any other creature. Selfishness keeps man blind through life, and he scarcely knows when he has caused harm to another. In this struggle of life, if a man can be considerate enough to keep his eyes open to all around him and see in what way he can be of help to them, he becomes rich; he inherits the kingdom of God. *Hazrat Inayat Khan*

In the name of Allah, the Beneficent, the Merciful
Let man consider his food. (80:24 Quran)
How We pour water in showers. (80:25 Quran)
Then split the earth in clefts. (80:26 Quran)
And cause the grain to grow therein. (80:27 Quran)
And grapes and green fodder. (80:28 Quran)
And olive-trees and palm-trees. (80:29 Quran)
And garden-closes of thick foliage. (80:30 Quran)
And fruits and grasses. (80:31 Quran)
Provision for you and your cattle. (80:32 Quran)

The Kingship of God ~ Hazrat Inayat Khan

The God-ideal has been regarded by different men differently. Some have idealized God as the King of earth and Heaven. Some have a conception of God as a person, others think of God as an abstraction. Some believe in God, others do not. Some raise the ideal of the Deity to the highest Heaven, others bring it down to the lowest depth of earth.

Some picture God in Paradise, others make an idol and worship it. There are many ideas and many beliefs, different names, such as pantheism, idolatry belief in a formless God, or belief in many gods and goddesses. But all are striving after something in one way or another.

There is a story told in the East of a man who used to avoid going to the house of prayer, who showed no outward sign, so that his wife often wondered if he had any belief in God; and she thought a great deal about this, and was very anxious about it. Then one day she said to her husband: 'I am very happy today.' The man was surprised, and asked what made her happy, and she said: 'I was under a false impression, but now I have found out the truth I am glad.' He asked: 'What has made you glad?' and she replied: 'I heard you saying the Name of God in your sleep.' He said 'I am very sorry.' It was too precious, too great for him to speak of, and he felt it was a great blow after having hidden this secret in the deepest part of his being because it was too sacred to speak of. He could not bear it, and he died.

We cannot say from the outward appearance who believes, and who does not believe. One person may be pious and orthodox and it may mean nothing; and another may have a profound love for the Deity and a great knowledge of Him and no one may know it.

What benefit does man receive from believing in the Kingship of God? How does he derive real help from his belief? He must begin by realizing the nobility of human nature. Not that one must expect everything to be good and beautiful, and if one's expectation is not realized, think there is no hope of progress, for man is limited, his goodness is limited. No one has ever proved to be your ideal; you may make an ideal of your imagination and whenever you see goodness to be lacking, you may give from your own heart and so complete the nobility of human nature. This is done by patience, tolerance, kindness, forgiveness. The lover of goodness loves every little sign of goodness. He overlooks the faults and fills up the gaps by pouring out love and filling up that which is lacking. And this is real nobility of soul.

Religion, prayer, worship are all intended to ennoble the soul, not to make it narrow, sectarian, bigoted. One cannot arrive at true nobility of spirit if one is not prepared to forgive imperfect human nature. For all, worthy or unworthy, require forgiveness, and only in this way can one rise above the lack of harmony and beauty, until at last one arrives at the stage when one reflects what one has collected. All the riches of love, kindness, tolerance, good manners, a man then reflects and he throws the light on to the other person and brings out those virtues in that other, just as watering a plant makes the leaves and buds open and the flowers blossom. This brings one nearer to the perfection of God in Whom alone one sees all that is perfect, all that is divine.

Surah Eighty-One

At Takwir

The final victory in the battle of life for every soul is when he has risen above the things which once he most valued.

The final victory in the battle of life for every soul is when he has abandoned, which means when he has risen above, what once he valued most. For the value of everything exists for man only so long as he does not understand it. When he has fully understood, the value is lost, be it the lowest thing or the highest thing.

Do not, therefore, be surprised at the renunciation of sages. Perhaps every person in the spiritual path must go through renunciation. It is not really throwing things away or disconnecting ourselves from friends; it is not taking things to heart as seriously as one naturally does by lack of understanding. No praise, no blame is valuable; no pain or pleasure is of any importance. Rise and fall are natural consequences, so are love and hatred; what does it matter if it be this or that? It matters so long as we do not understand. Renunciation is a bowl of poison no doubt, and only the brave will drink it; but in the end it alone proves to be nectar, and this bravery brings one the final victory. Hazrat Inayat Khan

In the name of Allah, the Beneficent, the Merciful

That this is in truth the word of an honored messenger. (81: 19 Quran)

Mighty, established in the presence of the Lord of the Throne. (81:20 Quran)

One to be obeyed and trustworthy. (81:21 Quran)

And your comrade is not mad. (81:22 Quran)

Surely he beheld him on the clear horizon. (81:23 Quran)

And he is not avid of the Unseen. (81:24 Quran)

Nor is this the utterance of a devil worthy to be stoned. (81:25 Quran)

Wither then go ye? (81:26 Quran)

This is naught else but a reminder unto creation. (81:27 Quran)

Unto whomsoever you willeth to walk straight. (81:28 Quran)

And ye will not, unless it be that Allah willeth, the Lord of Creation. (81:29 Quran)

The Religion of the Heart ~ Hazrat Inayat Khan

When we think of the different religions which are known to humanity we shall find that each of them brought to the world the message of love in some form or other. And now the question arises who brought religion in the world? And the answer is that religion has always existed in the heart of man. Religion is the outcome of the heart, and among all races, however primitive, a certain religion has existed, perhaps incomprehensible to people more evolved in different directions. For religion is instinctive, and as it is instinctive, not only in the world of man but also in the lower creation one sees a glimpse of religious tendency. For instance, one finds among pet animals, such as the dog, the cat, the horse, some such faithful creatures, and sometimes one has such experiences with them that one cannot today expect from mankind.

Besides this, the absorption that one sees among the birds, the little sparrows in the morning absorbed in the beauty of nature; so to speak, singing a song, a hymn to God — that all is religion; if we can understand it. For man has made his religion so narrow that he is not able to appreciate the broad religion of nature. By being narrow he has named his creed a religion, or the particular place of worship a religion, or the book religion, or the form of service religion. If one would only think that the religion when one goes in the woods, in the forests, and stands alone in the forest near the silent trees standing in contemplation through the summer and winter, through all seasons! That silent contemplation, what does it give one, what thought arises? It lifts one up and makes one think that there is a religion.

One may call it a legend or a superstition or a story, but still there are experiences — we have the experiences in India with the cobras — they never bite unless someone hurts them. The affection and the attachment that the doves shown to their mates, it is something to learn and to understand. And there are many instances, many experiences of thoughtfulness, of consideration, and of the nature of attachment that one sees in the lower creation, and that makes one think that there is an instinctive religion.

But then, there are stories known in the East about the elephants. In the herd of elephants there is one who always leads them and he has a stem of a tree in his trunk, and he goes on feeling the earth — if there be a pit or if it be a good way for the elephants to pass. And if there was a pit, he gives a warning to his followers that they may not fall victims to this. When we consider the birds we see that there is among them a leader who knows and understand the coming and continuing of rain and storm, and according to that he guides them, and they all follow him. By what is it all accounted for? This taking care of those who depend upon one, and then to yield to respond, to trust someone who guides one, it is not only in the human beings, but even more in the animals. And man who is always supposed to have a religion and thinks that he has a religion, has always opposed in all ages the ones who have served him, those who have wished to awaken him from his errors. The saints and the sages and the great souls who have continually tried to work for him they have always had to suffer and they were the ones who found opposition from all directions and in this way man has shown a lesser tendency to religion than the animals.

But what is love? Love is a continual sacrifice. And what does sacrifice mean? Sacrifice means forgetting of the self. As Rumi says in his poem, the Mathnawi: The Beloved is all in all, the lover merely veils him. The Beloved is all that lives, the lover a dead thing. *Mathnawi I, 30*

Surah Eighty-Two

Al Infitar

When power leads and wisdom follows, the face of wisdom is veiled and she stumbles; but when wisdom leads and power follows, they arrive safely at their destination.

The head power is not enough to give the Message to humanity. The heart power is needed—the heart first, the head comes after. If the head is first and the heart follows, then the heart will become weak, the head will get the upper hand. It is the development of the heart quality that will enable us to work in a field of wisdom and to bring to those who come in contact with us the Message we are destined to bring. The first thing that is desirable, or that which is most desirable in life, is wisdom. The next is power. As a foolish man would not be able to make good use of his wealth, so a person with psychic power without wisdom is apt to harm himself with his own power rather than to do any good. Every atom in this world has its peculiar charm and attraction, and mankind, so attracted by things that seem for the moment attractive, whether wealth, power, position or a friend, does not necessarily know the outcome of their attainment.

Every man is as blind in his desire of attainment as a child attracted to anything beautiful, be it a toy or a knife. And when man cannot attain to it he feels as disappointed as a child that is not allowed to play with the knife. And it is keen sight into life that makes man see what is really good for him in his life. Selfish both are, the wise and the foolish; only that the foolish with his selfishness meets with disappointment while the wise with his selfishness gets the benefit. The nature of power is to cover the eyes and hide from one's sight the true nature of the things he wishes to attain. Hazrat Inayat Khan

In the name of Allah, the Beneficent, the Merciful

When the heaven is cleft asunder. ((82:1 Quran)

When the planets are dispersed. (82:2 Quran)

When the seas are poured forth. (82:3 Quran)

And the sepulchers area overturned. (82:4 Quran)

A soul will know what it hath sent before it and what left behind. (82:5 Quran)

O man! What had made thee careless concerning thy Lord, the Bountiful. (82:6 Quran)

Who created thee, then fashioned, then proportioned thee? (82:7 Quran)

The Religion of the Heart (3) ~ Hazrat Inayat Khan

The power of love is seen in all things, and in whatever form it acts, it shows in it a great virtue. And one does not know always what power love has behind it, that there is nothing in the world which is more powerful than love. Think of the hen with its little chickens. At the time when they are so young that they seek her protection, if the horse came, if the elephant came she would fight in defense.

What is religion? Religion is what breaks away the barriers of falsehood and guides man toward the truth. What we call kindness, helpfulness, gentleness, meekness, or humility, what do all these virtues come from? Are they all not made of love? They are different forms of love. That shows that there is only one stream of virtue and that is love; and all different virtues that man knows, they are all different drops falling in different directions. And the idea of right and wrong good and bad, we can find among all different people in different ways, but in love we all unite, whether from East or South, or West or North, for none who is thoughtful will argue on the question that cruelty is virtue and kindness a sin. Therefore from the point of view of love, we can all unite in one conception of good and bad, of right and wrong. All that is guided by the principle of love has its virtue and all that is done by coldness, it is that which is wrong.

And when we think of the condition through which humanity has passed in all different times—in the name of religion there have been wars and battles—one wonders if it was taught by the religion. Not at all, religion was the pretense that men by this pretense wanted to cause bloodshed, absorbed in selfishness. And if ever there has been a kind of accusation against any religion in the world, it is not against the religion, it is against the misunderstanding of that religion by the followers of that religion.

There are many political institutions, social institutions, and moral institutions, but what is most necessary today is the awakening of the religion of the heart. It does not matter what religion they profess if they know the depth of the religion, which is love. And then, all the different forms, the forms of religious service and the forms of prayer, behind them what secret is there? The secret is to prepare the heart of that bliss which love only can give.

The school of the Sufis, in whatever age, has been the school of the mystics. Its religion has been the religion of the heart, and it is therefore that there is a verse of Abul Ala, who says, 'Quran, the Bible, or a martyr's bone, all these my heart can tolerate, since my religion is love alone.' For the religion of love is the religion of tolerance, the religion of love is the religion of forgiveness.

And if there is any inspiration, any revelation, that also is attained by a loving heart. The life's purpose is to make use of this shrine which is the human heart and which was made for God. And if there is a shrine and no God, the shrine is purposeless. And if there is a heart and the heart has not yet attained to that ideal, the only ideal which is worthy of love, that heart has not yet attained its purpose.

But no doubt it can be worthless if a person says, 'I love God, but I do not love mankind.' That profession is worthless. It is like saying, 'Friend, I love you very much, but I cannot look at your face.' The creation is the manifestation of God. It is in the art of the artist that we recognize him. If we refuse to acknowledge the art, we do not know the artist. The man who does not express his love, who does not forget himself in love, expressing it as a respect, tolerance, forgiveness, does not know religion.

Surah Eighty-Three

At Tatfif
Man's whole conduct in life depends upon what he holds in his thought.

The heart, which is called a mirror in Sufi terms, has two different actions which it performs. Whatever is reflected in the heart does not only remain a reflection but becomes a creative power, productive of a phenomenon of a similar nature. For instance a heart which is holding in itself and reflecting the rose, will find roses everywhere. Roses will be attracted to that heart; roses will be produced from it and for it. As this reflection becomes stronger, so it becomes creative of the phenomenon of roses. The heart that holds and reflects a wound will find wounds everywhere, will attract wounds, will create wounds; for that is the nature of the phenomenon of reflection. There is another aspect of this reflection, and that is what one thinks, one becomes. One becomes identified with it. Therefore, the object which is in one's thought becomes one's own property, one's own quality.

A person (lacking mastery) holds a thought in mind, whether it is beneficial to him or not, without knowing the result which will come from it. It is like a child who holds a rattle in his hand and hits his head with the rattle and cries with the pain, and yet does not throw the rattle away. There are many who keep in their mind a thought of illness or a thought of unkindness done to them by someone and suffer from it, yet not knowing what it is that makes them suffer so, nor understanding the reason of their suffering.

Man's whole conduct in life depends upon what he holds in his thought. The thought of the wicked produces in him wickedness, and the thought of the good creates goodness. The love of Rasul, the divine ideal, enables one to concentrate upon this ideal. Since all in the garb of matter are to be separated one day in life, good or wicked, friends or foes, what alone is reliable is the ideal which man creates within himself, call it Christ, Buddha, Krishna or Muhammad. Hazrat Inayat Khan

In the name of Allah, the Beneficent, the Merciful

Nay but the record of the righteous is in Iliyin. (83:18 Quran)

Ah what will convey unto thee what Iliyin is? (83:19 Quran)

A written record. (83:20 Quran)

Attested by those who are brought near unto their Lord. (83:21 Quran)

Lo! The righteous verily are in delight. (83:22 Quran)

On couches, gazing. (83:23 Quran)

Thou wilt know in their faces the radiance of delight. (83:24 Quran)

They are given to drink of a pure wine, sealed. (83:25 Quran)

Whose seal is musk—For this let all those who strive who strive for bliss. (83:26 Quran)

And mixed with water of Tasnim. (83:27 Quran)

A spring whence those brought near to Allah drink. (83:28 Quran)

The Message (2) ~ Hazrat Inayat Khan

As we all in this world, according to our little ability, serve God, consciously or unconsciously, we all perform that service, though it be without knowing it. There is a saying of a great philosopher of Persia, Rumi; 'Fire, water, air, and earth are God's servants; and whenever He wishes them to work for Him, they are ready to obey His command.' If the elements are the obedient servants of God, and if the elements become the instruments of God, can man not be a greater and better instrument? In reality man must be the best instrument of God for the accomplishment of the purpose of His creation. And in this way those who have been the instruments for a community He has used as instruments for a community; those who have been instruments for a nation He has used as instruments for a nation; and the souls that have been instruments for the whole humanity have been used by God for that purpose. In whatever capacity in life, as a king, as a prophet, as a reformer, as a preacher, they have served God. The great service of God is the work that is done by the prophet, to bring humanity close to perfection. For every soul is born for this purpose and that every soul should reach, so to speak, the feet of God.

And since the Prophet brings the Message of God, it is the Message of God, it is the Message from the same Source whenever it comes. If it came a hundred thousand years ago it was His Message; and if it came two thousand years ago it was His message; and if it came today it is His message. And how ignorant man has been through all ages, and he shows his ignorance even today! For whenever the message has come, man has fought and disputed and argued. Man has held to one prophet and ignored the other, he esteemed one, and he despised the other. And the reason is that he knew the Messenger but he did not know the Message, he has taken the book as his religion, but he does not know the Message. If that were not the tendency of the generality, then how could Jesus Christ with his most spiritual Message have been crucified? There had been prophecies and, besides prophecies, the Master himself was the evidence of his Message, as there is a saying: What you are speaks louder than what you say. And how thickly veiled man's eyes must be by the religion, the faith, the belief he held for him to accept one Messenger and to reject the Message, not knowing that there is one Message, there cannot be two!

Yes, the way in which it is given are different ways, because of the mentality of humanity at each time. Every prophet had to speak in the manner of the time at which he lived, according to the evolution of that time. Another thing is that the custom of each country differs from that of other countries the manners and life differ. If the Messenger is born in one country and has to give his Message in one country, surely he has to consider the way in which the people of that country look at life and to give his Message according to that. But the Message is from God. This is the reason why the external study of Buddhism will make one feel that Hinduism is different from Buddhism, and external study of Christianity and Islam will make one feel that Christianity is different from Islam. But if one saw that underlying thread that connects all religions, one would see that all religion is one, as Truth is one, as life is one, as God is one.

Surah Eighty-Four

Al Inshiqaq

He who can be detached enough to keep his eyes open to all those whom circumstances have placed about him, and see in what way he can be of help to them, he it is who becomes rich — he inherits the kingdom of God.

Those who are inclined to do kindness in life must not discriminate among the people around them, between those to whom they must be kind and those to whom they need not be kind. However kind and good a person may be to those he likes, to those he wishes to be kind to, he cannot for this be called kind by nature; real kindness is that which gushes out from the heart to the worthy and to the unworthy. In the Quran it is said, 'God alone is rich, and everyone on earth is poor.' Man is poor with his myriad needs, his life's demand. The wants of his nature; and when one keenly observes life, it seems that the whole world is poverty-stricken, everyone struggling for the self. In this struggle of life, if a man can be considerate enough to keep his eyes open to all around him and see in what way he can be of help to them, he becomes rich; he inherits the kingdom of God.

The soul of the spiritually inclined man is constantly thirsty, looking for something, seeking for something; and when it thinks it has found it, the thing turns out to be different; and so life becomes a continual struggle and disappointment. And the result is that instead of taking interest in all things, a kind of indifference is produced; and yet in the real character of this soul there is no indifference, there is only love. Hazrat Inayat Khan

In the name of Allah, the Beneficent, the Merciful

Thou, verily, O man, are working toward thy Lord a work which thou wilt meet in His presence. (84:6 Quran)

Nay, but lo! His Lord is ever looking on him. (84:15 Quran)

Oh, I swear by the afterglow of the sunset. (84:16 Quran)

And by the night and all that is underneath. (84:17 Quran)

And by the moon when she is at the full. (84:18 Quran)

That ye shall journey on from plane to plane (85:19 Quran)

The God Ideal (3) ~ Hazrat Inayat Khan

The existence of God is a question which arises in every mind, whether in the mind of the believer in God or in the mind of the unbeliever. And there are moments when the greatest believer in God questions His existence—whether there really is a God. He finds it, at the second thought, sacrilegious to have a notion such as this; and he tries to get rid of it. But often this question rises in the heart of the unbeliever: if it is really true; if there is some such a thing as God. The idea of God is inborn in man. The God-Ideal is the flower of the human race; and this flower blooms in the realization of God.

As everything in the objective world has its tendency to rise upward, so the tendency of the soul can be seen in human aspiration, which always soars upwards, whatever be the sphere of man's consciousness.

The man who is only conscious of the material life, his aspirations reach as far as they can reach in material gains. And yet he proceeds higher and higher, and remains discontented with all that he achieves through life, owing to the immensity of life in every phase. This craving for the attainment of what is unattainable gives the soul a longing to reach life's upmost heights.

It is the nature of the soul to try and discover what is behind the veil: it is the soul's constant longing to climb such heights which are beyond its power, it is the desire of the soul to see something that it has never seen; it is the constant longing of the soul to know something it has never known. But the most wonderful thing about it is that the soul already knows that there is something behind this veil, the veil of perplexity; that there is something to be sought for in the highest spheres of life; that there is some beauty to be seen; that there is someone to be known who is knowable. This desire, this longing is not acquired. This desire is a dim knowledge of the soul which it has in itself.

Their disbelief in the God-Ideal is nothing but a condition which is brought about by the vapors arising from the material life of illusion and covering as clouds the light of the soul, which is its life. It is therefore that the unbeliever is not satisfied with his disbelief. Yes, sometimes his vanity is fed by it, to think that he is wise in not believing in someone whose existence is believed in by numberless blind beings. So he begins to think: after all, to believe in God is not a difficult thing; any simpleton can believe in the God-Ideal. He takes, therefore, the opposite direction, of refusing to believe. He is honest, and yet he is like someone who stands before a wall which hinders his path to progress.

Seeking for God is a natural outcome of the maturity of the soul. There is a time in life when a passion is awakened in the soul which gives the soul a longing for the unattainable. And if the soul does not take that direction, then it certainly misses something in life which is its innate longing and in which lies its ultimate satisfaction.

Surah Eighty-Five

Al Buruj
True justice cannot be perceived until the veil of selfishness has been removed from the eyes.

The development of the sense of justice lies in unselfishness; one cannot be just and selfish at the same time. The selfish person can be just, but only for himself. He has his own law most suited to himself, and he can change it, and his reason will help him to do so, in order to suit his own requirements in life. A spark of justice is to be found in every heart, in every person, whatever be his stage of evolution in life; but the one who loves fairness, so to speak blows on that spark, thus raising it to a flame, in the light of which life becomes more clear to him.

We cannot be a judge of the action of another until we ourselves are selfless. Only then will justice come to us; only then will we understand the nature of justice. Self is the wall between us and justice. There is only one thing that is truly just, and that is to say, 'I must not do this.'

Real justice cannot be perceived until the veil of selfishness has been removed from his eyes. The least spark of selfishness will prevent man from being just. He will continue to have a partial interest, because he will be looking after his own interest. Whatever furthers his own interests, he will call his right and his justice.

The prophets and the holy ones have all recognized the justice of God as the only real justice. What is the nature of the justice of God? It can only be learned from the self within after selfishness has been removed. Our limited self is like a wall separating us from the Self of God. God is as far away from us as that wall is thick. The wisdom and justice of God are within us, and yet they are far away under the covering of the veil of the limited self. Whoever has arrived at that realization of the nature of God's justice is able to see things in a different way from others. His whole outlook on life becomes different. Hazrat Inayat Khan

In the name of Allah, the Beneficent, the Merciful

By the heaven holding mansions of stars. (85:1 Quran)

And by the Promised Day. (85:2 Quran)

And by the witness of that whereunto he beareth testimony. (85:3 Quran)

Lo! He it is Who produceth, then reproduceth. (85:13 Quran)

And He is the Forgiving, the Loving. (85:14 Quran)

Lord of the Throne of Glory. (85:15 Quran)

Doer of What He will. (85:16 Quran)

Hath there come unto thee the story of the hosts. (85:17 Quran)

The Pharaoh and the tribe of Thamud? (85:18 Quran)

Nay, but those who disbelieve live in denial. (85:19 Quran)

And Allah, all unseen, surroundeth them. (85:20 Quran)

Nay, but it is a glorious Quran. (85:21 Quran)

On a guarded tablet. (85:22 Quran)

The God Ideal (4) ~ Hazrat Inayat Khan

There are different conceptions of God existing in various periods and known to different people. The people, in all ages, seeking for the Deity have pictured Him in some form or other. It is natural with man. If he is told about someone he has never seen or known, he makes a conception of that person and he holds his conception as his knowledge of that person until he sees him. There are some who make a conception in their mind of a person they have not seen, almost as real as the person. The human heart is an accommodation which conceives the idea of God and pictures Him according to man's mentality.

The Buddha of China has Chinese features, and that of Japan has the eyes of Japan, the Buddha of India has the Indian likeness. Man cannot conceive of an angel being any different from a human being, except that he attaches two wings to the angel in order to make it a little different. If the angel were not pictured as man it would not be an attraction to a human being. Therefore it is natural that in every period people have conceived the personality of God as a human personality. And no better conception could they have given, for there is nothing in the world which is a more finished personality than the human personality.

People have called God He, recognizing the might and power of the Deity. People have called God She, recognizing in the Deity that Mother-principle and beauty. And it is the differences of conception from which have come the many gods and goddesses. And it is true, too; for as many conceptions, so many gods. And yet many gods means many conceptions of the One Only God. By ignorance of this truth many have fought over their different gods; and yet the wise man in every period of the world has understood God to be the One and Only Being. For the ordinary mind, to feel the existence of someone in the idea is not sufficient. It is too vague. One wants to feel the existence of someone with his own hands, then only he can acknowledge something to be existent.

The wise, therefore, have given different objects to such mentalities, and pointed them out to the people as gods. Some said: see God in the sun, and the person understood. He was not satisfied to think that God was in the idea; he was much more pleased to know now that God is seen by him, and God is incomparably even as the sun, and that God is not reachable. Some wise men have said: He is in the fire. Some said, to a simpleton who asked to see God: Go in the forest and find out a certain tree, and that tree is God. The search for that tree gave something for that man to do, which was the first essential thing. And the patience with which he sought the tree also did something in his soul. And the joy of finding a rare tree was also a pleasure, and in the end he found, for God is everywhere.

Surah Eighty-Six

At Tariq

Our thoughts have prepared for us the happiness or unhappiness we experience.

All our possessions, all that we collect in life, all these things which we shall have to leave one day are transitory; but that which we have created in our thought, in our mind, that lives. A person thinks, 'Someday I should like to build a factory.' At this time he has no money, no knowledge, no capability; but a thought came, 'Someday I should like to build a factory.' Then he thinks of something else. Perhaps years pass, but that thought has been working constantly through a thousand minds, and a thousand sources prepare for him that which he once desired. If we could look back to all we have thought of at different times, we would find that the line of fate or destiny, Kismet as it is called in the East, is formed by our thought. Thoughts have prepared for us that happiness or unhappiness which we experience. The whole of mysticism is founded on this.

Every good or bad word or deed is reproduced before us, though it seems as in a dream. If we watched life keenly, we should see how true this is. Joy, sorrow, love, all depend on our thought, on the activity of our mind. If we are depressed, if we are in despair, it is still the work of our mind; our mind has prepared that for us. If we are joyful and happy, and all things are pleasant, that also has been prepared for us by our mind. It is only when our mind works without control that unhappiness, sorrow, trouble, pain, or whatever we experience comes without our intention. No one could wish to create hell for himself; all would create heaven for themselves if they could; and yet how many allow their minds to create these things for them, regardless of their own intention. *Hazrat Inayat Khan*

In the name of Allah, the Beneficent, the Merciful
By the heaven and the Morning Star. (86:1 Quran)
Ah what will tell thee what the Morning Star is? (86:2 Quran)
No human soul but hath a guardian over it. (86:3 Quran)
So let man consider from what he is created. (86:4 Quran)
He is created from a gushing fluid. (86:5 Quran)
That issued from heaven between ribs and loins. (86:6 Quran)
Lo! He verily is Able to return him unto life. (86:7 Quran)
Lo! This Quran is a conclusive word. (86:13 Quran)

The God Ideal (5) ~ Hazrat Inayat Khan

The conception of many gods has come from two sources. One was the idea of the wise to make every kind of power and attribute in a form of deity and to call it a certain god. It was done in order to give the ordinary mind the most needed thought that God is in everything and that God is all power. Many afterwards misunderstood the idea, and the wisdom behind it became obscured. Therefore some wise men had to fight against the ideas of the other wise men. And yet they did not fight with the idea, they fought with the misconception of it.

But now, at the present time, when there exists no such idea in Europe of many gods, many have lost their faith after the recent war, saying: if God is all goodness, all justice, all powerful, why has such a dreadful thing as war been allowed to take place? If the same people were accustomed to see, among their many gods, as the Hindus have worshipped for generations, Kali, the goddess of war, it would not have been a new thing for them to know that if all is from God, not only peace, but even war is from God.

The mystics of all ages have therefore given God many Names. The Sufi schools of esotericism have possessed their different names of God, with their nature and secret; and have used them in different meditations along the path of spiritual attainment. Therefore the Sufis have not many gods but many Names of God, each expressive of a certain attribute. Suppose these Names which the Sufis have used were not the Names of God – if they had only held in thought words such as: mercy, compassion, patience, it would have been a merit, not a person. Merit is not creative, and merit is only something which is possessed. Therefore attributes is not important, the important one is the possessor of the attribute. Therefore, instead of thinking of success, the Sufi calls upon the God of success. For him the God of success is not a different God, there is only one God. But only by calling upon that Name of God which is expressive of success he attaches his soul to that perfect Spirit of success.

The other source from whence the idea of many gods has come is the deep thinkers and philosophers, who have seen God in every soul and every soul making a God of its own according to its stage of evolution. Therefore there is a saying among the Hindus: 'There are as many gods as there are strains of music.' In other words, there are numerous imaginations and numberless gods. And if ever this idea was taught to the people, it was to break that ignorance of some people who made God confined to heaven, and kept the earth free from His divine presence. They waited for death to come, when they might be taken into the presence of God, Who was sitting on the throne of justice in the hereafter. By this they tried to show to the people that God is in every soul, and so as many souls, so many gods; some advanced, some not advanced, some further advanced; and yet all gods. If there is a struggle, it is a conflict between gods, if there is harmony, it is a friendship between gods. By these terms they wished to make man realize the most essential truth that God is all. No doubt those who misunderstand will always misunderstand.

This idea brought about corruption also, and made people who regard many gods interested in the legends of the past which narrated the wars and battles which took place among gods. Therefore the wise had again to come to their rescue, and teach them again of the one God; that by this teaching they may again come to the realization of the oneness of life, which is best realized in the God-Ideal.

Surah Eighty-Seven

Al Aala

Love is the best means of making the heart capable of reflecting the soul-power and love in the sense of pain rather than of pleasure. Every blow opens a door whence the soul-power comes forth.

Love is the best means of making the heart capable of reflecting the soul-power—love in the sense of pain rather than as pleasure. Every blow, it seems, opens a door in the heart whence the soul-power comes forth. The concrete manifestations of the soul-power can be witnessed in the depth of the voice, in the choice of words, in the form of a sentence or a phrase, in every movement, pose, gesture, and especially in the expression of the man. Even the atmosphere speaks, though it is difficult for everyone to hear it.

The heart may be likened to soil. Soil may be fertile or a barren desert, but the soil which is fertile is that which bears fruit. It is that which is chosen by living beings to dwell in, although many are lost in the soil of the desert, and lead in it a life of grief and loneliness. Man has both in him, for he is the final manifestation. He may let his heart be a desert where everyone abides hungry and thirsty, or he may make it a fertile and fruitful land where food is provided for hungry souls, the children of the earth, strong or weak, rich or poor, who always hunger for love and sympathy. *Hazrat Inayat Khan*

In the name of Allah, the Beneficent, the Merciful
Praise the name of thy Lord Most High. (87:1 Quran)
Who createth, then disposeth. ((87:2 Quran)
Who measureth, then guidest. (87:3 Quran)
Who bringeth forth the pasturage. (87:4 Quran)
Then turneth it into russet stubble. (87:5 Quran)
We shall make thee read O Muhammad, so that thou shalt not forget. (87:6 Quran)
Save that which Allah willeth. Lo, He knoweth the disclosed and that which still is hidden. (87:7 Quran)

The God Ideal (6) ~ Hazrat Inayat Khan

Very often many who are ready to accept the God-Ideal question the personality of God. Some say: If all is God, then God is not a person; for 'all' is not a person, 'all' is what is expressed by the word all. This question can be answered that, though the seed does not show the flower in it, yet the seed culminates in a flower, and therefore the flower has already existed in the seed. And if one were to say that in the image of the seed the flower was made, it would not be wrong, for the only image of the seed is the flower.

If God has no personality, how can we human beings have a personality, who come from Him, out of His Own Being, and we who can express the divine in the perfection of our souls? If the bubble is water, certainly the sea is water. How can the bubble be water and the sea not be water? Only the difference between the human personality and the Divine Personality, God's Personality is that the human personality can be compared, God's personality has no comparison. Human personality can be compared because of its opposite; God has no opposite, so His Personality cannot be compared. To call God all is like saying: a number of objects all of which exist somewhere together. The word all does not give that meaning which can explain the God-Ideal; the proper expression for God is the Only Being.

Many would ask if it would not be deceiving oneself by making a God of one's imagination. Someone who is not seen in the objective world. The answer is that we are the germs of imagination, our whole life is based and constructed on imagination; and all that is in this objective world, if it were put together — there is one thing which is more lasting in life, which is imagination. The one incapable, who has no value for imagination, is void of art and poetry, of music, manner, and culture. He can very well be compared to a rock, which never troubles to imagine.

Man is not capable of picturing God other than a person, a person with all the best qualities, the ideal person. This does not mean that all that is ugly and evil does not belong to the universe of God, or, in other words, is not in God Himself. But the water of the ocean is ever pure in spite of all the things that may be thrown into it. The Pure One consumes all impurities, and turns them all into purity. Evil and ugliness is to man's limited conception; in God's great Being these have no existence. Therefore he is not wrong who makes God in his imagination the God of all beauty, free from ugliness; the God of all the best qualities, free from all evil. For by that imagination he is drawn nearer and nearer every moment of his life to that Divine Ideal which is the seeking of his soul. And once he has touched divine perfection, in it he will find the fulfillment of his life.

Surah Eighty-Eight

Al Ghashiyah

Every experience on the physical, astral or mental plane is just a dream before the soul.

The soul in itself alone is not other than consciousness, which is all pervading. But when the same consciousness is caught in a limitation through being surrounded by elements, in that state of captivity, it is called soul. Every experience on the physical or astral plane is just a dream before the soul. It is ignorance when it takes this experience to be real. It does so because it cannot see itself; as the eye sees all things, but not itself. Therefore, the soul identifies itself with all things that it sees, and changes its own identity with the change of its constantly changing vision.

The soul has no birth, no death, no beginning, and no end. Sin cannot touch it, nor can virtue exalt it. Wisdom cannot open it up, nor can ignorance darken it. It has been always and always it will be. This is the very being of man, and all else is its cover, like a globe on the light. The soul's unfoldment comes from its own power, which ends in its breaking through the ties of the lower planes. It is free by nature, and looks for freedom during its captivity. All the holy beings of the world have become so by freeing the soul, its freedom being the only object there is in life. *Hazrat Inayat Khan*

In the name of Allah, the Beneficent, the Merciful
Will they not regard the camels, how they are created? (88:17 Quran)
And the heavens, how it is raised? (88:18 Quran)
And the hills, how they are set up? (88:19 Quran)
And the earth, how it is spread? (88:20 Quran)
Remind them, for thou art but a remembrancer. (88:21 Quran)
Thou art not at all a warder over them. (88:22 Quran)

Belief and Disbelief in God ~ Hazrat Inayat Khan

If it were in the power of the person to make another believe, then every great soul that came in the world would have made the world believe in him and his word. Belief is according to the power of one's self-confidence. You find the tendency to trust in a brave man, in a wise man, in a great man; but the tendency to doubt and disbelieve you will find in the weak and insignificant man, who does not know what he believes. This shows that he who trusts himself will trust all; and he who does not trust himself cannot trust anybody. The person who trusts another and does not trust himself, his trust is an illusion, his trust is not alive. It may appear as strength, but it is a weakness. He holds on to something he does not know, and it seems trust. A person who cannot believe in himself cannot believe in a friend, and he who does not believe in another, how can he believe in God, who is beyond the comprehension of man?

Now, coming to the idea of the belief in God: Everything in this world we each of us see according as our sight allows us to see it. Therefore one chooses for oneself a particular color. One chooses blue, another red, another violet. If one color had the same effect upon every person's eye and mind, everyone would choose the same color. And so with form. Then coming to feeling: Although we can understand by words such as love, gratefulness, sincerity, beauty yet the sense of love, sincerity, gratefulness, or beauty in the heart of one person cannot in any way be compared with the same feelings in the heart of another person. Therefore each person's belief is peculiar to himself. It is not only that there are so many different faiths in the world, but in one particular Church how many differences! When you come to think of this subject still further, if you think of the people attending one church, if you examine the feelings of each person, they are different.

Everything in the world that has a name is imaginable; the One and Only Being the imagination cannot reach is God. And yet as God is manifested in all things and in all beings, so in all things and in all beings there is always a part which is unimaginable. That itself is the proof that God is not only a separate God beyond comprehension, God is all and all is God. Man can reach God only as far as his imagination can take him. But the most sensible thing man can do in the pursuit of God is to humble himself and bend in all humility, and say: 'Thou art farther than I can ever reach, and all I can do is to accept Thee in all humility.' The one who, by understanding the idea 'God in man', claims: 'I am God', he, besides all errors, deprives himself of the great beauty of journeying from man to God.

There is a saying in the Hindu language that the diamond does not require to tell its price; its nature, its light, proves it. Those who came with the Divine Spirit gave light, the Message from Above, and their work proved what they brought. Man has always shown his childish tendency. Man is not only a child when he is young, but often man is a child all his life. In every period of the world's history people have fought together, some for one Master or scripture and some for another. It is just like people from one country fighting people from another country, saying: 'Your country cannot produce diamonds;' or 'On your coast there are no pearls to be found, but on our coast there are plenty.' Man clings to the exterior form of scripture and teaching, and has lost hold of the spirit, whose light pervades all over the earth. People have given up their religion, but still churches exist and scriptures exist. What is lost? It is the Light which illuminates and gives man his belief.

Doubt acts as a cover over all things, right and wrong. Today doubt is a cover over multitudes, over nations, over races and communities. Can you remember one instance, in history when one race distrusted, not another nation, but a whole race. The friendship between men and races and nations and religions is all for interest. The central theme of the whole life is selfishness, not that confidence and belief that Christ has taught to man. Religion without confidence is a religion without foundation, but a religion based upon confidence, that is the true belief!

Surah Eighty-Nine

Al Fajr

The fire of devotion purifies the heart of the devotee and leads to spiritual freedom.

Overlooking the faults of others with politeness, tolerance, forgiveness, and resignation is regarded as a moral virtue in the East. Man's heart is visualized as the shrine of God, and even a small injury in thought, word, and deed against it is considered as a great sin against God, the Indwelling One. Gratitude is shown by the loyalty of the Orient and by being true to the salt; the hospitality of a day is remembered throughout all the years of life, while the benefactor never forgets humility even in the midst of his good deeds. There is an Eastern saying, 'Forget thy virtues and remember thy sins.'

'Chained with gold chains about the feet of God.' — Tennyson

Thus the heart, developed by religion and morality, becomes first capable of choosing and then of retaining the object of devotion without wavering for a moment. Yet in the absence of these qualities it remains incapable of either choice or retention.

There have been innumerable devotees in the East, Bhakta or Ashiq, whose devotional powers are absolutely indescribable and ineffable. To the ignorant the story of their lives may appear exaggerated, but the joy of self-negation is greater than that of either spiritual or material joy.

Devotion sweetens the personality, and is the light on the path of the disciple. Those who study mysticism and philosophy while omitting self-sacrifice and resignation grow egoistic and self-centered. Such persons are apt to call themselves either God or a part of God, and thus make an excuse for committing any sins they like. Regardless of sin or virtue they misuse and malign others, being utterly fearless of the hereafter. Yet they forget that 'strait is the gate, and narrow is the way, which leadeth unto life', as the Bible says. *Hazrat Inayat Khan*

In the name of Allah, the Beneficent, the Merciful

By the Dawn. And ten nights. And the Even and the Odd. (89:1-3 Quran)

And the night when it departeth. (89:4 Quran)

There surely is an oath for thinking man. (89:5 Quran)

Dost thou not consider how thy Lord dealt with the tribe of Aad. (89:6 Quran)

With many-columned Irem. (89:7 Quran)

The like of which was not created in the lands. (89:8 Quran)

And with the tribe of Thamud who clove the rocks in the valley. (89:9 Quran)

But ah! Thou soul at peace. (89:27 Quran)

Return unto thy Lord, content in His good pleasure. (89:28 Quran)

Enter thou among my bondmen. (89:29 Quran)

Enter thou My Garden! (89:30 Quran)

The God Ideal (7) ~ Hazrat Inayat Khan

In the terms of the Sufis the Self of God is called Zat, and His qualities, His merits, are named Sifat. The Hindus call the former aspect of God Purusha and the latter Prakriti, which can be rendered in English by the words spirit and nature. Zat, the Spirit of God, is incomprehensible. The reason is that that which comprehends itself is Intelligence, God's real Being; so comprehension has nothing to comprehend in its own Being. No doubt, in our usual terms it is the comprehending faculty in us which we call comprehension; but in this it is not meant so, for intelligence is not necessarily intellect.

Merit is something which is comprehensible; it is something which is clear and distinct, so it can be made intelligible. But intelligence is not intelligible except to its own self. Intelligence knows: I am; but it does not know: what I am. Such is the nature of God. Intelligence would not have known its own power and existence if it had not known something besides itself. So God knows Himself by the manifestation. The manifestation is the self of God, but a self which is limited, a self that makes Him know that He is perfect when He compares His own Being with this limited self which we call nature. Therefore the purpose of the whole Creation is the realization that God Himself gains by discovering His own perfection through this manifestation.

Surah Ninety

Al Balad

When love's fire produces its flame, it illuminates like a torch the devotee's path in life, and all darkness vanishes.

As love is the source of creation and the real sustenance of all beings, so, if man knows how to give it to the world around him as sympathy, as kindness, as service, he supplies to all the food for which every soul hungers. If man knew this secret of life he would win the whole world, without any doubt.

Love can always be discerned in the thought, speech, and action of the lover, for in his every expression there is a charm which shows as a beauty, tenderness, and delicacy. A heart burning in love's fire has a tendency to melt every heart with which it comes in contact. Love is like the fire; its glow is devotion, its flame is wisdom, its smoke is attachment, and its ashes detachment. Flame rises from glow, so it is with wisdom, which rises from devotion. When love's fire produces its flame it illuminates the devotee's path in life like a torch, and all darkness vanishes.

All deeds of kindness and beneficence take root in the soil of the loving heart. Generosity, charity, adaptability, an accommodating nature, even renunciation, are the offspring of love alone. The great, rare and chosen beings, who for ages have been looked up to as ideal in the world, are the possessors of hearts kindled with love. All evil and sin come from the lack of love.

People call love blind, but love in reality is the light of the sight. The eye can only see the surface; love can see much deeper. All ignorance is the lack of love. As fire when not kindled gives only smoke, but when kindled, the illumination flame springs forth, so it is with love. It is blind when undeveloped, but, when its fire is kindled, the flame that lights the path of the traveler from mortality to everlasting life springs forth.

In the name of Allah, the Beneficent, the Merciful
Ah what will covey to thee what the Ascent is? (90: 12 Quran)
It is to free a slave. (90: 13 Quran)
And to feed in the day of hunger. (90:14 Quran)
An orphan near of kin. (90:14 Quran)
Or some poor wretch in misery (90:15 Quran)
And to be of those who believe and exhort one another to perseverance and exhort one another to pity. (90:16 Quran)

The God-Ideal (8) ~ Hazrat Inayat Khan

Why God is called the Creator? Because the creation itself is the evidence of some wisdom working. No mechanical creation could result in such perfection as is nature. All the machine of the scientists are built on the model of nature's mechanism, and every inspiration that the artist gets, he receives it from nature. Nature is so perfect in itself that in reality it needs no scientific or artistic improvement upon it, except that, to satisfy the limited human fancies, man develops science and art.

And yet it is still the creation of God expressed in art and science through man; as in man God is not absent but more able in some ways to finish His creation which necessitates His finishing it as man. No better evidence is needed for a sincere enquirer into the Creator-God. If he only concentrates his mind upon nature, he certainly must sooner or later get an insight into the perfect wisdom which is hidden behind it. The soul that comes into the world is nothing but a divine ray. The impressions it gets on its way while coming to the earth also are from God. For no movement is possible without the command of God. And therefore in all creation, in its every aspect, in the end of search and examination God alone proves to be the only creator.

The word Sustainer is attached to His Name. Jesus Christ said, 'Consider the lilies of the field. They toil not, neither do they spin; yet even Solomon in all his glory was not arrayed as one of these.' And Rumi explains it further in the Masnavi: 'Even the spider is not neglected by God, but is supplied with its food.' If the smallest germ and worm, insignificant as it is, had depended for its supply upon man, who cannot even always supply himself, how would the creation have gone on? It seems that the creatures who do not worry for their supply, to their mouth their food is conveyed.

Man's struggle, it seems, for his supply is greater than all other living beings in the lower creation. But what makes it so? It is not God, it is man himself, who is selfish and who is unfair to his brother, absorbed in his own interests in life. In spite of all famines the world still has sufficient supplies; but imagine the amount of food that has been sunk in the sea how many years the earth, in which man's food is prepared, was neglected by men busy killing one another! If the result of this causes hunger and greater strife, is God to be blamed? It is man who deserves all blame.

Sadi very subtly explains human nature in regard to Providence — it is the most beautiful expression: 'The Creator is always busy preparing for me the supply, but my anxiety for my supply is my natural illness.' Life is such a phenomenon, if only we dive deep into it, that we find no question is without an answer. It never is so that we need something and are not provided with it. Only the difference is between what we think we need and what we really need. For the supply is always greater than our need. And therefore Providence is always a phenomenon. Sometimes we look at it with smiles, at other times with tears. But it is something real and living; and more real it will prove to be if we look at it by climbing to the top of our reason.

But what we can marvel most at in life is to know that, in spite of His great justice, God is the Forgiver. He forgives even more than He judges. For justice comes from His Intelligence, but forgiveness comes from His Divine Love. When His Divine Love rises as a wave it washes away the sins of a whole life in a moment. For law has no power to stand before love, the stream of love sweeps it away.

Surah Ninety-One

Ash Shams

It is mistrust that misleads; sincerity always leads straight to the goal.

With regard to trusting people, a person may think. 'Is it right to believe in anything a person says? Is it right to trust everybody? There are many people who are not worthy of trust; shall we then trust everybody in order to develop our trust?' The answer is yes. Perhaps we will have failures, but we will only trust another person when we trust ourselves, when we have faith in ourselves then we will have faith in another. Without faith in ourselves we can never have faith in another; to have faith in another is to have faith in ourselves. It does not matter if once or twice we are disappointed, but if we are afraid of being disappointed even once in our lives, perhaps we will doubt all through life, and so there will never come a time when we will be able to trust anybody, even ourselves. Hazrat Inayat Khan

In the name of Allah, the Beneficent, the Merciful

By the sun and his brightness. (91:1 Quran)

And the moon when she followeth him. (91:2 Quran)

And the day when it revealeth him. (91:3 Quran)

And the night when it enshroudeth him. (91:4 Quran)

And the heavens and Him who built it. (91:5 Quran)

And the earth and Him who spread it. (91:6 Quran)

And a soul and Him who perfected it. (91:7 Quran)

And inspired it with conscience of what is wrong for it and what is right for it. (91:8 Quran)

He is indeed successful who causes it to grow. (91:9 Quran)

And he is indeed failure who stunneth it. (91:10 Quran)

The God-Ideal (9) ~ Hazrat Inayat Khan

God is called King of Heaven and of the earth, and of the seen and unseen beings only because we have no better words than the words we use for all the things of this world. To call God King does not raise Him in anyway higher that the position He has, it only helps us to make his power and glory more intelligible to our mind. And yet there are certain characters which are kingly characters, and such characters may be seen in God in their perfection. It does not mean that every person has not that character. It only means that from a higher position a soul shows out that character more, perhaps, than in an ordinary capacity. And that character is love hidden behind indifference. In Sufic terms this character is denoted by a Persian word, *bi-niyaz,* which means hidden. It does not mean: the hidden God, it means, hidden beauty. Love expressed is one thing and love hidden is another thing. Under the veil of indifference, love is often hidden, and the Sufi poets have pictured it most beautifully in their verses, which are nothing but pictures of human life and nature.

There are examples in the histories of the kings which show this character. Sometimes a person whom the king favored the most was kept back from being the prime minister. This did not mean that it was not the wish of the king, it only meant that the king considered the sympathy and admiration he had for the person more than the prime ministership. In other aspects one sees it: the king did not speak to a person for a long time; this did not mean that the king disfavored him so, it only meant that the king knew that he would understand. There are instances that the patience of the saints and sages has been tried to the uttermost. The pain and suffering that the spiritual souls have sometimes gone through has been greater than the average person's. Behind this indifference there are many reasons.

And then one sees the other part of kingliness: that those who; sometimes, the king cared little for were graciously received and amply rewarded. And the ordinary mind could not conceive the reason behind. The one who is responsible for his subjects as a king, he understood rightly, like a gardener who knows which plant to rear and which tree had better be out of the garden. In spite of all opposition from all around the kings have held to their idea, conscious of their duty. So it is with God.

But, King apart, even the manner and method of a responsible person is not always understood by another whose responsibility is not the same. So how can man always understand the ways of God, the only King in the true sense of the word, before whom all other kings are nothing but imitations? And it is the Kingship of God which manifests in the blooming of every soul. When a soul arrives at its full bloom, it begins to show the color and spread the fragrance of the Divine Spirit of God.

Surah Ninety-Two

Al Leyl

Love lies in service; only that which is done not for fame or name, not for the appreciation or thanks of those for whom it is done, is love's service.

The lover shows kindness and beneficence to the beloved. He does whatever he can for the beloved in the way of help, service, sacrifice, kindness, or rescue, and hides it from the world and even from the beloved. If the beloved does anything for him he exaggerates it, idealizes it. Makes it into a mountain from a molehill. He takes poison from the hands of the beloved as sugar, and love's pain in the wound of his heart is his only joy. By magnifying and idealizing whatever the beloved does for him and by diminishing and forgetting whatever he himself does for the beloved, he first develops his own gratitude, which creates all goodness in his life.

The Sufi moral is this: Love another and do not depend upon his love; and: Do good to another and do not depend upon receiving good from him; serve another and do not look for service from him. All you do for another out of your love and kindness, you should think that you do, not to that person, but to God. And if the person returns love for love, goodness for goodness, service for service, so much the better. If he does not return it, then pity him for what he loses; for his gain is much less than his loss.

Do not look for thanks or appreciation for all the good you do to others, nor use it as a means to stimulate your vanity. Do all that you consider good for the sake of goodness, not even for a return of that from God. *Hazrat Inayat Khan*

In the name of Allah, the Beneficent, the Merciful
By the night enshrouding. (92:1 Quran)
And the day resplendent. (92:2 Quran)
And Him Who hath created male and female. (92:3 Quran)
Lo! Your effort is dispersed toward divers ends. (92:4 Quran)
And for him who giveth and is dutiful toward Allah. (92:5 Quran)
And believeth in goodness. (92:6 Quran)
Surely We will ease his way unto the state of ease. (92:7 Quran)

The God-Ideal (10) ~ Hazrat Inayat Khan

The reason why the soul seeks for the God-Ideal is that it is dissatisfied with all that momentarily satisfies it. All beauty and goodness and greatness which man attributes to God is something he admires and seeks through life. He admires these things in others and strives to attain them for himself; and when, at the end of examination, he finds that all that he touches as good, great, or beautiful falls short of that perfection which is his soul's seeking, he then raises his eyes towards the sky and seeks for the One Who has beauty, goodness, and greatness, and that is God.

The one who does not seek for God, he has, in the end of his journey of illusion, a disappointment. For through the whole journey he did not find the perfection of beauty, goodness and greatness on the earth, and he neither believed nor expected to meet such an ideal in Heaven. All disappointments, which are the natural outcome of this life of illusion, disappear when once a person has touched the God-Ideal, for what one seeks after in life one finds in God.

Now the question is: all beauty, goodness and greatness, however small and limited, can be found on the earth, but where can the same be found in the perfection called God? This may be answered that what is first necessary is the belief that there is such a Being as God, in whom goodness, beauty and greatness is perfect. In the beginning it will seem nothing but a belief; but in time, if the belief is kept in sincerity and faith, that belief will become like the egg of the phoenix, out of which the magic bird is born. It is the birth of God which is the birth of the soul.

Every soul seeks for happiness, and after running after all objects which, for the moment, seem to give happiness, finds out that nowhere is there perfect happiness except in God. This happiness cannot come by merely believing in God. Believing is a process. By this process the God within is awakened and made living. It is the living of God which gives happiness. When one sees the injustice, the falsehood, the unfriendliness of human nature, and to what degree this nature develops, and that it culminates in tyranny of which individuals and the multitude become victims, there seems to be only one Source, and that is the center of the whole life, which is God, in whom there is the place of safety from it all, and the source of peace, which is the longing of every soul.

Surah Ninety-Three

Ad Duha

The soul is all light; darkness is caused by the deadness of the heart; pain makes it alive.

Those who have avoided love in life from fear of its pain have lost more than the lover, who by losing himself gains all. The loveless first lose all, until at last their self is also snatched away from their hands. The warmth of the lover's atmosphere, the piercing effect of his voice, the appeal of his words, all come from the pain of his heart. The heart is not living until it has experienced pain. Man has not lived if he has lived and worked with his body and mind without heart. The soul is all light, but all darkness is caused by the death of the heart. Pain makes it alive. The same heart that was once full of bitterness, when purified by love

becomes the source of all goodness. All deeds of kindness spring from it.
Hazrat Inayat Khan

In the name of Allah, the Beneficent, the Merciful

By the morning hours. (93:1 Quran)

And by the night when it is stillest. (93:2 Quran)

Thy Lord hath not forsaken thee nor doth He hate thee. (93:3 Quran)

And verily the latter portion will be better for them than the former.
(93:4 Quran)

And verily thy Lord will give unto thee so that thou wilt be content.
(93:5 Quran)

Did He not find thee an orphan and protect thee? (93:6 Quran)

Did He not find thee wandering and direct thee? (93:7 Quran)

Did He not find thee destitute and enrich thee. (93:8 Quran)

Therefor the orphan oppress not. (93:9 Quran)

Therefor the beggar drive not away. (93:10 Quran)

Therefor of the bounty of thy Lord be thy discourse. (93:11 Quran)

The God-Ideal (11) ~ Hazrat Inayat Khan

The God-Ideal is meant to waken in the soul God, that he may realize His Kingship. The Kingdoms of the earth, from the time man has evolved so as to understand his affairs, have been established, where man has learned the first lesson when he first knew what a king means, what a kingdom means, he knew that there was someone whose command was obeyed by all, great and small; in the kingdom; who is the upraiser and the judge of all those who deserve honor and respect, who possess a treasure in the kingdom; who is as a Mother and Father of his subjects. Once this was learned, it gave the person an education to understand what a king means, as a child after playing with her dolls begins to understand the cares of the household.

The next step was taken in the spiritual path when the spiritual hierarchy was recognized. The prophet, or the high-priest was recognized, representing the spiritual head. Then there was the hierarchy. And in this way the next step was taken with the realization that it is not the outer environments, money and possession, which make a king, but it is the spiritual realization which can make a person greater than a king with all his kingly surroundings. And this was proved to people when the king, who was accepted as the principal and head of the community, went before the high-priest with bent head, and knelt down in the place of prayer. This gave the next lesson, that kingship is not in outer wealth but in spirituality that even the king stands humbly at the door of the God-realized man.

When once this step was taken, then there was the third step. And that was to see that the high-priest considered was such even by the king knelt down and bent his head low to the Lord, King of humanity, showing his greatness as dust before God, to Whom alone belongs all greatness. When the greatness of God was realized, God was glorified and the purpose of aristocracy was fulfilled, for it was nothing but a rehearsal before the battle. Once man realized that it is God alone before Whom man should bow, it is God alone Who really is rich and all are poor, it is God alone whose wisdom and justice are perfect, then before him the kingship of the king and the holiness of the high-priest faded away: before him remained only one King, the King of kings; on Him he depended and under Him he sought refuge under all the different circumstances in life.

After one had taken these three steps towards the goal, he found the goal to be quite different from the way that he had taken. And the goal was the finding of the traces of that King within oneself; a spark of that divine light which is the illumination of one's own heart; a ray of that Sun which is the light of the whole universe. And so self-realization developed, in which the soul found that wisdom, illumination and peace which was the purpose of the God-Ideal.

Surah Ninety-Four

Al Inshirah
The quality of forgiveness that burns up all things except beauty is the quality of love.

Nature is such that no two things are created alike; and the human being cannot expect his or her mate, whom nature made, to be as docile and flexible as that creature whom his imagination alone conceives. To make a friend, forgiveness is required which burns up all things, leaving only beauty.

Love is the fire that burns all infirmities. By criticizing, by judging, by looking at wickedness with contempt, one does not help the wicked or the stupid person. The one who helps is he who is ready to overlook, who is ready to forgive, to tolerate, to take disadvantages he may have to meet with patiently.

To resist evil, however, usually means to participate in and be guilty of the same evil. There is a story told of Muhammad, that a man who had always maligned him and behaved as a bitter and treacherous enemy, came to see him. His disciples, hoping for revenge, were disappointed and indignant to find that Muhammad treated his despicable enemy with courtesy, even deference, granting his request. 'Did you not see the gray in his beard?' asked Muhammad after the man had gone. 'The man is old, and his age at least called for my courtesy.' It is forgiveness and that forbearance which is a recognition of the freedom and dignity of the human being, that consume all ugliness and burn up all unworthiness, leaving only beauty there. *Hazrat Inayat Khan*

In the name of Allah, the Beneficent, the Merciful

Have We not caused thy bosom to dilate. (94:1 Quran)

And eased thee of burden. Which weighed down thy back. (94:2-3 Quran)

And exalted thy fame. (94:4 Quran)

But Lo! With hardship goeth ease. (94:5 Quran)

Lo! With hardship goeth ease. (94:6 Quran)

So when thou are relieved, still toil. (95:7 Quran)

And strive to please thy Lord. (94:8 Quran)

God the Infinite ~ Hazrat Inayat Khan

The Infinite God is the Self of God, and all that has manifested under name and form is the outward aspect of God. When we take all the forms existing and all the names put together, it becomes one form which is the Form of God. In other words, all names are the Name and all forms are the Form of God. But as God is One, His Form is also one; and that is the sum-total of all names and forms; there is no thing or being which is not the Being of God. In order to teach this the wise have said there is God in everything, God is in every being.

Many have wondered: if He is in everything, how does He live in everything, and as what; and if He is in man, where is He to be found, and what part of man's being is to be considered God? Many answers may be given, and yet no answer will satisfy. For the true answer is that all is God and God is all, none exists save He. And the question: what we are then — may be answered by the phrase in the Bible that 'We live and move and have our being in God.' God is we, but we are not gods. The difference between God and our being is not of the Being; in Being, God and we are one. The difference is in our limitation and the perfection of God.

How are we to conceive the idea of God the Absolute? We are not meant to conceive that. We, as limited beings, are not able to know perfection, but perfection itself knows perfection. We can imagine and make a God of our own, to make God intelligible to us, to make it easy for us to advance on the spiritual path. And as we advance, the Unlimited Being working through us makes His own way and realizes His perfection. For in this realization He only realizes Himself, which is not at all difficult for Him.

Man thinks that religion or philosophy or mysticism, all this he has learned as he has evolved. Yes, it is true. But the result of all this learning and evolution is realized to a certain degree, not only by unevolved human beings, but even by the animals and birds. They all have their religion, and they all worship God in their own way. The birds, while singing in the forest, feel that exaltation even more than man feels it after he has worshipped God. For all men who join in the prayers may not be as sincere as the birds in the forest; not one of them says its prayers without sincerity. If a soul were wakened to feel what they feel when singing in the forest at dawn, he would know that their prayer is even more exalting than his own, for their prayer is more natural. The godly, therefore, worship their God with nature, and in this manner or worship they experience perfect exaltation as the result of their prayer.

Man thinks he is able to meditate and that he can concentrate, but he cannot do better meditation and concentration than the animals and birds in the forest. The cobra attracts its food by a thought. There are certain cobras whose food comes and falls into their mouth. They fast patiently for a long time, not worrying about the food for the morrow. There are men who, on the contrary, are anxiously busy about their breakfast, they are not even certain of their luncheon. They have no confidence in their own power nor faith in the providence of God.

In short, spirituality is attained by all beings; not only by man but by the beasts and the birds; and each has its own religion, its principle, its law, and its morals. For instance, a bird, whose honor it is to fly over the heads of those who walk on the earth, feels it beneath its dignity to be touched by an earthy being, it feels it is polluted. And if a bird is touched once by a human being, its fellow-creatures will not rest till they have killed it, for it is outcast for them; they dwell in the air and it is their dignity to be so.

The study of nature is not only of interest for the student of science; the one who treads the path of spirituality, for him the study of nature is of immense interest. Man will find in the end of his search in the spiritual line that all beings — including trees and plants, rocks and mountains — all are prayerful, and all attain to that spiritual perfection which is the only longing of all souls.

Surah Ninety-Five

At Tin

Each individual composes the music of his own life; if he injures another he breaks the harmony and there is discord in the melody of his life.

All the trouble in the world, and all the disastrous results arising out of it, all come from lack of harmony. And this shows that the world needs harmony today more than ever before. The true use of music is to become musical in one's thoughts, words, and actions. We must be able to give the harmony for which the soul yearns and longs every moment. All the tragedy in the world, in the individual and in the multitude, comes from lack of harmony. And harmony is best given by producing harmony in one's own life.

The whole of life is as music and in order to study life we must study it as music. It is not only study, it is also practice which makes man perfect. If someone tells me that a certain person is miserable or wretched or distressed, my answer will be that he is out of tune.

The Sufi harmonizes with everybody whether good or bad, wise or foolish, by becoming like the key-note. All races, nations, classes and people are like a strain of music based upon one chord, where the key-note, the common interest, holds so many personalities in a single bond of harmony. By a study of life the Sufi learns and practices the nature of its harmony. He establishes harmony with the self, with others, with the universe and with the infinite. He identifies himself with another, he sees himself, so to speak, in every other being. He cares for neither blame nor praise, considering both as coming from himself. He overlooks the faults of others, considering that they know no better. He hides the faults of others, and suppresses any facts that would cause disharmony.

His constant fight is with the Nafs (self-interest), the root of all disharmony and the only enemy of man. By crushing this enemy man gains mastery over himself; this wins for him mastery over the whole universe, because the wall standing between the self and the Almighty has been broken down. Gentleness, mildness, respect, humility, modesty, self-denial, conscientiousness, tolerance and forgiveness are considered by the Sufi as the attributes which produce harmony within one's own soul as well as within that of another. *Hazrat Inayat Khan*

In the name of Allah, the Beneficent, the Merciful

By the fig and the olive. (95:1 Quran)

By Mount Sinai. (95:2 Quran)

And by this land made safe. (95:3 Quran)

Surely We created man of best stature. (95:4 Quran)

Then We reduced him to the lowest of the low. (95:5 Quran)

Save those who believe and do good works and theirs is a reward unfailing. (95:6 Quran)

So who henceforth will give the lie to thee about the judgment? (95:7 Quran)

Is not Allah the most conclusive of all judges? (95:8 Quran)

Divine Blessing ~ Hazrat Inayat Khan

Heaven can be defined in three ways. One way is the conception of creeds, as in Arabia, when the Bedouin came to the Prophet, and asked him, what is Heaven? he said, 'Heaven is a place where there are rivers of milk, tanks of honey, and emeralds and pearls and rubies and diamonds is to be found, and all that is good and beautiful is to be found there.' They said, that is the place we are looking for. And the Prophet said, that place you will only enter if you will do good. But if you will lie and thieve and rob you will go to the other place, then he showed the other place with all kinds of torture. That is the place which is taught to the ordinary man.

Then there is a Heaven which is reached above. What is above us is Heaven. The plane where we stand is the earth, and the plane to which we look forward is Heaven. And we all look forward to something, not only human beings, but also the earth is reaching upwards in the form of mountains and hills. The water is reaching upwards in the form of rising waves. Birds try to reach upwards by flying, and the animals try to reach upwards by standing on their hind legs. And in this way every creature is trying to reach upwards, though he does not know where he wants to, and what he wants to, reach. But he wants to reach upwards.

And when we look upwards what do we find? We find stars and the moon and the sun. And it is more pleasant to look at it than to look at the earth with all its beauties. And it is the climate in the Western countries which does not allow us to look at Heaven, but in the tropical countries you can sit for hours. That is the only thing which can lift you up, and make you free from all the worries of this dense earth. What do we see? We only see light. The light inspires us, attracts us, and gives us such a feeling of upliftment, what nothing can give. It shows us that light is the thing that we seek after, even light in its visible form, as we see in the Heaven. But that is symbolical Heaven, real Heaven is where there is no light that our eyes can see, but there is light that our soul can see. And that light is the Grace of God, that light is the soul's unfoldment, that light is wakening to the secret of life; and it is that wakening which is Heaven.

And there is a third description, which is description of Omar Khayyam. That the Heaven of each person is what gives him a joy; as in the Vadan it is said: Whether you are at the top of the mountain or at the foot, if you are happy where you are, that is all that matters. If you are happy at the foot, you are just as much in Heaven as when you are at the top. And if you are happy at the top you are just as much in Heaven as when you are at the foot. It is the soul experiencing something, wakening to a certain consciousness, which give on a joy. And the joy comes as a fulfillment of life, and it is that joy which can be called Heaven.

Surah Ninety-Six

Al Alaq
He who with sincerity seeks his real purpose in life is himself sought by that purpose.

One may ask, 'What is the best way for a person to understand his life's purpose?' If one follows the bent of one's own mind, if one follows the track to which one is attracted, if one follows one's own inclination, which is not satisfied with anything else, one feels, 'There is something waiting for me (which one does not know at the time), which will bring me satisfaction.' Besides, if one is intuitive and mystical, it is easier still, because then one is continually told what the purpose of one's life is. For nature has such a perfection of wisdom. One sees that the insects are given the sense to make their little houses and to protect themselves and make a store of their food. The bees, who have the gift of making honey, are taught how to make honey. So nature has taught every soul to seek its purpose.

When a person has arrived at this stage, he has risen above the limitations of the world. Then he has become entitled to experience the joy of coming near to the real purpose of life. It is then that in everything that he says or does, he will be accomplishing that purpose. We come to understand by this that the further we go the more tolerant we become. Outward things matter little. It is the inward realization which counts. However sacred duty may be, however high may be the hope of paradise, however great the happiness one may experience in the pleasures of the earth, however much satisfaction one may find in earthly treasures, the purpose of life is in rising above all these things. Therefore, in this fulfillment it is not that man attained, but that God Himself has fulfilled His purpose. Hazrat Inayat Khan

In the name of Allah, the Beneficent, the Merciful
Read: In the name of thy Lord who createth. (96:1 Quran)
Createth man from a clot. (96:2 Quran)
Read: And thy Lord is the Most Bounteous. (96:3 Quran)
Who teacheth by the pen. (96:4 Quran)
Teacheth man that which he knew not. (96:5 Quran)
Nay, but verily man is rebellious. (96:6 Quran)
That he Thinketh himself independent! (96:7 Quran)
Lo! Unto thy Lord is the return. (96:8 Quran)
Hast thou seen him who dissuadeth. (96:9 Quran)
A slave when he prayeth? (96:10 Quran)

Hast thou seen if he relieth on the guidance of Allah. (96:11 Quran)
Or enjoineth piety? (96:12 Quran)

Divine Grace ~ Hazrat Inayat Khan

There is a saying that the one who troubles much about the cause, is far removed from the cause. Many wonder: if I am happy in life, what is the cause of it? If I am sorry in life, what is the cause of it? Is it my past life from where I have brought something which brings me happiness or unhappiness or is it my action in this life which is the cause of my happiness or unhappiness? And one can give a thousand answers to it and at the same time one cannot satisfy the questioner fully. When people think much about the law, they forget about love. When they think that the world is constructed according to a certain law, then they forget the Constructor Who is called in the Bible: Love, God is Love.

Many know the Grace of God. And what it means? It means a wave of favor, a rising of love, a manifestation of compassion which sees no particular reason. One may say: 'Does God close His eyes? Why must it be like this?' But in human nature we see the same thing. The Divine nature can be recognized by human nature. Ask a lover who loves someone: 'What is the beauty of that person? What is in that person that makes you love her? He may try to explain: 'It is because this person is kind, or because this person is beautiful, or because this person is good, or because this person is compassionate, or intellectual, or learned.' But that is not the real cause. If really he knows what makes him love, he will say: 'Because my beloved is beloved; that is the reason. There is no other reason.' One can give a reason for everything. One can say': I pay this person because he is good in his work: I pay for this stone because it is beautiful; but I cannot give a reason why I love; there is no reason for it.'

Love stands beyond law, beyond reason. The love of God works beyond reason, that Divine Love which is called the Grace of God, no piety, no spirituality, no devotion can attract it. No one can say: 'I will draw the Divine Grace.' God apart, can anyone say in this world: 'I shall draw the friendship of someone.' No one can say this. This is something which comes by itself. No one can command or attract it, or compel anyone to be his friend. It is natural. God's Grace is God's friendship, God's Grace is God's Love, God's Compassion. No one has the power to draw it, to attract it; no meditation, no spirituality, no good action can attract it. There is no commercial business between God and man, God stands free from rules which humanity recognizes. That aspect makes him the Lord of His own creation. As the wind blows, as the wind comes when it comes, so the Grace of God comes when it is its time to come.

God's compassion cannot be returned by all life's good actions. The relation of God and man apart, can one return a real thought of love, all a friend has done to us? We can love that friend, his loving kindness, and his compassion. But we can never pay it. In all our life we cannot pay it. And when we see the kindness and compassion of God which is always hidden from our view because we are always seeing what is lacking, the pain, the suffering, and the difficulties. Man is so absorbed in them that he loses the vision of all the good that is there. We can never be grateful enough, if we saw like this, that it is not the law, but that it is the Grace of God which governs our life. And it is the trust and confidence in this Grace which does not only console a person, but which lifts him and brings him nearer and nearer to the Grace of God.

Surah Ninety-Seven

Al Qadir

Through motion and change, life becomes intelligible; we live a life of change, but it is constancy we seek. It is this innate desire of the soul that leads man to God.

Man placed in the midst of this ever-changing world yet appreciates and seeks for constancy somewhere. He does not know that he must develop the nature of constancy in himself; it is the nature of the soul to value that which is dependable. But is there anything in the world on which one can depend, which is above change and destruction? All that is born, all that is made, must one day face destruction. All that has a beginning has also an end; but if there is anything one can depend upon it is hidden in the heart of man, it is the divine spark, the true philosopher's stone, the real gold, which is the innermost being of man.

What is this mortal world? What is this physical existence? What is this life of changes? If it were not for belief, what use is it all? Something which is changing, something which is not reliable, something which is liable to destruction. Therefore it is not only for the sake of truth, but for life itself that one must find belief in oneself, develop it, and nurture it. Allow it to grow every moment of one's life that it may culminate in faith. It is that faith which is the mystery of life, the secret of salvation.

Hazrat Inayat Khan

In the name of Allah, the Beneficent, the Merciful

Lo! We revealed it on the Night of Power. (97:1 Quran)

Ah! What will convey unto thee what the Night of Power is? (97:2 Quran)

The Night of Power is better than a thousand months. (97:3 Quran)

The angels and the spirits descend therein by the permission of their Lord with all decrees. (97:4 Quran)

That night is Peace until the rising of the dawn. (97:5 Quran)

Belief and Superstition ~ Hazrat Inayat Khan

Every country seems to have certain beliefs which are called beliefs by the believers and superstitions by those who do not believe. There are beliefs which arise from some subtle experiences of life, and some which spring from intuition, and they are believed by some who are inclined to believe and they are mocked at by some who cannot understand their meaning, and often by those who do not wish to trouble themselves to investigate the truth in them. It is easy to laugh at things, and it takes patience to endure and tolerate things that cannot appeal to one's reason. And it is difficult to investigate the truth of such beliefs, for it requires something more than reason to probe the depths of life. Those from whom the beliefs come, naturally could not give the explanation of those beliefs to everybody; for the man who is capable of believing a thing is not necessarily capable of understanding it by an analytical explanation. There are natures which would be willing to believe a thing if it is for their good, if it comes from someone who they trust, but it is too much trouble for them to go deeply into the matter. For some among them it is better that they should not have an analytical knowledge of a belief, for to some the belief is helpful but its explanation confusing. It is a certain grade of evolution that enables man to understand a certain belief, and a man must not be told what he is incapable of understanding, for, instead of helping him, it puts him off.

Surah Ninety-Eight

Al Beyyinah
Love is the essence of all religion, mysticism and philosophy.

Love is the practice of the moral of Suluk, the way of beneficence. The lover's pleasure is in the pleasure of the beloved. The lover is satisfied when the beloved is fed. The lover is vain when the beloved is adorned. 'Who in life blesses the one who curses him? Who in life admires the one who hates him? Who in life proves faithful to the one who is faithless? No other than a lover.' And in the end the lover's self is lost from his vision and only the beloved's image, the desired vision, is before him forever.

Love is the essence of all religion, mysticism, and philosophy, and for the one who has learnt this, love fulfills the purpose of religion, ethics, and philosophy, and the lover is raised above all diversities of faiths and beliefs.

For the Sufi there is one principle which is most essential to be remembered and that is consideration for human feeling. If one practices in his life this one principle he need not learn much more; he need not trouble about philosophy, he need not follow an old or a new religion, for this principle in itself is the essence of all religions. God is love, but where does God dwell? He abides in the heart of man.

Hazrat Inayat Khan

In the name of Allah, the Beneficent, the Merciful

Those who disbelieve among the People of the Scripture and the idolaters could not have left off erring till clear proof came unto them. (98:1 Quran)

A messenger from Allah, reading purified pages. (98:2 Quran)

Containing correct scriptures. (98:3 Quran)

Nor were the People of the Scripture divided until after the clear proof came unto them. (98:4 Quran)

And they are ordered naught else than to serve Allah, keeping religion pure for Him, as men by nature is upright, and to establish worship and to pay the poor due. That is true religion. (98:5 Quran)

Belief ~ Hazrat Inayat Khan

The term 'belief' is used of an idea that one believes and for which one cannot give reason. When such ideas are of an ordinary nature they are termed superstitions, and when they are of a sacred nature they are called beliefs.

Often man confuses belief with truth. Many people, without understanding their own belief hold it not as a truth but as *the* truth, and thereby ignore every other belief which seems to them different from the truth they possess. In reality belief is not the truth nor is the truth a belief. When a person has risen to the understanding of the truth it is no more a belief for him, it is a conviction.

The beliefs of a sacred nature, which come in the realm of religion, are as steps towards the goal which is called truth, and when man stops at a belief the belief holds him and he holds the belief. Neither can the belief push him onward nor can he advance. In many cases belief, which should serve as wings on which to soar toward the height, becomes as nails fixing man onto the earth. Every belief in the beginning is a step in the dark, but as man draws nearer to the goal, he at every step becomes more and more illuminated. Therefore there is hope for the believer, but the case of the unbeliever is hopeless.

There are souls who are capable of believing, even capable of understanding their belief, who yet for some reason or other are not willing to believe and reject a belief before the understanding comes. The wise course in life would be to try to become a pupil, a pupil of one teacher as well as a pupil of all beings; it is then that one will become the pupil of God. Then the wise course would be to investigate the truth of belief instead of giving up one's belief, also to be patiently tolerant of the belief of another until one sees from his point of view the truth of his belief. When man sees only from his own point of view, he sees with one eye and the other eye is closed. The complete view is in seeing from both points of view, however contrary they may be. It is this tendency which will balance things and will give the right idea of things. In order to view a building one must stand in the street and view it, instead of standing inside it and wanting to see the outside.

In understanding beliefs one must be able to neutralize one's spirit, and to the extent to which it is neutralized man becomes capable of seeing the belief in its right sense. When man says, on hearing something from another, 'That is not what I believe', he shows his weakness, he shows his incapacity to view the belief of the other from the point of view of that other. Knowledge comes by readiness to learn, and when we refuse it in life it is by lack of readiness. No matter from what source knowledge may seem to come, it is from one source in reality, and when the mind becomes a free receptacle knowledge flows freely into the heart. There is some truth hidden in every religious belief, and often it is of greater value than it may seem to be. And believing in a thing without understanding is a first step forward to knowledge, and refusing to believe when a belief is presented means taking a step backward. When a person is content with his belief that is a comfortable state of being, but it is the understanding of the belief which is ideal.

Surah Ninety-Nine

Az Zilzal

Every being has a definite vocation and his vocation is the light that illuminates his life. The man who disregards his vocation is as a lamp unlit.

We find with many people that somehow they never happen to find their life's vocation. And what happens then is that in the end they consider their life a failure. All through their life they go from one thing to another, yet as they do not know their life's object they can accomplish so little. When people ask why they do not succeed, the answer is: because they have not yet found their object. As soon as a person has found his life's object he begins to feel at home in this world, where before he had felt himself in a strange world. No sooner has a person found his way than he will prove to be fortunate, because all the things he wants to accomplish will come by themselves.

Even if the whole world were against him, he will get such a power that he can hold on to his object against anything. He will get such a patience that when he is on the way to his object no misfortune will discourage him. There is no doubt that as long as he has not found it he will go from one thing to another, and again to another; and he will think that life is against him. Then he will begin to find fault with individuals, conditions, plans, climate, with everything. Thus what is called fortunate or successful is really having the right object. When a person is wearing clothes which were not made for him, he says they are too wide or too short, but when they are his clothes he feels comfortable in them. Everyone should therefore be given freedom to choose his object in life. And if he finds his object one knows that he is on the right path. Hazrat Inayat Khan

In the name of Allah, the Magnificent, the Merciful
When the earth is shaken with her final earthquake. (99:1 Quran)
And earth yieldeth up her burdens. (99:2 Quran)
And man saith: what aileth her? (99:3 Quran)
That day she will relate her chronicles. (99:4 Quran)
Because thy Lord inspireth her. (99:5 Quran)
That day mankind will issue forth in scattered groups to be shown their deeds. (99:6 Quran)
And whoso doeth good an atom's weight will see it then. (99:7 Quran)
And whoso doeth ill an atom's weight will see it then. (99:8 Quran)

The Origin of the Custom of the Seclusion of Women ~ Hazrat Inayat Khan

The custom of the seclusion of women has its source in mystical thought. There used to be the mystical orders of people in the East who contemplated in solitude and lived in seclusion. The magnetism and power of influence that they developed by seclusion was in itself a marvel. This gave power to their gaze, power in their word, and influence in their atmosphere. This custom of seclusion was then imitated by the kings and people of high rank.

They had two ways of veiling themselves when away from home. One was to put a covering over the back of the head, which was made to hang down in front, so that the eyes could be half-covered; and the other was to put a veil over the face. It was a sort of mantle that they put on their head. Every prophet of Beni Israel had this. In the ancient pictures of the prophets of the Semitic race one will always see the head covered with a mantle. In the Hindu race also many orders of Buddhists and Yogis wore a mantle over the head. The veil which the kings also used, which was called *Makna*, later became customary in the East, and ladies of high rank wore what is called in Turkish the *Yashmak*. For thousands of years it has been the custom among Parsis that during their religious services the priest covers his head with a turban together with a mantle, and the Parsi women have kept the custom of covering the head with a white cloth, though it is less observed at the present time. In India, among Hindus as well as among Muslims, there is a custom at weddings of veiling the faces of bride and bridegroom with a veil of jasmine flowers.

Under all these different customs of veiling the head and face one finds a mystical significance. Man's form is considered by Sufis as consisting of two parts, the head and the body, the body for action and the head for thought. Since the head is for thought its radiance is incomparably greater than that of the body, and the hairs are as rays of that radiance in a physical form. It is a constant outpouring of light that one observes in man's life. Every action of looking, or breathing, or speaking, robs so much of the radiance out of man's life. By preserving this radiance the mystic develops within him that influence, power and magnetism which in the average person are wasted. For instance, closing the eyes, which is a custom among mystics, not only helps in concentration and repose of mind, but during the moment when the eyes are closed, it preserves the radiance from flowing out. These customs were helpful to the kings and commanders for developing their power and influence, and they were valued for ladies of rank for preserving their beauty and charm. We learn by this that a life but little exposed to the outer world, whether through seclusion, or silence, or a perfect state of repose with the closed eyes, clasped hands and crossed legs, has a great influence.

Surah One Hundred

Al Aadiyat
The heart sleeps until it is awakened to life by a blow; it is as a rock, and the hidden fire flashes out when struck by another rock.

It is the thoughts that spring from the depths of the heart which become inspirations and revelations, and these come from the hearts of awakened souls, called by the Sufis, *Sahib-i Dil*. The bringers of joy are the children of sorrow. Every blow we get in life pierces the heart and awakens our feelings to sympathize with others, and every swing of comfort lulls us to sleep, and we become unaware of all. This proves the truth of these words, 'Blessed are they that mourn.'

Every atom, every object, every condition and every living being has a time of awakening. Sometimes there is a gradual awakening, and sometimes there is a sudden awakening. To some persons it comes in a moment's time—by a blow, by a disappointment, or because their heart has broken through something that happened suddenly. It seemed cruel, but at the same time the result was a sudden awakening and this awakening brought a blessing beyond praise. The outlook changed, the insight deepened; joy, quiet, independence and freedom were felt, and compassion showed in the attitude. A person who would never forgive, who liked to take revenge, who was easily displeased and cross, a person who would measure and weigh, when his soul is awakened, becomes in one moment a different person.

The heart is like a being which is asleep and receiving a sharp blow it awakens. Also the heart is like a stone and the fire which is hidden within it can only he brought to life when it is struck by a hard material. Then the fire appears. So it is with the heart. The fire which is life, love and feeling and which is the most sacred thing in us, is hidden in the heart as the fire in the stone. When it is struck hardly the fire appears. That is why we receive great blows in life. The person becomes thoughtful as soon as the fire appears. And he looks at things differently. But of life's changes and great blows the wise realize that joy, rest and peace come.

Hazrat Inayat Khan
In the name of Allah, the Beneficent, the Merciful
By the morning coursers. (100:1 Quran)
Striking sparks of fire. (100:2 Quran)
And scouring to the raid at dawn. (100:3 Quran)
Then, therewith, with their trail of dust. (100:4 Quran)
Cleaving as one, the center. (100:5 Quran)
Lo! Man is an ingrate unto his Lord. (100:6 Quran)
And lo! He is a witness unto that. (100:7 Quran)
And lo! In the love of wealth he is violent. (100:8 Quran)
Knoweth he not that, when the contents of the grave are poured forth. (100:9 Quran)
And the secrets of the breasts are made known. (100:10 Quran)
On that day will their Lord be perfectly informed concerning them. (100:11 Quran)

The Custom of the Seclusion of Women (1) ~ Hazrat Inayat Khan

The custom of the seclusion of the mystics remains only in the mystical Orders, but one finds the seclusion of women prevalent in the East. When a custom takes root in a section of society certainly it can be used and abused as people may choose. No doubt jealousy, which is in human nature, is a proof of love, but jealousy can be the source of a great many crimes. Man has always guarded the treasures that he values most in all sorts of coverings, and since that which man can love most is woman he has often ignorantly tried to guard her in the same way as all things of value and importance. And the custom of seclusion has been in his hand a means that has enabled him to control his household in the manner he likes.

However, it is not true that this custom was the outcome of the teaching of the Prophet. There are only two places in the records where an utterance of the Prophet on the subject is to be found. In one place it is told that when some coarse dances were going on among the peasants of his land, he said that women must be clad properly. In the other place that when the ladies of the Prophet's household were returning home after taking care of the Prophet and his army during a battle, they were disinclined to look at the battle-field and to show themselves to their enemies, and the only thing that could be advised by the Prophet was that now that peace had been made if they did not like to show themselves they might veil their faces.

In India one sees the custom that an aged woman covers her face, a widow covers her face and a bride veils her face. There is some little psychological meaning in it. It is the nature of every soul to wish to hide its sorrow, and by veiling her face the widow veils her sorrow from others. And the veil that one sees on the face of an aged woman is there for the reason that in age the emotions become more visible and one has little control so as to hide them from; others, and when the heart has become softened at every little touch, however gentle, it is easily moved, and the covering is as a shield over it. On the face of a bride the veil is for the preservation of her charm, of the magnetism; at the same time the finest beauty in human nature is modesty, in whatever form it appears.

The Custom of the Seclusion of Women (2) ~ Hazrat Inayat Khan

From the physical as well as the occult point of view, woman is more impressionable than man. The task of woman as a mother is of a greater importance than that of man on any position. Woman with her thought and feeling molds the character of the child, and as she is susceptible to outward impressions, her impressions always have their influence on her child. During the period before motherhood very great care must be taken, for any word spoken to her reaches the depth of her being, and it re-echoes in the soul of the child. If a word made her bitter at the time or cross at a moment, it can create bitterness or crossness in the child. Especially during that period woman is more sensitive and susceptible to all impressions, beautiful or ugly. Anything striking impresses her soul deeply. A color, lightning, thunder, storm, all make impressions upon her. Conditions of life, misery or joy, all tell upon her more than on every person. Having this in consideration, the custom of seclusion has been kept in the East, and still exists among certain communities.

No doubt there is another side to consider: that home and state are not two separate things. Home is the miniature of the state; and if woman performs a part equally important at home, why must she not perform an equally important part in the outward life. No doubt these ancient customs, even with their psychological importance, often make an iron bar before the progress of the generality. In the East, for the maid and mistress both, there are days set apart for rest in every month, in all different religions, among Hindus, Parsis, and Muslims. The life in the world is a constant battle, and a hard battle one has to fight, if one has any fineness of feeling, any decency of manner. The position of woman in this battle is worse than that of man. It greatly robs her of her womanly fineness and delicacy of sentiment. Man is more dependent upon woman than woman on man. From the first moment any child, whether boy or girl, opens his eyes in the world, he seeks the protection of woman. Woman, as his mother, sister, daughter, friend, or wife, in every form, is the source of his happiness, comfort and peace. In whatever form man may express it—in a crude custom like the seclusion in the East or in many different ways—to guard her against the hard knocks which fall on every soul living in this world of selfishness is the first duty of a thoughtful man.

Surah One Hundred One

Al Qariah

The awakened heart says, "I must give, I must not demand." Thus it enters a gate that leads to a constant happiness.

An unhappy person, being himself unhappy, cannot make others happy. It is a wealthy person who can help the one who is hard up, not a poor person, however much desire of helping he may have. So it is with happiness, which is a great wealth; and a happy person can take away the unhappiness of another, for he has enough for himself and for others.

Why does a mystic attribute such great importance to harmony? Because to a mystic, his whole life is one continuous symphony, a playing of music, with each soul contributing his particular part to the symphony. A person's success therefore depends upon the idea he has of harmony. Very few people in the world pay attention to harmony. They do not know that without it, there is no chance of happiness. It is only the harmonious ones who can make others happy and partake of that happiness themselves; and apart from them, it is hard to find happiness in the world.

The method of attainment is to endeavor always to make others happy and by experiencing happiness in the happiness of others. In the terms of the Sufi, it is Suluk. Any selfishness prevents us from appreciating another's happiness and therefore we shall be kept back, for the happiness of others is the gate to our own happiness. Real happiness is entering the gate. We must feel satisfaction in another's satisfaction. If a person needs a certain thing and we can supply it, we should be happy, however small the thing may be. *Hazrat Inayat Khan*

In the name of Allah, the Beneficent, the Merciful

The Calamity? What is the Calamity? (101:1-2 Quran)

Ah! What will convey unto thee what the Calamity is? (101:3 Quran)

A day wherein mankind will be as thickly scattered moths. (101:4 Quran)

And mountains would become as carded wool. (101:5 Quran)

Then, as for him whose scales are heavy with good works. (101:6 Quran)

He will live a pleasant life. (101:7 Quran)

The Symbology of Religious Ideas ~ Hazrat Inayat Khan

Shaqqu's-Sadr, the Opening of the Breast of the Prophet

There exists a legend in the world of Islam, and some believe that it really did occur—some say once, and some say it happened more than once—that the angels from heaven descended on earth and cut open the breast of the Prophet; they took away something that was to be removed from there, and then the breast was made as before.

According to the Sufi point of view this is a symbolical legend. It explains what is necessary in the life of man, to allow the plant of divine love to grow in the heart. It is to remove that element which gives the bitter feeling. Just as there is a poison in the sting of the scorpion, and there is a poison in the teeth of the snake, so there is poison in the heart of man, which is made to be the shrine of God. But God cannot rise in the shrine, which is as dead by its own poison. It must be purified first and made real for God to arise. The soul who had to sympathize with the whole world was thus contempt, resentment and ill feeling against another, was destroyed first. So many talk about the purification of the heart, and so few really know what it is. Some say to be pure means to be free from all evil thought, but there is no evil thought. Call it evil or call it devil, if there is any such thought it is the thought of bitterness against another. No one with sense and understanding would like to keep a drop of poison in his body, and how ignorant it is on the part of man when he keeps and cherishes a bitter thought against another in his heart. If a drop of poison can cause the death of the body, it is equal to a thousand deaths when the heart retains the smallest thought of bitterness.

In this legend cutting open the breast is the cutting open of the ego, which is a shell over the heart. And taking away that element is that: every kind of thought or feeling against anyone in the world was taken away, and the breast, which means the heart, was filled with love alone, which is the real life of God.

Surah One Hundred Two

At Takathur
The worlds are held together by the heat of the sun; each of us are atoms held in position by that eternal Sun we call God. Within us is the same central power we call the light, or the love of God; by it we hold together the human beings within our sphere, or, lacking it, we let them fall.

A close study of the formation of the sun and of its influence on everything in life will help us to understand the divine Spirit. Heat, gas-light, electric light, the coal fire, the wood fire, the candle, the flame of the oil-lamp, all these different manifestations of light have their source in the sun; it is the sun which is showing itself in all these different forms, although we generally consider the sun to be separate from all other aspects of light. In the same way the supreme Spirit is manifested in all forms, in all things and beings, in the seen and unseen worlds; and yet it stands remote, as the sun stands remote from all other forms of light. The Qur'an says, 'God is the light of heaven and of earth'; and in reality all forms, however dense they may be, are to some degree the radiance of that spirit which is all light. All the different colors are different degrees of that same light.

Each one has his circle of influence, large or small; within his sphere so many souls and minds are involved; with his rise, they rise; with his fall, they fall. The size of a man's sphere corresponds with the extent of his sympathy, or we may say, with the size of his heart. His sympathy holds his sphere together. As his heart grows, his sphere grows; as his sympathy is withdrawn or lessened, so his sphere breaks up and scatters. If he harms those who live and move within his sphere, those dependent upon him or upon his affection, he of necessity harms himself.

The worlds are held together by the heat of the sun. Each of us are atoms held in position by that eternal sun we call God. Within us is that same central power, we call it the light of God, or the love of God, and by it we too hold up the human beings within our sphere; or lacking it, we let them fall. So God keeps all, and so we keep our friends and surroundings. With this knowledge life in the world becomes a glorious vision. Not that we are compelled to keep away from sin, but we learn what power virtue has. *Hazrat Inayat Khan*

In the name of Allah, the Beneficent, the Merciful

Rivalry in worldly increase distracteth you. (102:1 Quran)

Until ye come to the graves. (102:2 Quran)

Nay, but ye will come to know. (102:3 Quran)

Nay, but ye will come to know (102:4 Quran)

The Symbology of Religious Ideas ~ Hazrat Inayat Khan

Miraj, the Dream of the Prophet

A story exists in Islam about the dream of the Prophet, a dream which was an initiation in the higher spheres. Many take it literally and discuss it, and afterwards go out by the same door by which they came in. It is by the point of view of a mystic that one can find out the mystery.

It is said that the Prophet was taken from Jerusalem to the inner city of peace. A Buraq was brought for the Prophet to ride on. Jabril--Gabriel accompanied the Prophet on the journey to guide him. Buraq is said to be an animal of heaven which has wings, the body of a horse and the face of a human being. It signifies the body together with the mind. The wings represent the mind, the head represents perfection. Also this is the picture of the breath. Breath is the Buraq which reaches from the outer world to the inner world in a moment's time. Jabril in this story represents reason.

It is said that the Prophet saw on his way, Adam, who smiled looking to one side and shed tears looking to the other side. This shows that the human soul when it develops in itself real human sentiment rejoices at the progress of humanity. The Buraq could not go beyond a certain point, which means that breath takes one a certain distance in the mystical realization, but there comes a stage when the breath cannot accompany one. When they arrived near the destination Jabril also retired, which means that reason cannot go any further than its limit. Then the Prophet arrived near that curtain which stands between the human and the divine, and called aloud the name of God, saying, 'None exists save Thou,' and the answer came, 'True, true.' That was the final initiation, from which dated the blooming of Muhammad's prophetic message.

Surah One Hundred Three

Al Asr

When a man dives within, he finds that his real self is above the perpetual motion of the universe.

The soul of man is a dweller in heaven. It is able to see more than the eyes can see. It is able to hear more than the ears can hear. The soul is able to expand further than man can journey. The soul is able to dive deeper than any depths that man can ever touch. The soul is able to reach higher than man can reach by any means. Its life is freedom, it knows nothing but joy and sees nothing but beauty. Its own nature is peace, and its being is life itself. It is not intelligent. It is intelligence itself. It is spirit. Its nature is not human but divine. Man is a process, manifestation is a process through which the spirit goes from one condition to another condition, from one pole to another pole. And through this whole process the attempt of the spirit is to find itself. The highest perception of freedom comes when a person has freed himself from the false ego, when he is no longer what he was. All the different kinds of freedom will give a momentary sensation of being free, but true freedom is in ourselves. When one's soul is free, then there is nothing in this world that binds one; everywhere one will breathe freedom, in heaven and on earth.

It is therefore that the Sufi seeks God as his love, lover and beloved, his treasure, his possession, his honor, his joy, his peace; and his attainment in its perfection alone fulfills all demands of life both here and hereafter. *Hazrat Inayat Khan*

In the name of Allah, the Beneficent, the Merciful

By the declining day. (103:1 Quran)

Lo! Man is in a state of loss. (103:2 Quran)

Save those who believe and do good works, and exhort one another to truth and exhort one another to endurance. (103:3 Quran)

Taqwa Taharat— Everyday Life   Hazrat Inayat Khan

It is a very necessary thing in the life of an adept for him to adapt his mind and body to the spiritual life, in other words, it is necessary for a man to become his natural self before he begins his journey in a spiritual path. It is this naturalness which is called by the orthodox purity. For pure water, or pure milk, means water or milk in its own essence; when another element is mixed with it then its purity is lost. To become spiritual means to purify one's spirit from the foreign elements which take away the natural feeling of the spirit. Concentration, meditation, all these help to make the spirit its natural self again, but the vehicles that the spirit uses in order to experience life must help the spirit to become natural. These vehicles are the mind and the body. However great the musician, if the instrument is out of tune he can do nothing with it. To say that only the spirit matters and the body does not count is not right. Therefore it is necessary that first both mind and body be fit vehicles for the spirit to use.

The difference between a pious person and a spiritual person is this, that the pious person makes his mind and body ready for his own spirit to use, and the spiritual person, after making them ready, gives them to God. Piety is the first step and spirituality the next. There is no exaggeration in the saying that cleanliness in next to godliness. The body must be considered as the temple of God, and this sacred house of God is reflected in it.

Beasts and birds all have a tendency to be clean and pure, and for man it is necessary that he should develop this tendency. It helps, not only on the spiritual path, but also in the development of mind. To the artist in his art, to the scientist in his science, in all aspects of life it gives happiness. When man neglects it, that does not mean that he does not like it, it is only out of negligence that he overlooks things that are of the first importance. One's body is of all things in the world the closest to oneself, and its influence has a great effect, and an immediate effect, upon one's mind and soul. A great many illnesses are caused by the lack of consideration of the necessary cleanliness of the body, which is a science and an art in itself. On the soul and mind one's own body makes the first impression, all other things come afterwards. Yet, there are souls who have arrived at such a plane of spirituality that the condition of the body does not matter to them. But they are not to be followed as examples. It is the normal path which is safe and is for all. The question, 'Would this not give one too much the thought of self?' may be answered thus: the thought of oneself exists when the light of God is absent; in the presence of every beautiful thing man forgets himself.

Surah One Hundred Four

Al Humazah
Man's pride and satisfaction in what he knows limits the scope of his vision.

One wishes to be admired for his clothes, his jewels, his possessions, his greatness and position, and, and he is as blind toward others. This ego, so to speak, restricts life, because it limits a person.

All the knowledge that man possesses he has acquired by belief. When he strengthens his belief by knowledge then comes disbelief in things that his knowledge cannot cope with, and in things that his reason cannot justify. He then disbelieves things that he once believed in. An unbeliever is one who has changed his belief to disbelief; disbelief often darkens the soul, but sometimes it illuminates it. There is a Persian saying, 'Until belief has changed to disbelief, and, again, the disbelief into a belief, a man does not become a real Muslim.' But when disbelief becomes a wall and stands against the further penetration of mind into life, then it darkens the soul, for there is no chance of further progress, and man's pride and satisfaction in what he knows limit the scope of his vision. *Hazrat Inayat Khan*

In the name of Allah, the Beneficent, the Merciful

Woe unto every slandering traducer. (104:1 Quran)

Who had gathered wealth of this world and arranged it. (104:2 Quran)

He thinketh that his wealth will render him immortal. (104:3 Quran)

Any, but verily he will be flung to the Consuming One. (104:4 Quran)

The Instrument of Our Body   Hazrat Inayat Khan

The body is an instrument for experiencing life; both the worlds, that within and without, are reflected in this instrument. Therefore purity of the body is the first essential thing, and the most essential, in the path of spiritual attainment. Every civilization has a peculiar method of cleanliness. But the mystic is not satisfied with the customary manner.

Mystics have two views: one view is that external cleanliness matters nothing to them, and the other is that it is most important. As the work of an astronomer depends upon a telescope, and as it is necessary for him to keep the telescope as clean as possible, so it is necessary in the life of the mystic to keep the body in a fit condition.

All the passages in the body are connected with the centers, which are most important in spiritual development, and it is upon the cleanliness and purity of these passages that spiritual development depends. Besides these nine passages it is also necessary to keep the skin in a proper condition for spiritual purposes. It is from the mystical conception that humanity first learned the idea of clothes. There have been times when certain races painted their skin, and by certain *yogis* the body was covered with ashes. In ancient times the body was covered with the bark of trees. But behind all this there was always an inclination to keep the skin in a proper condition. It is upon the cleanliness of the body that sensitiveness depends; therefore people who have no regard to the cleanliness of the body are less sensitive than those who have regard to it. Besides the cleanliness of the outer part of the body, it is equally important, perhaps more important, to consider the cleanliness of the inner part of the body. Mystics, therefore, take precaution about what they eat and drink, and have methods of cleansing the inner part of the body also. No mystic in the East guides a pupil who has not first prepared his body for spiritual purposes. Cleanliness of the body, besides its importance for spiritual and moral development, also prevents serious disease.

Surah One Hundred Five

Al Fil

Man must first create peace in himself if he desires to see peace in the world; for lacking peace within, no effort of his can bring any result.

Our spirit is the real part of us. The body is but a garment. There is absolute peace in the abode from whence the spirit came, and the true happiness of the soul lies in that peace. As man would not find peace at the tailor's just because his coat came from there, so the spirit cannot get true happiness from the earth just because the body belongs to the earth. The soul experiences life through the mind and body and enjoys it, but its true happiness lies in peace.

In order to gain this peace we have to begin with ourselves. There are fights going on within us between spirit and matter. Struggles for our daily bread, and want of peace in our surroundings. We must first get this peace within ourselves before we can talk of peace in the world. Then we must be at peace with our surroundings, and never do or say anything that disturbs that peace. All thoughts, words, and actions that disturb the peace are sin, and all thoughts words, and actions that create peace are virtue.

It is natural to experience peace, but life in the world is not natural. Animals and birds all experience peace, but not mankind, for man is the robber of his own peace. He has made his life so artificial that he can never imagine how far he is removed from what may be called a normal, natural life for him to live. It is for this reason that we need the art of discovering peace within us; we shall not experience peace by improving outside conditions. Man has always longed for peace and he has always brought about wars. At the same time every individual says he is seeking for peace. Then where does war come from? It comes because the meaning of peace has not been fully understood. Man lives in a continual turmoil, in a restless condition, and in order to seek for peace he seeks war; if this goes on we shall not have peace till every individual begins to seek peace within himself first. What is peace? Peace is the natural condition of the soul.

O peace-maker, before trying to make peace throughout the world, first make peace within thyself! Hazrat Inayat Khan

In the name of Allah, the Beneficent, the Merciful

Hast thou not seen how thy Lord dealt with the owners of the Elephant? (105:1 Quran)

Did He not bring their stratagem to naught? (105:2 Quran)

And send against them swarms of flying creatures. (105:3 Quran)

Which pelted them with stones of baked clay. (105:4 Quran)

And made them like green crops devoured by cattle. (105:5 Quran)

Fasting ~ Hazrat Inayat Khan

The reason why fasting is practiced by those who live in retirement is to let the breath pass through every vein and tube of the body. This can be made possible only when there is no foreign substance, such as food or even drink, in the body to block the channels. When the breath has touched every particle of the body, the body naturally becomes more sensitive and the pores of the skin open, making the centers transparent, so as to feel, outwardly and inwardly, all that is to be felt. This can be understood by seeing the difference between the intelligence and the intuitive faculty of a fine person and a dense person.

Continence also helps, not only to keep the channels clear, but it conserves all the energy in every particle of the body and especially in the centers where it is most needed. Another thing is that continence keeps every outer element away. By this the adept is better able to keep his body and centers free from every foreign element, becoming at the same time a reservoir of energy, which expresses itself as radiating magnetism. Professed celibacy is an assumption of chastity that must sooner or later break by nature, together with man's profession of the same. The true celibacy, therefore, can be practiced without profession and without any outward appearance or the attributing to it any religious rank, only for a certain time and for a certain purpose.

Surah One Hundred Six

Ash Shita

The knowledge of self is the essential knowledge; it gives knowledge of humanity. In the understanding of the human being lies that understanding of nature which reveals the law of creation.

What we need most is the understanding of that religion of religions and that philosophy of philosophies which is self-knowledge. We shall not understand the outer life if we do not understand ourselves. It is the knowledge of the self that gives the knowledge of the world.

If a person goes through his whole life most cleverly judging others, he may go on, but he will find himself to be more foolish at every step. At the end, he reaches the fullness of stupidity. But the one who tries, tests, studies and observes himself, his own attitude in life, his own outlook on life, his thought, speech, and action, who weighs and measures and teaches himself self-discipline, it is that person who is able to understand another better. How rarely one sees a soul who concerns himself with himself through life, in order to know! Mostly, every soul seems to be busily occupied with the lives of others. And what do they know in the end? Nothing. If there is a kingdom of God to be found anywhere, it is within oneself.

And it is, therefore, in the knowledge of self that there lies the fulfillment of life. The knowledge of self means the knowledge of one's body, the knowledge of one's mind, the knowledge of one's spirit; the knowledge of the spirit's relation to the body and the relation of the body to the spirit; the knowledge of one's wants and needs, the knowledge of one's virtues and faults; knowing what we desire and how to attain it, what to pursue and what to renounce. And when one dives deep into this, one finds before one a world of knowledge which never ends. And it is that knowledge which gives one insight into human nature and brings one to the knowledge of the whole of creation. And in the end one attains to the knowledge of the divine Being. *Hazrat Inayat Khan*

In the name of Allah, the Beneficent, the Merciful

For the taming of the Quraysh. (106:1 Quran)

For their taming We cause the caravans to set forth in winter and summer. (106:2 Quran)

So let them worship the Lord of this House. (106:3 Quran)

Who hath fed them against hunger. (106:4 Quran)

And hath made them safe from fear. (106:5)

Belief ~ Hazrat Inayat Khan

BELIEF is a natural tendency to accept knowledge without doubt. Every soul is born with this tendency to accept every knowledge that is given to it, in whatever way or form. Therefore no soul in the world is born an unbeliever.

Belief has two tendencies. One is the tendency of water that runs and the other is that of water that becomes frozen. Some people who have a belief like to keep that belief unchanged as a rock, and identify their ego with that belief. People of this temperament are steady in their belief, but often they lack progress. If they happen to have a right belief, there is no danger of their giving it up. But if it is not right, they are perplexed. Those whose belief is like running water perhaps go from one belief to another and they may not seem steady in their belief, yet their life is progressive. The progressive soul can never hold one belief, and must change and go on changing until it arrives at the ultimate truth. For a simple person steadiness of belief is more advantageous than change, for change may lead him astray. But for an intelligent person it is natural and necessary that he must go from belief to belief until he arrives at his final convictions.

Belief is of four kinds. The first kind is a belief accepted because it is believed by all. The second is a belief accepted because it is believed by someone in whom the believer trusts. The third belief is the belief that reason helps one to believe. The fourth belief is conviction of which one is as sure as if one were an eyewitness.

The four kinds of belief are held by souls of different grades of evolution in life and different temperaments. There is a knowledge which one can perceive with the senses. There is a knowledge which one can perceive with the mind alone, and a knowledge which can be realized by the soul. And it is for this reason that when a person wishes to touch a thing which can only be perceived, and when a person wishes to feel a thing which can only be realized spiritually, he naturally becomes an unbeliever.

In point of fact one person's belief cannot be another person's belief. Every belief is peculiar to the person who holds it. Even if two persons held one belief, there would still be the difference of the point of view, even though it be as small as the difference between two roses. Therefore it is unjust, no doubt, on the part of one person to try to press his own belief on another. At the same time the person who refuses to try to understand the belief of another, from bigotry or pride, closes the door of his heart, that otherwise would have let that knowledge come in.

There are two tendencies that can be developed in a person, either constantly to try to believe whatever comes before him, or to try to disbelieve whatever is presented to him. And there is an advantage and a disadvantage in each of these tendencies. The advantage of the believing tendency is the taking of every chance of acquiring knowledge, the disadvantage is that one takes the chance of often and readily falling into error. But the advantage of the disbelieving tendency is only the protection from error, and its disadvantage is the prevention of every chance of further acquisition of knowledge.

Nature has very many covers. Its activity covers and uncovers it. At every covering and uncovering, it is natural that the belief of the individual should change. Therefore when a Sufi is asked, 'Do you believe in this, or that?' he says, 'My belief is for me, yours is for you, there is no faith to which I give my unchanging belief, nor any belief that I reject without having investigated it.' If you are asked, 'What belief does the Sufi teach?' you may say, 'No belief, but he helps the pupil to seek and find within himself his own belief.

Surah One Hundred Seven

Al Maun

While man blames another for causing him harm, the wise man first takes himself to task.

By a study of life the Sufi learns and practices the nature of its harmony. He establishes harmony with the self, with others, with the universe and with the infinite. He identifies himself with another, he sees himself, so to speak, in every other being. He cares for neither blame nor praise, considering both as coming from himself. If a person were to drop a heavy weight and in so doing hurt his own foot, he would not blame his hand for having dropped it, realizing himself in both the hand and the foot. In like manner the Sufi is tolerant when harmed by another, thinking that the harm has come from himself alone. He overlooks the faults of others, considering that they know no better. He hides the faults of others, and suppresses any facts that would cause disharmony. His constant fight is with the Nafs (the self-centered ego), the root of all disharmony and the only enemy of man.

The mystic develops a wider outlook on life, and this wider outlook changes his actions. He develops a point of view that may be called a divine point of view. Then he rises to the state in which he feels that all that is done to him comes from God, and when he himself does right or wrong, he feels that he does right or wrong to God. To arrive at such a stage is true religion. There can be no better religion than this, the true religion of God on earth. This is the point of view that makes a person God-like and divine. He is resigned when badly treated, but for his own shortcomings, he will take himself to task, for all his actions are directed towards God. *Hazrat Inayat Khan*

In the name of Allah, the Beneficent, the Merciful
Hast thou observed him who believeth religion? (107:1 Quran)
That is he who repelleth the orphan. (107:2 Quran)
And urgeth not the feeding of the needy. (107:3 Quran)
Ah, woe unto worshippers. (107:4 Quran)
Who are heedless of their prayers. (107:5 Quran)
Who would be seen at worship. (107:6 Quran)
Yet refuse small kindnesses. (107:7 Quran)

Faith ~ Hazrat Inayat Khan

Faith can be defined by two words, 'self-confidence' and 'certainty in expectation.' Faith in no way signifies certainty without expectation, nor confidence with evidence. All things in life are appointed from eternity for a certain time. Every experience and every knowledge comes in its own time. No doubt in this free will plays a certain part, as destiny plays a great part. We make our road in life by our expectations. Things that we have not attained to we look forward to and hope to attain. Ideals that we wish to reach we expect to reach some day. And that which determines our success in attaining our ideal is faith. It is faith that uncovers things veiled with a thousand covers. It is faith that attracts things almost out of reach. The distance between heaven and earth, the difference between life and death can be bridged by faith.

There is blind faith, and there is faith, which is not blind. Faith is blind when its power is small and reason does not support it. Then faith may be called blind. But in fact the mind has all power. Every expectation that it has will certainly be fulfilled sooner or later. It may not be fulfilled in a certain limited time, but in eternity it will be fulfilled. Faith is the power of mind. Without faith the mind is powerless. When faith leads and reason follows, success is sure, but when reason leads and faith follows, success is doubtful. Faith causes the attitude of the mind. The influence of the attitude of the mind works psychically upon every affair. The belief, 'My friend is faithful to me and is helping me', by itself influences the helper. And when there is a doubting attitude—'Perhaps my friend or my agent is faithful to me, perhaps not'—then the fact is made doubtful. Faith can bring a surer and speedier cure than medicine, and both success and failure in life depend very much upon faith. Man rides upon the elephant and controls tigers by the power of faith. The great people of the world, the greatest people, are great more by their faith than by anything else, because mostly great people have been adventurous and at the back of a venture is faith, nothing else.

As all things in this artificial world are made by faith so the whole creation is made by the faith of the divine mind. Therefore as the divine mind has been able to create all by faith, so man by this divine attribute can rise to the source of his being.

Thought, speech, and action without faith are as body without life. All things by faith are made alive, for faith is the life of all things. Think what joy trust brings, and what a feeling of suffocation doubt brings! When a person does not trust another that means he has no confidence in himself. He is not happy through this. It would be no exaggeration to say that material loss resulting from misplaced confidence is better than all profit resulting from justified suspicion.

Surah One Hundred Eight

Al Kauthar

Whatever their faith, the wise have always been able to meet each other beyond those boundaries of external forms and conventions which are natural and necessary to human life, but which nonetheless separate humanity.

There are two aspects of intelligence: intellect, and wisdom. Intellect is the knowledge of names and forms, their character and nature, gathered from the external world. Wisdom is contrary to the above-named knowledge. It is the knowledge which is illumined by the light within; it comes with the maturity of the soul, and opens up the sight to the similarity of all things and beings, as well as the unity in names and forms. The wise man penetrates the spirit of all things; he sees the human in the male and female, and the racial origin which unites nations. He sees the human in all people and the divine immanence in all things in the universe, until the vision of the whole being becomes to him the vision of the One Alone, the most beautiful and beloved God.

When a person opposes or hinders the expression of a great ideal, and is unwilling to believe that he will meet his fellow men as soon as he has penetrated deeply enough into every soul, he is preventing himself from realizing the unlimited. All beliefs are simply degrees of clearness of vision. All are part of one ocean of truth. The more this is realized the easier is it to see the true relationship between all beliefs, and the wider does the vision of the one great ocean become. Limitations and boundaries are inevitable in human life; forms and conventions are natural and necessary; but they none the less separate humanity. It is the wise who can meet one another beyond these boundaries. *Hazrat Inayat Khan*

In the name of Allah, the Beneficent, the Merciful

Lo, We have given thee abundance. (108:1 Quran)

So pray unto thy Lord and sacrifice. (108:2 Quran)

Lo, it is thy insulter, and not thou, who is without posterity. (108:3 Quran)

Tolerance ~ Hazrat Inayat Khan

Tolerance is the first lesson of morals, and the next is forgiveness. A person who tolerates another through fear, through pride, from a sense of honor, or by the force of circumstances does not know tolerance. Tolerance is the control of the impulse of resistance by will. There is no virtue in tolerance which one practices because one is compelled by circumstances to tolerate, but tolerance is a consideration by which one overlooks the fault of another and gives no way in oneself to the impulse of resistance. A thoughtless person is naturally intolerant, but if a thoughtful person is intolerant, it shows his weakness. He has thought, but has no self-control. In the case of the thoughtless, he is not conscious of his fault, so it does not matter much to him, but a thoughtful person is to be pitied if he cannot control himself owing to the lack of will. The activities in the worldly life cause many disturbances, and it is a constant jarring effect upon a sensitive soul. If one does not develop tolerance in nature, one is always subject to constant disturbances in life. To wish to live in the world and to be annoyed with its activities is like wanting to live in the sea and be constantly resisting its waves. This life of the world, full of different activities constantly working, has much in it to be despised, if one has a tendency to despise. But at the same time there is much to admire if one turns one's face from left to right. It is in our own power to choose the view of imperfection or the vision of perfection, and the difference is only looking down, or looking upwards. By a slight change of attitude in one's outlook on life one can make the world into heaven or hell. The more one tolerates, the stronger one becomes in this way. It is the tolerant who is thoughtful. And as thought becomes greater, one becomes more tolerant. The words of Christ, 'Resist not evil', teach tolerance.

Surah One Hundred Nine

Al Kafirun
It is the message that proves the messenger, not the claim.

The prophet brings love, the love of God, the Father and Mother of the whole humanity, a love that is life itself. No words nor actions can express that love. The presence of the prophet, his very being, speaks of it, if only the heart had ears to listen. Verily, to the believer all is right, and to the unbeliever all is wrong.

The principal work of the prophet is to glorify the Name of God and to raise humanity from the denseness of the earth, to open the doors of the human heart to the divine beauty which is everywhere manifested and to illuminate souls which are groping in darkness for years. The prophet brings the message of the day, a reform for that particular period in which he is born. A claim of a prophet is nothing to the real prophet. The being of the prophet, the work of the prophet, and the fulfillment of his task is itself the proof of prophethood.

There was a time when the world was not capable of seeing. Humanity did not have enough realization to recognize the message that is why the claim of prophecy had to be made. But now the world can recognize, sooner or later, what is right and what is wrong. The warner, the master, the messenger of today will not claim. He will only work. He will leave his work to prove for itself whether it is true or false. *Hazrat Inayat Khan*

In the name of Allah, the Beneficent, the Merciful
Say: O disbelievers. (109:1 Quran)
I worship not that which ye worship. (109:2 Quran)
Nor worship ye that which I worship. (109:3 Quran)
And I shall not worship that which ye worship. (109:4 Quran)
Nor will ye worship that which I worship. (109:5 Quran)
Unto you your religion, and unto me my religion. (109:6 Quran)

Forgiveness ~ Hazrat Inayat Khan

They say, 'Forgive and forget.' Which is very expressive of the process of forgiveness. It is impossible to forgive unless you can forget. What keeps man from forgiving his fellow man is that he holds the fault of another constantly before his view. It is just like sticking a little thorn in one's own heart and keeping it there and suffering the pain. It may also be pictured as putting a drop of poison in one's own heart and retaining it until the whole heart becomes poisoned. Verily, blessed are the innocent, who do not notice anybody's fault, and the greater credit is to the mature souls, who, recognizing a fault, forget it and so forgive. The limitations of human life make man subject to faults. Some have more faults, some have less, but there is no soul without faults. As Christ says, 'Call me not good.'

Forgiveness is a stream of love, which washes away all impurities wherever it flows. By keeping this spring of love, which is in the heart of man, running, man is able to forgive, however great the fault of his fellow man may seem. One who cannot forgive closes his heart. The sign of spirituality is that there is nothing you cannot forgive, there is no fault you cannot forget. Do not think that he who has committed a fault yesterday must do the same today, for life is constantly teaching and it is possible in one moment a sinner may turn into a saint.

At times it is hard to forgive, as it is hard to take away the thorn that has gone deep into one's heart. But the pain that one feels in taking away the thorn deepest in the heart is preferable to keeping the thorn in the heart constantly. The greater pain of a moment is better than the mild pricking going on constantly. Ask him who forgives what relief there is in forgiveness. Words can never explain the feeling of the heart when one has cast out the bitter feeling from one's heart by forgiving and when love spreads all over within oneself, circulating like warm blood through one's whole being.

Surah One Hundred Ten

An Nasr
Every soul has a definite task, and the fulfillment of each individual purpose can alone lead man aright; illumination comes to him through the medium of his own talent...

It is in unfoldment that the purpose of life is fulfilled, and it is not only so with human beings but also with the lower creation; even with all the objects that exist the fulfillment of their existence lies in their unfoldment. We learn from this that every being and every object is working towards that unfoldment which is the fulfillment of its purpose. There is a saying of a Persian poet, Sadi, that every being is intended to be on earth for a certain purpose, and the light of that purpose has been kindled in his heart. In all different purposes which we see working through each individual, there seems to be one purpose which is behind them all, and that is the unfoldment of the soul.

The ultimate purpose, for which the soul is seeking every moment of our life, is our spiritual purpose. And you may ask how to attain to that purpose. The answer is that what you are seeking for is within yourself. Instead of looking outside, you must look within. The way to proceed to accomplish this is for some moments to suspend all your senses such as sight, hearing, smell, touch, in order to put a screen before the outside life. And by concentration and by developing that meditative quality you will sooner or later get in touch with the inner Self which is more communicative, which speaks more loudly than all the noises of this world. And this gives joy, creates peace, and produces in you a self-sufficient spirit, a spirit of independence, of true liberty. The moment you get in touch with your Self you are in communion with God. It is in this way, if God-communication is sought rightly, that spirituality is attained.

Everything a person does, spiritual or material, is only a stepping-stone for him to arrive at the inner purpose. When the desire to live brings one in touch with one's real life, a life which is not subject to death, then the purpose of that desire is accomplished. When one has been able to perceive fully the knowledge of one's own being, in which is to be found divine knowledge and the mystery of the whole manifestation, then the purpose of knowledge is attained. When one is able to get in touch with the Almighty Power, then the desire for power is achieved. When one has been able to find one's happiness in one's own heart, independent of all things outside, the purpose of the desire for happiness is fulfilled; when one is able to rise above all conditions and influences which disturb the peace of the soul and has found one's peace in the midst of the crowd and away from the world, in him the desire for peace is satisfied. It is in the fulfillment of these five desires that one purpose is accomplished, the purpose for which every soul was born on earth. *Hazrat Inayat Khan*

In the name of Allah, the Beneficent, the Merciful

When Allah's succor and the triumph cometh. (110:1 Quran)

And thou seest mankind entering the religion of Allah in troops. (110:2 Quran)

Then hymn the praises of thy Lord, and seek forgiveness of Him. Lo! He is ever ready to show mercy. (110:3 Quran)

Tawakkul—Dependence Upon God ~ Hazrat Inayat Khan

Dependence is nature and independence is the spirit. The independent spirit becomes dependent through manifestation. When One becomes many, then each part of the One, being limited, strives to be helped by the other part, for each part finds itself imperfect. Therefore we human beings, however rich with the treasures of heaven and earth, are poor in reality, because of our dependence upon others. The spiritual view makes one conscious of this, and the material view blinds man, who then shows independence and indifference to his fellow man. Pride, conceit and vanity are the outcome of this ignorance. There come moments when even the king has to depend upon a most insignificant person. Often one needs the help of someone before whom one has always been proud and upon whom one has always looked with contempt. As individuals depend upon individuals so the nations and races depend upon one another. As no individual can say, 'I can get on without another person', so no nation can say. 'We can be happy while another nation is unhappy.' But an individual or a multitude depends most upon God, in Whom we all unite. Those who depend upon the things of the earth certainly depend upon things that are transitory and they must some day or other lose them. Therefore there remains only one object of dependence that is God, Who is not transitory, and Who always is and will be. Sadi has said, 'He who depends upon Thee will never be disappointed.'

No doubt it is the most difficult thing to depend upon God. For an average person, who has not known or seen, who never had any idea of such a personality existing as God, but has only heard in church that there exists someone in the Heavens Who is called God and has believed it, it is difficult to depend entirely upon Him. A person can hope that there is a God, that by depending upon Him he will have his desire fulfilled, a person can imagine that there can be Someone Whom people call God, but for him also it is difficult to depend entirely on God. It is for them that the Prophet has said, 'Tie your camel and trust in God.' It was not said to Daniel, 'Take your sword and go among the lions.' One imagines God, another realizes God. There is a difference between these two persons. The one who imagines can hope, but he cannot be certain. The one who realizes God, he is face to face with his Lord, and it is he who depends upon God with certainty. It is a matter of struggling along on the surface of the water, or courageously diving deep, touching the bottom of the sea. There is no greater trial for a person than dependence upon God. What patience it needs, besides the amount of faith it requires, to be in the midst of the world of illusion and yet to be conscious of the existence of God! To do this man must be able to turn all what is called life into death, and to realize in what is generally called death — in that death, the true life. This solves the problem of false and real.

Surah One Hundred Eleven

Al Masad

While man judges another from his own moral standpoint, the wise man looks also at the point of view of another.

A mystic removes the barrier that stands between himself and another person by trying to look at life not only from his own point of view, but also from the point of view of another. All disputes and disagreements arise from people's misunderstanding of each other. Mostly, people misunderstand each other because they have their fixed points of view and are not willing to move from them. This is a rigid condition of mind. The more dense a person is, the more fixed he is in his own points of view. Therefore, it is easy to change the mind of an intelligent person, but it is most difficult to change the mind of a foolish person once it is fixed. It is this dense quality of mind which becomes fixed on a certain idea and that clouds the eyes so that they cannot see from the point of view of another person.

The condition today is that people are rich, they have all convenience and comfort—but what is lacking is understanding. Home is full of comfort, but there is no understanding, there is no happiness. It is such a little thing, and yet so difficult to obtain. No intellectuality can give understanding. This is where man makes a mistake: he wants to understand through his head. Understanding comes from the heart. The heart must be glowing, living. When the heart becomes feeling then there is understanding, then you are ready to see from the point of view of another as much as you can see from your own point of view.

Is it not amusing to think that the foolish person disagrees more with others than the wise? One would think that he knows more than the wise one. The wise one agrees with both the foolish and the wise; he is ready to understand everybody's point of view. It may not be his idea, his way of looking, but he is capable of looking at things from the point of view of others. I. *Hazrat Inayat Khan*

In the name of Allah, the Beneficent, the Merciful

The power of Abu Lahab will perish, and he will perish. (111:1 Quran)

His wealth and gains will not exempt him. (111:2 Quran)

He will be plunged in flaming fire. (111:3 Quran)

And his wife, the wood-carrier. (111:4 Quran)

Will have upon her neck a halter of palm-fiber. (111:5 Quran)

Qaza and Qadr—The Will, Human and Divine ~ Hazrat Inayat Khan

The question of the will, human and divine, may be seen from two points of view, from the wisdom point of view and from the point of view of the ultimate truth. If words can explain something, it is from the former point of view. The latter point of view allows no word to be spoken in the matter, for in the absolute truth two do not exist, there is no such a thing as two, there is one alone. From the wisdom point of view one sees one weaker, one stronger, and one has to give in to the power of the other. This one sees in all aspects of the creation. The larger fish eats the little fish, but the little fish lives upon smaller fishes. So there is no one in this world so strong that there is not another person stronger still. And there is no one in this world so weak that there is not another that is weaker still. The other thing one can think about is the opposing conditions and situations which stand before a willing mind and a striving person like a stone wall, so that with every wish of doing and accomplishing one does not find one's way. It is this experience which has made man say, 'Man proposes, God disposes.' The Hindu philosophers have called these two great powers, one of which is as an intention and the other the power of destruction, by the names Brahma, the Creator, and Shiva, the Destroyer. And the most wonderful part in this creation and destruction is that what Brahma creates in a thousand years, Shiva destroys in one moment. Since God is almighty, the wise see the hand of God in the greater power, manifesting either through an individual or by a certain condition or situation, and instead of struggling too much against the difficulties in life and instead of moaning over the losses which cannot be helped, they are resigned to the will of God.

In short, every plan that a person makes and his desire to accomplish that plan are often an outcome of his personal will, and when his will is helped by every other will that he comes in contact with in the path of the attainment of a certain object, then he is helped by God, as every will goes in the direction of his will and so his will becomes strengthened, and often a person accomplishes something which perhaps a thousand people would not have been able to accomplish. Then there is another person who has a plan or a desire, and finds opposition from every side. Everything seems to go wrong, and yet he has the inner urge which prompts him to go on in the path of attainment. There also is the hand of God behind his back, pushing him on, forward in his path, even though there might seem oppositions in the beginning of his strife — but all's well that ends well.

The saintly souls, who consider it as their religion to seek the pleasure of God and to be resigned to His will, are really blessed, for their manner is pleasing to everyone, for they are conscientious lest they should hurt the feelings of anyone, and if by mistake they happen to hurt someone's feelings they feel they have hurt God Whose pleasure they must constantly seek, for the happiness of their life is only in seeking the pleasure of God. They watch every person and every situation and condition, and their heart becomes so trained by constantly observing life keenly, as a lover of music whose ears become trained in time, who distinguishes between the correct and the false note. So they begin to see in every desire that springs in their heart, if it is in accordance with the will of God. Sometimes they know the moment the desire has sprung. Sometimes they know when they have gone halfway in the path of its pursuit. And sometimes they know at the end of strife. But even then, at the end of it, their willingness to resign to the will of God becomes their consolation, even in the face of disappointment. The secret of seeking the will of God is in cultivating the faculty of sensing harmony, for harmony is beauty and beauty is harmony. The lover of beauty in his further progress becomes the seeker of harmony, and by trying always to maintain harmony man will tune his heart to the will of God.

Surah One Hundred Twelve

At Tauhid

While man rejoices over his rise and sorrows over his fall, the wise man takes both as the natural consequences of life.

It makes no difference to me if I am so praised that I am raised from earth to heaven, nor if I am so blamed that I am thrown from the greatest heights to the depths of the earth. Life to me is an ever-moving sea in which the waves of favor and disfavor constantly rise and fall.

In sorrow one may look to God, and in joy one may thank Him. One does not bemoan the past, nor worry about the future; one tries only to make the best of today. One should know no failure, for even in a fall there is a stepping-stone to rise; but to the Sufi the rise and fall matter little. One does not repent for what one has done, since one thinks, says, and does what one means. One does not fear the consequences of performing one's wish in life, for what will be, will be.

What will rise must fall, and what will fall must rise. Rise and fall are natural to life. No rise is permanent, or fall lasting. It is reality behind it all which is steady and dependent. Life is one living stream, continually running without beginning or end. Death is man's illusion. The change that hides man's existence from him he calls death. Life is still, but its flow, which is ever-moving, rises and fall in waves; it is this that created an illusion of rise and fall. All this we see is the manifestation of one Spirit in many and varied forms.

The quality of the saints is to be resigned to all that comes—but then they do not even form a wish. They take all that comes, flowers or thorns;

everything that comes, they take it. They look into thorns and see that they are flowers. With praise and with blame they are contented. They are contented with rise and fall; they take all that comes, they take life as it is. *Hazrat Inayat Khan*

In the name of Allah, the Beneficent, the Merciful
Say: He is Allah, the One! (112:1 Quran)
Allah, the eternally besought of all. (112:2 Quran)
He begetteth not nor was begotten. (112:3 Quran)
And there is none comparable to Him. (112:4 Quran)

The Word 'Sin' ~ Hazrat Inayat Khan

Many wonder if sin is an attitude or an action or a situation or a result, and the answer is that all these combined together make either a virtue or a sin. The absence of one from it makes it incomplete, but all these together make it a complete virtue or sin. Now the question is where it is originated, what is the source of it, and the answer is that its origin is in wrong thinking. Wrongdoing comes from wrong thinking and wrong thinking comes from wrong feeling. And yet it is difficult to distinguish between feeling right and wrong. In short, as a definition of the word I would give this: Every attitude, word, or action that deprives one of the expected result, the result which is expected not only by the mind but by the soul, may be called sin. That which deprives one of peace, freedom, happiness, tranquility of mind, and ever-increasing power of will may be called sin, whatever be the action. It may be an action which all the orthodox call virtue, and yet it cannot be a virtue. Why virtue is called a virtue? Because it brings happiness. It is not because it is a particular kind of action, it is because it brings to one what one's whole being is desiring. It brings freedom, it brings the air of happiness, and it gives by its pressure upon one's mind an increase of will power that is why it is called virtue. It is therefore that no person in the world can judge another person, whether superior to him in evolution or inferior. The person himself is the best judge of his action.

In the Messages of the past it was necessary that a kind of standard of virtue should be given to the world as a law given from the Prophets of God, but at this period it is not necessary. The Sufi Message does not bring to the world a law made so plain as to say which is which, but the principle of the Message is to waken in the spirit of those who receive this Message that spirit that they may recognize what is right and what is wrong, that they may become masters of their destiny, and by their realization of this their progress on the spiritual path may become much higher as compared to those who during the period of the prophets depended on being directed in their lives by the law made by the prophets and carried out by the priests. The Sufi Message does not bring this. It brings the spirit of freedom, the air of happiness that which gives happiness with increased will power, which opens up freedom for those who can recognize for themselves the difference between right and wrong, and in that evolution of humanity is brought a step forward from what it was before.

After a certain time the same principle that the Sufi Message has brought to the world will culminate and will appear as a law among nations, because the Message is the throwing of the seed. Just now you do not see the fruits and leaves, just now you see the seed which is hidden under the dust and on the ground. But time will show the tree with its fruit and its leaves. When the nations will recognize the divine law and the law of the time then humanity will no longer be ruled by the laws made by a few intellectual people for their convenience and as they think right, but the law will recognize the divine indication which is constantly working through every soul, guiding it on the path, showing it the way of its destiny. And when such a time will come there will not be a necessity for so many laws, and as many laws so many lawyers, and probably as many lawyers so many law courts, and no end of prisons and no limit to the prisoners! This will cease to exist. There will not be the necessity of strict laws and severe punishments for nothing.

If one could only see that among one hundred people who are sentenced by the courts there is hardly one to be blamed, to be held responsible for his fault. And if there is anyone to be held responsible, it is all we human beings. Why do we not all work, why do we not all help them to kindle the light in their soul that would show them their path plainly? It is not necessary that the clergyman, the priest only should be responsible for the evolution of each individual. We must work in the capacity of brother and sister to everyone. In the realization of the brotherhood in the Fatherhood of God we must hold it as our duty, our sacred task, to waken in our brother, with love, with respect, with modesty, with humility, that power of understanding what is really for his best, what can really benefit him. It is not the mission of one person, it is the mission of every person. And if we each considered our share of work in the Message and showed it by our own example in the world we should be doing a great duty toward God and humanity.

Surah One Hundred Thirteen

Al Falaq
It is the lover of God whose heart is filled with devotion who can commune with God, not he who makes an effort with his intellect to analyze God.

Science is learned by analysis and esotericism by synthesis. If a person who wants to obtain esoteric knowledge breaks things up into bits, he is analyzing them; and as long as he does this he will never come to understand esotericism. In psychology two things are needed: analysis and synthesis; and when through a better understanding of psychology one has accustomed oneself to synthesize as well as to analyze, then one prepares oneself to synthesize only, which leads to a fuller understanding of esotericism. Therefore, the acquisition of esoteric knowledge is quite different from the study of science.

It is the lover of God whose heart is filled with devotion, who can commune with God; not the one who makes an effort with his intellect to analyze God. In other words, it is the lover of God who can commune with Him, not the student of His nature. It is the 'I' and 'you', which divide, and yet it is 'I' and 'you', which are the necessary conditions of love. Although 'I' and 'you' divide the one life into two, it is love that connects them by the current which is established between them; and it is this current which is called communion, which runs between man and God. *Hazrat Inayat Khan*

In the name of Allah, the Beneficent, the Merciful
Say: I seek refuge in the Lord of the Daybreak. (113:1 Quran)
From the evil of that which He created. (113:2 Quran)
From the evil of the darkness when it is intense. (113:3 Quran)
And from the evil of malignant witchcraft. (113:4 Quran)
And from the evil of the envier when he envieth. (113:5 Quran)
It is simpler to find a way to heaven than to find a way on earth.

A person whose soul has awakened becomes awake to everything he sees and hears. It is this awakening of the soul which is mentioned in the Bible, 'Unless the soul is born again it will not enter the kingdom of heaven'. Being born again means that the soul is awakened after having come on earth, and entering the kingdom of heaven means that this world, the same kingdom in which we are standing just now, turns into heaven as soon as the point of view has changed. Is it not interesting and most wonderful to think that the same earth we walk on is earth to one person and heaven to another? And it is still more interesting to notice that it is we who change it; we change it from earth into heaven, or we change it otherwise. This change comes not by study, nor by anything else, but only by the changing of our point of view.

The higher life is so much simpler than life on the surface of the earth, but man does not know what he is. He does not know that he is a drop on the surface of the ocean, and yet an ocean himself in his innermost part; that there is nothing that is not within him. A person who says to himself, 'I do not possess this faculty', 'I cannot put up with this', 'I am sorry but I could not think of such a thing', and so forth, well, all these ideas are his imagination, part of the confusion of his thought and lack of understanding of what he is. If a person understood what he is he would never say, 'I cannot do this.' Instead he would become a real man, that which a man ought to be. The mystic only says, 'I cannot' or 'I have not' very seldom, and he believes these words still less often.

When God is with you everything is with you; when God is in you everything is in you. Inspiration, knowledge, light, all are then within you. But if you find joy in confusion, if you confuse yourself and keep yourself in darkness, you may do so. However, you have inherited from the heavenly Father His inspiration, His Light, His power. You have inherited might from the Almighty God; you have inherited light from the Light of the universe. Therefore you are blessed with all these things, if you can only open your eyes and see the blessing. *Hazrat Inayat Khan*

Narrowness is primitiveness; it is the breadth of heart that proves evolution.

One person will do something and consider that there is great wisdom in his sacrifice, while another who is not evolved enough to understand it will say, 'How very foolish!' Remember therefore that not only to the wise person the man of little sense seems foolish, but even to the foolish person the wise one seems foolish. The points of view of both are different: one looks from the top of the tower, the other standing on the ground. So there is a vast difference in the range of their sight.

It is a man's outlook on life which makes him broad or narrow, and it is the grade of his evolution which gives man the illumination of sacrifice. What a man was not inclined to do last year, he may be inclined to do this year; the sacrifice one could not make yesterday, one can make today, for the rate of speed of man's evolution cannot be limited to a particular standard. A broad outlook enriches man and a high point of view ennobles the soul.

Once you have linked yourself with love, a flood of inspiration is revealed to you, whatever the subject, whatever the problem in life may be. Whatever it be that your eye casts its glance upon, it will disclose itself. Then you are on the real road, and what a joy this is!

Breadth of heart is what is needed for all this. It is the breadth of heart that makes a man great, whereas it is narrowness of heart that makes him small. The great heart does not think about how troublesome a person is, and why he should be bothered like this. It is only the narrow of heart that thinks, 'I will cause him some trouble.' It may be justified, but still it is a narrow thought. The one with a broad heart thinks, 'This is a small thing, I can put up with it; not much harm will come from it.'

The Nizam wrote this verse, 'The width of the land and the water cannot be compared with the width of man's heart. If man's heart is wide enough there is nothing greater than that.' The heart becomes wide by forgetting the self, and narrow by thinking of the self and by pitying one's self. To gain a wide and broad heart you must have something before you to look upon and to rest your intelligence upon, and that something is the God ideal. This is the prescription for killing the self, and to kill the self is the basis of every religion. *Hazrat Inayat Khan*

Surah One Hundred Fourteen

An Nas

Do not bemoan the past, do not worry about the future, but try to make the best of today.

There is not anything one should not be ready to tolerate, and there is nobody whom one should not forgive. Never doubt those whom you trust; never hate those whom you love; never cast down those whom you once raise in your estimation. Wish to make friends with everyone you meet; make an effort to gain the friendship of those you find difficult No one is either higher or lower than oneself. In all sources that fulfill one's need, one may see one source, God, the only source; and in admiring and in bowing before and in loving anyone, one may consider one is doing it to God. In sorrow one may look to God, and in joy one may thank Him. One does not bemoan the past, nor worry about the future; one tries only to make the best of today. One should know no failure, for even in a fall there is a stepping-stone to rise.

In Fitzgerald's translation of Omar Khayyam: 'O my Beloved, fill the cup that clears today of past regrets and future fears. Why, tomorrow I may be myself, with yesterday's sev'n thousand years!' By this he means: Make the best of this moment; it is now that you can clearly see eternity, if you live in this moment. But if you keep the world of the past or the world of the future before you, you do not live in eternity but in a limited world. In other words, live neither in the past nor in the future, but in eternity. It is now that we should try to discover that happiness which is to be found in the freedom of the soul. Hazrat Inayat Khan

In the name of Allah, the Beneficent, the Merciful
Say: I seek refuge in the Lord of mankind. (114:1 Quran)
The King of mankind. (114:2 Quran)
The God of mankind. (114:3 Quran)
From the evil of the sneaking whisperer. (114:4 Quran)
Who whispereth in the hearts of mankind. (114:5 Quran)
Of the jinn and of mankind. (114:6 Quran)

Memorial Note: Hazrat Inayat Khan born in the city of Baroda in India July 5, 1882

Following a bout with pneumonia, Hazrat Inayat Khan departed from this world on February 5, 1927, at the Tilak Lodge, located along the river Yamuna near Delhi, India. His burial tomb is in the Basti Nizamuddin neighborhood of Delhi. Hazrat Inayat Khan described the essence of his spiritual message with the following words, which are offered here to commemorate his life and teachings:

Our sacred task is to awaken among those around us and among those whom we can reach in the first place the spirit of tolerance for the religion, scripture, and the ideal of devotion of one another; our next task is to make man understand people of different nations, races and communities, also of different classes.

By this we do not mean to say that all races and nations must become one, nor that all classes must become one; only what we have to say is that whatever be our religion, nation, race or class, our most sacred duty is to work for one another, in one another's interest, and to consider that as the service of God.

The central theme of the Sufi Message is one simple thing, and yet most difficult, and that is to bring about in the world the realization of the divinity of the human soul, which hitherto has been overlooked, for the reason that the time had not come.

The principal thing that the Message has to accomplish in this era is to create the realization of the divine spark in every soul that every soul according to its progress may begin to realize for itself the spark of divinity within. This is the task that is before us.

Now you may ask, what is the Message? The Message is this: that the whole humanity is as one single body, and all nations and communities and races as the different organs, and the happiness and well-being of each of them is the happiness and well-being of the whole body. If there is one organ of the body in pain, the whole body has to sustain a share of the strain of it. That by this Message mankind may begin to think that his welfare and his well-being is not in looking after himself, but it is in looking after others, and when in all there will be reciprocity, love and goodness towards another, the better time will come.

The need of the world today is not learning, but how to become considerate towards one another. To try and find out in what way happiness can be brought about, and in this way to realize that peace which is the longing of every soul; and to impart it to others, thereby attaining our life's goal, the sublimity of life. *Hazrat Inyat Khan*

M. R. Bawa Muhaiyaddeen

'My son! This is a Hadith of Rasulullha (Sal.) about Islam:

Brothers in Islam! You who are Iman-Islam! You must not see differences between yourselves and your neighbors. You must not discriminate against any religion. You must not oppress or harm any man, no matter what religion or race he may be. Islam is one and Allah is one; just as we in Islam see Allah as one, we must see all mankind as one.

All the prophets brought the words of Allah, and all the words they brought are true. Allah sent His messages through each of the prophets, and they brought His commandments step by step. In the revelations contained in the Quran, Allah has given the entirety of His teaching. The Quran is the ultimate and final teaching, showing everything in its fullness.

All the children of Adam (A. S.) are brothers and sisters. They are not different. Although they may stand on different steps of the teachings brought by the prophets in their respective times, you must not discriminate against any of them. You must not harass their places of worship, their bodies, or their hearts. You must protect them as you would protect your own life.

To comfort the hunger of your neighbor, no matter who he is or what religion he belongs to, is Islam. When someone dies, to join together and give him a decent burial is Islam. To realize the pain and suffering of others and offer your hands in assistance, helping to alleviate their suffering, is Islam.

To see division is not Islam. To see other men as different is not Islam. In this world and the next, there must be no prejudice in our hearts, for all will come together on the Day of Reckoning and the Day of Judgment. All of us will come together in heaven. Therefore, we must not see any differences or create any divisions here. Where Allah does not see a difference, we must not see a difference. We must not despise anyone whom Allah loves—and Allah loves everyone. He belongs equally to everyone, just as Islam belongs equally to everyone. Islam is unity, not division.

Hurting another is not Islam. Failing to comfort the hunger of your neighbor is not Islam. The purity of Islam is to avoid hurting others; you must regard others as you regard yourself. You must accept Allah's word totally. There must be no discrimination in your heart against the children of Islam.

You who are Muslim must understand what halal is and what haram is, what is permissible and what is forbidden. You must understand that there is only One worthy of worship. You must understand Qiyamah, the Day of Reckoning and the Day of Judgment.'

Conclusion:

'We must look at the Quran in two different ways. There are the opposites of Khair and sharr or good and evil, dhat and sifat God's grace and essence and the manifested creation, and halal and haram or permissible and impermissible. One section exists as the laws and justice of God, and the other exists as the section of darkness.

In this state, we who are the children of Adam (A. S.) must realize that we must discard all that is evil and accept and act upon only what is good. That is the law of righteousness. We must simply discard what is evil; we need not denounce or attack anything.

What is called Islam was brought as perfect purity by the Quran. It is brotherly unity. Islam is to bring together as one family all the children of the one mother who have divided into four separate sections. The Quran teaches us to see what is good as good, while discarding what is evil. It is the law of justice. It shows us patience, inner patience, contentment, surrendering all to the will of God, and giving all praise to God. We, the children of Adam (A. S.) must understand this.

The Quran and its explanations are very deep in meaning. Therefore, we who are the children of Adam (A. S.) should not hold up the Quran as a banner for the slightest reason. We should not quote from the Quran and use it for waging wars, for our fights and quarrels, of our anger toward others, or to gain things of this world. The world which is sharr, evil, and has to be discarded. The opposite, khair, which is goodness, must be accepted and put into action. The Quran should only be used for what is good. It shows brotherhood and unity, not divisiveness and discrimination. It soothes those who are weeping in sorrow. It gives solace to those who are suffering and makes them smile. It comforts those who are ill and protects them. It explains the wealth of God to those who are poor. It gives peace to those who are mentally ill. It gives wisdom to those without wisdom. It creates faith in those without faith and makes them bow in reverence to God. What is called the Quran is, in reality, something that has great value and very deep meaning.

The true meaning of Islam and the Quran is quite different from what people accept today, in the midst of so much fighting and strife. People quote Islam and wave the Quran as a banner for their wars. This is not correct. The Quran discards what is evil and shows only goodness, unity and tolerance. Tawakkul-alallah, giving all responsibility to God, and giving all praise to God, saying, "Al-hamdu lillah," with every breath is the Quran and the Islam.

No matter how large the ocean is, it cannot quench our thirst, can it? The ocean cannot quench the thirst of any life. But if there is a pond, however small it may be, it can comfort many lives, appeasing thirst and dispelling fatigue. Like that, the Quran comforts so many lives, dispelling fatigue and hunger and clearing away the dirt. This is the meaning of the Quran and Islam. When you quote from the Quran, those words must only demonstrate peace and equality. When you say "Islam", you must show patience, equality, and peace. When you show what is good, that goodness points to Islam, but when you show what is evil, that evil is something that has been discarded from the Quran.

The Treasures, kingdoms, and titles of this world are all sharr and have been discarded from the Quran. Fighting and waging war for those worldly things, seeking vengeance, committing treacherous acts, telling lies for worldly gain, eating haram or impermissible foods, lying out of jealousy for the sake of titles and positions—all these cannot be called Islam. And you cannot quote the Quran, saying that these actions appear there, because these actions are totally contrary to the Quran.

The Quran shows the brotherhood where we live as one family and eat off the same plate in unity. The Quran shows the brotherhood where we live in harmony, the way it is in the church or the mosque, where the beggar and the king are equal. It shows the brotherhood where we embrace each other, whether in the place of prayer or in the home. If two people have a fight, the next time they meet, they will look each other in the face and embrace and beg forgiveness from each other. The Quran and Islam tell us to ask forgiveness from God for our own faults, to dispel our anger, and to embrace each other in the next moment.

These are the explanations of the laws of the Quran from the beginning of creation to the hereafter. Lying, vengeance, treachery, jealousy, and murder should never be done in the name of Islam. Islam is brotherly unity, tolerance, and peacefulness. It is to purify each heart with the water of the Kalimah which the Rasul (Sal.) brought, washing away the darkness and creating peace.

But there are some people who hold up the Quran with anger, jealousy, and selfishness, using the Quran and Islam for their own self-gain and pride. The Quran should never be mentioned with these qualities, but should be mentioned only where there is righteousness. Anger, treachery, deceit, discrimination, divisiveness, and all that is impermissible have been thrown out of the Quran. All these sections belonging to the world have been eliminated from the Quran, and they must be eliminated from man, too. Man must take what is khair and eliminate what is sharr. In this way, the Quran must be used to show what is good and to eliminate what is evil, and this is Islam. The word Islam means unity, brotherhood, and harmony. It does not see differences among people; it only sees peace and harmony among all lives. This is Islam. This is the Quran. Every one of the children of Adam (A. S.) must realize this.

One who calls himself Muslim will never harm anyone, take revenge, or be treacherous toward anyone. We must realize this. Islam must realize this. The name "Islam" has very deep meaning and is of inestimable value, and it should never be held up for falsehood, robbery, or murder. Islam is brotherly unity that can appease the thirst of the entire world. This is the Islam which was brought by Prophet Muhammad (Sal.). All of everything, all the universes, and all of creation is contained within the Quran. But failing to understand this, we hold up and quote the Quran and Islam for the slightest reasons.

We who are in the world must realize that the Quran is the divine law of righteousness, which was given to show brotherly unity, to make lives peaceful, to forgive in the presence of faults, to teach patience and compassion and to comfort all lives. We must have sabur, shakur, tawakhul and al-hamdu lillah. This is the Quran and Islam. All my brothers and sisters who have Iman, perfect faith in

God, must realize this, Amin, Amin.' M. R. Bawa Muhaiyaddeen

Bibliography:

Pickthall, Marmaduke: The Meaning of the Glorious Koran. Alfred A. Knopf. 1992

Hazrat Inayat Khan. The Complete Sayings of Hazrat Inayat Khan. Omega Publications. 1978

Works of Hazrat Inayat Khan, published and unpublished, by kind permission of his grandson Pir Zia Inayat Khan

About the Author

Farzana Moon is a poet, historian and a playwright. Writes Sufi poetry, historical, biographical accounts of the Moghul emperors and plays based on stories from religion and folklore. Her published works in religion and spirituality are: *Irem of the Crimson Desert; Sufis and Mystics of the World; Prophet Muhammad: The First Sufi of Islam; No Islam But Islam; Sharia Exposed.* Published works in the sequels of the Moghul emperors are: *Babur, The First Moghul In India; The Moghul Exile; Divine Akbar and Holy India; The Moghul Hedonist: Glorious Taj and Beloved Immortal; The Moghul Saint of Insanity; Poet Emperor of the Last of the Moghuls: Bahadur Shah Zafar.* Another of her published book in history is about the partition of India and Pakistan, *Holocaust of the East.* Her play *Osama The Demented* had a staged reading in Stockholm. Another of her play, *Russian Roulette,* is being considered for production. Latest published book, Friends Incarnate. Currently working on a book, *The American Queen,* about the wife of Hazrat Inayat Khan, Ora Ray Baker who was born in Albuquerque, New Mexico USA.

ALL THINGS THAT MATTER PRESS

FOR MORE INFORMATION ON TITLES AVAILABLE FROM
ALL THINGS THAT MATTER PRESS, GO TO
http://allthingsthatmatterpress.com
or contact us at
allthingsthatmatterpress@gmail.com

**If you enjoyed this book, please post a review on Amazon.com
and your favorite social media sites.
Thank you!**